CHAMPIONS LEAGUE
YEARBOOK 2007/2008

EVERY GAME, EVERY GOAL, EVERY FACT!

Know The Score Books Publications

MATCH OF MY LIFE
Twelve Stars Relive Their Favourite Games

Relive a dozen of the greatest games in history through the eyes of twelve legends who were on the pitch creating history

SPURS
ISBN: 9781905449583
£16.99 Available Now
includes Ossie Ardiles, Clive Allen, Cliff Jones

ENGLAND WORLD CUP
ISBN: 1905449526
£16.99 Available Now
includes Tony Adams, David Platt, Sir Bobby Robson

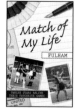

FULHAM
ISBN: 1905449518
£16.99 Available Now
includes Sean Davis, Simon Morgan, Gordon Davies

EUROPEAN CUP FINALS
ISBN: 1905449577
£16.99 Available Now
includes Jamie Carragher, Alec Stepney, Paolo Rossi

LEEDS
ISBN: 1905449542
£16.99 Available Now
includes Peter Lorimer, Allan Clarke, Brendan Ormsby

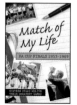

FA CUP FINALS 1953-1969
ISBN: 9781905449538
£16.99 Pub. Date: October 2006
includes Bert Trautmann, Dave Mackay, Peter McParland

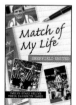

SHEFFIELD UNITED
ISBN: 1905449623
£16.99 Available Now
includes Tony Currie, Keith Edwards, Phil Jagielka

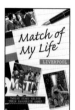

LIVERPOOL
ISBN: 190544950X
£16.99 Available Now
includes Jamie Carragher, John Barnes, Tommy Smith

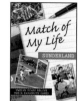

SUNDERLAND
ISBN: 1905449607
£16.99 Available Now
includes Niall Quinn, Marco Gabbiadini, Gary Rowell

MANCHESTER UNITED
ISBN: 9781905449590
£16.99 Available Now
includes Bryan Robson, Frank Stapleton, Gary Pallister

STOKE CITY
ISBN: 9781905449552
£16.99 Available Now
includes Mike Sheron, Mark Stein, Denis Smith

WOLVES
ISBN: 1905449569
£16.99   Available Now
includes Steve Bull, Bert Williams,
John Richards

ASTON VILLA
ISBN: 9781905449651
£16.99   Pub. Date: March 2008
includes Stan Collymore, Ian Taylor,
Nigel Spink, Olof Mellberg

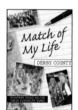

DERBY COUNTY
ISBN: 9781905449682
£16.99   Pub. Date: November 2007
includes Steve Howard, Roger Davies,
Marco Gabbiadini

CULT HEROES
**Examining the reasons why the twenty biggest
cult heroes in a club's history won the hearts of
their fans, revealing many new stories and
behind-the-scenes anecdotes**

CHELSEA
by Leo Moynihan
ISBN: 1905449003
£16.99   Available Now
includes Gianfranco Zola, John Terry,
Peter Osgood

NEWCASTLE
by Dylan Younger
ISBN: 1905449038
£16.99   Pub Date: October 2006
includes Alan Shearer, Paul Gascoigne,
Jackie Milburn

SOUTHAMPTON
by Jeremy Wilson
ISBN: 1905449011
£16.99   Available Now
includes Matt Le Tissier, Mick Channon,
Terry Paine

WEST BROM
by Simon Wright
ISBN: 190544902X
£16.99   Available Now
includes Jeff Astle, Cyrille Regis,
Bob Taylor

MANCHESTER CITY
by David Clayton
ISBN: 9781905449057
£16.99   Available Now
includes Giorgi Kinkladze, Rodney Marsh,
Bert Trautmann

RANGERS
by Paul Smith
ISBN: 9781905449071
£16.99   Pub. Date: November 2007
includes Barry Ferguson, Ally McCoist,
Davie Cooper

NOTTINGHAM FOREST
by David McVay
ISBN: 9781905449064
£16.99   Available Now
includes Brian Clough, Jason Lee,
Stuart Pearce

CARLISLE
by Paul Harrison
ISBN: 9781905449088
£16.99   Available Now
includes Kevin Gray, Jimmy Glass,
Ivor Broadis

OTHER TITLES

TACKLES LIKE A FERRET
by Paul Parker
ISBN: 190544947X
£18.99 Available Now
The autobiography of England,
Manchester United, QPR and Fulham's
springheeled defender

BURKSEY
The Autobiography of a Football God
by Peter Morfoot
ISBN: 1905449496
£9.99 Available Now
'Burksey does for football what Spinal Tap did
for rock bands' Non-League Paper

HOLD THE BACK PAGE
Football's Tabloid Tales
by Harry Harris
ISBN: 1905449917
£16.99 Available Now
The true stories behind the headlines, the
bungs, the court cases and the scandals of
Harry's thirty years investigating football's
shady underbelly

OUTCASTS
The Lands That FIFA Forgot
by Steve Menary
ISBN: 9781905449316
£16.99 Available Now
How football thrives amongst the 'nations'
which FIFA refuses to recognise, such as
Gibraltar and Tibet

UNITED IN TRIUMPH AND TRAGEDY
The Autobiography of Bill Foulkes
by Bill Foulkes
ISBN: 9781905449781
£17.99 Pub. Date: December 2007
The Manchester United legend gives a
candid assessment of his 15 years at the
club, great players such as Best, Charlton and
Law and his own tale of the Munich disaster

MARTIN JOL: DUTCH MASTER
A Biography of the Spurs Manager
by Harry Harris
ISBN: 9781905449774
£19.99 Pub. Date: November 2007
An in-depth look at how the Spurs manager
became the most loved Premiership
manager amongst football fans

2006 WORLD CUP DIARY
by Harry Harris
ISBN: 1905449909
£14.99 Available Now
Every game, every goal and every fact
about the fabulous tournament in Germany

PARISH TO PLANET
How Football Came To Rule The World
by Eric Midwinter
ISBN: 97819054497309
£17.99 Pub. Date: November 2007
Tracing the origins of football from the
backyards of England into the greatest
global passion the world has ever seen

**MARCUS HAHNEMANN'S
PREMIERSHIP DIARY**
by Marcus Hahnemann
ISBN: 97819054497330
£16.99 Available Now
behind the scenes with the colourful
American goalkeeper during Reading's
incredible odyssey through the weird
and wonderful world of the Premiership
in 2006/07

To pre-order or order any of these books, postage free, please
send a cheque made out to Know The Score Books to:

Know The Score Books Ltd, 118 Alcester Road,
Studley, Warwickshire, B80 7NT
Tel: 01527 454482   Fax: 01527 452183
Email: info@knowthescorebooks.com
or visit our website where signed copies may also be purchased

CHAMPIONS LEAGUE
YEARBOOK 2007/2008

EVERY GAME, EVERY GOAL, EVERY FACT!

Know The Score Books Limited
118 Alcester Road
Studley
Warwickshire
B80 7NT
United Kingdom
www.knowthescorebooks.com

A CIP catalogue record is available for this book from the British Library
ISBN 978-1-905449-93-4

Jacket and book design by Lisa David

Printed and bound by Butler & Tanner, England

Mixed Sources
Product group from well-managed
forests and other controlled sources
www.fsc.org Cert no. SGS-COC-1722
© 1996 Forest Stewardship Council
FSC

Welcome

The 2006/07 UEFA Champions League was a breathtaking, colourful and sometimes controversial orgy of football.

The tournament was blessed with wonderful goals by Didier Drogba, Ronaldinho, Peter Crouch, Shunsuke Nakamura, Kaka, Wayne Rooney and Thierry Henry.

In this book we focus on the British clubs, but never lose sight of the jamboree of football across the continent of Europe, and sometimes even beyond. Incisive commentary is provided by award-winning journalist Harry Harris of Express Group Newspapers and stunning photographs by Action Images.

Along the way we chart the pre-tournament shenanigans which almost saw eventual winners AC Milan barred from taking part, Manchester United's awesome blitz of Roma in the quarter-finals, Chelsea's second defeat at the semi-final stage in three seasons at the hands of Liverpool and the record-breaking progress of Celtic into the knockout stages of the tournament for the first time in its current format.

If that wasn't enough, amongst other special features, Jamie Carragher recalls that amazing night in Istanbul, which set up the revenge match in this season's final and we pay tribute to a Champions League legend – Ferenc Puskas – who left us for good during the season.

We would very much like to thank all the journalists who have contributed their thoughts and articles to this book including Tom Green, Steve Menary, Leo Moynihan and Jeremy Wilson, plus the assistance of Jim Baldwin, Andy Searle, Lisa David, Aardman Animation, Nathan Harmer, Graham Hales and Kay Hoffman in creating the best possible book for your enjoyment.

We would also like to thank Vodafone for supporting this fabulous venture in its first season, alongside their first season of sponsorship of the UEFA Champions League.

We've packed in every statistic, goal and fascinating fact that we could possibly think of during the competition, plus a whole lot more and hope that this book brings vividly to life the Champions League season of 2006/07.

Enjoy the trip.

Simon Lowe
Editor-in-Chief
Know The Score Books Ltd

Contents

Section Five – Knockout Stage

Section Six – The Final

Section Seven – 2007/08 UEFA Champions League

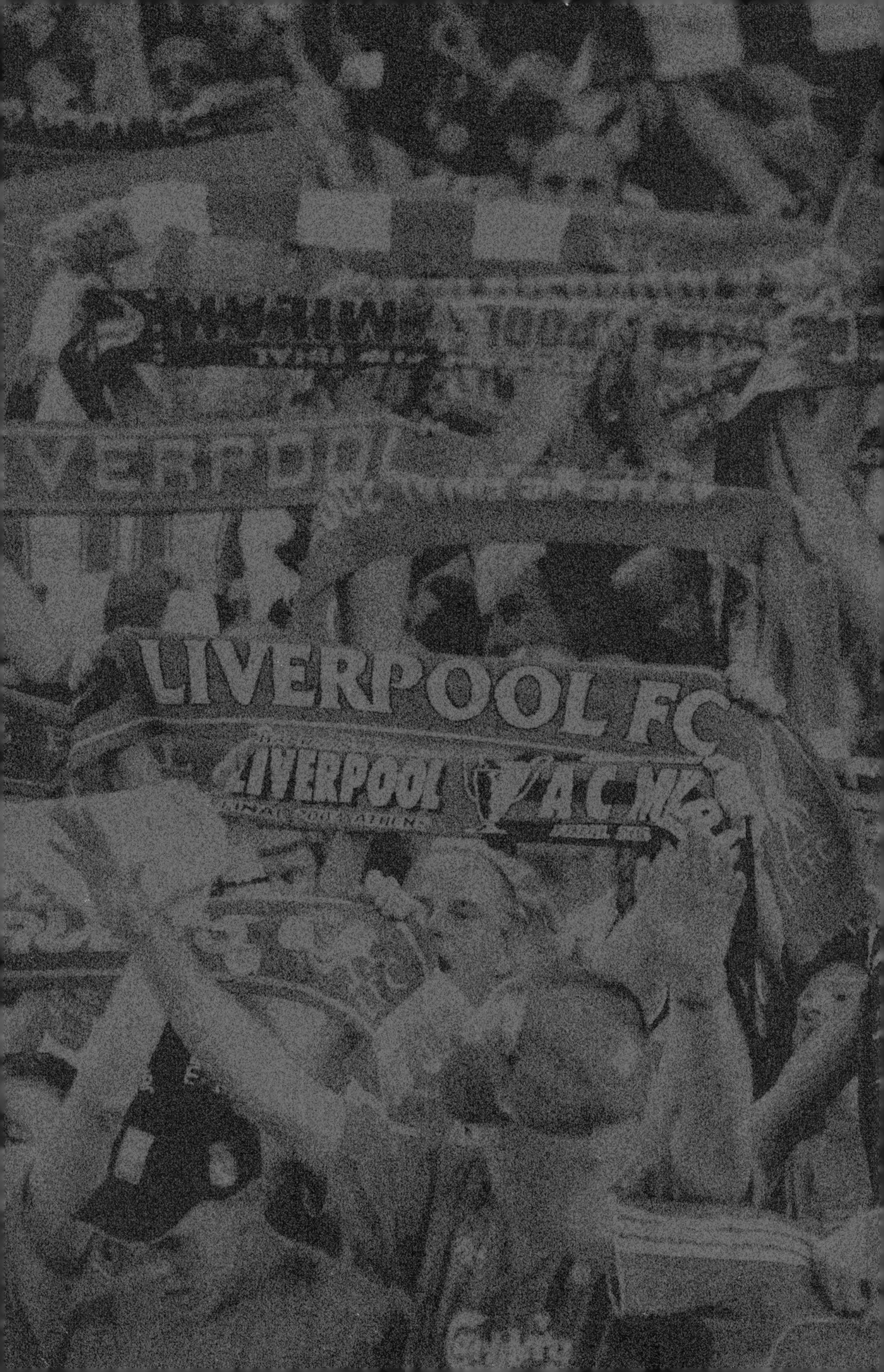
LIVERPOOL FC
LIVERPOOL
A C M

section one

introduction

Introduction

Bayern Munich fans rejoice as their side defeat Inter Milan

It's the beautiful, exciting and all-consuming game. Wherever you go, football permeates people's consciousness and it is at the centre of Vodafone's love of sport which sees us involved in everything from Formula 1 to the England Cricket team.

Communication is the modern way to follow Sport, and particularly football. Whether it be by phoning friends to let them know what is happening at a match, by texting them to give them updates, or sending photo-messages to bring them your own unique perspective on the atmosphere surrounding a game, mobile communications have become part and parcel of football and, especially, UEFA Champions League nights when the action comes thick and fast around Europe.

At Vodafone we pride ourselves on bringing fans closer together and closer to the game. The services we offer, which we endeavour to consistently improve, are designed to help you keep in touch with what's happening on the pitch, what your mates are doing off it, and allow you to enjoy all the pride and passion, skill and endeavour, humour and hubris, glitz and glamour of the Champions League in the process.

We also love to have fun and hope that you, the fans, do too.

This first Vodafone Champions League Yearbook will help bring football fans closer to the greatest club football competition on the planet and there is no better way to celebrate the first season of our sponsorship than with this fabulous look back through a great UEFA Champions League campaign, which culminated in victory for AC Milan over Liverpool in the final which was sweet revenge for the incredible turnaround which had occurred in Istanbul two years earlier.

We would like to say a big thank you to all our partners in putting this book together and to you the fans for reading it. Enjoy following the UEFA Champions League over the coming season, which promises to be every bit as good as the last – possibly even better!

David Wheldon
Global Brand Director
& Customer Experience, Vodafone

Filippo Inzaghi shows all the passion and ecstasy that scoring the winning goal in the UEFA Champions League final imbues

Parkhead celebrates as only it knows how

The Champions League Story

Europe's premier club competition was launched one month after UEFA's first Congress, held in Vienna on 2 March 1955 yet, curiously, the so-called "European Cup" was not a UEFA initiative.

French Founders

Whereas many of UEFA's founder members were more interested in establishing a national team competition, the French sports daily L'Equipe and their then-editor Gabriel Hanot, were championing the cause for a European-wide club competition. Hanot, together with colleague Jacques Ferran, designed a blueprint for a challenge tournament to be played on Wednesdays under floodlights.

Sporting Record

The tournament initiated by L'Equipe did not stipulate that the participating teams had to be champions of their country, but they invited clubs who they considered had the most fan appeal. Representatives of 16 clubs were invited to meetings on 2 and 3 April 1955 and the L'Equipe rules were unanimously approved. The first European Champions Clubs' Cup fixture was played in Lisbon and Sporting Clube de Portugal were held to a 3-3 draw by FK Partizan. The Yugoslav side won the return leg in Belgrade 5-2 to advance to the next round.

Madrid Dominate

Real Madrid immediately made the tournament their own by winning the first five finals. Since then, other clubs have also enjoyed fruitful runs in the competition with Ajax and Bayern Munich both completing three consecutive wins. However, no one club has been able to claim long-term domination. Ajax waited 22 years to add a fourth title to the hat-trick obtained in the early 1970s; Madrid's win in 1998 was their first in 32 years; and Bayern's penalty shoot-out success in Milan in 2001 ended a 26-year wait for their fourth success.

Liverpool Success

Liverpool's four victories between 1977 and 1984 deserve special mention and the Reds' European pedigree shone brightly again in 2005 when they battled back from 3-0 down to defeat AC Milan on penalties in what was perhaps the competition's most exciting and memorable final; a fitting 50th anniversary present.

Honours List

Real Madrid have been the most successful side in the UEFA Champions League, since the competition was revamped in 1992/93, winning the Cup three times. They are also the most successful side overall with nine triumphs, followed by six for current holders AC Milan, five for Liverpool and four each for Bayern and Ajax. Madrid also hold the record for final appearances, with 12. Milan's 2002/03 success came after a marathon 19 games from the third qualifying round of the competition all the way to their penalty shoot-out success against Juventus FC in the final.

The legendary 1960 Real Madrid side celebrate their classic 7-3 victory over Eintracht Frankfurt

Manchester United celebrate only the second ever treble of domestic cup and league plus the celebrated UEFA Champions League trophy

Competition Format

Eligibility

The UEFA Champions League is open to each national association's domestic champions, as well as selected clubs who finish just behind them in their respective domestic championship. The number of clubs that can be entered by an association and their entry point in the competition depends on the association's position in UEFA's coefficient ranking list.

Evolving Format

The European Champion Clubs' Cup was a purely knock-out competition until the format was changed in 1992/93 with the inception of the UEFA Champions League. That year the competition began with three knockout rounds with the winners advancing to a group stage involving two sets of four clubs playing home and away. The popularity of the group phase has witnessed the competition grow from eight to 32 teams with games taking place on Tuesdays and Wednesdays across Europe. Initially, the two group winners contested the final. A similar format was used the following season, with the addition of a two-legged semi-final stage involving the top two clubs from both groups.

Competition Expansion

The competition expanded further for the 1994/95 season with one preliminary round required before the clubs divided into four groups of four clubs. The top two clubs in each group advanced to the knockout stage, which this time began at the quarter-final stage. The 1997/98 season saw another phase of expansion to reflect the growth of UEFA members thanks to the split of both the Soviet Union and Yugoslavis into separate, smaller countries. Two qualifying rounds were introduced and the group stage expanded to six groups of four clubs each. The six group winners and the two best runners-up advanced to the knockout stages.

Additional Round

An additional qualifying round was introduced for the 1999/2000 season to generate two group stages, firstly with 32 teams – eight groups of four – who played six matches apiece to reduce the competition to 16 teams for the second group stage, with the eight third-placed teams moving to the UEFA Cup third round. At the end of the second group stage, eight teams remained to contest the knock-out stage.

Evolution

Since its inception in 1992/93, the UEFA Champions League has continued to evolve, maintaining a mixture of round-robin group matches as well as its traditional knock-out format. The current format was introduced in 2003/04. After three qualifying rounds, 32 teams contest the group stage, divided into eight groups of four. The group winners and runners-up advance to the knockout stages, the eight third-placed teams move into the UEFA Cup third round, and the eight fourth-placed teams are eliminated.

Knock-out Rounds

A draw determines who each of the 16 clubs will play in the first knock-out stage, with ties decided over two matches on a home and away basis. The club that scores the greater aggregate of goals advances, or in the event of both teams scoring the same number of goals, the team which scores more away goals. If the away-goals rule proves inconclusive, extra time of two periods of 15 minutes is played after the second match. If during extra time both teams score the same number of goals, away goals count double (i.e. the visiting team advances). If no goals are scored during extra time, the winner is decided by penalty kicks. The two teams that advance from the knock-out round contest the final, held as a single match in May.

Daniele Massaro (back L) and Dietmar Hamann with young AC Milan and Liverpool fans before the 2007 final in Athens. In 2007/08 the Holy Grail is to reach Moscow

Four Stars of the 2006/07 UEFA Champions League

KAKÁ

His real name is Ricardo Izecson dos Santos Leite, but the world knows him as Kaká. AC Milan triumphed in the 2006/07 Champions League in large part due to the brilliance of the maturing Brazilian playmaker and his smiling good looks could see him rivalling David Beckham as the pin-up of choice in world football.

His extra-time winner over dogged Celtic in the first knockout round showed the difference this ball-playing genius can make to his side and he regularly provides the spark which makes the UEFA Champions League holders ignite into action.

Kaká began his club career with São Paulo at the age of 8. He signed a contract at 15, made his São Paulo senior debut in January 2001 and scored 12 goals in 27 appearances, leading the club to its first and only Torneio Rio-São Paulo championship.

Not surprisingly his performance was soon attracting attention from European clubs. Gaziantepspor in Turkey looked set to sign him, but balked at the $1.5 million fee. AC Milan, fresh from winning the Champions League in 2003, had no such qualms. Coach Carlo Ancelloti signed the 21 year-old for $8.5 million, a fee described in hindsight as "peanuts" by club owner Silvio Berlusconi.

Within a month, he graduated to the starting lineup, and has remained there ever since. Kaká scored 10 goals in 30 games in his first season as the Rossoneri won the Scudetto and the European Super Cup.

Kaká was an integral part of Milan's five-man midfield in the 2004/05 season, usually playing in a withdrawn role behind striker Andriy Shevchenko. He scored 7 goals in 36 domestic appearances as Milan lost a famous Champions League final to Liverpool. He was nonetheless voted the best midfielder of the tournament, and also finished ninth, with 19 votes, in the running for the 2005 Ballon D'Or.

The 2005/06 season saw Kaká score his first hat-tricks in domestic and European competition; a feat he matched with his treble against Anderlecht in the 2006/07 UEFA Champions League. Three goals in the semi-final against Manchester United, including two superb strikes at Old Trafford, proved his class.

After finishing as the competition's top scorer with 10 goals, four clear of the field. As a member of the organisation Atletas de Cristo ("Athletes of Christ"), his goal celebration sees him point to the sky as a sign of thanks to God after every goal. You get the feeling we'll be seeing a lot more of it.

Kaká is a common form of endearment in Brazil for youngsters named Ricardo, so it is completely wrong when the media refer to the brilliant Brazilian as 'Ricky Kaká'

GENNARO GATTUSO

The most influential player of the entire tournament almost single-handedly shackled the entire Manchester United midfield in the semi-final second leg after being substituted in the first leg at Old Trafford and given little chance of playing in that game. His performance that night was his crowning glory, but Gattuso was the heart of the Milan side throughout their campaign, particularly in the vital away win in the second leg of the quarter-final in Munich, when a 2-0 win announced Milan as one of the serious contenders for the 2006/07 Champions League.

Gattuso started his career at the Italian side Perugia, but moved to Rangers in July 1997 at the age of 19. When Dick Advocaat replaced manager Walter Smith, who had brought Gattuso to Glasgow, the young Italian fell out of favour and, after being played out-of-position as a right-back, he was sold to Salernitana for £4 million in October 1998.

Just a year later AC Milan spent £8 million on bringing Gattuso to the San Siro and his rugged tackling and fierce determination allowed manager Carlo Ancellotti to free midfielder Andrea Pirlo to adopt a more attacking approach. Gattuso's style has earned him the nickname of Ringhio or "the Snarler". It is not without substance. In December 2005, at the final whistle of Milan's 3-2 defeat of Schalke 04 in the Champions League, Gattuso taunted Schalke's midfielder Christian Poulsen as a reaction to Poulsen's taunting of Kaká in the first leg. Indeed, his temper has caused him regular problems. In a Champions League group stage match against Ajax in September 2003, he was sent off during second-half injury time after striking Ajax striker Zlatan Ibrahimovic. But his competitive spirit, when properly channelled, makes him a fearsome foe.

The British press has frequently reported that Gattuso's ambition is to join Manchester United, although the Italian has publicly denied these rumours and he extended his current deal with Milan until 2011 in February 2007.

Having also been an integral part of Italy's World Cup-winning side in Germany, Gattuso can now truly lay claim to being the best defensive midfielder in the world. How long can a player of his influence and ability be denied one of the great individual prizes such as World Player of the Year?

Perhaps Gattuso's most notorious moment came during his post-match celebration after Italy won the World Cup, during which he removed his shorts and ran around the pitch in just his pants, until FIFA officials forced him to cover up

JOSE 'PEPE' REINA

Out-psyching Chelsea's penalty-takers in the tense semi-final shootout lifted Spanish custodian Reina into the top rank of global goalkeepers. But it wasn't the first time Reina had emerged victorious from a vital shootout as Liverpool had won the 2006 FA Cup final thanks to a penalty-kick victory over West Ham United.

Although he was born in Madrid, Reina started his career with Barcelona, making his debut at the age of 18. But to get some first team football he joined Villareal on loan in 2002 and made the switch permanent in 2004. The unfashionable Spanish side were enjoying a boom period, winning the Intertoto Cup twice in succession in 2003 and 2004 to qualify for the UEFA Cup for the first time, and Reina helped the club secure a Champions League spot by finishing third in La Liga at the end of the 2004/05 season, saving seven out of nine penalty kicks along the way.

He was signed by Liverpool in July 2005 taking over as first choice goalkeeper from 2005 Champions League final hero Jerzy Dudek. At the start of that season Reina made his international debut for Spain in a friendly match against Uruguay which Spain won 2-0.

Reina proved a huge success as he notched up various new Liverpool records. He surpassed David James' club record of five successive clean sheets in the Premiership era. Reina's incredible run ended at eight league games when Everton's James Beattie headed past him into the Liverpool net in Liverpool's 3-1 win in December 2005.

On 16 April 2006 Reina celebrated his 50th appearance for Liverpool by keeping yet another a clean sheet against Blackburn. As a result he holds a Liverpool record for the fewest number of goals conceded by a keeper in their first fifty games at 29, beating the previous record held by Ray Clemence in 1970/71 for conceding only 32 goals.

In May 2006 Reina was awarded the Premier League's Golden Gloves award for keeping 20 clean sheets that season.

In the final domestic game of the season – the FA Cup Final – Reina made a number of errors to allow the Hammers to lead 3-2. Steven Gerrard saved Reina's blushes with a late equaliser, and then Reina made a crucial save in extra-time. The match ended 3-3 and went to penalties, where Reina saved three out of four kicks to win the Cup.

After the 2006/07 Champions League semi-final first-leg against Chelsea, Reina was awarded Man of the Match by Liverpool supporters thanks to a string of superb saves, including two stunning stops from England midfielder Frank Lampard. He repeated his good form in the second-leg, keeping a clean sheet. The match went to a penalty shootout where Reina reinforced his penalty-saving reputation, stopping two out of the three Chelsea kicks, from Arjen Robben and Geremi, as Liverpool won 4-1.

Only beaten in the final by a wickedly deflected free-kick and then in a late one-on-one when his manager had removed his defensive cover in an attempt to grab an equaliser, Reina conceded just 7 goals in 12 matches in the 2006/07 Champions League.

If manager Rafa Benitez's claim in 2005 on signing the young keeper that Reina was the best in the world was premature, then 2006/07 showed that he now lays serious claim to that crown. Even Steven Gerrard says so.

Reina has only conceded two out of seven spot-kicks in shootouts for Liverpool

CARLO ANCELOTTI

Masterminding AC Milan's victory in the 2006/07 means that there is only one candidate for best coach of the UEFA Champions League campaign.

Many would feel that Liverpool coach Rafa Benitex would qualify as the most tactically astute around, but Ancelotti's approach to the final, which contrasted markedly with the gung-ho tactics of the 2005 final, saw determined Milan take a growing grip on the game, dominate the second half and gain revenge for that painful defeat in Istanbul.

In fact Milan's victory meant Ancelotti became a member of an elite club, being only the fifth coach to win the Champions League as both a player and a coach. As a player, "Carletto" appeared 26 times for Italy, including playing in Italia 90. He started his club career in 1976 with Parma. In 1979, he transferred to Roma, as captain and midfielder, where he won the Italian championship and the Italian Cup 4 times. From 1987 until 1992 he played for AC Milan, and was part of the legendary squad that won consecutive European Cups in 1989 and 1990.

Ancelotti's first coaching job was with Serie B side Reggiana in 1995, winning promotion to Serie A in his only year at the club. Ancelotti then returned to Parma and promptly won the 1997 UEFA Cup. He became the successor to Marcello Lippi at Juventus in 1999, but went trophyless during his two-year stint, finishing runner-up twice in Serie A. That all changed when he joined AC Milan in 2001 as a replacement for the fired Fatih Terim. The Rossoneri had foundered domestically and in Europe since their last Scudetto victory in 1999. Yet, in his first full season, Ancelotti lead them to the semi-finals of the 2001/02 UEFA Cup. The following season, Ancelotti developed his squad, converting budding striker Andrea Pirlo to playmaker alongside Rui Costa. At the same time, the striking partnership of Filippo Inzaghi and Andriy Shevchenko was dominant and dynamic. Milan won the Champions League, beating Ancelotti's old team, Juventus, 3-2 on penalties, and lifted the Scudetto and Coppa Italia in 2004.

Then came the horrific defeat to Liverpool in the 2005 Champions League final, when Milan blew a 3-0 half-time lead. Two years later, though, came sweet revenge as Ancellotti outwitted Benitez and, admittedly, enjoyed his slice of luck which had so clearly deserted him in Istanbul.

Having created a young, dynamic side, Ancelotti's Milan will be the team to beat for some time to come.

Ancelotti is currently the longest-serving manager in Italian football, yet his hobby is singing and he serenaded his victorious players after their 2006/07 Champions League triumph at the club's celebratory party at the San Siro. He also ranks second in terms of number of Milan matches coached with 322, trailing Nereo Roco (459)

Managers
by Jeremy Wilson

MOURINHO

More semi-final heartache for Jose Mourinho had the British press casting doubt over his future under Roman Abramovich at Chelsea

For different managers, the 2006/07 UEFA Champions League meant different things. At Liverpool and AC Milan it was the most important competition of the season and that was reflected in the way they prioritised those matches and each reached a second final in three years. For Real Madrid, it remains the ultimate prize and this could not have been better illustrated by Fabio Capello's demise following their exit to Bayern Munich in the last 16, even though he went on to win La Liga – Real's first trophy in four years. Elsewhere, domestic success was Manchester United's priority, likewise for

Inter Milan while Chelsea had a genuine chance of winning an unprecedented clean sweep of four major trophies. In the final analysis, those competing priorities came at a price on the European stage.

For Jose Mourinho at Chelsea, it also had appeared likely that Champions League failure would cost him his job. The club's owner, Roman Abramovich, is known to crave European success and the additions last year of Andriy Shevchenko and Michael Ballack were a clear indication of that priority. After three attempts now with Chelsea, Mourinho is already clear about the importance of the Champions League this season. "Winning is a habit, winning

is culture," he said. "I just feel the last step is to take this feeling, or this little bit of luck, to European competition. Chelsea played three UEFA Champions League semi-finals in the last four years, which is fantastic, but couldn't play one single final. This club wants more and we want more. I won it before, but past is past; I want to do it with Chelsea. The players, they want to do it but we have to do it without being obsessed because being obsessed doesn't help."

Mourinho believes that small details can make the difference. A second semi-final loss in three years at the hands of Liverpool came about only after extra-time and penalties. Earlier in the competition, Mourinho had guided Chelsea through a difficult

FERGUSON

Domestic title success allowed Sir Alex Ferguson some respite from chasing his goal of a second Champions League success, but it seems as if the old maestro won't retire until he's got his hands on the famous old trophy once again

group containing Werder Bremen and Barcelona before beating Porto and Valencia in the knock-out phase. Even in defeat, Mourinho was the highest profile manager in the competition although the pre-match 'mind games' appeared to backfire against Rafael Benitez and his Liverpool side.

Prior to the tie, there was friction between the rival managers. Mourinho pointed to Chelsea's league ascendancy over Liverpool, before suggesting that he would have been sacked if he had Benitez's Premiership record. Unusually, Mourinho also set a negative tone for his team by saying that the clubs' respective schedules would give Liverpool an advantage. Benitez kept his calm, smiled at Mourinho's 'games' and kept a psychological edge that was arguably decisive in his victory. It remains to be seen whether this latest Champions League disappointment will leave a lasting scar on Mourinho and Chelsea. Gianfranco Zola, for one, doubts it: "It shouldn't become a mental problem. They've got a master in handling mental situations in Mourinho, he's very good at these type of things."

Despite his club's eventual defeat in the final, the Champions League has continued to enhance Benitez's reputation as an astute tactician, particularly

CAPELLO

Fabio Capello went through dark times during 2006/07, especially after a second round exit from the Champions League to Bayern Munich, yet emerged to lift the Spanish title for Real Madrid the first time since 2003

WENGER

Arsène Wenger watches Arsenal's dream die yet again as a late goal at the Emirates sends them crashing out to PSV Eindhoven

Boudewijn Zenden who were given the job of hugging the touchline and supplying the ammunition for Dirk Kuyt and Steven Gerrard in attack. It was a specific plan which almost worked, but you had to wonder whether the Liverpool players' familiarity (or lack of) with this formation was a problem. There is a fine line between sensible rotation of players and constant tinkering.

Ultimately, though, after a rather fortuitous goal put them ahead, it was a clinical finish from Filippo Inzaghi which proved the difference for a hugely experienced Milan team. Champions League success was something that no-one at Milan could have dreamt of achieving at the beginning of the season and it certainly arrived as vindication for the manager Carlo Ancelotti after the traumas of managing a team to defeat in the final against Liverpool at Istanbul in 2005 despite a 3-0 half-time advantage. Milan were perhaps fortunate to be allowed in the competition after being engulfed in the scandal which shook Italian football in 2006, but they were also probably helped by being able to concentrate fully on the competition once their hopes in Serie A had been ended by the deduction of eight points. "Our season is like a happy-ending story," concluded Ancelotti.

Earlier in the competition, Milan had suffered mixed experiences in overcoming Celtic and Manchester United. Managed by Gordon Strachan, Celtic had qualified for the knock-out phase for the first-time in their history with performances which included a memorable win over Manchester United, before facing Milan in the last 16. Strachan's dogged team kept Milan at bay until extra-time of the second leg at the San Siro when Kaká scored the only goal in 210 minutes of football. "If there was a trophy for sheer guts and determination then we'd have a chance of winning it," said Strachan, whose own managerial reputation continues to grow.

Milan, however, saved their best for the second leg of the semi-final against Manchester United which they won 3-0 after losing 3-2 at Old Trafford. Despite winning the European Cup Winners'

in the intense environment of knock-out football. It is something that Mourinho knows to his personal cost after now losing three head-to-head semi-finals against Benitez, including the 2006 FA Cup semi-final.

Perhaps most impressive, though, was the way in which Benitez masterminded success over the defending champions Barcelona in the last 16 and then PSV Eindhoven in the quarter-finals. Both matches were won courtesy of their performances away from

home in the first leg of the matches with respective 2-1 and 3-0 victories. In both ties, Benitez's tactics were implemented to perfection. His decision to prioritise the Champions League from a relatively early stage of the season was also crucial.

The final, however, revealed limitations in his managerial style. Milan sat back in the first-half, but Liverpool, totally dominant, could not take advantage. Benitez sent out a side with two wingers in Jermaine Pennant and

Cup with both Aberdeen and United, as well as the Champions League of 1999, silverware in Europe remains relatively scarce on Ferguson's managerial record. Milan players spoke of their preference for playing against United's more open and attacking style as opposed to the more cautious Liverpool. United, of course, had set the competition alight with a 7-1 win over Roma, but when the crunch came the likes of Wayne Rooney and Cristiano Ronaldo – so dominant in the Premiership – were unable to exert the same influence on the European stage.

Like Chelsea, United had mitigating circumstances. Their preparations were undermined by injury and the team looked weary as they struggled to counteract Milan's slick passing. In truth, the gruelling and relentless nature of the head-to-head for the Premiership between Ferguson and Mourinho had probably done most to determine the UEFA Champions League finalists. For

different reasons, another European success would be a defining moment in the careers of either Ferguson or Mourinho. The evidence of this season is that they might have to sacrifice something domestically in order to fulfil that particular ambition.

Of the other managers at English clubs, the Champions League provided scant comfort for Arsenal. Having reached the final in 2006, Thierry Henry's last match for the club proved to be defeat at the hands of a rather ordinary PSV Eindhoven. Of the big four clubs in England, Arsène Wenger remains the only manager who lacks a European trophy on an otherwise hugely impressive CV. After the turmoil of the end to Arsenal's first season at their new stadium, can Wenger magic up a team to challenge in Europe? With the competition becoming ever more intense between the top managers and clubs, the task will prove ever more difficult in 2007/08.

Carlo Ancelotti worked a minor miracle to take AC Milan from third qualifying round to Champions of Europe

BENITEZ

Liverpool manager Rafa Benitez seems much more at home in the tactical jousting of European competition than the blood and thunder of the Premiership

Every Game, Every Goal, Every Fact!

Kaká (AC Milan), leading scorer in the 2006/07 UEFA Champions League

Ryan Giggs (Manchester United), who provided the most assists thoroughout the competition

TOP GOALSCORERS		
Kaká	AC Milan	10
Peter Crouch	Liverpool	7
Ruud van Nistelrooy	Real Madrid	6
Fernando Morientes	Valencia	6
Didier Drogba	Chelsea	6
Raúl González	Real Madrid	5
Filippo Inzaghi	AC Milan	4
Nicolae Dica	Steaua Bucharest	4

ASSISTS		
Ryan Giggs	Manchester United	7
Juninho Pernambucano	Lyon	5
Cristiano Ronaldo	Manchester United	5
Steve Finnan	Liverpool	4
Clarence Seedorf	AC Milan	4
Craig Bellamy	Liverpool	3
Hasan Salihamidciz	Bayern Munich	3
Kaká	AC Milan	3

SHOTS ON TARGET		
Kaká	AC Milan	28
Cristiano Ronaldo	Manchester United	22
Didier Drogba	Chelsea	15
Steven Gerrard	Liverpool	14
Ruud van Nistelrooy	Real Madrid	13
Filippo Inzaghi	AC Milan	13
Francesco Totti	AS Roma	13
David Villa	Valencia	13

SHOTS OFF TARGET		
Cristiano Ronaldo	Manchester United	18
Didier Drogba	Chelsea	18
Kaká	AC Milan	16
Francesco Totti	Roma	15
Wayne Rooney	Manchester United	15

RULED OFFSIDE

Didier Drogba	Chelsea	20
Jefferson Farfán	PSV Eindhoven	17
Mohamed Tchite	Anderlecht	17
Francesco Totti	AS Roma	17
Hélder Postiga	Porto	14

RED CARDS

Dirk Marcellis	PSV Eindhoven	1
Michael Lamey	PSV Eindhoven	1
Daniele Bonera	AC Milan	1
Mahamadou Diarra	Real Madrid	1
Bastian Schweinsteiger	Bayern Munich	1

YELLOW CARDS

Mark van Bommel	Bayern Munich	5
Claudio Pizarro	AS Roma	5
David Albelda	Valencia	5
Roberto Ayala	Valencia	5
Sergio Ramos	Real Madrid	4

FOULS COMMITTED

Jefferson Farfán	PSV Eindhoven	30
Didier Drogba	Chelsea	29
Mark van Bommel	Bayern Munich	25
Paul Scholes	Manchester United	25
Massimo Ambrosini	AC Milan	25

FOULS SUFFERED

Francesco Totti	Roma	36
Cristiano Ronaldo	Manchester United	32
Didier Drogba	Chelsea	29
Kaká	AC Milan	29
Deco	Barcelona	25

Paul Scholes receives red against Roma

Roma's Francesco Totti was the most fouled player in 2006/07

section two

2006/07 uefa champions league competing clubs

The Competitors

AC MILAN
Milan, Italy
Ground: San Siro
Capacity: 85,700

EUROPEAN CLUB COMPETITION RECORD

Competition	Pld	W	D	L	GF	GA
ECCC	198	108	46	44	349	168
ECWC	30	17	10	3	47	20
UCUP	60	31	11	18	93	57
SCUP	11	6	3	2	10	10
IC	0	0	0	0	0	0
WCC	10	4	1	5	17	15
Total	309	166	71	72	516	270

UEFA WINNERS
European Cup – 1962/63, 1968/69,
1988/89, 1989/90
UEFA Champions League – 1993/94, 2002/03
UEFA Cup Winners' Cup – 1967/68, 1972/73
World Club Championship – 1969, 1989, 1990
UEFA Super Cup – 1989, 1990, 1994, 2003

AJAX AMSTERDAM
Amsterdam, Netherlands
Ground: Amsterdam ArenA
Capacity: 50,200

EUROPEAN CLUB COMPETITION RECORD

Competition	Pld	W	D	L	GF	GA
ECCC	155	77	37	41	249	150
ECWC	28	18	2	8	53	22
UCUP	80	44	12	24	160	75
SCUP	6	2	1	3	11	4
IC	0	0	0	0	0	0
WCC	3	1	2	0	4	1
Total	272	142	54	76	477	252

UEFA WINNERS
European Champions Clubs' Cup – 1970/71,
1971/72, 1972/73
UEFA Champions League – 1994/95
UEFA Cup Winners' Cup – 1986/87
World Club Championship Cup – 1972, 1995
UEFA Super Cup – 1973, 1995
UEFA Cup – 1991/92

AKTOBE
Aktobe, Kazakhstan
Ground: Tsentralny Stadium
Capacity: 13,161

EUROPEAN CLUB COMPETITION RECORD

Competition	Pld	W	D	L	GF	GA
ECCC	2	0	1	1	1	2
ECWC	0	0	0	0	0	0
UCUP	0	0	0	0	0	0
SCUP	0	0	0	0	0	0
IC	0	0	0	0	0	0
WCC	0	0	0	0	0	0
Total	2	0	1	1	1	2

2005/06 was Aktobe's first Champions League
season after their first ever Kazakh league title

AEK ATHENS
Athens, Greece
Ground: Spiridon Louis,
Olympic Stadium
Capacity: 67,199

EUROPEAN CLUB COMPETITION RECORD

Competition	Pld	W	D	L	GF	GA
ECCC	60	16	20	24	70	92
ECWC	22	10	3	9	33	27
UCUP	78	30	14	34	115	118
SCUP	0	0	0	0	0	0
IC	0	0	0	0	0	0
WCC	0	0	0	0	0	0
Total	160	56	37	67	218	237

AEK stands for Athletic Union of Constantinople,
as the club was established by Greek refugees
from that city in 1924 during the Greco-Turkish war

ANDERLECHT
Anderlecht, Belgium
Ground: Vanden Stock Stadium
Capacity: 26,361

EUROPEAN CLUB COMPETITION RECORD

Competition	Pld	W	D	L	GF	GA
ECCC	158	61	34	63	227	238
ECWC	44	29	3	12	86	34
UCUP	84	42	21	21	150	88
SCUP	4	2	0	2	9	6
IC	0	0	0	0	0	0
WCC	0	0	0	0	0	0
Total	290	134	58	98	472	366

UEFA WINNERS
UEFA Cup Winners' Cup – 1975/76, 1977/78
UEFA Super Cup – 1976, 1978
UEFA Cup – 1982/83

APOLLON LIMASSOL
Limassol, Cyprus
Ground: Tsirion Stadium
Capacity: 14,400

EUROPEAN CLUB COMPETITION RECORD

Competition	Pld	W	D	L	GF	GA
ECCC	6	1	1	4	5	9
ECWC	16	3	2	11	16	50
UCUP	20	6	5	9	32	39
SCUP	0	0	0	0	0	0
IC	4	1	0	3	4	13
WCC	0	0	0	0	0	0
Total	46	11	8	27	57	111

Apollon are named after the Greek god of sun, Apollo, who features on the club badge

ARSENAL
London, England
Ground: Emirates Stadium
Capacity: 60,432

EUROPEAN CLUB COMPETITION RECORD

Competition	Pld	W	D	L	GF	GA
ECCC	101	46	27	28	146	101
ECWC	27	15	10	2	48	20
UCUP	25	12	4	9	45	32
SCUP	2	0	1	1	0	2
IC	0	0	0	0	0	0
WCC	0	0	0	0	0	0
Total	155	73	42	40	239	155

UEFA WINNERS
UEFA Cup Winners' Cup – 1993/94

AUSTRIA VIENNA
Vienna, Austria
Ground: Franz-Horr-Stadion
Capacity: 11,800

EUROPEAN CLUB COMPETITION RECORD

Competition	Pld	W	D	L	GF	GA
ECCC	63	22	13	28	90	97
ECWC	39	10	15	14	41	54
UCUP	54	20	14	20	80	70
SCUP	0	0	0	0	0	0
IC	20	4	4	12	27	34
WCC	0	0	0	0	0	0
Total	176	56	46	74	238	255

The club was formed by members of the Vienna Cricket Club

B36 TORSHAVN
Torshavn, Faroe Islands
Ground: Gundadalur Stadium
Capacity: 8,020

EUROPEAN CLUB COMPETITION RECORD

Competition	Pld	W	D	L	GF	GA
ECCC	8	1	1	6	8	22
ECWC	2	0	1	1	1	2
UCUP	10	1	2	7	8	28
SCUP	0	0	0	0	0	0
IC	4	0	0	4	2	15
WCC	0	0	0	0	0	0
Total	24	2	4	18	19	67

B36 means 'Ball Club 36', referring to 1936 as the date of the club's foundation

BAKU
Baku, Azerbaijan
Ground: Tofik Bakhramov Stadium
Capacity: 29,858

EUROPEAN CLUB COMPETITION RECORD

Competition	Pld	W	D	L	GF	GA
ECCC	2	1	0	1	1	2
ECWC	0	0	0	0	0	0
UCUP	4	1	0	3	3	10
SCUP	0	0	0	0	0	0
IC	2	0	2	0	2	2
WCC	0	0	0	0	0	0
Total	8	2	2	4	6	14

Baku's first trophy was the Azerbaijan Cup in 2004/05, which they followed by winning their national league title a season later

BARCELONA
Barcelona, Spain
Ground: Camp Nou
Capacity: 98,934

EUROPEAN CLUB COMPETITION RECORD

Competition	Pld	W	D	L	GF	GA
ECCC	169	95	38	36	320	177
ECWC	85	50	18	17	178	87
UCUP	78	40	17	21	149	75
SCUP	11	3	4	4	9	13
IC	0	0	0	0	0	0
WCC	1	0	0	1	1	2
Total	344	188	77	79	657	354

UEFA WINNERS
European Champions Clubs' Cup – 1991/92
UEFA Champions League – 2005/06
UEFA Cup Winners' Cup – 1978/79, 1981/82, 1988/89, 1996/97
UEFA Super Cup – 1992, 1997

BAYERN MUNICH
Munich, Germany
Ground: Allianz Arena
Capacity: 69,901

EUROPEAN CLUB COMPETITION RECORD

Competition	Pld	W	D	L	GF	GA
ECCC	216	115	55	46	400	215
ECWC	39	19	14	6	67	36
UCUP	54	33	7	14	118	63
SCUP	5	1	0	4	5	11
IC	0	0	0	0	0	0
WCC	3	2	1	0	3	0
Total	317	170	77	70	593	325

UEFA WINNERS
European Champions Clubs' Cup – 1973/74, 1974/75, 1975/76
UEFA Champions League – 2000/01
UEFA Cup Winners' Cup – 1966/67
EUSA Cup – 1976, 2001
UEFA Cup – 1995/96

BENFICA
Lisbon, Portugal
Ground: Estádio da Luz
Capacity: 65,647

EUROPEAN CLUB COMPETITION RECORD

Competition	Pld	W	D	L	GF	GA
ECCC	174	84	40	50	320	182
ECWC	42	21	12	9	67	34
UCUP	70	33	17	20	106	79
SCUP	0	0	0	0	0	0
IC	0	0	0	0	0	0
WCC	5	1	0	4	6	15
Total	291	139	69	83	499	310

UEFA WINNERS
European Champions Clubs' Cup –
1960/61, 1961/62

BIRKIRKARA
Birkirkara, Malta
Ground: Ta'Qali Stadium
Capacity: 17,000

EUROPEAN CLUB COMPETITION RECORD

Competition	Pld	W	D	L	GF	GA
ECCC	4	0	1	3	4	11
ECWC	0	0	0	0	0	0
UCUP	18	1	5	12	7	39
SCUP	0	0	0	0	0	0
IC	2	0	0	2	1	5
WCC	0	0	0	0	0	0
Total	24	1	6	17	12	55

Despite representing the largest town on the island of Malta, Birkirkara first qualified for Europe by finishing second in the league in 1996/97

BORDEAUX
Bordeaux, France
Ground: Stade Chaban
Delmas
Capacity: 34,327

EUROPEAN CLUB COMPETITION RECORD

Competition	Pld	W	D	L	GF	GA
ECCC	34	11	14	9	35	37
ECWC	10	6	1	3	14	10
UCUP	90	48	16	26	135	95
SCUP	0	0	0	0	0	0
IC	6	5	1	0	18	3
WCC	0	0	0	0	0	0
Total	140	70	32	38	202	145

UEFA WINNERS
UEFA Intertoto Cup – 1995

CELTIC
Glasgow, Scotland
Ground: Celtic Park
Capacity: 60,506

EUROPEAN CLUB COMPETITION RECORD

Competition	Pld	W	D	L	GF	GA
ECCC	118	60	20	38	194	124
ECWC	38	21	4	13	75	37
UCUP	69	33	13	23	113	67
SCUP	0	0	0	0	0	0
IC	0	0	0	0	0	0
WCC	3	1	0	2	2	3
Total	228	115	37	76	384	231

UEFA WINNERS
European Champions Clubs' Cup – 1966/67

CHELSEA
London, England
Ground: Stamford Bridge
Capacity: 42,055

EUROPEAN CLUB COMPETITION RECORD

Competition	Pld	W	D	L	GF	GA
ECCC	62	32	16	14	93	50
ECWC	39	23	10	6	81	28
UCUP	8	4	1	3	11	10
SCUP	1	1	0	0	1	0
IC	0	0	0	0	0	0
WCC	0	0	0	0	0	0
Total	110	60	27	23	186	88

UEFA WINNERS
UEFA Cup Winners' Cup – 1970/71, 1997/98
UEFA Super Cup – 1998

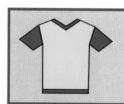

CHIEVO VERONA
Verona, Italy
Ground: Marc'Antonio
Bentegodi
Capacity: 42,160

EUROPEAN CLUB COMPETITION RECORD

Competition	Pld	W	D	L	GF	GA
ECCC	2	0	1	1	2	4
ECWC	0	0	0	0	0	0
UCUP	4	1	1	2	2	5
SCUP	0	0	0	0	0	0
IC	0	0	0	0	0	0
WCC	0	0	0	0	0	0
Total	6	1	2	3	4	9

Chievo are owned by cake company, Paluani

COPENHAGEN
Copenhagen, Denmark
Ground: Park Stadion
Capacity: 41,781

EUROPEAN CLUB COMPETITION RECORD

Competition	Pld	W	D	L	GF	GA
ECCC	24	10	4	10	37	39
ECWC	14	7	3	4	26	15
UCUP	36	13	10	13	49	40
SCUP	0	0	0	0	0	0
IC	6	3	2	1	8	8
WCC	0	0	0	0	0	0
Total	80	33	19	28	120	102

Copenhagen's local rivals in the capital city of
Denmark are Brondby, the club part-owned by
Peter Schmeichel

CORK CITY
Cork, Republic of Ireland
Ground: Turner's Cross
Stadium
Capacity: 9,000

EUROPEAN CLUB COMPETITION RECORD

Competition	Pld	W	D	L	GF	GA
ECCC	8	2	1	5	7	12
ECWC	4	1	0	3	2	9
UCUP	14	2	3	9	6	20
SCUP	0	0	0	0	0	0
IC	14	4	5	5	10	11
WCC	0	0	0	0	0	0
Total	40	9	9	22	25	52

The club is one of the youngest competing in the
top level of European football, only having been
founded in 1984

CRVENA ZVEZDA
Belgrade, Serbia
Ground: Stadion Crvena
Zvezda
Capacity: 51,328

EUROPEAN CLUB COMPETITION RECORD

Competition	Pld	W	D	L	GF	GA
ECCC	105	55	18	32	214	133
ECWC	34	12	10	12	64	43
UCUP	90	41	20	29	150	116
SCUP	1	0	0	1	0	1
IC	0	0	0	0	0	0
WCC	1	1	0	0	3	0
Total	231	109	48	74	431	293

UEFA WINNERS
European Champions Clubs' Cup – 1990/91
Super Cup – 1991

CSKA MOSCOW
Moscow, Russia
Ground: Dinamo Stadion
Capacity: 36,540

EUROPEAN CLUB COMPETITION RECORD

Competition	Pld	W	D	L	GF	GA
ECCC	36	14	10	12	39	38
ECWC	4	2	0	2	5	5
UCUP	27	11	8	8	37	22
SCUP	1	0	0	1	1	3
IC	0	0	0	0	0	0
WCC	0	0	0	0	0	0
Total	68	27	18	23	82	68

UEFA WINNERS
UEFA Cup – 2004/05

DEBREÇEN
Debreçen, Hungary
Ground: Stadion Oláh
Gábor Út
Capacity: 10,200

EUROPEAN CLUB COMPETITION RECORD

Competition	Pld	W	D	L	GF	GA
ECCC	6	2	1	3	10	11
ECWC	0	0	0	0	0	0
UCUP	16	6	4	6	20	23
SCUP	0	0	0	0	0	0
IC	10	4	3	3	18	13
WCC	0	0	0	0	0	0
Total	32	12	8	12	48	47

Debrecen's nickname is Loki,
from Lokomotiv, stemming from its long-standing
ties with the railways

DJURGÅRDEN
Stockholm, Sweden
Ground: Stockholms
Stadion
Capacity: 14,500

EUROPEAN CLUB COMPETITION RECORD

Competition	Pld	W	D	L	GF	GA
ECCC	16	4	5	7	17	28
ECWC	8	1	4	3	10	11
UCUP	18	7	4	7	26	26
SCUP	0	0	0	0	0	0
IC	4	2	0	2	15	6
WCC	0	0	0	0	0	0
Total	46	14	13	19	68	71

Teddy Sheringham once had a brief loan spell at
the club as a 19 year-old in 1985

F91 DUDELANGE
Dudelange, Luxembourg
Ground: Stade Jos Nosbaum
Capacity: 4,600

EUROPEAN CLUB COMPETITION RECORD

Competition	Pld	W	D	L	GF	GA
ECCC	16	4	5	7	17	28
ECWC	8	1	4	3	10	11
UCUP	18	7	4	7	26	26
SCUP	0	0	0	0	0	0
IC	4	2	0	2	15	6
WCC	0	0	0	0	0	0
Total	46	14	13	19	68	71

Dudelange was formed in 1991 by the alliance of three clubs in the southern Luxembourg town

DYNAMO KIEV
Kiev, Ukraine
Ground: Stadion NSK Olimpiyskiy
Capacity: 83,160

EUROPEAN CLUB COMPETITION RECORD

Competition	Pld	W	D	L	GF	GA
ECCC	172	78	36	58	256	200
ECWC	30	20	6	4	72	27
UCUP	34	12	11	11	36	32
SCUP	3	2	0	1	3	1
IC	0	0	0	0	0	0
WCC	0	0	0	0	0	0
Total	239	112	53	74	367	260

UEFA WINNERS
UEFA Cup Winners' Cup – 1974/75, 1985/86
UEFA Super Cup – 1975

EKRANAS
Panevezys, Lithuania
Ground: Aukstaitija Stadium
Capacity: 10,000

EUROPEAN CLUB COMPETITION RECORD

Competition	Pld	W	D	L	GF	GA
ECCC	6	1	0	5	6	12
ECWC	2	0	1	1	4	5
UCUP	10	4	1	5	9	17
SCUP	0	0	0	0	0	0
IC	4	0	2	2	2	4
WCC	0	0	0	0	0	0
Total	22	5	4	13	21	38

In 2004 the club was expelled from the Lithuanian top flight for one day for a match-fixing scandal, and then reinstated

ELBASANI
Elbasan, Albania
Ground: Stadiumi Ruzhdi Bizhuta
Capacity: 13,000

EUROPEAN CLUB COMPETITION RECORD

Competition	Pld	W	D	L	GF	GA
ECCC	4	1	0	3	1	9
ECWC	0	0	0	0	0	0
UCUP	2	0	2	0	1	1
SCUP	0	0	0	0	0	0
IC	0	0	0	0	0	0
WCC	0	0	0	0	0	0
Total	6	1	2	3	2	10

Elbasani celebrated their second league title in 2006 by staging Albania's first ever open-topped bus ride

FENERBAHÇE
Istanbul, Turkey
Ground: Fenerbahçe Sükrü Saraçoglu
Capacity: 53,530

EUROPEAN CLUB COMPETITION RECORD

Competition	Pld	W	D	L	GF	GA
ECCC	67	19	9	39	69	125
ECWC	9	3	1	5	11	11
UCUP	54	18	10	26	72	91
SCUP	0	0	0	0	0	0
IC	0	0	0	0	0	0
WCC	0	0	0	0	0	0
Total	130	40	20	70	152	227

The Turkish club celebrates its centenary in 2007

GALATASARAY
Istanbul, Turkey
Ground: Ali Sami Yen Stadi
Capacity: 26,000

EUROPEAN CLUB COMPETITION RECORD

Competition	Pld	W	D	L	GF	GA
ECCC	131	48	32	51	172	187
ECWC	32	12	7	13	42	55
UCUP	33	10	11	12	38	47
SCUP	1	1	0	0	2	1
IC	0	0	0	0	0	0
WCC	0	0	0	0	0	0
Total	197	71	50	76	254	290

UEFA WINNERS
UEFA Cup – 1999/00
UEFA Super Cup – 2000

NK GORICA
Nova Gorica, Slovenia
Ground: Sportni Park Gorica
Capacity: 4,200

EUROPEAN CLUB COMPETITION RECORD

Competition	Pld	W	D	L	GF	GA
ECCC	12	5	1	6	20	25
ECWC	0	0	0	0	0	0
UCUP	22	4	2	16	18	42
SCUP	0	0	0	0	0	0
UIC	0	0	0	0	0	0
EUSA	0	0	0	0	0	0
Total	34	9	3	22	38	67

Gorica won a hat-trick of Slovenian league titles from 2004-2006

HAFNARFJÖRDUR
Hafnarfjördur, Iceland
Ground: Kaplakrikavöllur Stadium
Capacity: 4,800

EUROPEAN CLUB COMPETITION RECORD

Competition	Pld	W	D	L	GF	GA
ECCC	6	1	1	4	5	10
ECWC	0	0	0	0	0	0
UCUP	12	4	4	4	14	18
SCUP	0	0	0	0	0	0
IC	4	1	1	2	6	7
WCC	0	0	0	0	0	0
Total	22	6	6	10	25	35

The town is renowned as being one of the most popular residences for Elves in Iceland

HAMBURG
Hamburg, Germany
Ground: AOL Arena
Capacity: 55,000

EUROPEAN CLUB COMPETITION RECORD

Competition	Pld	W	D	L	GF	GA
ECCC	43	19	9	15	72	56
ECWC	34	20	7	7	81	39
UCUP	80	40	13	27	130	93
SCUP	4	0	2	2	1	9
IC	24	14	6	4	42	21
WCC	1	0	0	1	1	2
Total	186	93	37	56	327	220

UEFA WINNERS
European Champions Clubs' Cup – 1982/83
UEFA Cup Winners' Cup – 1976/77
UEFA Intertoto Cup – 2005

HEART OF MIDLOTHIAN
Edinburgh, Scotland
Ground: Tynecastle
Capacity: 18,300

EUROPEAN CLUB COMPETITION RECORD

Competition	Pld	W	D	L	GF	GA
ECCC	8	2	1	5	8	16
ECWC	10	3	3	4	16	14
UCUP	38	17	6	15	46	44
SCUP	0	0	0	0	0	0
IC	0	0	0	0	0	0
WCC	0	0	0	0	0	0
Total	56	22	10	24	70	74

The club was named after a local dance hall, where it was founded, which in turn was named after a novel by famed author Sir Walter Scott

INTER MILAN
Milan, Italy
Ground: San Siro
Capacity: 85,700

EUROPEAN CLUB COMPETITION RECORD

Competition	Pld	W	D	L	GF	GA
ECCC	119	59	36	24	174	106
ECWC	12	6	2	4	22	9
UCUP	149	73	36	40	222	129
SCUP	0	0	0	0	0	0
IC	0	0	0	0	0	0
WCC	5	3	1	1	6	1
Total	285	141	75	69	424	245

UEFA WINNERS
European Champions Clubs' Cup –
1963/64, 1964/65
EUSA Cup – 1964, 1965/66
UEFA Cup

LEGIA WARSAW
Warsaw, Poland
Ground: Stadion Wojska Polskiego
Capacity: 15,278

EUROPEAN CLUB COMPETITION RECORD

Competition	Pld	W	D	L	GF	GA
ECCC	38	18	5	15	46	43
ECWC	37	14	12	11	53	39
UCUP	50	21	12	17	87	63
SCUP	0	0	0	0	0	0
IC	0	0	0	0	0	0
WCC	0	0	0	0	0	0
Total	125	53	29	43	186	145

The club was founded in March 1916 during military operations among the 'legions' of Polish Soldiers on the eastern front of World War I

LEVSKI SOFIA
Sofia, Bulgaria
Ground: Georgi Asparoukhov
Capacity: 28,150

EUROPEAN CLUB COMPETITION RECORD

Competition	Pld	W	D	L	GF	GA
ECCC	48	12	12	24	61	74
ECWC	36	14	5	17	70	55
UCUP	74	28	17	29	103	101
SCUP	0	0	0	0	0	0
UIC	0	0	0	0	0	0
EUSA	0	0	0	0	0	0
Total	158	54	34	70	234	230

Levski is the only club that has never been relegated from the Bulgarian top flight

LILLE
Lille France
Ground: Felix-Bollaert Stadium, Lens
Capacity: 41,810

EUROPEAN CLUB COMPETITION RECORD

Competition	Pld	W	D	L	GF	GA
ECCC	24	7	9	8	22	17
ECWC	0	0	0	0	0	0
UCUP	18	9	6	3	19	11
SCUP	0	0	0	0	0	0
IC	12	7	4	1	17	7
WCC	0	0	0	0	0	0
Total	54	23	19	12	58	35

UEFA WINNERS
UEFA Intertoto Cup – 2004

LINFIELD
Belfast, Northern Ireland
Ground: Windsor Park
Capacity: 20,332

EUROPEAN CLUB COMPETITION RECORD

Competition	Pld	W	D	L	GF	GA
ECCC	51	6	15	30	53	100
ECWC	6	2	0	4	6	11
UCUP	18	3	6	9	18	39
SCUP	0	0	0	0	0	0
IC	0	0	0	0	0	0
WCC	0	0	0	0	0	0
Total	75	11	21	43	77	150

Linfield once drew 2-2 away at Nottingham Forest in the FA Cup

LIVERPOOL
Liverpool, England
Ground: Anfield
Capacity: 45,400

EUROPEAN CLUB COMPETITION RECORD

Competition	Pld	W	D	L	GF	GA
ECCC	143	82	31	30	256	113
ECWC	29	16	5	8	57	29
UCUP	73	40	19	14	116	55
SCUP	7	4	1	2	16	10
IC	0	0	0	0	0	0
WCC	2	0	0	2	0	4
Total	254	142	56	56	445	211

UEFA WINNERS
European Cup – 1976/77, 1977/78, 1980/81, 1983/84
UEFA Champions League – 2004/05
UEFA Super Cup – 1977, 2001, 2005
UEFA Cup – 1972/73, 1975/76, 2000/01

OLYMPIQUE LYONNAIS
Lyon, France
Ground: Stade
de Gerland
Capacity: 41,184

EUROPEAN CLUB COMPETITION RECORD

Competition	Pld	W	D	L	GF	GA
ECCC	66	34	14	18	113	68
ECWC	22	9	5	8	31	28
UCUP	40	23	5	12	71	57
SCUP	0	0	0	0	0	0
IC	8	7	0	1	21	7
WCC	0	0	0	0	0	0
Total	136	73	24	39	236	160

UEFA WINNERS
UEFA Intertoto Cup – 1997

MACCABI HAIFA
Haifa, Israel
Ground: Kiryat
Eli'ezer Stadium
Capacity: 14,002

EUROPEAN CLUB COMPETITION RECORD

Competition	Pld	W	D	L	GF	GA
ECCC	20	6	4	10	34	36
ECWC	18	9	2	7	29	22
UCUP	26	9	8	9	26	36
SCUP	0	0	0	0	0	0
IC	6	2	0	4	4	11
WCC	0	0	0	0	0	0
Total	70	26	14	30	93	105

Maccabi were the club who discovered
Eyal Berkovic, who played for Manchester City,
West Ham and Celtic amongst others

MANCHESTER UNITED
Manchester, England
Ground: Old Trafford
Capacity: 76,212

EUROPEAN CLUB COMPETITION RECORD

Competition	Pld	W	D	L	GF	GA
ECCC	180	99	41	40	352	181
ECWC	31	16	9	6	55	35
UCUP	20	6	10	4	19	16
SCUP	2	1	0	1	1	1
IC	0	0	0	0	0	0
WCC	3	1	1	1	2	2
Total	236	123	61	52	429	235

UEFA WINNERS
European Cup – 1967/68
UEFA Champions League – 1998/99
UEFA Cup Winners' Cup – 1990/91
World Club Championship – 1999
UEFA Super Cup – 1991

METALURGS
Liepajas, Latvia
Ground: Daugava
Stadions
Capacity: 5,083

EUROPEAN CLUB COMPETITION RECORD

Competition	Pld	W	D	L	GF	GA
ECCC	4	1	1	2	3	9
ECWC	8	2	2	4	7	20
UCUP	18	5	4	9	33	39
SCUP	0	0	0	0	0	0
IC	4	3	0	1	7	9
WCC	0	0	0	0	0	0
Total	34	11	7	16	50	77

The club is named after the metallurgical
factory in the seaside resort of Liepajas in
which it was founded

MLADÁ BOLESLAV
**Boleslav , Czech Republic
Ground:
ll Mestsky stadion
Capacity: 8,121**

EUROPEAN CLUB COMPETITION RECORD

Competition	Pld	W	D	L	GF	GA
ECCC	4	1	2	1	8	9
ECWC	0	0	0	0	0	0
UCUP	6	1	3	2	6	6
SCUP	0	0	0	0	0	0
IC	0	0	0	0	0	0
WCC	0	0	0	0	0	0
Total	10	2	5	3	14	15

From 1919 to 1949 the club included
'Aston Villa' in its name

MYLLYKOSKEN PALLO-47
**Anjalankoski, Finland
Ground: Anjalankosken
Jalkapallokenttä
Capacity: 4,067**

EUROPEAN CLUB COMPETITION RECORD

Competition	Pld	W	D	L	GF	GA
ECCC	4	2	1	1	4	4
ECWC	6	1	1	4	4	9
UCUP	24	5	8	11	24	40
SCUP	0	0	0	0	0	0
IC	4	0	2	2	7	9
WCC	0	0	0	0	0	0
Total	38	8	12	18	39	62

MyPa, as they are better known, were the club who
discovered Jari Litmanen and Sami Hyppia

OLYMPIAKOS
**Piraeus, Greece
Ground: Karaiskaki
Stadium
Capacity: 33,334**

EUROPEAN CLUB COMPETITION RECORD

Competition	Pld	W	D	L	GF	GA
ECCC	94	26	22	46	110	159
ECWC	33	14	6	13	43	47
UCUP	44	20	6	18	57	68
SCUP	0	0	0	0	0	0
IC	0	0	0	0	0	0
WCC	0	0	0	0	0	0
Total	171	60	34	77	210	274

The club has 17 different sporting departments
including basketball, Athletics, Volleyball
and Water Polo

OSASUNA
**Pamplona, Spain
Ground: Estadio Reyno
de Navarra
Capacity: 19,553**

EUROPEAN CLUB COMPETITION RECORD

Competition	Pld	W	D	L	GF	GA
ECCC	2	0	2	0	1	1
ECWC	0	0	0	0	0	0
UCUP	26	11	7	8	29	21
SCUP	0	0	0	0	0	0
IC	0	0	0	0	0	0
WCC	0	0	0	0	0	0
Total	28	11	9	8	30	22

'Osasuna' is the Basque word for 'health'

PORTO
Porto, Portugal
Ground: Estádio do Dragão
Capacity: 50,106

EUROPEAN CLUB COMPETITION RECORD

Competition	Pld	W	D	L	GF	GA
ECCC	151	64	37	50	222	166
ECWC	41	21	7	13	58	44
UCUP	57	29	10	18	95	58
SCUP	4	2	0	2	3	3
IC	0	0	0	0	0	0
WCC	2	1	1	0	2	1
Total	255	117	55	83	380	272

UEFA WINNERS
European Champions Clubs' Cup – 1986/87
UEFA Champions League – 2003/04
World Club Championship – 1987, 2004
UEFA Super Cup – 1987/88
UEFA Cup – 2002/03

PSV EINDHOVEN
Eindhoven, Netherlands
Ground: Philips Stadion
Capacity: 36,500

EUROPEAN CLUB COMPETITION RECORD

Competition	Pld	W	D	L	GF	GA
ECCC	137	53	32	52	189	163
ECWC	26	14	5	7	52	22
UCUP	73	32	18	23	126	83
SCUP	2	1	0	1	1	3
IC	0	0	0	0	0	0
WCC	1	0	1	0	2	2
Total	239	100	56	83	370	273

UEFA WINNERS
European Champions Clubs' Cup – 1987/88
UEFA Cup – 1977/78

PYUNIK
Yerevan, Armenia
Ground: Hanrapetakan Stadium
Capacity: 14,968

EUROPEAN CLUB COMPETITION RECORD

Competition	Pld	W	D	L	GF	GA
ECCC	16	4	5	7	17	21
ECWC	0	0	0	0	0	0
UCUP	0	0	0	0	0	0
SCUP	0	0	0	0	0	0
IC	0	0	0	0	0	0
WCC	0	0	0	0	0	0
Total	16	4	5	7	17	21

Pyunik have won six consecutive Armenian league title from 2001 to present

RABOTNICKI
Skopje, FYR Macedonia
Ground: City Stadium
Capacity: 18,104

EUROPEAN CLUB COMPETITION RECORD

Competition	Pld	W	D	L	GF	GA
ECCC	10	3	3	4	13	10
ECWC	0	0	0	0	0	0
UCUP	4	0	0	4	2	11
SCUP	0	0	0	0	0	0
IC	0	0	0	0	0	0
WCC	0	0	0	0	0	0
Total	14	3	3	8	15	21

Rabotnicki is owned by the Kometal company, run by the Mayor of Skopje

REAL MADRID
Madrid, Spain
Ground: Santiago Bernabeau Stadium
Capacity: 80,354

EUROPEAN CLUB COMPETITION RECORD

Competition	Pld	W	D	L	GF	GA
ECCC	299	173	52	74	654	334
ECWC	31	16	9	6	57	24
UCUP	64	33	10	21	111	75
SCUP	3	1	0	2	4	4
IC	0	0	0	0	0	0
WCC	7	3	1	3	10	8
Total	404	226	72	106	836	445

UEFA WINNERS
European Champions Clubs' Cup – 1955/56, 1956/57, 1957/58, 1958/59, 1959/60, 1965/66
UEFA Champions League – 1997/98, 1999/00, 2001/02
UEFA Cup – 1984/85, 1985/86
UEFA Super Cup – 2002
WCC Cup – 1960, 1998, 2002

ROMA
Rome, Italy
Ground: Stadio Olimpico
Capacity: 82,922

EUROPEAN CLUB COMPETITION RECORD

Competition	Pld	W	D	L	GF	GA
ECCC	49	16	16	17	53	57
ECWC	29	12	9	8	34	24
UCUP	94	52	14	28	150	82
SCUP	0	0	0	0	0	0
IC	0	0	0	0	0	0
WCC	0	0	0	0	0	0
Total	172	80	39	53	237	163

Club anthem 'Roma Roma Roma' by folksinger Antonello Vendetti is played and sung before each home match

RUZOMBEROK
Ruzomberok, Slovakia
Ground: MAK Ruzomberok
Capacity: 5,030

EUROPEAN CLUB COMPETITION RECORD

Competition	Pld	W	D	L	GF	GA
ECCC	4	1	0	3	3	7
ECWC	0	0	0	0	0	0
UCUP	6	2	2	2	6	9
SCUP	0	0	0	0	0	0
IC	0	0	0	0	0	0
WCC	0	0	0	0	0	0
Total	10	3	2	5	9	16

The club celebrated its centenary in 2006 by winning its first silverware – and did it in style by winning the Slovakian League and Cup double

SALZBURG
Salzburg, Austria
Ground: Stadion Salzburg
Capacity: 18,686

EUROPEAN CLUB COMPETITION RECORD

Competition	Pld	W	D	L	GF	GA
ECCC	16	5	5	6	13	17
ECWC	2	0	0	2	0	8
UCUP	28	11	3	14	33	43
SCUP	0	0	0	0	0	0
IC	12	4	3	5	22	19
EUSA	0	0	0	0	0	0
Total	58	20	11	27	68	87

Red Bull bought the club on 6 April 2005 and redesigned the kit to closely reflect their own branding

SEVILLA
Seville, Spain
Ground: Ramón Sánchez Pizjuán
Capacity: 55,000

EUROPEAN CLUB COMPETITION RECORD

Competition	Pld	W	D	L	GF	GA
ECCC	6	2	2	2	9	13
ECWC	2	1	0	1	2	4
UCUP	58	30	15	13	90	49
SCUP	1	1	0	0	3	0
IC	0	0	0	0	0	0
WCC	0	0	0	0	0	0
Total	67	34	17	16	104	66

UEFA WINNERS
UEFA Super Cup – 2006
UEFA Cup – 2005/06

SHAKHTAR DONETSK
Donetsk, Ukraine
Ground: Stadion Shakhtar
Capacity: 31,718

EUROPEAN CLUB COMPETITION RECORD

Competition	Pld	W	D	L	GF	GA
ECCC	40	16	8	16	58	59
ECWC	18	8	5	5	32	24
UCUP	44	20	6	18	59	63
SCUP	0	0	0	0	0	0
IC	4	1	1	2	5	8
WCC	0	0	0	0	0	0
Total	106	45	20	41	154	154

Owner Rinat Akhmatov has publicly declared he will bring European glory to Shakhtar and its fans

SHAKHTAR SOLIGORSK
Soligorsk, Belarus
Ground: Shakhtsyor Stadion
Capacity: 5,000

EUROPEAN CLUB COMPETITION RECORD

Competition	Pld	W	D	L	GF	GA
ECCC	2	0	0	2	0	2
ECWC	0	0	0	0	0	0
UCUP	4	0	1	3	4	8
SCUP	0	0	0	0	0	0
IC	6	3	1	2	15	9
WCC	0	0	0	0	0	0
Total	12	3	2	7	19	19

Soligorsk once went 60 home games unbeaten in the Belorussian Premier League

FC SHERIFF
Tiraspol, Moldova
Ground: Malaya Arena
Capacity: 9,300

EUROPEAN CLUB COMPETITION RECORD

Competition	Pld	W	D	L	GF	GA
ECCC	24	8	5	11	23	28
ECWC	0	0	0	0	0	0
UCUP	4	0	3	1	1	4
SCUP	0	0	0	0	0	0
IC	0	0	0	0	0	0
WCC	0	0	0	0	0	0
Total	28	8	8	12	24	32

FC Sheriff was the first Moldovan club to import players from Brazil and Africa

SIONI BOLNISI
Bolnisi, Georgia
Ground: Tamaz Stepania
Capacity: 3,000

EUROPEAN CLUB COMPETITION RECORD

Competition	Pld	W	D	L	GF	GA
ECCC	4	1	0	3	2	5
ECWC	0	0	0	0	0	0
UCUP	2	0	0	2	0	6
SCUP	0	0	0	0	0	0
IC	0	0	0	0	0	0
WCC	0	0	0	0	0	0
Total	28	8	8	12	24	32

Sioni was named after the nearby Church of Sioni
in the town of Bolnisi

SIROKI BRIJEG
Siroki Brijeg,
Bosnia-Herzegovina
Ground: Pecara Stadium
Capacity: 10,000

EUROPEAN CLUB COMPETITION RECORD

Competition	Pld	W	D	L	GF	GA
ECCC	6	3	1	2	4	5
ECWC	0	0	0	0	0	0
UCUP	10	5	0	5	14	16
SCUP	0	0	0	0	0	0
IC	0	0	0	0	0	0
WCC	0	0	0	0	0	0
Total	16	8	1	7	18	21

The club's fans call themselves 'Skipari', which
means 'Crusaders' and refers to freedom fighters
against the old communist regime of Yugoslavia

SLOVAN LIBEREC
Liberec, Czech Republic
Ground: U Nisy Stadion
Capacity: 10,000

EUROPEAN CLUB COMPETITION RECORD

Competition	Pld	W	D	L	GF	GA
ECCC	4	1	1	2	3	4
ECWC	0	0	0	0	0	0
UCUP	26	12	6	8	39	33
SCUP	0	0	0	0	0	0
IC	18	10	4	4	28	13
WCC	0	0	0	0	0	0
Total	48	23	11	14	70	50

In 1994 Slovan changed their name to include
Vratislav, the name of a local beer who sponsored
the club that season

SPARTAK MOSCOW
Moscow, Russia
Ground:
Luzhniki Stadion
Capacity: 84,745

EUROPEAN CLUB COMPETITION RECORD

Competition	Pld	W	D	L	GF	GA
ECCC	96	34	24	38	141	137
ECWC	18	10	4	4	31	17
UCUP	87	48	16	23	139	97
SCUP	0	0	0	0	0	0
IC	6	3	1	2	9	5
WCC	0	0	0	0	0	0
Total	207	95	45	67	320	256

Spartak are named after Spartacus, the slave who
led a rebellion against Rome, played by Kirk
Douglas in the film of the same name

SPORTING LISBON
Lisbon, Portugal
Ground: Estádio
José Alvalade
Capacity: 50,300

EUROPEAN CLUB COMPETITION RECORD

Competition	Pld	W	D	L	GF	GA
ECCC	52	13	12	27	63	86
ECWC	40	18	9	13	82	49
UCUP	101	49	21	31	164	111
SCUP	0	0	0	0	0	0
IC	0	0	0	0	0	0
WCC	0	0	0	0	0	0
Total	193	80	42	71	309	246

UEFA WINNERS
UEFA Cup Winners' Cup – 1963/64

STANDARD LIEGE
Liege, Belgium
Ground: Stade
Maurice Dufrasne
Capacity: 29,173

EUROPEAN CLUB COMPETITION RECORD

Competition	Pld	W	D	L	GF	GA
ECCC	42	23	4	15	75	51
ECWC	38	20	5	13	71	51
UCUP	60	24	16	20	85	78
SCUP	0	0	0	0	0	0
IC	20	8	10	2	25	16
WCC	0	0	0	0	0	0
Total	160	75	35	50	256	196

The club was founded in 1900 by students of the College of Saint-Servais in Liege

STEAUA BUCHAREST
Bucharest, Romania
Ground:
Stadionul Steaua
Capacity: 27 063

EUROPEAN CLUB COMPETITION RECORD

Competition	Pld	W	D	L	GF	GA
ECCC	97	38	26	33	148	135
ECWC	40	14	12	14	51	54
UCUP	62	23	18	21	81	72
SCUP	1	1	0	0	1	0
IC	0	0	0	0	0	0
WCC	1	0	0	1	0	1
Total	201	76	56	69	281	262

UEFA WINNERS
European Champions Clubs' Cup – 1985/86
UEFA Super Cup – 1986

THE NEW SAINTS
Llansantffraid, Wales
Ground: Recreation Field
Capacity: 2,000

EUROPEAN CLUB COMPETITION RECORD

Competition	Pld	W	D	L	GF	GA
ECCC	6	0	1	5	2	14
ECWC	2	0	1	1	1	6
UCUP	8	0	0	8	3	29
SCUP	0	0	0	0	0	0
IC	0	0	0	0	0	0
WCC	0	0	0	0	0	0
Total	16	0	2	14	6	49

In summer 2006 the club offered the sponsorship rights to its name on ebay

TVMK Tallinn
Tallinn, Estonia
Ground: Kalevi Keskstaadion
Capacity: 12,000

EUROPEAN CLUB COMPETITION RECORD

Competition	Pld	W	D	L	GF	GA
ECCC	2	0	1	1	3	4
ECWC	0	0	0	0	0	0
UCUP	8	0	2	6	6	17
SCUP	0	0	0	0	0	0
IC	4	0	1	3	2	9
WCC	0	0	0	0	0	0
Total	14	0	4	10	11	30

TVMK won their only Estonian league title in 2005 to qualify for the 2006/07 Champions League

VALERENGA
Oslo, Norway
Ground: Jordal Amfi Arena
Capacity: 5,500

EUROPEAN CLUB COMPETITION RECORD

Competition	Pld	W	D	L	GF	GA
ECCC	14	4	3	7	17	25
ECWC	8	1	4	3	11	17
UCUP	12	0	7	5	6	16
SCUP	0	0	0	0	0	0
IC	2	1	0	1	1	2
WCC	0	0	0	0	0	0
Total	36	6	14	16	35	60

Valerenga's 2005 league title was their first for 21 years

WERDER BREMEN
Bremen, Germany
Ground: Weserstdion
Capacity: 42,466

EUROPEAN CLUB COMPETITION RECORD

Competition	Pld	W	D	L	GF	GA
ECCC	44	20	8	16	78	66
ECWC	21	11	3	7	39	22
UCUP	74	32	17	25	145	91
SCUP	2	0	1	1	2	3
IC	22	14	4	4	36	20
WCC	0	0	0	0	0	0
Total	163	77	33	53	300	202

UEFA WINNERS
UEFA Cup Winners' Cup – 1991/92
UEFA Intertoto Cup – 1998

FC ZURICH
Zurich, Switzerland
Ground: Letzigrund Stadion
Capacity: 23,605

EUROPEAN CLUB COMPETITION RECORD

Competition	Pld	W	D	L	GF	GA
ECCC	29	12	2	15	38	52
ECWC	12	4	4	4	24	16
UCUP	34	14	6	14	55	59
SCUP	0	0	0	0	0	0
IC	6	3	1	2	11	5
WCC	0	0	0	0	0	0
Total	81	33	13	35	128	132

The Letzigrund Stadion is also the home of the annual 'Weltklasse' athletics meeting, part of the IAAF Golden League series

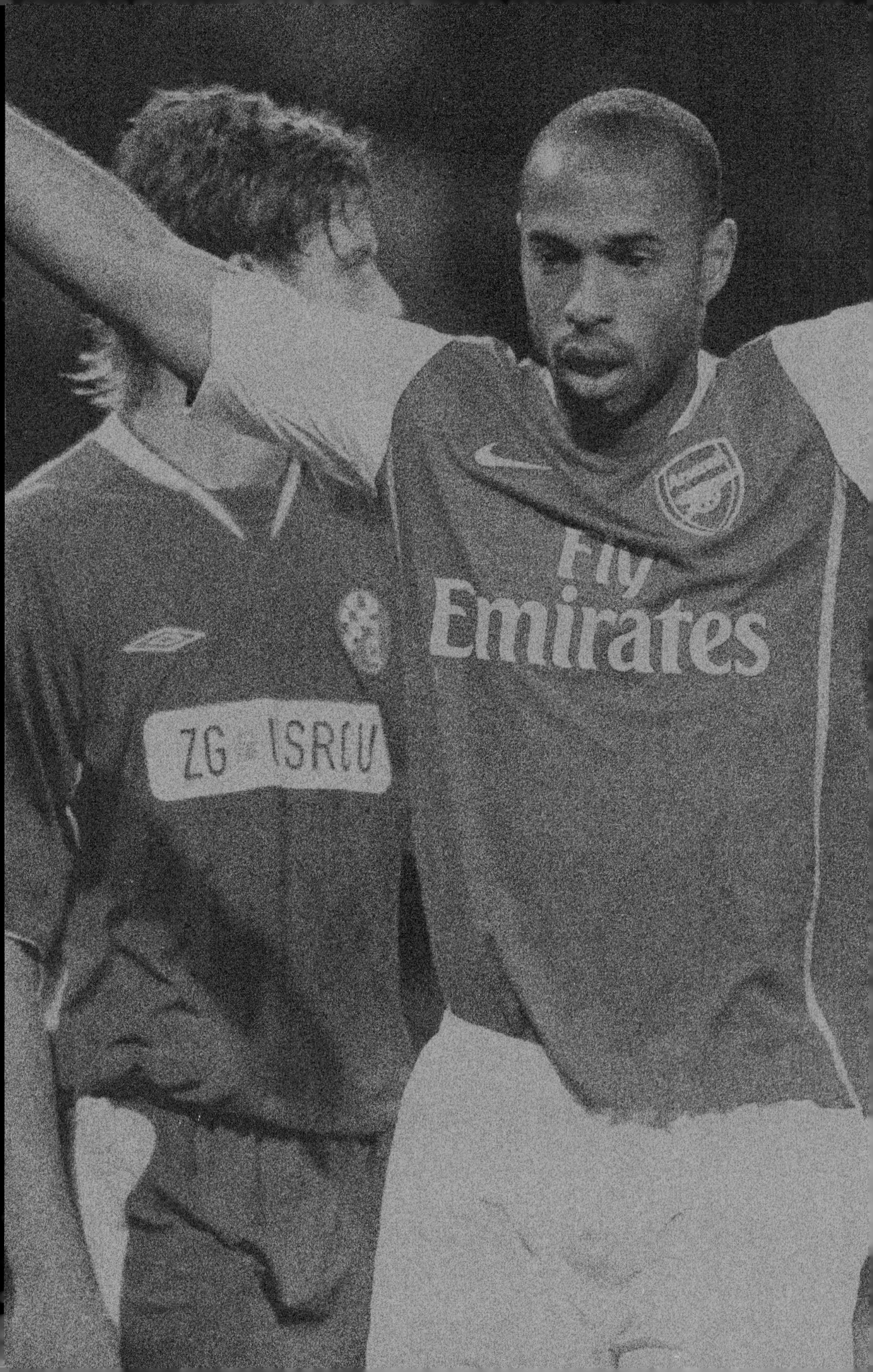
Fly Emirates

section three

qualifying rounds

1st Qualifying Round
11-19 July 2006

The UEFA Champions League got underway just two days after Italy lifted the World Cup in the final in Berlin.

Cork City's Billy Woods scored a stunning winner in their first leg against Limassol, while Dan Murray's header 15 minutes from the end of the return sent Cork through. Welsh side TNS bowed out 2-0 on aggregate to Finnish Champions MyPa, while Siroki Brijeg of Bosnia edged out Shaktor Soligorsk of Belarus for the right to play Scottish club Hearts in the second round. There were also close fought wins for Rabotnicki of Macedonia over Luxembourg's Dudelange and Latvia's Metalurgs over Kazakhstani champions Aktobe, while the only side to comeback from a first leg deficit was Ekranas of Lithuania, who overcame Albania's finest; Elbasani.

DID YOU KNOW?
Cork City's record appearance maker is John Caulfield, who played 455 games and scored a record 129 league goals in his career at Turner's Cross

Dudelange of Luxembourg's Joly Thierry (R) tackles Rabotnicki Kometal's Pance Stojanov during the second leg match in Skopje

	Agg.		First leg	Second leg
Elbasani	1-3	**Ekranas**	1-0	0-3
Sioni Bolnisi	2-1	Baku	2-0	0-1
FC Dudelange	0-1	**Rabotnicki**	0-1	0-0
Pyunik	0-2	**Sheriff**	0-0	0-2
Birkirkara	2-5	**B36 Torshavn**	0-3	2-2
Linfield	3-5	**NK Gorica**	1-3	2-2
TVMK Tallin	3-4	**Hafnarfjördur**	2-3	1-1
Metalurgs	2-1	Aktobe	1-0	1-1
MyPa	2-0	TNS	1-0	1-0
Cork City	2-1	Apollon Limassol	1-0	1-1
Shakhtyor Soligorsk	0-2	**Siroki Brijeg**	0-1	0-1
First-leg home team shown first				
First-leg home team score shown first for both legs				
Winning team shown in bold				

2nd Qualifying Round
25 July – 2 August 2006

The second round saw a number of high-scoring ties and the entry into the competition of returning big names, desperate to make their mark on Europe once again.

Hearts, making their first appearance in the competition for 46 years, comfortably defeated Siroki Brijeg thanks to a 3-0 first leg victory at Murrayfield. Cork City bowed out to Crvena Zvezda, otherwise better known as Red Star Belgrade, the Champions of Europe in 1991, despite a fabulous performance in the home leg, where they only succumbed 1-0. Zvezda's prize was a third qualifying round meeting with giants AC Milan, only recently allowed back into the competition after a match-fixing scandal which rocked Italia football. Other well-known clubs entering the fray included Spartak Moscow, who just sneaked through against FC Sheriff, the Champions of Moldova, and Dynamo Kiev, rather more convincing winners against Metalurgs 8-1, on aggregate. Perhaps the surprise of the round was Ruzomberok from Slovakia defeating Djurgarden of Sweden 3-2 on aggregate after overturning a first leg deficit.

Dinamo Zagreb progressed comfortably to meet Arsenal and Fenerbahce thrashed Icelandic Champions B36 9-0, while Steaua Bucharest easily disposed of NK Gorica.

Crvena Zvezda's Bulgarian Blagoy Georgiev (R) fights for the ball with Cork City's Admir Softic

	Agg.		First leg	Second leg
Ekranas	3-9	**Dinamo Zagreb**	1-4	2-5
Fenerbahce	9-0	B36 Torshavn	4-0	5-0
Mladá Boleslav	5-3	Valerenga	3-1	2-2
Sheriff	1-1	**Spartak Moscow** (ag)	1-1	0-0
Metalurgs	1-8	**Dynamo Kiev**	1-4	0-4
Hafnarfjördur	0-3	**Legia Warsaw**	0-1	0-2
FC Copenhagen	4-2	MyPa	2-0	2-2
NK Gorica	0-5	**Steaua Bucharest**	0-2	0-3
Levski Sofia	4-0	Sioni Bolnisi	2-0	2-0
FC Zürich	2-3	**Salzburg**	2-1	0-2
Djurgarden	2-3	**Ruzomberok**	1-0	1-3
Cork City	0-4	**Crvena Zvezda**	0-1	0-3
Hearts	3-0	Siroki Brijeg	3-0	0-0
Debrecen	2-5	**Rabotnicki**	1-1	1-4
Agg. – Aggregate score over two legs				
(ag) – Match decided on away goals				
First-leg home team shown first				
First-leg home team score shown first for both legs				
Winning team shown in bold				

3rd Qualifying Round
Tuesday 8 August 2006 – First Legs

On The Mark

Chilean winger Mark Gonzalez nets a vital goal as Liverpool come from behind to see off Maccabi Haifa and negotiate their way through a tricky tie

Great Guns

Arsenal see off the challenge of Dinamo Zagreb thanks to newboy Tomas Rosicky

Broken Hearts

Despite taking the lead against AEK Athens, Hearts fail to make it through to the Group Stage

"We know how important [qualification] is to the club, both financially and to us as a team."

Arsène Wenger, Arsenal manager

Dinamo Zagreb 0 v Arsenal 3

Maksimir Stadium
Attendance: 28,500

DINAMO Z'B 0	v	ARSENAL 3

Referee
Lubos Michel (BUL)

Scorers

Fabregas **63', 78'**
van Persie **64'**

Teams

01	Turina	Almunia	24
03	Cale	Djourou	20
05	Corluka	Eboue	27
06	Cvitanovic	Hoyte	31
04	Nowotny	Toure	05
02	Buljat	Gilberto Silva	19
10	Modric	Fabregas	04
24	Eduardo	Hleb	13
28	Mamic	Rosicky	07
30	Vugrinec	Adebayor	25
07	Etto	van Persie	11

Substitutes

27'	11 Agic / 30 Vugrinec	30 Aliadiere / 25 Adebayor	82'
90'	07 Santos Carlos / 03 Cale	16 Flamini / 07 Rosicky	82'
90'	20 Vukojevic / 02 Buljat		

Discipline

13'	Corluka	Hleb	60'
		Hoyte	80'

1	Yellow cards	2
0	Red cards	0
2	Shots on target	12
9	Shots off target	8
8	Fouls committed	15
4	Corners	2
2	Offsides	1
43%	Ball. Poss. (%)	57%

Alexandr Hleb hurdles a challenge from Jasmin Agic of Zagreb

Cesc Fabregas and Robin van Persie destroyed Dinamo Zagreb with an impressive display of finishing. Fabregas hit two fabulous second half goals and van Persie added another in a final thirty minutes which gave the lie to a tricky first hour.

The Spanish youngster struck first in the 63rd minute, racing onto a van Persie pass to smash the ball past Dinamo keeper Ivan Turina, as Arsenal appeared to be struggling to overcome the Croatian champions. Van Persie then got in on the act 78 seconds later with a fine finish from Alexander Hleb's fantastic pass and Fabregas rounded off

Cesc Fabregas scores a splendid third goal in Zagreb

Robin van Persie turns on a few tricks

> **"I feel that Tomas Rosicky was ready to play and that Reyes, with all the noises he has made about moving to Real Madrid, didn't have the right mentality to play."**
> **Arsène Wenger, Arsenal manager**

the night in sensational fashion with a wonder goal 11 minutes from time to mark his 100th appearance for the club. The win gave boss Arsène Wenger some respite from a difficult start to the season with ructions over Ashley Cole's imminent departure to Chelsea and Jose Antonio Reyes' desire to quit the club for Real Madrid, which saw him left out of this Champions League qualifier. Wenger left the Spanish winger on the bench so that he would not become ineligible for the Champions League should he complete the expected £10 million move. The 22 year-old star had insisted for the past 18 months that he wanted to return to his homeland and eventually did so, although only on a season-long loan basis.

Wenger always insists his young Gunners are at their best with their backs to the wall and they proved it yet again with three stunning goals symbolic of the steely resolve within the Gunners team which simply refused to cave in.

With the likes of Cole and Henry at home in London for differing reasons (Henry because of an injury which would decimate his season), the confirmation that Reyes was on the bench added further expectation to a 40,000 crowd baying for an upset. But new Czech signing Tomas Rosicky – who had played just 30 minutes of preseason football after a summer of football for his country in the World Cup – was a star in fighting the Arsenal cause.

Austria Vienna 1 v Benfica 1
Ernst Happel Stadium
Attendance: 19,600

AUS. VIENNA 1 v **BENFICA 1**

Referee
Referee: S Farina (ITA)

Scorers

36'	Blanchard	Nuno Gomes	16'

Teams

01	Safar	Quim 12
30	Papac	Anderson 03
08	Radomski	Katsouranis 08
05	Tokic	Luisao 04
03	Troyanski	Nelson 22
15	Blanchard	Paulo Jorge 15
14	Lasnik	Ricardo Rocha 33
10	Vachousek	Manu 18
25	Wimmer	Petit 06
11	Aigner	Rui Costa 10
07	Wallner	Nuno Gomes 21

Substitutes

46'	> 19 Ceh < 23 Wimmer		07 Marco Ferreira > 18 Manu <	67'
46'	> 33 Mila < 11 Aigner		17 Kikin > 21 Nuno Gomes <	80'
82'	> 17 Pichlmann < 14 Lasnik		25 Nuno Assis > 15 Paulo Jorge <	88'

Discipline

35'	Lasnik	Katsouranis	36'
44'	Radomski	Jorge	62'
59'	Tokic	Rocha	66'
3	Yellow cards		3

THIRD QUALIFYING ROUND
FIRST LEG

Austria Vienna's demonstrative coach Frankie Schinkels shows what the Champions League means to him during the third round first leg match against Benfica in Vienna

"No-one in Austria expects us to knock Benfica out... not even my wife."
Frenkie Schinkels, Vienna coach

Benfica earned a creditable 1-1 draw in Vienna, against Austria, thanks to a well-worked goal from Portugal striker Nuno Gomes. He backheeled the ball in after a textbook series of passes between Rui Costa, Konstantinos Katsouranis, Paulo Jorge and Manu. The technically superior Portuguese then took charge of the match until Jocelyn Blanchard fired home from 22 metres after defender Ferdinand Troyansky had knocked down a free kick by Andreas Lasnik.

3rd Qualifying Round
Wednesday 9 August 2006 – First Legs

LIVERPOOL 2 v **MACCABI H. 1**

Referee
Wolfgang Stark (GER)

Scorers

32'	Bellamy	Boccoli	29'
87'	González		

Teams

25	Reina	Davidovitch	01
23	Carragher	Harazi	03
03	Finnan	Keinan	21
04	Hyypia	Magralishvili	18
06	Riise	Olarra	19
14	Alonso	Anderson	05
08	Gerrard	Bokoli	07
22	Sissoko	Dirceu	15
32	Zenden	Masudi	10
17	Bellamy	Colautti	09
16	Pennant	Katan	20

Substitutes

55' > 10 Luis Garcia < 32 Zenden		12 Melicsohn > 20 Katan <	85'
65' > 15 Crouch < 17 Bellamy		14 Meshumar > 10 Masudi <	79'
85' > 11 Gonzalez < 08 Gerrard			

Discipline

64'	Sissoko	Magralishvili	40'
		Colautti	79'

1	Yellow cards	2
0	Red cards	0
4	Shots on target	3
12	Shots off target	2
15	Fouls committed	17
5	Corners	5
3	Offsides	5
64%	Ball. Poss. (%)	36%

THIRD QUALIFYING ROUND

FIRST LEG

Liverpool 2 v Maccabi Haifa 1
Anfield
Attendance: 40,058

Policemen keep watch over Maccabi Haifa fans after the worsening political situation in the Middle East caused concern for safety at Liverpool's home game

The Israelis of Haifa shocked Anfield by taking the lead in the first half and, although Liverpool equalised four minutes later with Craig Bellamy's first goal since his move from Blackburn, they were largely unconvincing until Chile's Mark González, a late substitution for Steven Gerrard, scored a second goal with only a couple of minutes remaining to hand the Reds a slender advantage.

Despite their performance and good result, the political situation back home seemed set to destabilise the Israeli challenge. "If the second leg were in Tel Aviv I believe we would stand a wonderful chance," said Roni Levy, Maccabi's coach. The second leg will, UEFA decided, be played in neutral Kiev, much to the disappointment of the Israeli club.

Although they created a limited number of chances, Maccabi were unfortunate to concede such a late goal against a Liverpool side fast running out of ideas. González had had trouble getting to Anfield because of work-permit difficulties, but for him and Rafael Benítez it was clearly well worth the wait.

"The goal was fantastic for him, as was Bellamy's. Maccabi will need to go forward more in the second leg, so it will be a different game and we will have more space," said Benítez, clearly worried by the away goal. "We have a little bit of an advantage, but the outcome is 50-50. I said before that they were a good team and now people will believe me."

Unexpectedly Benitez started Peter Crouch on the bench, although he eventually replaced Bellamy, whose pace had brought a new dimension to

Haifa head coach Roni Levy expressed his concern that Liverpool would be handed an unfair advantage if the second leg had to be played at a neutral venue

Liverpool's attacking play, midway through the second half.

Maccabi, in their emerald strip, were anything but green and Anfield fell silent when Liverpool's initial

attacks failed to provide any chances. It was John Arne Riise who raised the temperature with a flashing left-foot shot which skidded on the wet turf wide of Nir Davidovitch, the Maccabi

Haifa fans go ballistic as their side takes the lead at Anfield

Bellamy scores against Haifa to make it 1-1

However, with Liverpool becoming a little frustrated Maccabi suddenly broke to take the lead in the 29th minute. Roberto Colautti and Gustavo Boccoli neatly exchanged passes, leaving Boccoli to sprint clear and hit a low right-foot shot beyond the thoroughly exposed José Reina.

Liverpool were quick to respond. Four minutes later another Pennant-led thrust down the right ended with Gerrard touching the ball to Momo Sissoko, who unleashed a drive which Davidovitch could only parry, leaving Bellamy a virtually open goal.

When González replaced Gerrard most Liverpool fans had accepted the inevitability of a draw, but the Chilean then popped up like a latter-day David Fairclough to earn plaudits as a super sub.

goalkeeper, and the goal. Initially Bellamy was not getting the support he needed, but Pennant finally managed to get in a low cross from the right, with which the rushing Bellamy just failed to connect.

Mark Gonzalez nets Liverpool's winner

Hearts 1 v AEK Athens 2
Murrayfield
Attendance: 32,459

HEARTS 1 v **AEK ATHENS 2**

Referee
Nicolai Vollquart (DEN)

Scorers

62'	Mikoliunas	Kapetanos	89'
		Berra (og)	90'

Teams

Hearts		AEK Athens	
01	Gordon	Sorrentino	28
20	Berra	Cirillo	05
03	Fyssas	Dellas	55
25	Karipidis	Georgeas	31
02	Neilson	Koutroumanos	19
04	Pressley	Emerson	25
08	Aguiar	Ivic	17
07	McCann	Pautasso	13
12	Bednar	Julio Cesar	99
16	Mikoliunas	Kapetanos	35
11	Pospisil	Nikos Liberopoulos	33

Hearts' Saulius Mikoliunas celebrates his goal which gave his side a 1-0 lead over AEK

Hearts' first taste of UEFA Champions League football ended in disappointment after two late goals from AEK Athens.

But it had all started so well. The home side went ahead in the 61st minute when midfielder Saulius Mikoliunas slammed the ball into the net from close range after Roman Bednar's effort had rebounded off the post.

Then it began to go pear-shaped. Four minutes later, Hearts midfielder Bruno Aguiar was sent off for two yellow cards, the second for kicking the ball away after the home side conceded a foul in the middle of the park.

With a minute of normal time remaining, Pantelis Kapetanos flicked a cross by substitute Stavros Tziortziopoulos past the helpless Gordon and in off the post. And then, in a devastagingly cruel finale, four minutes into injury time, Christophe Berra deflected a shot from Nikos Liberopoulos into his own net.

The Edinburgh club had hoped to beat their European attendance record of 37,500 set against Standard Liege at Tynecastle in 1958, but although less than that figure turned up at the Jambos' adopted stadium Murrayfield, an atmosphere befitting a Champions

League game greeted both sides as they emerged from the tunnel.

It was the slick-moving visitors who started brighter, forcing two corners in as many minutes. And from Julio Cesar's second effort from the right, Greek striker Liberopoulos crashed his header from six yards against the bar before the ball was eventually scrambled away to safety.

Substitutes

55'	> 09 Jankauskas < 25 Karipidis	23 Lakis > 19 Koutroumanos <	65'
69'	> 23 Wallace < 12 Bednar	14 Tziortziopoulos > 13 Pautasso <	80'
82'	> 22 Elliot < 11 Pospisil	88 Tozser > 99 Julio Cesar <	90'

Discipline

28'	Aguiar	Georgeas	13'
76'	McCann		
66'	Aguiar		

3	Yellow cards	1
1	Red cards	0

A young Hearts fan soaks up the pre-match atmosphere

THIRD QUALIFYING ROUND

FIRST LEG

Disaster strikes for Hearts as Athens' Pantelis Kapetanos celebrates the winning goal

The Gorgie side seemed paralysed with nerves, but in the 11th-minute, midfielder Mikoliunas offered encouragement when he hammered a left-footed shot from the edge of the box off the near post with the help of a deflection from Athens defender Bruno Cirillo.

But the Greeks were clearly still in control and the subdued home support sat in almost silence as the Tynecastle men tried to stem the tide.

Athens fans celebrate a magnificent late comeback

In the 19th minute, Hearts' best move of the game involving midfielder Neil McCann and Takis Fyssas ended with Mikoliunas blazing the ball over the bar from 16 yards out, following the Gorgie defender's cross to the far side of the penalty area.

Hearts, who had built their recent success on pace and power, were often chasing shadows as AEK swept the ball around Murrayfield in impressive style.

On the half-hour mark, another Cesar corner from the right caused havoc in the Hearts defence before Berra calmly cleared the danger.

Most of the traffic continued on its way to the Hearts goal in the second half, but there must have been some encouragement for the home side because, for all their dominance, the Greek side could not get the goal their superiority deserved. And then in the 61st minute, Murrayfield erupted when the Jambos did get the opening goal. Substitute Edgaras Jankauskas, on minutes earlier for Karipidis, broke free on the left and, when his pass came to Bednar, the Hearts striker slammed his right-footed shot from 12 yards past Athens keeper Stefano Sorrentino but off the post. However, Mikoliunas gleefully drove the rebound home from barely eight yards out.

But then came Aguiar's dismissal and the initiative shifted back to the Greeks. Cesar sent a 25-yard free-kick inches past the post with Gordon rooted to the spot and in the closing stages Hearts were hanging on in desperation. But the home side's luck ran out in the 89th minute.

Salzburg 1 v Valencia 0
Lehen Stadium
Attendance: 15,000

SALZBURG 1 v **VALENCIA 0**

Referee
Peter Fröjdfeldt (SWE)

Scorers
73'	Pitak

Teams
Salzburg		Valencia	
01	Ochs	Canizares	01
02	Bodnar	Torres	23
03	Dudic	Moretti	24
04	Linke	Navarro	17
31	Vargas	Albelda	06
05	Carboni	Albiol	20
27	Janocko	Baraja	08
11	Jezek	Vicente	14
06	Kovac	Angulo	10
16	Pitak	Morientes	09
07	Zickler	Regueiro	11

Substitutes
51'	> 28 Aufhauser < 27 Janocko	07 Villa > 11 Regueiro <	62'
77'	> 33 Winklhofer < 11 Jezek	21 Silva > 14 Vicente <	74'

Discipline
07'	Vargas

1	Yellow cards	0

Salzburg's Alexander Zickler, Vladimir Janocko, Timo Ochs,
Milan Dudic and Nico Kovac celebrate a famous win over Valencia

Salzburg shocked Spanish group stage regulars Valencia when Karel Pitak headed past goalkeeper Cañizares after a pass from Jezek after 73 minutes at the Wals-Siezenheim stadium.

AC Milan 1 v Crvenza Zvezda 0
San Siro
Attendance: 55,000

AC Milan's Gennaro Gattuso (R) challenges Nenad Kovacevic
of Crvena Zvezda for the ball

AC MILAN 1	v	CRVENA ZV 0

Referee
Jan Wegereef (NED)

Scorers

22'	Inzaghi	

Teams

01	Dida	Randjelovic	01
05	Costacurta	Basta	30
02	Cafu	Bisevac	06
22	Kaká	Gueye	05
17	Simic	Miladinovic	24
08	Gattuso	Pantic	04
21	Pirlo	Jankovic	08
20	Seedorf	Kovacevic	16
27	Serginho	Perovic	11
11	Gilardino	Georgiev	17
09	Inzaghi	Zigic	25

Substitutes

72'	> 27 Ambrosini < 11 Gilardino	13 Tutoric > 11 Perovic <	66'
79'	> 19 Favalli < 02 Cafu	09 Djokic > 24 Miladinovic <	86'
81'	> 57 Gourcuff < 21 Pirlo	10 Krivokapic > 08 Jankovic <	89'

Discipline

	Perovic	14'

0	Yellow cards	1

AC Milan earned a slender first leg led thanks to a superb defensive display by Crvena Zvezda, better known as Red Star Belgrade.

Milan attacked from the start and Gilardino thought he had scored after 11 minutes but his header from point-blank range was well saved by Ivan Randjelovic in the Red Star goal. After 22 minutes their early pressure paid off as they took the lead when Kaká split the Red Star defence with a trademark pass and Inzaghi raced clear to score against the 1991 European and world champions. Inzaghi, celebrating his 33rd birthday and a member of Italy's World Cup winning squad, had another chance 11 minutes later, but Randjelovic saved well to deny the hitman.

In the second half a free-kick from another World Cup hero Andrea Pirlo forced Randjelovic into prompt action and the Red Star goalkeeper made another fine stop on the hour mark to foil Gilardino to give Milan further problems on top of their point deduction in Serie A.

There were also solid wins for Ajax, Lille, CSKA Moscow, Galatasaray and Dynamo Kiev all of whom seemed set fair to progress.

DID YOU KNOW?
Crvena Zvezda's 1991 European Cup-winning side included midfielders Robert Prosinecki, Dejan Savicevic and Sinisa Mihajlovic, who all went on to become world stars

COPENHAGEN 1	v	AJAX 2

Referee
Manuel Enrique Mejuto Gonzalez (ESP)

Scorers

45'	Hangeland	Huntelaar 37', 83'

Teams

01	Christiansen	Stekelenburg	01
15	Bergdolmo	Emanuelson	05
14	Gravgaard	Heitinga	02
05	Hangeland	Maduro	06
02	Jacobsen	Stam	03
10	Gronkjaer	Vermaelen	04
13	Hutchinson	Gabri	18
06	Linderoth	Sneijder	10
08	Silberbauer	Huntelaar	09
11	Allback	Perez	11
09	Berglund	Rosales	07

Substitutes

68'	> 20 Pimpong < 09 Berglund	08 Babel > 11 Perez <	67'
79'	> 23 Kvist < 08 Silberbauer	19 Rosenberg > 07 Rosales <	78'

Discipline

39'	Allback	Huntelaar	42'
60'	Hutchinson	Perez	54'
79'	Jacobsen	Heitinga	74'
		Emanuelson	78'

3	Yellow cards	4

ST'D LIEGE 2 v STEAUA BUCH. 2

Referee
Valentin Ivanov (RUS)

Scorers

18', 15' Rapaic	Paraschiv	09'
	Marin	81'

Teams

16 Renard	Carlos	13
02 Deflandre	Ghionea	24
19 Sarr	Goian	03
22 Geraerts	Marin	18
11 Rapaic	Nesu	15
03 Nuno Coelho	Dica	10
08 Defour	Lovin	28
27 Fellaini	Paraschiv	22
23 Jovanovic	Nicolita	16
20 Matias	Oprita	07
76 Sa Pinto	Badea	09

Substitutes

80' > 24 Pelaic < 08 Defour		14 Cristocea > 09 Badea <	63'
90' > 09 Bouchouari < 76 Sa Pinto		11 Bostina > 16 Nicolita <	80'
		17 Baciu > 07 Oprita <	90'

Discipline

70'	Fellaini	Ghionea	15'
89'	Geraerts	Mihai Nesu	17'

2	Yellow cards	2

HAMBURG 0 v OSASUNA 0

Referee
Tom Henning Ovrebo (NOR)

Teams

12 Kirschstein	Ricardo	13
20 Demel	Cuellar	05
10 Kompany	Javier Flano	17
04 Reinhardt	Josetxo	14
28 De Jong	Lopez	16
09 Paolo Guerrero	Delporte	23
14 Jarolim	Punal	10
15 Trochowski	Raul Garcia	06
23 van der Vaart	Milosevic	09
07 Mahdavikia	Soldado	18
17 Sanogo	Monreal	27

Substitutes

74' > 11 Lauth < 15 Trochowski		11 Lopez > 23 Delporte >	70'
		08 Romeo > 18 Soldado <	79'
		24 Nekounam > 09 Milosevic <	90'

Discipline

22'	Trochowski	Cuellar	35'
		Josetxo	37'
		Delporte	64'
		Lopez	90'

1	Yellow cards	4

CSKA MOSCOW 3 v RUZOMBEROK 0

Referee
Referee: Florian Meyer (GER)

Scorers

58', 65' Olic		
83'	Vágner Love	

Teams

35 Akinfeev	Hajduch	21
06 Berezutsky	Dvornik	19
04 Ignashevich	Laurinc	13
02 Semberas	Pospisil	12
22 Aldonin	Silva	22
10 Jo	Bozok	15
17 Krasic	Sapara	27
25 Rahimic	Sedlak	04
18 Zhirkov	Zofcak	09
07 Daniel Carvalho	Nezmar	07
09 Olic	Robert Rak	25

Substitutes

58' > 11 Vágner Love < 10 Jo	10 Tomcak > 15 Bozok <	63'
73' > 20 Dudu < 09 Olic	20 Rychlik > 25 Rak <	84'
86' > 08 Gusev < 07 Daniel Carvalho		

Discipline

32'	Berezutsky	Laurinc	26'
42'	Aldonin	Zofcak	56'
88'	Semberas		

3	Yellow cards	2

THIRD QUALIFYING ROUND
FIRST LEG

THIRD QUALIFYING ROUND
FIRST LEG

THIRD QUALIFYING ROUND
FIRST LEG

Qualifying Rounds

DYNAMO KIEV 3 v FENERBAHCE 1

Referee
Valeri Lobanovski Stadium

Scorers

01', 67'	Rincon	Aurelio	48'
83'	Yussuf		

Teams

01	Shovkovskiy	Rustu	34
30	Kadouri	Ozat	
81	Markovic	Turaci	
44	Rodrigo	Alex	
13	Sablic	Appiah	
37	Yussuf	Arat	
15	Rincon	Aurelio	
20	Gusev	Balci	
05	Rebrov	Metin	
16	Shatskikh	Anelka	
07	Correa	Sanli	

Substitutes

62'	> 25 Milevskiy < 05 Rebrov	25 Boral > 11 Metin <	74'
80'	> 08 Belkevich < 20 Gusev	23 Senturk > 39 Anelka <	74'

Discipline

86'	Kadouri	Appiah	34'
		Ozat	44'
		Balci	46'
		Balci	76'

1	Yellow cards	4
0	Red cards	1

LILLE 3 v RABOTNICKI 0

Referee
Vladimir Hrinak (SVK)

Scorers

60'	Stojanovsk (og)
70'	Bastos (pen)
72'	Fauvergue

Teams

01	Sylva	Pacovski	01
26	Lichtsteiner	Vajs	28
25	Plestan	Ignatov	23
05	Schmitz	Ilievski	07
20	Tafforeau	Lazarevski	14
07	Cabaye	Nedzipi	10
17	Makoun	Stankovski	30
08	Bastos	Stojanovski	21
13	Fauvergue	Trajcov	22
23	Keita	Carlos	16
11	Youla	Pejcic	20

Substitutes

45'	> 21 Chalme < 26 Lichtsteiner	05 Stepanovski > 14 Lazarevski <	60'
52'	> 14 Odemwingie < 11 Youla	15 Janker > 10 Nedzipi <	66'
76'	> 27 Mirallas < 23 Keita	02 Stojanov > 23 Ignatov <	86'

Discipline

74'	Chalme	Lazarevski	28'
		Ignatov	40'
		Stepanovski	64'
		Trajcov	71'

1	Yellow cards	4

GALATASARAY 5 v MLADA BOL'V 2

Referee
Konrad Plautz (AUT)

Scorers

10'	Ilic (pen)	Brezinsky	83'
45, 62'	Turan	Kulic	85'
49'	Hakan Sukur		
90'	Sarioglu		

Teams

01	Mondragon	Kucera	01
05	Ak	Brezinsky	09
04	Song	Riegel	25
02	Tomas	Sevinsky	03
18	Akman	Smerda	17
06	Buruk	Vit	21
19	Haspolatli	Matejovsky	08
22	Ilic	Pecka	16
55	Sarioglu	Polacek	12
66	Turan	Vaculik	05
09	Sukur	Kulic	10

Substitutes

70'	> 67 Penbe < 05 Ak	04 Rolko > 12 Polacek <	69'
85'	> 11 Sas < 22 Ilic		

Discipline

42'	Akman	Kucera	07'
		Vaculik	65'

1	Yellow cards	2

THIRD QUALIFYING ROUND
FIRST LEG

THIRD QUALIFYING ROUND
FIRST LEG

THIRD QUALIFYING ROUND
FIRST LEG

SHAKHTAR D. 1 v LEGIA WAR'W 0

Referee
Frank De Bleeckere (BEL)

Scorers

39' Elano (pen)

Teams

12	Shutkov	Fabianski	01
03	Hubschman	Alcantara	05
18	Lewandowski	Choto	04
26	Rat	Edson	27
07	Fernandinho	Guerreiro	06
09	Matuzalem	Szala	03
33	Srna	Surma	08
04	Tymoschuk	Szalachowski	20
17	Aghahowa	Vukovic	10
36	Blumer	Brandao	28
25	Brandau	Wlodarczyk	09

Substitutes

| 57' | > 38 Jadson < 36 Blumer | 24 Balde > 10 Vukovic < | 80' |
| 63' | > 29 Marica < 17 Aghahowa | | |

Discipline

| 70' | Fernandinho | Szala | 52' |
| | | Balde | 89' |

| 1 | Yellow cards | 2 |

LEVSKI SOFIA 2 v CHIEVO VER. 0

Referee
Jaroslav Jara (CZE)

Scorers

08' Domovchiyski
90' Bardon (pen)

Teams

01	Petkov	Sicignano	01
04	Tomasic	Lanna	23
11	Topuzakov	Mantovani	04
20	Angelov	Moro	27
07	Borimirov	Scurto	26
17	Domovchiyski	Brighi	33
06	Eromoigbe	Giunti	08
35	Korudzhiev	Semioli	07
21	Telkiyski	Zanchetta	10
27	Bardon	Amauri	11
10	Yovov	Tiribocchi	90

Substitutes

74'	> 28 Angelov < 17 Domovchiyski	20 Marcolini > 10 Zanchetta <	63'
83'	> 88 Mihailov < 21 Telkiyski	11 Pellissier > 90 Tiribocchi <	67'
90'	> 03 Milanov < 04 Tomasic		

Discipline

| 14' | Topuzakov | Brighi | 61' |

| 1 | Yellow cards | 1 |

SLOVAN LIB. 0 v SP. MOSCOW 0

Referee
Alain Hamer (LUX)

Teams

24	Cech	Kowalewski	30
14	Kostal	Jiranek	15
19	Singlar	Rodriguez	17
05	Zapotocny	Shishkin	49
07	Bilek	Stranzl	03
20	Frejlach	Kalinichenko	25
10	Hodur	Kovac	15
17	Janu	Kovalchuk	27
03	Pudil	Mozart	24
28	Blazek	Cavenaghi	19
11	Pospech	Pavluchenko	10

Substitutes

46'	> 23 Papousek < 20 Frejlach	07 Boyarintsev > 10 Pavluchenko <	72'
52'	> 25 Holenda < 28 Blazek	32 Bazhenov > 07 Boyarintsev <	87'
81'	> 15 Parks < 11 Pospech		

Discipline

| 15' | Bilek | Kovac | 27' |
| 84' | Kostal | Kalinichenko | 62' |

| 2 | Yellow cards | 2 |

3rd Qualifying Round
Tuesday 22 August 2006 – Second Legs

MACCABI HAIFA 1 v LIVERPOOL 1

Referee
Referee: Roberto Rosetti (ITA)

Scorers

63'	Colautti	Crouch	54'

Teams

01	Davidovitch	Reina	25
03	Harazi	Agger	05
21	Keinan	Finnan	03
18	Magralishvili	Hyypia	04
19	Olarra	Alonso	14
05	Anderson	Gonzalez	11
07	Bokoli	Luis Garcia	10
15	Dirceu	Pennant	16
10	Masudi	Sissoko	22
09	Colautti	Warnock	28
20	Katan	Crouch	15

Substitutes

65'	> 14 Meshumar < 21 Keinan	12 Aurelio > 28 Warnock <	28'
71'	> 12 Melikson < 05 Anderson	08 Gerrard > 22 Sissoko <	67'
80'	> 11 Arbaitman < 10 Masudi	17 Bellamy > 16 Pennant <	86'

Discipline

43'	Keinan	Alonso	31'
45'	Ariderson	Hyypia	73'
90'	Meshumar		

3	Yellow cards	2
0	Red cards	0
3	Shots on target	7
2	Shots off target	11
31	Fouls committed	20
1	Corners	3
8	Offsides	4
48%	Ball. Poss. (%)	52%

DID YOU KNOW?
Dutchman Jan Krompamp was a non-playing substitute for Liverpool against Haifa, but played against the Reds later in the competition for PSV Eindhoven after moving to the Dutch Champions

Maccabi Haifa 1 v Liverpool 1
(Liverpool win 3-2 on aggregate)
Valeri Lobanovski Stadium, Kiev
Attendance: 12,500

Rafa Benitez mounts a solid defence of his team gaining an advantage by not having to play in war-torn Israel

Not that anyone was surprised to see Liverpool and AC Milan progress at the expense of Maccabi Haifa and Crvena Zvezda respectively, but little did anyone know that two eventual finalists were winning their way through to the group stage.

With Israel off limits due to the worsening political situation between Palestinians and Israelis, Rafael Benitez arrived in the neutral venue of Kiev to face accusations of cowardice and conspiracy, but it was a relieved Liverpool manager who left the Ukrainian capital after a 1-1 draw saw the Reds through.

His presence as the public face of Liverpool protests against staging this second leg of the third qualifying round on Israeli soil had provoked an angry, emotional response from Haifa, who deemed UEFA's decision to switch the tie to a neutral venue as an affront and a sign of favouritism towards Europe's leading clubs.

Stranded for more than an hour on their chartered plane from John Lennon Airport in the morning Liverpool were then forced to wait 90 minutes to retrieve their luggage upon arrival in the Ukraine. It was, therefore, a tetchy Benitez who arrived late for the obligatory pre-match press conference at the Radisson hotel, and his mood deteriorated when he was instantly besieged by Israel journalists who demanded, almost to the point of hysteria, a full explanation for his reluctance to play Haifa in Tel Aviv.

To all the neutrals in a crowded, chaotic room off the foyer at the

Liverpool team HQ the answer appeared as clear as UEFA's ruling that no European ties should be played in Israel at this volatile time. Yet the issue had dominated Haifa's preparations for the first leg and now, having kept alive hopes of an astonishing upset at Anfield, the loss of home advantage resonated more than ever. Emotions and a sense of grievance were running high through the Israeli camp.

"Why do you keep asking these questions? Look, we have a lot of respect for Haifa, their manager and their players, but I am not going to answer any more of your hypothetical questions," bristled a riled Benitez when asked for the fifth time if he was afraid of the Israeli champions and whether he would consider holidaying in the country now that the fighting, apparently, has stopped.

Those passions were transferred into another belligerent display from the Israeli players, but ultimately their grievance at being deprived of home advantage was compounded as Liverpool survived several late scares to edge into the group stage and claim a guaranteed £12m in prize money.

Liverpool's financiers had budgeted for Champions' League qualification long before they took the Spaniard's total spending to £89.9m with the £10m acquisition of Dirk Kuyt, the Dutch striker, ineligible to face Haifa. An early exit, in the words of one Anfield official, would therefore have been "catastrophic".

Relief at securing the kudos and euros on offer from Europe's premier event was not confined to Benitez and his squad. The Anfield hierarchy, having budgeted for Champions League football before backing their manager to the tune of £25m over the summer, will also take their seats in Monaco in silent prayer to Peter Crouch's 54th-minute header at the Valeri Lobanovskiy Stadium.

"We are happy and we are relieved," admitted the Liverpool manager. "We created a lot of clear chances in the first half, but their goalkeeper was fantastic, for me the man of the match, and the more chances we missed the more

our opponents believed they could keep going. In the end they gave us a lot of problems."

Benitez's assessment of a tense night for his side contained many truths. Liverpool did indeed dominate the opening hour, showing a threat that Haifa initially failed to match if relying too heavily on the long ball from a defence that was clearly intent on sitting deep and preserving the slender lead secured by Mark Gonzalez's winner at Anfield. Crouch and Xabi Alonso both shot narrowly wide early on while the Haifa goalkeeper, Nir Davidovitch, was inspired in denying Jermaine Pennant and Luis Garcia, twice, from close range before half-time.

It was a strangely subdued performance from Liverpool, but their outlets were provided by the width of Pennant and Gonzalez, and it was the £6.5m summer signing from Birmingham who created the breakthrough for Crouch when he skipped clear of a feeble challenge from Haifa left back Hain Magrashvili and crossed for the England international to head home at the near post.

Instead of deflating at the setback, Haifa rallied, and found renewed hope nine minutes later when Anderson and Yaniv Katan combined to slice open the

Liverpool defence, and Roberto Colautti pounced from close range after Reina could only parry Anderson's shot.

Liverpool held out in a fraught finale, but progress came at a price. Having lost Jamie Carragher and John Arne Riise to injury during a league match the previous Saturday, and Steven Gerrard to a stomach complaint before kick-off, Liverpool suffered further disruption when the influential Mohamed Sissoko was carried off with a knee injury and left back Stephen Warnock limped off with an ankle problem.

However, the greatest misery was reserved for the Haifa coach, Roni Levy. "I am proud of my team, but disappointed with the situation. We would have had a much better chance if we had played on our soil in front of our fans."

Peter Crouch is mobbed after netting the vital goal

CRVENA ZV. 1 v **AC MILAN 2**

Referee
Claus Bo Larsen (DEN)

Scorers

80'	Djokic	Inzaghi	29'
		Seedorf	79'

Teams

01	Randjelovic	Dida	01
04	Pantic	Costacurta	05
30	Basta	Cafu	02
03	Gueye	Simic	17
06	Bisevac	Gattuso	08
16	Kovacevic	Kaká	22
32	Milovanovic	Pirlo	21
17	Georgiev	Seedorf	10
08	Jankovic	Serginho	27
09	Djokic	Gilardino	11
25	Zigic	Inzaghi	09

Substitutes

53'	> 11 Perovic < 08 Jankovic	23 Ambrosini > 09 Inzaghi <	68'
61'	> 20 Purovic < 04 Pantic	19 Favalli > 02 Cafu <	82'
71'	> 03 Andjelkovic < 32 Milovanovic	30 Borriello > 11 Gilardino <	88'

Discipline

48'	Gueye	Kaká	57'
1	Yellow cards		1

Crvena Zvezda 1 v AC Milan 2
(AC Milan win 3-1 on aggregate)
Crvena Zvezda Stadium
Attendance: 49,862

Clarence Seedorf celebrates his goal which saw Milan through a tricky tie 3-1 on aggregate

New AC Milan signing Ricardo Oliveira declared he was not worried about having to fill the boots of Andriy Shevchenko following his move to the Italian giants.

The 26 year-old, who joined Milan on a five-year deal from Real Betis with midfielder Johann Vogel travelling in the opposite direction, was handed the number seven shirt vacated by Shevchenko when he moved to Chelsea over the summer. However, Brazilian Oliveira denied the responsibility will be an extra weight despite the Ukrainian's celebrity status at Milan.

"I have no problem with it," Oliveira said. "I am a striker arriving at one of the best clubs in the world and I understand the responsibility that brings, but I am not worried."

Oliveira watched his new team-mates ease past a potentially tricky tie in Belgrade thanks to another Inzaghi strike on the half hour. Clarence Seedorf added a rare goal with ten minutes remaining to make it 3-0 on aggregate before Dusan Djokic pulled a goal back with a low right foot shot for Belgrade, but Milan cruised through.

DID YOU KNOW?
Crvena Zvezda midfielder Dejan Milovanovic's father Djordje played for Red Star Belgrade during the 1970s and was nicknamed 'Djoka bomb' in a nod to his prowess from long range

THIRD QUALIFYING ROUND

SECOND LEG
(AC MILAN WIN 3-1 ON AGGREGATE)

Osasuna 1 v Hamburg 1

(1-1 on aggregate Hamburg win on away goals)
El Sadar Stadium
Attendance: 19,000

OSASUNA 1 v **HAMBURG 1**

	Referee	
	Massimo Busacca (SUI)	

Scorers

06'	Cuellar	de Jong	74'

Teams

13	Ricardo	Kirschstein	12
05	Cuellar	Demel	20
17	Javier Flano	Kompany	10
14	Romero Josetxo	Reinhardt	04
27	Monreal	de Jong	28
16	David Lopez	Jarolim	14
23	Delporte	van der Vaart	23
10	Punal	Wicky	06
06	Raul Garcia	Lauth	11
09	Milosevic	Mahdavikia	07
18	Soldado	Sanogo	17

Substitutes

68'	> 15 Webo < 18 Soldado	30 Benjamin > 10 Kompany <	11'
80'	> 11 Valdo < 17 Javier Flano	09 Guerrero > 06 Wicky <	66'
		15 Trochowski > 11 Lauth <	79'

Discipline

62'	Punal	Demel	67'
		José Paolo Guerrero	88'

1	Yellow cards	2

Hamburg SV's Nigel de Jong (R) bundles in the vital goal against Osasuna and celebrates with his team mate Paolo Guerrero while goalkeeper Ricardo Lopez turns away in despair

Hamburg fought back from a goal down to claim a 1-1 draw at Osasuna that earned them an away-goals victory.

Primera Liga side Osasuna had looked on the verge of going through after Carlos Cuellar put them in front six minutes into the second leg of the third qualifying round tie. The defender squeezed a header past keeper Sascha Kirschstein at the far post after meeting an outswinging corner from David Lopez.

The Navarrans held their lead until 16 minutes from the final whistle when midfielder Nigel de Jong bundled in at the far post after Benjamin Lauth had sent a diving header across the front of the goal following a free-kick.

Osasuna poured forward for the remainder of the match, but they spurned a late chance to snatch victory when substitute Pierre Webo fired a close range header over the bar in the final minute.

DID YOU KNOW?

Hamburg are the only club to have played every season in the Bundesliga since its foundation in 1963

THIRD QUALIFYING ROUND

SECOND LEG
(1-1 on aggregate HAMBURG WIN ON AWAY GOALS)

VALENCIA 3 v SALZBURG 0

Referee
Referee: Lubos Michel (SVK)

Scorers

13'	Morientes
33'	Villa
90'	Silva

Teams

01	Canizares	Ochs	01
24	Moretti	Bodnar	02
17	Navarro	Dudic	03
06	Albelda	Linke	04
20	Albiol	Orosz	24
22	Edu	Vargas	31
21	Silva	Aufhauser	28
14	Vicente	Carboni	05
10	Angulo	Kovac	06
09	Morientes	Tiffert	13
07	Villa	Pitak	16

Substitutes

72'	> 11 Regueiro < 09 Morientes	09 Lokvenc > 24 Orosz <	46'
72'	> 19 Gavilan < 14 Vicente	19 Vonlanthen > 13 Tiffert <	57'
88'	> 05 Marchena < 22 Edu	11 Jezek > 06 Kovac <	65'

Discipline

37'	Angulo	Bodnar	18'
87'	Canizares	Tiffert	46'
		Vargas	58'

2	Yellow cards	3

One Spanish side did make it to the group stage when Valencia overturned a first leg deficit to see off Salzburg 3-1 on aggregate. First-half goals from Fernando Morientes and David Villa and an injury-time strike from David Silva gave Valencia, losing finalists in the competition in 2000 and 2001, a 3-0 win.

Valencia wiped out their 1-0 deficit from the first leg of the third qualifying round tie when Morientes put them ahead in the 13th minute. The former Liverpool and Real Madrid striker steered into the empty net when keeper Timo Ochs turned a Villa shot into his path after the Spain striker had raced past the Salzburg back four. The Primera Liga side took the aggregate lead 20 minutes later after Ezequiel Carboni had conceded a penalty for handling in the area when he came under pressure from Villa.

Ochs managed to turn Villa's spot kick on to the post, but the striker was on hand to smash the ball high into the net as it spun back into his path.

With Salzburg needing one goal to turn the tie, Valencia could never relax but they wrapped up an emphatic win when Silva curled a shot round Ochs and into the far corner from the right side of the area with the final kick of the game.

BENFICA 3 v AUST. VIENNA 0

Referee
Terje Hauge (NOR)

Scorers

21'	Rui Costa
45'	Nuno Gomes
57'	Petit

Teams

12	Quim	Safar	01
03	Anderson	Hill	04
04	Luisao	Papac	30
22	Nelson	Radomski	08
33	Ricardo Rocha	Tokic	05
08	Katsouranis	Troyanski	05
18	Manu	Blanchard	15
15	Paulo Jorge	Ceh	19
06	Petit	Mila	33
10	Rui Costa	Wimmer	25
21	Nuno Gomes	Wallner	07

Substitutes

66'	> 17 Fonseca < 10 Rui Costa	06 Schicker > 30 Papac <	29'
74'	> 16 Beto < 06 Petit	14 Lasnik > 33 Mila <	46'
85'	> 09 Mantorras < 15 Paulo Jorge	17 Pichlmann > 19 Ceh <	54'

Discipline

	Mila	10'
	Radomski	44'
	Schicker	73'
	Tokic	82'
	Wimmer	86'

0	Yellow cards	5

DID YOU KNOW?
Benfica's qualification for the Group Stage of the UEFA Champions League meant that Portugal boasted three teams through to this phase of the competition for the first time ever

3rd Qualifying Round
Wednesday 23 August 2006 – Second Legs

Arsenal 2 v Dinamo Zagreb 1
(Arsenal win 5-1 on aggregate)
Emirates Stadium
Attendance: 58,418

The teams enter the pitch for the first European tie at the Emirates stadium

ARSENAL 2 v **DINAMO Z'B 1**

Referee
Referee: Bertrand Layec (FRA)

Scorers

77'	Ljungberg	Eduardo	12'
90'	Flamini		

Teams

24	Almunia	Turina	01
20	Djourou	Carlos	15
27	Eboue	Corluka	05
31	Hoyte	Cvitanovic	06
05	Toure	Drpic	26
04	Fabregas	Eto	07
16	Flamini	Mamic	28
13	Hleb	Agic	11
08	Ljungberg	Modric	10
25	Adebayor	Vukojevic	20
11	van Persie	Eduardo	24

Substitutes

65'	> 14 Henry < 25 Adebayor	02 Buljat > 11 Agic <	69'
70'	> 19 Gilberto Silva < 13 Hleb	27 Ljubojevic > 20 Vukojevic <	89'
81'	> 32 Walcott < 11 van Persie	08 Tomic > 07 Eto <	90'

Discipline

08'	Flamini	Agic	14'
68'	Djourou	Drpic	43'
81'	Walcott	Buljat	72'
3	**Yellow cards**		3

Arsène Wenger's new look side made hard work of victory on the night, but had already sealed qualification for the group stage thanks to that good away performance

On a night when the Champions League bade farewell to one of the competition's greatest names, Arsenal completed the first step on the long road back to the Champions League final, but it was not without a stumble for the previous season's runners-up.

The departures of Dutch giants Ajax, Turkish side Fenerbahce and Chievo Verona of Italy did ruffle a few feathers; even more so that the likes of Shakhtar Donetsk, Copenhagen and Lille made it through to the group stage. But the Gunners made heavy weather of defending a seemingly impregnable three goal lead. They conceded early and could easily have had their aggregate lead cut further. However, an often frustrating night ended in joy with news of Chelsea's defeat to Middlesbrough in the Premiership adding a celebratory note to the relief felt when late goals from Freddie Ljungberg and Mathieu

THIRD QUALIFYING ROUND

SECOND LEG
(ARSENAL WIN 5-1 ON AGGREGATE)

Mathieu Flamini makes the score 2-1 to Arsenal

Flamini secured their first victory at their new home after an opening draw in the league against Aston Villa.

"It is a relief [to get through], and to win at home," said Arsène Wenger, "We know how important [qualification] is to the club, both financially and to us as a team. And if we did not win people would say, 'You can't win at the new stadium', so it is good to get that out of the way."

The knowledge that they were virtually assured of a place in the draw contributed to Arsenal's ponderous start. "It is difficult to put any urgency in when you are three-nil up," Wenger said. It took 12 minutes for Arsenal to be punished for allowing the visitors time to demonstrate their neat passing and technical quality. Eduardo exchanged passes with Etto, took advantage of a poor interception by Touré, and swept the ball past Almunia.

With Robin van Persie prominent in a deep-lying role, and the wide men pushing on, Arsenal pressed forward. Within 10 minutes Adebayor nodded a Cesc Fabregas free-kick down to van Persie but his shot was acrobatically cleared by Mario Cvitanovic. Van Persie, demonstrating clever sleight of foot, then brought a decent save from Ivan Turina. Ljungberg also tested the goalkeeper but, on the break, Zagreb could twice have struck, only for both Luka Modric and Etto to shoot into the side netting.

Arsenal's growing nerves should have been settled after 52 minutes as Justin Hoyte's cross found its way to Adebayor, unopposed and 15 yards from goal. The Togolese striker blasted over the bar. Wenger looked disgusted. This night of all nights he must have anticipated being able to enjoy the game; instead he had spent it fretting like a father in a maternity ward.

Finally, after both Thierry Henry and Gilberto Silva had been pressed into action, Ljungberg put him out of his misery, stooping to glance in van Persie's left-wing free-kick with 13 minutes remaining.

The party began, given further impetus by the introduction of Theo Walcott. In injury time the teenager delivered the cross from which Flamini, unmarked, tapped in to record the historic first home win at the new ground.

Eduardo celebrates a glimmer of hope after putting Zagreb ahead at the Emirates

AEK Athens 3 v Hearts 0
(AEK Athens win 5-1 on aggregate)
Spiros Louis Stadium
Attendance: 31,500

AEK Athens' Emerson challenges Edgaras Jankauskas of Hearts

AEK ATHENS 3 v **HEARTS 0**

Referee
Iouri Baskakov (RUS)

Scorers
79', 86'	Júlio César (1 pen)
82'	Liberopoulos

Teams
22	Chiotis	Gordon 01
05	Cirillo	Berra 20
55	Dellas	Fyssas 03
31	Georgeas	Neilson 02
25	Emerson	Pressley 04
17	Ivic	Brellier 28
19	Lagos	Cesnauskis 18
13	Pautasso	McCann 07
99	Cesar	Hartley 10
35	Kapetanos	Mikoliunas 16
33	Liberopoulos	Mole 35

Substitutes
54'	> 23 Lakis < 19 Lagos	09 Jankauskas > 10 Hartley <	61'
72'	> 88 Tozser < 13 Pautasso	23 Wallace > 18 Cesnauskis <	81'
84'	> 79 Kampantais < 33 Liberopoulos	19 Pinilla > 35 Mole <	89'

Discipline
16'	Liberopoulos	Neilson	07'
73'	Georgeas	Brellier	26'
80'	Julio Cesar	Brellier	30'
		Mikoliunas	41'
		Fyssas	57'
		McCann	63'

0	Yellow cards	5
0	Red cards	2

Julien Brellier and Neil McCann were both sent off as Hearts' hopes of reaching the Group Stage ended with a comprehensive 3-0 defeat away to AEK Athens, the Greeks completing a 5-1 win on aggregate.

Valdas Ivanauskas' team joined the other losers in the Third Qualifying round in the UEFA Cup draw, but that was scant consolation for the desperate manner of the ending of their first Champions League campaign. AEK man of the match Julio Cesar scored twice in the last 11 minutes, one from the penalty spot in the 79th minute after Deividas Cesnauskis had felled Vasilis Lakis in the right side of the penalty area, and another a fine side-footed strike from just inside the penalty area.

Ivanauskas had sprung a huge shock by including rookie striker Jamie Mole in his starting line-up for the game. The 18 year-old, who had not even played a single competitive game for Hearts this season previously.

Hearts survived a first half attacking onslaught from AEK after Brellier saw red on the half-hour mark when he was

THIRD QUALIFYING ROUND

SECOND LEG
(AEK ATHENS WIN 5-1 ON AGGREGATE)

AEK Athens' players Vassilis Lakis (L), Bruno Cirillo (C) and Nikos Liberopoulos celebrate AEK's second goal against Hearts

shown a second yellow card for an aerial challenge on AEK's Vladan Ivic in which he seemed to lead with his elbow. His first yellow had come just a couple of minutes earlier when he upset Russian referee Yuri Baskakov by coming onto the pitch without permission having been sent to take out an earring.

From then on it was backs to the wall for Hearts, who were fortunate to see Liberopoulos miss several golden opportunites to extend his team's advantage in the tie.

Things went from bad to worse when 20 minutes into the second half when Hearts were reduced to nine men when McCann foolishly lunged into a two-footed challenge on Ivic right in front of Baskakov, who had little option but to give the midfielder his marching orders. McCann's exit shattered the spirit of the Scots, who caved in in the latter stages under relentless AEK pressure.

Liberopoulos, who headed wide from an unmarked position following a corner midway through the first half, was presented with a chance to open

the scoring in the 67th minute when he was teed up on the edge of the penalty area by substitute Vasilis Lakis – but the striker shot straight at Gordon.

The hosts finally opened the scoring with 11 minutes left after winning a penalty courtesy of Lakis. The former Crystal Palace winger was felled in the box by Deividas Cesnauskis and the impressive Cesar slotted a left-footed shot home from the penalty spot.

Liberopoulos eventually found his range with eight minutes remaining, heading home AEK's second goal from a deep Nikos Georgeas left-wing cross. Hearts were well and truly on the rack with four minutes left on the clock as Cesar teased and tricked his way past defender Christophe Berra before grabbing his second and AEK's third goal of the game with a low sidefooted striker past Gordon from just inside the penalty area.

Post-match Hearts head coach Ivanauskas launched a scathing attack on Russian referee Yuri Baskakov, questioning both red cards and the

penalty decision. Ivanauskas glowered: "The referee's decisions have cost us the chance to win the game. We had chances in this match and played with heart. But I don't like to see these things from the referee. It was really unbelievable and I can't believe that they do these things in such important games."

Initially confusion surrounded Brellier's first booking, but Ivanauskas confirmed it was because of tape on an earring. But the clearly angry Hearts boss maintained that the Russian match official had checked the players before the game and given them the green light to play.

Despite his obvious anger with Baskakov, Ivanauskas still took the time to congratulate AEK, admitting that, over the two games, the Greek side deserved to go through to the lucrative UEFA Champions League group stages.

He said: "AEK were the best team over the two games. I offer them my congratulations and I wish them good luck."

Ajax Amsterdam 0 v FC Copenhagen 2

(FC Copenhagen win 3-2 on aggregate)
Amsterdam ArenA
Attendance: 35,000

AJAX 0 v **FC COPENH'N 2**

Referee
Herbert Fandel (GER)

Scorers

	Silberbauer	59'
	Vermaelen (o.g.)	77'

Teams

01	Stekelenburg	Christiansen	01
05	Emanuelson	Bergdolmo	15
02	Heitinga	Gravgaard	14
06	Maduro	Hangeland	05
03	Stam	Jacobsen	02
04	Vermaelen	Hutchinson	13
18	Gabri	Kvist	23
10	Sneijder	Linderoth	06
08	Babel	Pimpong	20
09	Huntelaar	Silberbauer	08
07	Rosales	Allback	11

Substitutes

61'	28 Vertonghen / 06 Maduro	09 Berglund / 20 Pimpong	58'
79'	11 Perez / 18 Gabri	16 Thomassen / 08 Silberbauer	89'
85'	19 Rosenberg / 07 Rosales		

Discipline

56'	Stam	Allback	50'
61'	Sneijder	Silberbauer	81'
2	Yellow cards		2

Ajax Amsterdam's defender Thomas Vermalen reacts after he scored an own goal to hand FC Copenhagen an unlikely win

FC Copenhagen struck twice in the second half to score a stunning 2-0 win at Ajax and qualify for the UEFA Champions League group stage for the first time with a shock 3-2 aggregate win.

Ajax, the four-time European champions, had won the first leg 2-1 in Denmark and expected a relatively easy night at the Amsterdam ArenA, but although the Dutch side dominated the first half and went close after eight minutes when exciting young winger Ryan Babel's deflected shot hit a post, they squandered a hatful of chances. Spaniard Gabri twice headed wide from close range, while a fierce strike from the edge of the penalty area was saved by goalkeeper Jesper Christiansen.

But just as in Copenhagen a fortnight earlier the Ajax defence proved vulnerable at set pieces. A 59th minute free kick from the left flank was netted at the far post by the unmarked Michael Silberbauer. Ajax defender Thomas Vermaelen then put through his own net after 77 minutes when he changed the direction of a cross from the right flank to hand Copenhagen their second goal of the night and put them 3-2 ahead over the two legs.

Ten minutes before time Klaas-Jan Huntelaar headed against the bar, but Ajax could not find the goal that would have taken the match into extra time and Copenhagen held on for a famous win.

FC Copenhagen's coach Stale Solbacken and his players celebrate their victory over Ajax Amsterdam

THIRD QUALIFYING ROUND

SECOND LEG
(FC COPENHAGEN WIN 3-2 ON AGGREGATE)

STEAUA BUCH. 2 v STAND'D LIEGE 1

Referee
Graham Poll (ENG)

Scorers

35', 51' Badea	Jovanovic 00'

Teams

13	Carlos	Renard	16
17	Baciu	Deflandre	02
09	Badea	Fellaini	27
03	Goian	Jovanovic	23
18	Marin	Onyewu	05
15	Nesu	Rogerio Matias	20
14	Cristocea	Sarr	19
10	Dica	Defour	08
20	Lovin	Geraerts	22
22	Paraschiv	Rapaic	11
16	Nicolita	Sa Pinto	76

Substitutes

70'	> 28 Coman < 22 Paraschiv	03 Coelho > 05 Onyewu <	64'
83'	> 07 Oprita < 09 Badea	09 Bouchouari > 02 Deflandre <	77'
88'	> 11 Bostina < 15 Nesu		

Discipline

04'	Marin	Jovanovic	03'
82'	Goian	Rapaic	22'
89'	Carlos	Fellaini	38'
		Sa Pinto	75'
		Sa Pinto	82'

3	Yellow cards	5
0	Red cards	1

THIRD QUALIFYING ROUND

SECOND LEG
(STEAUA BUCHAREST WIN 4-3 ON AGGREGATE)

DID YOU KNOW?
Steaua Bucharest reached the Group Stage for the first time since 1996/97

Steaua Bucharest 2 v Standard Liege 1
(Steaua Bucharest win 4-3 on aggregate)
Stadionul Ghencea
Attendance: 45,000

Standard Liege's Marouane Fellaini (R) fights for the ball with Steaua Bucharest's Valentin Badea

Steaua Bucharest came from behind to secure a close 4-3 win on aggregate over Standard Liege. Valentin Badea scored either side of half-time to overturn the lead given to the visitors by Milan Jovanovic's 2nd minute strike.

Liege Coach Johan Boskamp tears his hair out after losing the lead to Valentin Badea's brace

Fenerbahce 2 v Dynamo Kiev 2
(Dynamo Kiev win 5-3 on aggregate)
Sukru Saracoglu Stadium
Attendance: 38,793

Stephen Appiah's late goal for Fenerbahce was scant consolation for a sound beating by Dynamo Kiev

FENERBAHCE 2 v DYNAMO KIEV 2

Referee
Steve Bennett (ENG)

Scorers

36'	Appiah	Shatskikh	05',42'
57'	Kerim Zengin		

Teams

34	Rustu	Shovkovskiy	01
	Ozat	Markovic	81
	Turaci	Rodrigo	44
	Alex	Sablic	13
	Appiah	Yussuf	37
	Arat	Correa	07
	Aurelio	El Kaddouri	30
	Metin	Rotan	14
	Sanli	Gusev	20
	Senturk	Rebrov	05
	Zengin	Shatskikh	16

Substitutes

64'	> 53 Hacioglu < 23 Senturk	32 Gavrancic 20 Gusev	> <	66'
76'	> 25 Boral < 11 Metin	23 Verpakovskis 14 Rotan	> <	86'
84'	> 07 Yozgatli < 19 Turaci			

Discipline

32'	Ozat	Sablic	40'
		Shatskikh	77'
1	Yellow cards	2	

Maksim Shatskikh's two first half goals gave Dynamo Kiev plenty of breathing space after they had won the first leg against Fenerbahce 3-1. Shatskikh's two goals were scored through poor defensive play as Ümit Özat at left back, Can Arat and Önder Turacı in the centre and Kerim Zengin at the right were caught flat and out of position on many occasions.

Strikes by Stephen Appiah and Kerim Zengin added some respectability to the scoreline for the Zico's side, who were celebrating their centenary with a trip to the group stage.

DID YOU KNOW?
Dynamo Kiev was founded as a Soviet sporting society. The club was originally patronised by the NKVD, the Soviet Secret Police

SP'K MOSCOW 2 v SLOVAN LIB. 1

Referee
Luis Medina Cantalejo (ESP)

Scorers

23'	Mozart	Hodúr	73'
79'	Pavlyuchenko		

Teams

30	Kowalewski	Cech	24
13	Jiranek	Janu	17
17	Rodriguez	Kostal	14
49	Shishkin	Singlar	19
03	Stranzl	Zapotocny	05
23	Bystrov	Bilek	07
27	Covalciuc	Frejlach	20
15	Kovac	Hodur	10
24	Mozart	Pudil	26
19	Cavenaghi	Holenda	29
10	Pavluchenko	Pospech	11

Substitutes

75'	> 25 Kalinichenko < 23 Bystrov	28 Blazek > 29 Holenda <	54'
87'	> 32 Bazhenov < 19 Cavenaghi	09 Ancic > 20 Frejlach <	62'
		02 Matula > 17 Janu <	76'

Discipline

71'	Jiranek	Kostal	67'
37'	Zapotocny	Pudil	84'
37'	Zapotocny		
75'	Mozart		
84'	Kalinichenko		

5	Yellow cards	2
1	Red cards	0

Spartak Moscow 2 v Slovan Liberec 1
(Spartak Moscow win 2-1 on aggregate)
Luzhniki Stadium
Attendance: 35,000

Liberec captain Tomas Zapotocny (L) reacts in disbelief after he fails to put the ball past Spartak Moscow's Wojciech Kowalewski

Ivan Hodur's penalty seemed to have given Czech champions Slovan Liberec an unlikely win after the first leg against Spartak Moscow had ended goalless. Tomas Zapotocny had been dismissed for two yellow cards on the hour, but Hodur converted after Martin Jiranek's foul.

But a nailbiting encounter was won by Roman Pavluchenko's 79th minute fortuitous deflected goal, which sent Moscow through to the group stage after Brazilian Santos Batista Mozart's first half goal had given them the lead.

Spartak fans rejoice at safe passage into the group stage

CHIEVO VER. 2 v LEVSKI SOFIA 2

Referee
Lucilio Cardoso Cortez Batista (POR)

Scorers

48', 81'	Amauri	Telkiyski	34'
		Bardon	46'

Teams

01	Sicignano	Petkov	01
23	Lanna	Milanov	03
04	Malago	Tomasic	04
29	Mandelli	Topuzakov	11
04	Mantovani	Borimirov	07
08	Giunti	Domovchiyski	17
21	Sammarco	Eromoigbe	06
07	Semioli	Telkiyski	21
10	Zanchetta	Wagner	25
11	Amauri	Bardon	27
31	Pellissier	Yovov	10

Substitutes

59'	> 90 Tiribocchi < 31 Pellissier	28 E Angelov > 17 Domovchiyski <	72'
65'	> 20 Marcolini < 08 Giunti	20 Angelov > 21 Telkiyski <	76'
72'	> 05 Luciano < 07 Semioli	77 Koprivarov > 10 Yovov <	90'

Discipline

39'	Sammarco	Wagner	06'
83'	Lanna	Tomasic	45'
90'	Marcolini	Petkov	57'
		Wagner	90'

2	Yellow cards	4
1	Red cards	1

Levski Sofia became the first Bulgarian team to reach the group stages of the Champions League when they drew 2-2 with Chievo Verona to seal a 4-2 aggregate win over the Italian.

The Bulgarian champions went 1-0 ahead on the night when midfielder Dimitar Telkiyski took advantage of a poor Chievo clearance to score in the 35th minute. The Italian side tried to force their way back into contention, visiting keeper Giorgi Petkov turning a header by Brazilian striker Amauri round the post, but Cedric Bardon put Levski 2-0 ahead in the 47th minute.

Amauri pulled two goals back for Chievo, first heading in a corner and then sliding in to poke in a cross with his studs. But the gloss was taken off the Italians' good second-half performance, when defender Salvatore Lanna was red-carded for elbowing Emil Angelov and Levski's night was marred when Lucio was sent off for a second yellow card deep in stoppage time.

Benfica laid to rest any thoughts of failure to qualify with a 3-0 victory over Austria Vienna, with Portuguese international veterans Nuno Gomes and Rui Costa were amongst the scorers.

DID YOU KNOW?
Benfica sports club, of which the football arm is but one of many, has the largest registered paying membership of any sporting association in the world with 160,398 members according to the Guinness Book of Records 2006

MLADA BOLES. 1 v GALATASARAY 1

Referee
Martin Hansson (SWE)

Scorers

88'	Palat	Hasan Sas	73'

Teams

27	Miller	Mondragon	01
09	Brezinsky	Ak	05
06	Palat	Song	04
04	Rolko	Tomas	02
03	Sevinsky	Akman	18
23	Smerda	Buruk	07
08	Matejovsky	Haspolatli	19
16	Pecka	Ilic	22
12	Polacek	Sarioglu	55
05	Vaculik	Hasan Sas	11
07	Holub	Hasan Sukur	09

Substitutes

46'	> 11 Sedlacek < 12 Polacek	66 Turan > 22 Ilic <	71'
68'	> 15 Mikolanda < 23 Smerda	33 Ucar > 05 Ak <	76'
74'	> 25 Riegel < 07 Holub	23 Ozcan > 09 Sukur <	84'

Discipline

	Buruk	18'
	Hasan Sas	42'
	Sarioglu	90'

0	Yellow cards	3

RAB.KOMETAL 0 v LILLE 1

Referee
Costas Kapitanis (CYP)

Scorers
	Audel	18'

Teams

01	Pacovski	Malicki	16
16	Carlos	Lichtsteiner	26
03	Jeremic	Schmitz	05
28	Vajs	Tafforeau	20
15	Janker	Tavlaridis	04
21	Jankolovski	Cabaye	07
16	Nedzipi	Dumont	29
22	Trajcov	Makoun	17
08	Velkovski	Audel	09
20	Pejcic	Mirallas	27
30	Stankovski	Youla	11

Substitutes

60'	19 Karcev / 28 Vajs		21 Chalme / 17 Makoun		62'
76'	09 Aleksovski / 08 Velkovski		18 Robail / 07 Cabaye		76'

Discipline

19'	Jankolovski	Lichtsteiner	35'
20'	Vajs	Makoun	43'
83'	Jankolovski	Tavlaridis	70'

3	Yellow cards	3
1	Red cards	0

Shakhtar Donetsk recovered from an early scare to secure a 4-2 aggregate win over Legia Warsaw, who had taken an early lead through Piotr Wlodarczyk. But three goals in the last fifteen minutes of the first half saw Shakhtar home safely. Ciprian Marica scored twice and Luis Fernandinho once before Wlodarczyk netted in the last minute.

LEGIA WARSAW 2 v SHAKHTAR D. 3

Referee
Michael Riley (ENG)

Scorers
19', 88'	Wlodarczyk	Marica	25', 45'
		Fernandinho	29'

Teams

01	Fabianski	Shutkov	12
24	Balde	Hubschman	03
04	Choto	Lewandowski	18
27	Edson	Rat	26
32	Radovic	Sviderskiy	32
06	Roger	Elano	36
08	Surma	Fernandinho	07
20	Szalachowski	Matuzalem	09
28	Brandao	Tymoschuk	04
21	Gottwald	Brandau	25
09	Wlodarczyk	Marica	29

Substitutes

46'	13 Korzym / 21 Gottwald		98 Okoduwa / 25 Brandau		71'
65'	15 Janczyk / 28 Brandao		11 Vorobey / 29 Marica		71'
74'	19 Burkhardt / 08 Surma		38 Jadson / 09 Matuzalem		75'

Discipline

56'	Roger	Fernandinho	19'
		Matuzalem	23'

1	Yellow cards	2

RUZOMBEROK 0 v CSKA MOSCOW 2

Referee
Olegario Manuel Bartolo
Faustino Benquerença (POR)

Scorers
	Carvalho	08'
	Vágner Love	32'

Teams

21	Hajduch	Akinfeev	35
19	Dvornik	Berezutsky	06
13	Laurinc	Ignashevich	04
12	Pospisil	Semberas	02
22	Silva	Aldonin	22
15	Bozok	Dudu	20
27	Sapara	Jo	10
04	Sedlak	Krasic	17
09	Zofcak	Rahimic	25
07	Nezmar	Daniel Carvalho	07
25	Rak	Vagner Love	11

Substitutes

70'	08 Dovicovic / 04 Sedlak		18 Zhirkov / 11 Vagner Love		46'
70'	10 Tomcak / 15 Bozok		09 Olic / 07 D Carvalho		70'
78'	06 Babnic / 07 Nezmar		08 Gusev / 17 Krasic		86'

Rui Costa celebrates his goal in Benfica's 3-0 victory over Austria Vienna

Austria Vienna's Pichlmann (R) and team-mate Wallner walk away in despair after their defeat by Benfica

Is The Future Bright?

AJAX AMSTERDAM

Founded	March 1900
Stadium	Amsterdam ArenA
Nickname	Godenzonen (Sons of the Gods)
Team Honours	European Champions: 1971, 1972, 1972, 1995

Defeat by FC Copenhagen left the famous Ajax of Amsterdam consigned to the early stages of the UEFA Cup. It was a great surprise to see such a glorious name failing to compete in the Champions League group stage.

As one of the five teams who have earned the right to keep the European

Cup having won it in three consecutive seasons from 1971-1973 and then again in 1995, Ajax were also the first club to have won the treble of league title, national cup (KNVB Cup) and European Cup, the Godenzonen (Sons of the Gods) also won the World Club Championship in the same season – 1971/72. Currently only Manchester United in 1998/99 have matched that feat.

Formed in 1900, after coming to prominence in the late 1950s, when football belatedly went professional in the Netherlands, Ajax won their first Eredivisie (Dutch National Championship) in 1957. The great goalscorer of this time, Henk Groot, regularly topped the goalscoring charts, bagging 38 goals in 1959/60 as Ajax won the title again and having his personal best season in

1960/61 when he scored 41 times. But it wasn't until former player, the chain-smoking Rinus Michels, replaced Englishman Vic Buckingham as manager that the modern legend of Ajax was born. Michels' 'Total Football' revolution brought to the fore a generation of Dutch players whose style and flair flew against the predominant defensive tactical thinking of the late 1960s and early 1970s. Led by Johan Cruyff and including the likes of Arie Haan, Ruud Krol, Johan Neeskens, Piet Keizer and Gerrie Muhren, Ajax formed the basis for the great Dutch national side of the 1974 World Cup, which came so close to winning that tournament, but lost to hosts Germany after taking the lead in the first minute of the final.

The much vaunted youth policy which has seen four decades' worth of stars emerge from the Ajax finishing school – such as Cruyff, Frank Rijkaard, Marco van Basten, Marc Overmars, the de Boer twins, Dennis Bergkamp, Edgar Davids, Edwin van der Sar, Kanu and Patrick Kluivert, also now seems to have dried up. And the famous white shirt with the wide red central stripe doesn't carry quite the same fear in opponents' hearts as they take the field.

Since that success in winning the 1995 UEFA Champions League, Ajax have struggled in Europe's premier competition. Only a quarter-final appearance under manager Ronald Koeman in 2002/03, when Ajax conceded a heartbreaking last minute goal to AC Milan to go out, has offered any encouragement. In 2006/07 the club could only finish 2nd in the Eriedivisie to return to the Champions League 3rd qualifying round for 2007/08, losing out to PSV Eindhoven on goal difference on the last matchday.

A club partly tied to their glorious past, Ajax have now retired the famous number 14 Cruyff shirt. Star Spanish midfielder Roger became the last player to wear it in the 2006/07 season at the brand new Amsterdam ArenA, a stadium built to replace the ageing De Meer, Ajax's traditional home, in 1996 just when the club thought they were on the verge of

European domination having won the Champions League and then finished as runners-up to Juventus the following season. Sadly the changing face of football finance meant that the club could not hold on to its stars for the best part of their careers as they departed to seek riches available first in Spain and Italy and latterly in England.

Can Ajax come back to prominence under new coach Henk ten Cate? With Jaap Stam as captain and a squad burgeoned by the signings of Dennis Rommerdahl from Charlton and the returning veteran Edgar Davids, it could be that the fallen Dutch giant can return to the level of football to which they are accustomed on the European stage.

Happier days. Ajax captain Danny Blind lifts the 1995 European Cup

section four

group stage

Match Day 1
Tuesday 12 September 2006

Michael On The Spot

Ballack takes over the Chelsea penalty-taking duties from Frank Lampard and sparks a storm of controversy

United and Celtic Play Out Thriller

A fantastic game of flowing football sees Strachan's Hoops give his old mentor a fright

Galacticos Downed

The Madrid millionaires slump to defeat at hotly-tipped Lyon, managed by Gérard Houllier

"Something is happening with the English press in relation to Frank Lampard. I think you should respect him a bit more – I'm angry about the way you treat Frank Lampard."

Jose Mourinho, Chelsea manager

Chelsea 2 v Werder Bremen 0
Group A
Stamford Bridge
Attendance: 32,135

Michael Essien celebrates the opening goal

CHELSEA 2 v **WERDER BREMEN 0**

Referee
Kyros Vassaras (GRE)

Assistant Referee
Dimitrios Bozatzidis (GRE)
Dimitrios Saraidaris (GRE)

Fourth Official
Dimitrios Kalopoulus (GRE)

Scorers
| 24' | Essien |
| 68' | Ballack (pen) |

Teams
01	Cech	Reinke	01
09	Boulahrouz	Rodrigues	04
06	Ricardo Carvalho	Fritz	08
03	A Cole	Pasanen	03
26	Terry	Wome	05
13	Ballack	Baumann	06
05	Essien	Borowski	24
08	Lampard	Frings	22
04	Makelele	Diego	10
11	Drogba	Klasnic	17
07	Shevchenko	Klose	11

Substitutes
81'	10 J Cole / 07 Shevchenko	23 Almeida / 17 Klasnic	66'
86'	21 Kalou / 11 Drogba	09 Zidan / 06 Baumann	86'
90'	12 Mikel / 13 Ballack		

Discipline
52'	Terry	Baumann	61'
71'	Drogba		
82'	Lampard		
84'	Cole		

7	Shots on goal	4
3	Shots wide	8
17	Fouls	11
4	Corners	5
3	Offsides	2
29' 32"	Ball. Poss. (time)	26' 53"
53%	Ball. Poss. (%)	47%

The UEFA Champions League Group Stage got underway with a night of goals, surprising results, and controversy.

Stamford Bridge saw an absorbing rather than splendid game, but one which sparked plenty of column inches.

Jose Mourinho temporarily took away Chelsea's penalty-taking responsibility from Frank Lampard — and then launched a fierce attack on the England midfielder's critics. "Something is happening with the English press in relation to Frank Lampard," he said. "He is guilty because you have never had a player like him in the last 10 years. He is guilty because he scores so many goals and plays so many matches for Chelsea and England with 100% effort in every game. I think you should respect him a bit more – I'm angry about the way you treat Frank Lampard."

Lampard had been criticised for his England performances in the World Cup. Meanwhile Chelsea's summer signing of Ballack had led many to question whether there was room for both attack-minded players in the same midfield.

With the match against dangerous German side Werder Bremen still in the balance as Chelsea held a slender one goal lead, Mourinho observed that the importance of the second-half penalty had made Ballack the preferred option after Lampard's weekend penalty miss against Charlton Athletic and having missed three of his past four penalties

for club and country. "I told them that my confidence is 100% on Lampard, but I told them that, if the next penalty after a miss is crucial for the game, it's better that another player takes responsibility," said Mourinho. "But if the next penalty comes in a moment when Lamps is cool and in condition to take it, he will take it again. We have good penalty-takers. Lampard missed a penalty against Charlton, but in the last few years he scored more than 10 penalties, crucial penalties, and he never let us down."

Mourinho had further bees in his bonnet after his impassioned defence of Lampard. Four Chelsea players were booked, prompting the manager to suggest that referees were treating his players particularly harshly in European competition. "The difference between an easy group and a difficult group is that in an easy group you don't get

bookings because the game is soft, without pressure," he said. "Big matches, you have more yellow cards. At the same time, the reality is that there are no yellow cards tonight for Barcelona; Bayern Munich one yellow card; Liverpool no yellow cards; Valencia one yellow card; Roma one yellow card – and Chelsea four yellow cards."

Mourinho felt the bookings of Terry, Drogba and Lampard were unjust. "If Drogba is booked, a Werder Bremen player should be booked because it is exactly the same situation, an offside and he kicked the ball," he said. "Joe Cole I didn't see. John Terry is not [a booking] for me, although maybe later, and Lampard I don't think so. My team have a lot of fair players – in English football it is very difficult for them to get a yellow card. Then they go to European football and get a lot of cards."

None the less, had the referee Kyros Vassaras actually been malign he would have dismissed John Terry with a second yellow card for his foul on Ivan Klasnic soon after half-time.

Mourinho was more than happy, though, to begin the European campaign with a 2-0 win, and particularly the early contribution of his new signing Ashley Cole, a constant danger as he overlapped down the left flank.

"The result is fantastic," said Mourinho. "Using Ashley on the wings, coming forward, we used the ball well and created enough to be in front. But until the second goal in the second half they were better. After the penalty the game was under control."

Chelsea possessed a hint of potency even before Michael Essien's opener. Pressure from Lampard, which made the turning Petri Pasanen stumble in the 24th minute, saw the increasingly influential Essien

Frank Lampard doesn't seem to bear any grudges after Ballack's spot-kick hits the back of the net

take over to steer a finish beyond Andreas Reinke.

It took the Ballack penalty, smashed high past the left hand of Reinke after 66 minutes for his first goal at the club, to dim the brightness of Werder Bremen's spirit. Indeed Miroslav Klose's header against the bar had almost supplied the equaliser moments earlier. Chelsea should have had an earlier penalty had the referee noticed a Fritz foul on Lampard inside the area, but relief eventually did come when he spotted the same defender's barge on Drogba.

Only the post prevented Lampard from raising the margin to 3-0, but even Mourinho agreed that would have been unjust.

Barcelona 5 v Levski Sofia 0
Group A
Nou Camp
Attendance: 91,326

Ronaldinho acclaims his wonderstrike

Lilian Thuram made his European debut for Barca, but there was no place in the starting line-up for Argentina forward Lionel Messi. Sofia, meanwhile, only had one player in their side with any previous Champions League experience. And their baptism of fire could not have got off to a worse start in the cauldron of the Nou Camp, as they found themselves behind after only seven minutes.

Great running down the left flank by Ronaldinho found Samuel Eto'o on the edge of the penalty area, and his perfect lay-off teed up Andres Iniesta to fire the ball past the stranded Georgi Petkov and into the bottom left-hand

BARCELONA 5 V LEVSKI SOFIA 0

Referee
Konrad Plautz (AUT)
Assistant Referee
Egon Bereuter (AUT) Markus Mayr (AUT)
Fourth Official
Thomas Einwaller (AUT)

Scorers

07'	Iniesta
39'	Giuly
49'	Puyol
58'	Eto'o
90'	Ronaldinho

Teams

01	Valdes	Petkov	01
02	Belletti	Angelov	20
05	Puyol	Milanov	03
21	Thuram	Tomasic	04
12	van Bronckhorst	Topuzakov	11
20	Deco	Borimirov	07
08	Giuly	Eromoigbe	06
24	Iniesta	Telkiyski	21
05	Motta	Angelov	28
10	Ronaldinho	Bardon	27
09	Eto'o	Yovov	10

Substitutes

63'	07 Gudjohnsen / 08 Giuly		09 G Ivanov / 28 Angelov	45'
72'	06 Xavi / 24 Iniesta		14 Nikolov / 07 Borimirov	62'
79'	23 Oleguer / 21 Thuram		18 M Ivanov / 10 Yovov	69'

Discipline

	G Ivanov	64'
	Milanov	74'

14	Shots on goal	2
5	Shots wide	3
12	Fouls committed	13
3	Corners	2
1	Offsides	5
37' 27"	Ball. Poss. (time)	24' 21"
61%	Ball. Poss. (%)	39%

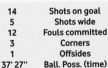

STATE OF PLAY					GROUP A		
	P	W	D	L	F	A	Pts
BARCELONA	1	1	0	0	5	0	3
CHELSEA	1	1	0	0	2	0	3
WERDER BREMEN	1	0	0	1	0	2	0
LEVSKI SOFIA	1	0	0	1	0	5	0

PSV EINDHOVEN 0 V LIVERPOOL 0

Referee
Massimo Busacca (SUI)

Assistant Referee
Stéphane Cuhat (SUI)
Francesco Buragina (SUI)

Fourth Official
Sascha Kever (SUI)

Scorers

Teams

01	Gomes	Reina 25
04	Alex	Agger 05
02	Kromkamp	Fabio Aurelio 12
03	Reiziger	Carragher 23
23	Salcido	Finnan 03
20	Afelley	Warnock 28
15	Culina	Pennant 16
11	Mendez	Sissoko 22
06	Simons	Zenden 32
17	Farfan	Bellamy 17
10	Koné	Kuyt 18

Substitutes

63'	> 16 Aisatti < 15 Culina	14 Alonso > 22 Sissoko <	62'
74'	> 07 Väyrynen < 20 Afelley	08 Gerrard > 17 Bellamy <	72'
		11 Gonzalez > 12 Aurelio <	82'

Discipline

4	Shots on goal	3
4	Shots wide	7
4	Fouls committed	7
3	Corners	3
2	Offsides	3
41' 34"	Ball. Poss. (time)	26' 05"
61%	Ball. Poss. (%)	39%

corner. The home side extended their advantage when Eto'o picked up the ball just past the half-way line and threaded a perfect through-ball into the path of Ludovic Giuly, who sent the keeper the wrong way.

After that it was one way traffic. On 49 minutes Petkov could only spill a driven free-kick from Ronaldinho into the path of Carles Puyol, and the Spain captain made no mistake in tapping in

his first goal in the UEFA Champions League for Frank Rijkaard's side.

Eto'o made it 4-0 nine minutes later with a superb individual goal which took him past four Sofia defenders before side-footing the ball past Petkov. But Ronaldinho saved the best until last, beating his man on the left corner of the penalty area to curl an audacious shot into Petkov's top corner and bring the Nou Camp crowd to their feet.

PSV Eindhoven 0 v Liverpool 0
Group C
Philips Stadion
Attendance: 30,000

Steven Gerrard and Xabi Alonso warm the bench while their team-mates fail to find a way past PSV's compact defence

A first clean sheet since mid-April secured Liverpool a vital point at PSV Eindhoven with a goalless draw. But it was a missed opportunity as Benítez's side passed up a chance to put some distance between them and the pack as the other game in Group C, Galatasaray versus Bordeaux, also finished goalless.

It was nearly a winning start, though. Ninety seconds from the end of normal time Steven Gerrard turned on the edge of the area and thrashed a dipping volley over the prone Heurelho Gomes

and onto the far post. It was the third time in four days that the Liverpool midfielder had struck woodwork, though the frustration was born less of the miss and more of the fact that Gerrard had spent 72 minutes of the match marooned on the bench.

His was a surprise omission, with Sunday's Premiership trip to Chelsea in mind, but given the impact he made in this cameo appearance it was a risk which did not pay off. "I think I've explained many, many times," said Benítez afterwards. "We cannot play all games at 100%. We played a very difficult game at Everton. If you have a good

Dirk Kuyt is foiled by PSV keeper Heurelho Gomes

Liverpool's Momo Sissoko loses out to Edison Mendez

know that Benítez changes things quite a bit, but to see Gerrard, Alonso and Hyypia not playing ..."

Liverpool had other chances but they were on the break and invariably arose through the pace of Bellamy and the rugged running of Kuyt. The Dutchman was thwarted for the best of them, Carlos Salcido diving in to smother a first-half shot after Fabio Aurelio had slipped the striker through.

A defence once renowned for its stinginess will feel slightly better for the shut-out, a first since Liverpool's 1-0 win at Blackburn 11 matches previously. Yet, much of their defending was still laced with indecision, with José Reina clearly traumatised by recent slips.

"We know the experience and the quality of PSV, so if we beat them at home a draw here will have been a good result," predicted Benítez.

> "We cannot play all games at 100%. I want to use all the players I have, and my selections depend on each game."
>
> Rafa Benítez, Liverpool manager

DID YOU KNOW?
PSV had not lost a group match at home in three years and did not concede a goal at home in the 2005/06 group stage

squad you can use different players, and I think we used [Gerrard] at the right moment. If you analyse how PSV play it was really important to work hard in defence to close their penetrating passes and be compact going forward. We did that with Craig Bellamy and Dirk Kuyt creating opportunities. The midfield did a lot of work, and Momo Sissoko was exhausted. But Gerrard and Xabi Alonso don't have the same stamina levels as Momo. I want to use all the players I have, and my selections depend on each game."

PSV, with the former Liverpool player Jan Kromkamp labouring at right-back and Alex floundering in the centre, appeared fallible. Yet without Gerrard, and with Alonso joining him on the bench for over an hour, Liverpool lacked a figure to impose himself on the contest. Boudewijn Zenden, for four years a PSV player, and Sissoko were rugged, but not too creative. PSV's Edison Méndez was the game's dominant force when it should have been Gerrard. "I was very surprised," admitted the PSV coach Ronald Koeman. "We

GALATASARAY 0 V BORDEAUX 0

Referee
Roberto Rosetti (ITA)
Assistant Referee
Marco Ivaldi (ITA) Angelo Carretta (ITA)
Fourth Official
Gianluca Rocchi (ITA)

Scorers

Teams

01	Mondragon	Ramé	16
25	Öztorun	Jemmali	13
04	Song	Jurietti	06
02	Tomas	Marange	23
22	Ilic	Planus	27
23	Inamoto	Ducasse	19
55	Sarioglu	Faubert	18
11	Hasan Sas	Micoud	14
66	Turan	Wendel	17
10	Ates	Chamakh	29
99	Karan	Darcheville	09

Substitutes

61'	> 58 Kabze < 99 Karan	07 Laslandes > 09 Darcheville <	84'
76'	> 19 Haspolatli < 11 Hasan Sas	12 Perea > 29 Chamakh <	85'
76'	> 14 Topal < 22 Ilic		

Discipline

| | | Ducasse | 25' |

0	Shots on goal	1
10	Shots wide	4
18	Fouls committed	19
4	Corners	2
3	Offsides	1
31' 34"	Ball. Poss. (time)	26' 45"
54%	Ball. Poss. (%)	46%

Galatasaray 0 v Bordeaux 0
Group C
Atatürk Stadium
Attendance: 60,000

Bordeaux's Florian Marange acknowledges fans after the goalless draw in Istanbul

In Istanbul, Galatasaray, the UEFA Cup winners in 2000, who were without veteran striker Hakan Sukur due to illness, were in control for much of the second half without prising the Bordeaux defence apart until the final minutes.

With 10 minutes remaining midfielder Arda Turan appealed for a penalty when he came down under a challenge in the area, but the referee waved away his claim to the frustration of the home fans.

Sabri volleyed over the middle of Ulrich Ramé's goal in the 86th minute and then three minutes later Necati fired just wide of Ramé's right post with his third shot of the night. The Girondins, second to Olympique Lyonnais in Ligue 1 last season and who were returning to the UEFA Champions League after a six-year absence, rarely threatened.

Sporting Lisbon 1 v Inter Milan 0
Group B
Jose Alvalade Stadium
Attendance: 30,222

SPORTING LISBON 1 v INTER MILAN 0

Sporting Lisbon's Marco Caneira (R) celebrates his goal against Inter Milan with team-mates Joao Moutinho (C) and Miguel Veloso

Referee
Alain Hamer (LUX)
Assistant Referee
Eric Castellani (FRA) Francis Crelo (LUX)
Fourth Official
Fredy Fautrel (FRA)

Scorers

65'	Caneira

Teams

01 Ricardo	Toldo 01
12 Caneira	Cordoba 02
78 Abel	Grosso 11
04 Polga	Maicon 13
13 Tonel	Samuel 25
24 Veloso	Dacourt 15
18 da Cunha	Figo 07
28 Moutinho	Stankovic 05
30 Romagnoli	Vieira 14
31 Liedson	Ibrahimovic 08
20 Yannick	Adriano 10

Substitutes

67'	19 Alecsandro / 30 Romagnoli	91 Gonzalez / 07 Figo	66'
83'	11 Tello / 18 da Cunha	18 Crespo / 10 Adriano	71'
		04 Zanetti / 11 Grosso	80'

Discipline

17'	Liedson	Cordoba	27'
21'	Moutinho	Toldo	32'
		Vieira	45'
		Vieira	68'

2	Shots on goal	3
8	Shots wide	1
22	Fouls committed	21
5	Corners	1
3	Offsides	3
31' 12"	Ball. Poss. (time)	25' 54"
55%	Ball. Poss. (%)	45%

The biggest shock of the night saw a brilliant goal from midfielder Marco Caneira gave Sporting a 1-0 win over 10-man Inter Milan in their opening Group B match.

"We said before that nothing is impossible in soccer, we knew about the difficulties we would face but managed to reduce those difficulties with excellent organisation," glowed proud Sporting coach Paulo Bento. "We were a team that was close to perfect." All the more so as the Lisbon team had been hit by injuries to several players, including Paraguayan international defender Carlos Paredes, and Bento had been forced to pick four young talents who impressed in a fine team performance.

Caneira scored in the 64th minute, chesting down a high crossfield ball from defender Tonel, touching it past Maicon and unleashing a dipping volley from outside the box that went in off the underside of the bar. Keeper Francesco Toldo leapt and managed to get a touch, but failed to turn the ball over.

"We have beaten a great team," said Caneira, whose goal was his first in the Champions League.

The Italian side were reduced to 10 men after 68 minutes when Patrick Vieira was sent off for head-butting Brazilian striker Liedson, the France midfielder's second bookable offence. Sporting stepped up the pace after Vieira was sent off and had more scoring opportunities, but Inter were poor, far from the team that would dominate the Italian league season over the coming months, and had few good chances. Zlatan Ibrahimovic was just wide with a late effort as Inter tried desperately to find an equaliser.

> **"We were a team that was close to perfect."**
> **Paulo Bento, Sporting Lisbon coach**

BAYERN 4 MUNICH v **SPARTAK 0 MOSCOW**

Referee
Alberto Undiano Mallenco (ESP)

Assistant Referee
Fermin Martinez Ibanez (ESP) Ramon Hernandez Hernandez (ESP)

Fourth Official
Vicente Lizondo Cortes (ESP)

Scorers
48'	Pizarro
52'	Santa Cruz
71'	Schweinsteiger
84'	Salihamidzic

Teams
01	Kahn	Kowalewski	30
03	da Silva	Géder	02
21	Lahm	Jiránek	13
02	Sagnol	Kovac	15
05	van Buyten	Rodriguez	17
23	Hargreaves	Stranzl	03
31	Schweinsteiger	Bistrov	23
17	van Bommel	Covaliciuc	27
14	Pizarro	Mozart	24
11	Podolski	Titov	09
24	Santa Cruz	Pavlyuchenko	10

Substitutes
70'	> 20 Salihamidzic < 14 Pizarro	49 Shishkin > 13 Jiránek <	31'
74'	> 07 Scholl < 17 van Bommel	32 Bazhenov > 15 Kovac <	62'
81'	> 08 Karimi < 24 Santa Cruz	14 Torbinskiy > 27 Covaliciuc <	77'

Discipline
40'	da Silva	Bistrov	28'

9	Shots on goal	7
3	Shots wide	2
13	Fouls committed	18
1	Corners	6
2	Offsides	2
37' 38"	Ball. Poss. (time)	25' 27"
60%	Ball. Poss. (%)	40%

STATE OF PLAY — GROUP B
	P	W	D	L	F	A	Pts
BAYERN MUNICH	1	1	0	0	4	0	3
SPORTING LISBON	1	1	0	0	1	0	3
INTER MILAN	1	0	0	1	0	1	0
SPARTAK MOSCOW	1	0	0	1	0	4	0

Bayern Munich 4 v Spartak Moscow 0
Group B
Allianz Arena
Attendance: 63,000

Bastian Schweinsteiger shadow boxes a corner flag after scoring a cracking volley for Bayern's fourth goal

Bayern Munich awoke from a first-half slumber to secure a 4-0 win over Spartak Moscow.

After a dreadful opening half, Claudio Pizarro put Bayern ahead in the 48th minute, taking a long ball from Willy Sagnol and smacking his shot just inside the post. Four minutes later Roque Santa Cruz doubled the lead after taking Mark van Bommel's pass, Bastian Schweinsteiger made it 3-0 with a beautifully controlled volley in the 71st and Hasan Salihamidzic tapped in with six minutes to go.

Spartak had made things difficult for Bayern in the first half, twice almost snatching the lead through Roman Pavlyuchenko and then Clemente Rodriguez on the counter-attack.

Bayern had not started well and when Lukas Podolski, Schweinsteiger and Owen Hargreaves made a mess of a free kick chance 10 minutes before the break – with Podolski managing to miss the ball altogether – it brought howls from the crowd and summed up the half pretty well.

Van Bommel, bought as a replacement for Michael Ballack, had looked lost in the first half, but he redeemed himself with a clever pass that set up Santa Cruz for a neat finish for the second goal. Spartak briefly roused themselves but the game was soon up as Schweinsteiger showed great technique to lean back and volley home from the edge of the box, and in the closing minutes Kahn pulled off a point-blank save from Vladimir Bistrov to cap a fine evening for the German champions.

AS Roma 4 v Shakhtar Donetsk 0
Group D
Stadio Olimpico
Attendance: 40,000

AS ROMA 4	V	SHAKHTAR 0 DONETSK

Referee
Bertrand Layec (FRA)
Assistant Referee
Patrick Reinbold (FRA) Franck Leloup (FRA)
Fourth Official
Thierry Auriac (FRA)

Scorers

67'	Taddei
76'	Totti
79'	De Rossi
89'	Pizarro

Teams

32	Doni	Shutkov	12
13	Chivu	Hubschman	03
21	Ferrari	Tymoschuk	04
02	Panucci	Duljaj	06
08	Aquilani	Elano	36
16	De Rossi	Lewandowski	18
30	Mancini	Matuzalem	09
20	Perrotta	Rat	26
11	Taddei	Srna	33
22	Tonetto	Brandao	25
10	Totti	Marica	29

Substitutes

62'	> 07 Pizarro < 08 Aquilani	17 Aghahowa > 25 Brandao <	63'
80'	> 09 Montella < 10 Totti	19 Gay > 09 Matuzalem <	72'
87'	> 77 Cassetti < 30 Mancini	38 Rodriguez > 19 Gay <	81'

Discipline

31'	Aquilani	Boruc	14'
		Tymoschuk	29'
		Hubschman	84'

5	Shots on goal	1
8	Shots wide	8
14	Fouls committed	25
8	Corners	0
3	Offsides	2
27' 36"	Ball. Poss. (time)	27' 54"
50%	Ball. Poss. (%)	50%

Roma's David Pizarro takes to the air alongside team-mate Daniele De Rossi after scoring the fourth goal against Shakhtar Donetsk

AS Roma also recovered from a poor start to score four goals in the final 24 minutes and crush UEFA Champions League new boys Shakhtar Donetsk 4-0.

The Serie A side, returning to the competition after a season's absence, were second-best for most of the first half and would have fallen behind if the Ukrainian side's strikers had been more incisive. But three goals in twelve second-half minutes killed off the contest long before David Pizarro fired in their fourth from long-range a minute before the end.

Roma had spent most of the night chasing the ball, mustering just one first half shot by Simone Perrotta, and struggled to find their rhythm. "We couldn't get the measure of them at all," admitted Roma coach Luciano Spalletti. "They were well-organised and in better physical condition than us. They made us suffer a lot, but I was pleased by the signs of maturity my team showed. Once we'd reorganised ourselves we were able to lift our game in the second half. And that made them more tentative."

The turning point came when Brazilian winger Mancini accelerated down the left and curled in a cross for Francesco Totti. The Roma captain was well-placed to score, but failed to

> "Their second goal came from a corner that was not a corner. The third was clearly offside."
> Mircea Lucescu, Shakhtar coach

STATE OF PLAY						GROUP D
	P	W	D	L	F	A	Pts
ROMA	1	1	0	0	4	0	3
VALENCIA	1	1	0	0	4	2	3
OLYMPIAKOS	1	0	0	1	2	4	0
SHAKHTAR DONETSK	1	0	0	1	0	4	0

OLYMPIAKOS 2 V VALENCIA 4

Referee
Terje Hauge (NOR)

Assistant Referee
Steinar Holvik (NOR)
Jan Petter Randen (NOR)

Fourth Official
Tommy Skjerven (NOR)

Scorers

28'	Konstantinou	Morientes 34', 35', 90'
66'	Castillo	Albiol 85'

Teams

71 Nikopolidois	Canizares 01
32 Anatolakis	Ayala 04
03 Domi	Marchena 05
14 Zewlakow	Miguel 02
07 Nery Castillo	Moretti 24
11 Djordjevic	Albiol 20
01 Kafes	Edu 22
17 Ouaddou	Martínez 19
06 Stoltidis	Angulo 10
23 Konstantinou	Morientes 09
10 Rivaldo	Villa 07

Substitutes

45'	> 30 Pantos < 14 Zewlakow	21 Silva > 19 Martínez <	72'
69'	> 55 César < 32 Anatolakis	11 Regueiro > 07 Villa <	81'
		18 Jorge Lopez > 09 Morientes <	90'

Discipline

44'	Ouaddou	Edu	75'
		Ayala	83'

7	Shots on goal	11
8	Shots wide	2
14	Fouls committed	15
4	Corners	5
5	Offsides	7
29' 39"	Ball. Poss. (time)	27' 55"
52%	Ball. Poss. (%)	48%

connect with the ball, which bounced between his legs and on to midfielder Rodrigo Taddei, unmarked at the far post, to blast past keeper Dmytro Shutkov – a piece of luck that infuriated Shakhtar coach Mircea Lucescu. "We played better for nearly 70 minutes and then – with their first chance – they scored," he complained.

The goal galvanised Roma's attack and in the 76th minute, Totti spun to sweep a corner into the top corner of Shutkov's goal. Three minutes later Daniele De Rossi powered in a close-range header, again from a corner, as Shakhtar's defence lost their composure. Pizarro's late strike completed a scoreline that flattered Roma's performance over the 90 minutes and left Lucescu fuming with anger at the injustice of it all. "Their second goal came from a corner than was not a corner. The third was clearly offside," he raged.

Olympiakos 2 v Valencia 4
Group D
Spiros Louis Stadium
Attendance: 48,000

Olympiakos' Michalis Konstantinou celebrates after scoring against Valencia

Olympiakos' goalkeeper Antonios Nikopolidis is beaten to the ball by Valencia's hat-trick hero Fernando Morientes

Arguably the best result of the night came in Greece where former Real Madrid and Liverpool striker Fernando Morientes gave new club Valencia the perfect start to Group D with a hat-trick in a 4-2 win over Olympiakos.

The scoreline, however, flattered the Spanish club, who spent much of the game soaking up Olympiakos pressure. The Greek side might even have won had Rivaldo not missed a great opportunity with the score tied at 2-2.

The Brazilian was prominent in the early part of the game when the Greek champions created a number of good chances, notably his own free-kick from the edge of the area that Santiago Canizares did well to palm away.

Olympiakos finally made the breakthrough in the 28th minute when Michalis Konstantinou latched on to a good through ball and popped it past the bleach-blond Valencia goalkeeper.

Morientes struck six minutes later when a David Villa cross found him unmarked in front of goal and a minute after that he followed up to fire home after Nikopolidis had saved from Miguel Angel Angulo.

Olympiakos came back in the second half and levelled through a wonderful strike from 22 year-old Uruguayan Nery Alberto Castillo on 66 minutes, but Rivaldo's miss proved fatal as they conceded two goals from corners in the last five minutes.

First Raul Albiol pounced on a scrambled clearance to rifle the ball into the net and then Morientes completed his hat-trick in the 90th minute with a powerful header that left Greece international goalkeeper Antonios Nikopolidis with no chance.

"Today we won because of our attack. It was the element of our game that worked the best and meant that in the end we did not pay for our mistakes," said Valencia coach Quique Sanchez Flores. "It was a good result on a bad surface and in front of a hostile crowd."

The result was disappointing for the home side, but Olympiakos coach Trond Sollied preferred to see the positives. "It was a very strange football game where the result could have gone either way," he said. "There are still 15 points to play for and I still think we can go through. Our aim is to make sure that we are still playing European football in the winter, whether it is in the Champions League or in the UEFA Cup."

"It was a good result on a bad surface and in front of a hostile crowd."
Quique Sanchez Flores, Valencia coach

DID YOU KNOW?
Fernando Morientes scored just 12 goals in 60 games for Liverpool, but bagged the same number in his first 28 games for Valencia

Match Day 1
Wednesday 13 September 2006

MAN UTD 3 v **CELTIC 2**

Referee
Lubos Michel (SVK)
Assistant Referee
Roman Slysko (SVK) Martin Balko (SVK)
Fourth Official
Vladimir Vnuk (SVK)

Scorers

30'	Saha (pen)	Vennegoor	21'
40'	Saha	Nakamura	43'
47'	Solskjaer		

Teams

01	van der Sar	Boruc	01
06	Brown	Caldwell	05
05	Ferdinand	McGeady	46
02	Neville	Naylor	03
27	Silvestre	Wilson	12
16	Carrick	Gravesen	16
24	Fletcher	Jarosik	20
11	Giggs	Lennon	18
18	Scholes	McManus	44
08	Rooney	Nakamura	25
09	Saha	Vennegoor of Hesselink	10

Substitutes

33'	> 20 Solskjaer < 11 Giggs		02 Telfer > 12 Wilson <	52'
80'	> 22 O'Shea < 18 Scholes		09 Miller > 20 Jarosik <	56'
86'	> 23 Richardson < 08 Rooney		29 Maloney > 46 McGeady <	70'

Discipline

27'	Silvestre	Boruc	29'
		Miller	90'

6	Shots on goal	4
7	Shots wide	0
16	Fouls committed	11
4	Corners	4
0	Offsides	1
32' 19"	Ball. Poss. (time)	25' 58"
56%	Ball. Poss. (%)	44%

STATE OF PLAY — GROUP F

	P	W	D	L	F	A	Pts
MANCHESTER UTD	1	1	0	0	3	2	3
BENFICA	1	0	1	0	0	0	1
COPENHAGEN	1	0	1	0	0	0	1
CELTIC	1	0	0	1	2	3	0

Manchester United 3 v Celtic 2
Group F
Old Trafford
Attendance: 75,453

Jan Vennegoor of Hesselink raises his arms to the heavens after opening the scoring

Ole Gunnar Solskjær was the hero as Manchester United opened their UEFA Champions League campaign with a pulsating 3-2 victory over Scottish champions Celtic.

There had been fears not so long ago that Solskjær, United's match-winner in the 1999 final against Bayern Munich, would never play again. After returning from an absence of almost two years, however, he reprised his super-sub routine here, showing his old sharpness with a close-range, and deserved, winner in the 47th minute.

Solskjær's strike settled a captivating contest which saw these two British heavyweights trade the lead, Celtic going ahead through Jan Vennegoor of Hesselink, Louis Saha then netting twice for the hosts before Shunsuke Nakamura made it 2-2.

With the two sides having such close historical links, this was never going to be a cagey affair and Wayne Rooney set the tone by twice charging down attempted clearances in the opening minutes. United carried the greater early menace, Saha looping a header wide from a Gary Neville cross. The Frenchman went close again on 17 minutes, flashing a volley just over the crossbar after seizing on Gary Caldwell's header.

At that stage, Celtic's sole threat had come when Vennegoor of Hesselink – operating as a lone striker – stole the ball off Rio Ferdinand but failed to punish the defender with a shot on target. Ferdinand enjoyed no such let-off in the 23rd minute, however, when from an Artur Boruc goal-kick, the Dutch forward beat him to the dropping ball, turned towards goal and let fire. Edwin van der Sar got a hand to the ball but failed to disturb its course to the bottom corner.

As the noise levels rose around the stadium, United went looking for an equaliser. Scholes blazed wide then saw his next effort blocked by three Celtic defenders. It was Saha, the man charged with replacing Ruud van Nistelrooy, who restored parity on the half-hour. Ryan Giggs went down under a challenge from Boruc, referee Lubos Michel pointed to the spot and Saha did the rest.

Ten minutes later and after Vennegoor of Hesselink had directed a free header straight at van der Sar, Saha struck again. Scholes supplied the low pass and the No 9 sent the ball low past the outcoming Boruc. United's advantage lasted just three minutes, though. Wes Brown upended Jiří Jarosík on the edge of the United box and Nakamura left van der Sar for dead with a sublime free-kick that sent the travelling support into ecstacy.

Two minutes into the second half, United were back in front. Boruc saved from Saha but Solskjær, a first-half substitute for the injured Giggs, was on hand to sweep the loose ball high into the net. After his long fight for fitness, it was the Norwegian's first Champions

Louis Saha makes it 2-1 to United

Artur Boruc shows his delight at Celtic's second goal

"Celtic? They showed the way football should be played."
Sir Alex Ferguson, Manchester United manager

League goal since 16 September 2003 and how Old Trafford celebrated. True to their tradition, United kept pushing forward. Saha, on a hat-trick, curled an effort just past the far post and saw his header smothered by Boruc. With the clock showing 68 minutes, Rooney poked Ferdinand's centre wide of an open goal.

Moments later he danced through the Celtic defence but could not beat Boruc. At the other end, substitute Kenny Miller crossed invitingly to Vennegoor of Hesselink but Ferdinand got there first. Van der Sar then kept out a low Gravesen drive, but it was United who finished the stronger.

Sir Alex Ferguson was at pains to praise the Scottish champions for their contribution. "You have to give Celtic great credit," said Ferguson. "We have a lot of teams who come here, put a bank of five across midfield and sit everyone on the edge of their own box. Not Celtic, though. They came here with a positive nature and had a real go. It's typical of their football club. We played Lille here last season and for the last 40 minutes we had 10 men yet they still didn't have one bloody shot at goal. It depressed me, that. They were happy playing for 0-0 with 10 men behind the ball and it was pathetic. Celtic? They showed the way football should be played. It wasn't

the cat-and-mouse stuff you normally get in Europe at all."

Ferguson eulogised about the Celtic supporters and he could not resist taking a swipe at the people Roy Keane had infamously labelled as the prawn-sandwich brigade. "Sometimes on a Saturday the supporters come here and they're half-asleep, waiting to be entertained," he said. "Tonight was totally different. The spirit of the game was great and the Celtic fans really played their part. I wish that everyone we faced brought 6,000 supporters with them because it created a really competitive element between the two sets of fans."

Ole Gunnar Solskjaer nets the winner

FC Copenhagen 0 v Benfica 0
Group F
Parken Stadion
Attendance: 40,085

FC COPENHAGEN 0 v   BENFICA 0

Benfica Head Coach Fernando Santos speaks during a news conference prior to their game against FC Copenhagen. To his left is Benfica's player Simao Sabrosa

Referee
Iouri Baskakov (RUS)

Assistant Referee
Tihon Kalugin (RUS)
Anton Averianov (RUS)

Fourth Official
Stanislav Sukhina (RUS)

Scorers

Teams

01	Christiansen	Quim	12
15	Bergdølmo	Alcides	13
14	Gravgaard	Leo	05
05	Hangeland	da Silva	04
02	Jacobsen	Rocha	33
10	Gronkjaer	Assis	25
13	Hutchinson	Katsouranis	08
06	Linderoth	Petit	06
04	Nørregaard	Simao	20
08	Silberbauer	Gomes	21
09	Berglund	Alves	15

Substitutes

45'	> 23 Kvist < 10 Gronkjaer	18 Evaristo > 20 Simao <	81'
73'	> 20 Pimpong < 09 Berglund	17 Fonseca > 21 Gomes <	90'

Discipline

45'	Nørregaard	Alcides	31'

4	Shots on goal	2
10	Shots wide	1
19	Fouls committed	13
1	Corners	6
1	Offsides	2
23' 15"	Ball. Poss. (time)	28' 21"
45%	Ball. Poss. (%)	55%

FC Copenhagen drew their first ever Champions League group stage game at home against former Champions Benfica 0-0.

The Danish champions dominated the first half, but squandered several opportunities inside the box, with Michael Gravgaard shooting over the bar and Hjalte Norregaard firing wide. Swedish international Marcus Allback was suspended, so Copenhagen relied on forwards Jesper Gronkjaer and Tobias Linderoth to create their chances. However, Linderoth wasted a free-kick when he fired over from the edge of the box in the 16th minute.

Former European champions Benfica, without injured playmaker Rui Costa, sat back and did not threaten Jesper Christiansen's goal until the 74th minute when Paulo Jorge hit the post. Brazilian centre back Luisao was Benfica's most dangerous player at corners, though he twice failed to find the target.

The pressure on the visitors eased after Gronkjaer injured his groin again and had to be substituted late in the first half. The home side only mustered long-range shots after that.

DID YOU KNOW?
Benfica remained unbeaten against Danish teams in European competition, with nine wins and two draws

DID YOU KNOW?
FC Copenhagen had returned UEFA Champions League group stage football to Denmark for the first time in eight years

STATE OF PLAY   **GROUP F**

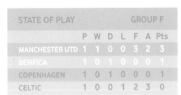

	P	W	D	L	F	A	Pts
MANCHESTER UTD	1	1	0	0	3	2	3
BENFICA	1	0	1	0	0	0	1
COPENHAGEN	1	0	1	0	0	0	1
CELTIC	1	0	0	1	2	3	0

HAMBURG 1 v **ARSENAL 2**

Referee
Peter Fröjdfeldt (SWE)

Assistant Referee
Stefan Wittberg (SWE)
Fredrik Nilsson (SWE)

Fourth Official
Daniel Stalhammar (SWE)

Scorers

90'	Sanogo	Gilberto (pen)	12'
		Rosicky	53'

Teams

12	Kirschstein	Lehmann 01
10	Kompany	Djourou 20
05	Mathijsen	Eboué 27
04	Reinhardt	Gallas 10
28	de Jong	Toure 05
20	Demel	Gilberto Silva 19
14	Jarolim	Fabregas 04
15	Trochowski	Hleb 13
06	Wicky	Rosicky 07
38	Ljuboja	Adebayor 25
17	Sanogo	van Persie 11

Substitutes

12'	> 01 Wächter < 06 Wicky		31 Hoyte > 05 Toure <	28'
54'	> 07 Mahdavikia < 20 Demel		16 Flamini > 13 Hleb <	69'
82'	> 09 Guerrero < 38 Ljuboja		09 Baptista > 11 van Persie <	69'

Discipline

10'	Kirshcstein

5	Shots on goal	7
9	Shots wide	7
9	Fouls committed	8
6	Corners	4
4	Offsides	2
27' 52"	Ball. Poss. (time)	34' 55"
44%	Ball. Poss. (%)	56%

Hamburg 1 v Arsenal 2
Group G
AOL Arena
Attendance: 51,839

Gilberto Silva nets Arsenal's penalty past replacement keeper Stefan Wachter after Kirschstein's dismissal

Arsenal began life in Group G with a bang, as their match in Hamburg threw up a penalty and a red card in the opening quarter of an hour.

The Champions League had provided a sanctuary for Arsenal last season and it seemed to be offering familiar relief for the team from a poor league start once again. Arsène Wenger's players may have been without a win in the Premiership, but they got a European victory at the first attempt, albeit against a side who played all but the first 12 minutes with 10 men.

A swift, incisive counter-attack brought the dismissal and Arsenal's penalty. Defence was turned into attack in classic fashion, and in a way some might have thought beyond them without the pace of Henry. Jens Lehmann threw the ball out to Alexander Hleb and the midfielder did well to retain possession, turn and pick out Emmanuel Adebayor. The leggy striker cut infield and had the awareness to find Robin van Persie in the box, and the Dutchman sent Kirschstein to ground with a shimmy close to goal before he tumbled over the keeper's raised left foot. Contact looked minimal, but van Persie was poised to stroke the ball into an empty net with his right foot, so the Swedish referee deemed it the denial of a clear goalscoring opportunity and sent off Kirschstein. Gilberto stroked in the penalty.

The omens had not looked positive for Arsenal, with Thierry Henry forced to remain in London because of a foot injury, but Wenger had been quietly confident of a response to their league travails. All the more so given that Hamburg had suffered their own nightmare start to the season, losing in the

	P	W	D	L	F	A	Pts
ARSENAL	1	1	0	0	2	1	3
CSKA MOSCOW	1	0	1	0	0	0	1
PORTO	1	0	1	0	0	0	1
HAMBURG	1	0	0	1	1	2	0

DID YOU KNOW?
The late strike by Boubacar Sanogo ended the personal record of Arsenal goalkeeper Jens Lehmann, who had not conceded in more than 850 minutes of top-flight European football

German Cup to Third Division Stuttgarter Kickers and had drawn all three of their Bundesliga fixtures.

Arsenal had seemed in little danger once Tomas Rosicky made it 2-0 with an excellent shot, but a late Hamburg burst saw Piotr Trochowski hit the bar and Boubacar Sanogo score from David Jarolim's cross.

There had been occasional alarms before Rosicky's goal, even though Hamburg were a man down. The Gunners dominated possession, but showed a lack of killer finishing, with Gilberto Silva heading wide from a corner.

Hamburg had sacrificed Raphael Wicky for a replacement goalkeeper, but still created flashes of danger even as Arsenal's eleven men monopolised the ball. When Hleb ignored his defensive responsibilities he was fortunate that Joris Mathijsen shot wide from a Sanogo cross. Soon afterwards Rosicky put his side 2-0 ahead with a spectacular

Hamburg's Boubacar Sanogo beats Emmanuel Eboué to score his late consolation goal

shot. The Czech was in a surprising amount of room when he collected a square pass from van Persie and as Hamburg failed to close he struck a powerful shot into the top corner from

about 25 yards. It was shooting ability of the sort he displayed against the United States at the World Cup, and only a save by Stefan Wachter denied Adebayor a third soon after.

Julio Baptista and Hamburg's Nigel de Jong battle it out

PORTO 0 v **CSKA MOSCOW 0**

Referee
Tom Henning Ovrebo (NOR)

Assistant Referee
Geir Age Holen (NOR) Erik Raestad (NOR)

Fourth Official
Per Ivar Staberg (NOR)

Scorers

Teams

#	Porto	CSKA Moscow	#
01	Helton	Akinfeev	35
14	Alves	Berezoutski	06
15	Ezequias	Ignashevitch	04
03	Pepe	Semberas	02
18	Assuncao	Aldonin	22
12	Bosingwa	Carvalho	07
08	González	Krasic	17
10	Anderson	Rahimic	25
07	Quaresma	Dudu	20
11	Sektioui	Zhirkov	18
28	Adriano	Vagner Love	11

Substitutes

	Porto	CSKA Moscow	
45'	> 23 Postiga < 11 T Sektioui	09 Olic > 11 Vagner Love <	76'
61'	> 02 Costa < 07 R Quaresma	24 Berezoutski > 20 Dudu <	88'
71'	> 09 López < ?? Louzada	08 Gusev > 07 Carvalho <	90'

Discipline

	Rahimic	36'
	Dudu	41'
	Zhirkov	46'

Porto		CSKA Moscow
11	Shots on goal	3
10	Shots wide	7
16	Fouls committed	16
9	Corners	6
2	Offsides	1
30' 55"	Ball. Poss. (time)	28' 53"
52%	Ball. Poss. (%)	48%

Porto 0 v CSKA Moscow 0
Group G
Estadio do Dragão
Attendance: 28,500

Porto's Adriano Vieira reacts after missing a chance against CSKA Moscow

The game between Porto and CSKA Moscow in Arsenal's group ended in a lacklustre goalless draw.

In a slow first half there was some open football, but the forwards of both teams failed to create many opportunities. Without injured midfielder Raul Meireles to protect the defence, Porto looked vulnerable at the back. However, they had two great chances when Brazilian youngster Anderson hit the post after 15 minutes and his compatriot Adriano failed to capitalise with a header nine minutes later. In injury time, CSKA keeper Igor Akinfeev helped to secure a point for his side with a brave save at the feet of Argentine substitute Lisandro Lopez.

"The result wasn't positive because our attacking efforts didn't work," said Porto's new coach Jesualdo Ferreira, who had replaced Dutchman Co Adriaanse at the start of the season. "Efficiency is something that one improves, even though we can't think it was just the forwards that failed, we have to train more on that."

STATE OF PLAY — GROUP G

	P	W	D	L	F	A	Pts
ARSENAL	1	1	0	0	2	1	3
CSKA MOSCOW	1	0	1	0	0	0	1
PORTO	1	0	1	0	0	0	1
HAMBURG	1	0	0	1	1	2	0

Lyon 2 v Real Madrid 0
Group E
Stade de Gerland
Attendance: 35,814

Lyon's Fred can't contain his joy at opening the scoring

LYON 2 v **REAL MADRID 0**

Referee
Wolfgang Stark (GER)
Assistant Referee
Carsten Kadach (GER) Harry Ehing (GER)
Fourth Official
Jochen Drees (GER)

Scorers

11'	Fred
31'	Tiago

Teams

01	Coupet	Casillas	01
20	Abidal	Cannavaro	05
03	Cris	Carlos	03
04	Müller	Cicinho	11
12	Reveillere	Sergio Ramos	04
10	Malouda	Beckham	23
08	Juninho	Diarra	06
21	Tiago	Emerson	08
28	Toulalan	Cassano	18
11	Fred	Raul	07
14	Govou	van Nistelrooy	17

Substitutes

73'	06 Kallstrom / 08 Juninho		19 Reyes / 18 Cassano		45'
78'	22 Wiltord / 11 Fred		14 Guti / 23 Beckham		55'
82'	02 Clerc / 14 Govou		10 Robinho / 07 Raul		69'

Discipline

38'	Reveillere	Sergio Ramos	32'
		Carlos	45'
		Cannavaro	61'
		Diarra	90'

13	Shots on goal	2
4	Shots wide	5
21	Fouls committed	20
4	Corners	5
1	Offsides	6
26' 41"	Ball. Poss. (time)	36' 54"
42%	Ball. Poss. (%)	58%

Lyon inflicted a painful defeat on Fabio Capello's Real Madrid in their opening Group E game, winning 2-0 at the Stade de Gerland.

The Galacticos, boasting global stars Beckham, Roberto Carlos, van Nistelrooy and Cannavaro in their starting line-up were soundly beaten.

Lyon's inspirational Brazilian midfielder Juninho forced goalkeeper Iker Casillas to make a dramatic save with one of his trademark free-kicks from 30 metres after seven minutes.

Juninho then set up his young compatriot Fred with a long-range pass for Lyon's opening goal in the 12th minute. Fred outsprinted Italy's World Cup-winning captain Fabio Cannavaro and, showing real composure, sent in a lob from just outside the box that gave Casillas no chance.

Tiago swept home a cross from Sidney Govou in the 31st minute to underline Lyon's superiority. Govou, playing only his second match of the season for his club, hit the woodwork and Fred narrowly missed the target before the interval with Casillas beaten

> "I can tell you that I'm really proud to be the coach of Olympique Lyon tonight. This was an outstanding performance on our part."
> Gérard Houllier

STATE OF PLAY — GROUP E

	P	W	D	L	F	A	Pts
STEAUA BUCHAREST	1	1	0	0	4	1	3
LYON	1	1	0	0	2	0	3
REAL MADRID	1	0	0	1	0	2	0
DYNAMO KIEV	1	0	0	1	1	4	0

Lyon's Tiago scores past Real Madrid goalkeeper Iker Casillas

DID YOU KNOW?
Lyon had beaten Real 3-0 exactly a year ago in their opening group match of the 2005/06 UEFA Champions League group stage

on both occasions. Real had little answer. The visitors created their best chance to narrow the gap when new Dutch striker Ruud van Nistelrooy shot wide 10 minutes from time.

"I can tell you that I'm really proud to be the coach of Olympique Lyon tonight," Gérard Houllier told a news conference. "This was an outstanding performance on our part. We ended up with a 2-0 victory but we could have won by a much bigger margin. The first half was simply flawless.

Tonight we showed we have great confidence, along with the kind of experience that could prove useful in the near future."

Real's new coach Fabio Capello said: "Lyon were superior to us technically and physically in the first 45 minutes. They created many chances to score and we were a bit weak in defence. There is still a lot of re-building work to do. We must keep believing in our ability. We are going to improve soon."

> **"There is still a lot of re-building work to do. We must keep believing in our ability. We are going to improve soon."**
> Fabio Capello, Real Madrid coach

Dynamo Kiev 1 v Steaua Bucharest 4
Group E
Valery Lobanovsky Stadium
Attendance: 45,000

Kiev fans celebrate Rebrov's goal, but they went home disappointed

DYNAMO KIEV 1 v   **STEAUA 4 BUCHAREST**

Referee
Paul Allaerts (BEL)
Assistant Referee
Peter Hermans (BEL) Eric Thiry (BEL)
Fourth Official
Jean-Baptist Bultynck (BEL)

Scorers

16'	Rebrov	Ghionea	03'
		Badea	24'
		Dica	43', 79'

Teams

01	Shovkovskiy	Fernandes	13
04	Rodolfo	Ghionea	24
81	Markovic	Goian	03
26	Nesmachniy	Nesu	15
44	Rodrigo	Saban	23
07	Correa	Cristocea	14
20	Gusev	Dica	10
15	Rincon	Lovin	20
37	Yussuf	Nicolita	16
05	Rebrov	Paraschiv	22
16	Shatskikh	Badea	09

Substitutes

59'	08 Belkevich / 07 Correa	21 Thereau / 09 Badea	70'
61'	11 Moreno / 81 Markovic	07 Oprita / 14 Cristocea	74'
74'	40 Otalvaro / 05 Rebrov	08 Petre / 10 Dica	82'

Discipline

	Nesu	13'
	Fernandes	27'
	Ghionea	73'

9	Shots on goal	5
8	Shots wide	2
10	Fouls committed	23
14	Corners	2
2	Offsides	3
28' 53"	Ball. Poss. (time)	21' 32"
57%	Ball. Poss. (%)	43%

Sergei Rebrov was on target for Dynamo Kiev against Steaua Bucharest in the group's other game, but the Ukrainians were overrun 4-1 at the Valery Lobanovskiy stadium, Nicolae Dica scoring twice for the visitors.

"It was just our day tonight," an ecstatic Steaua coach Cosmin Olaroiu proclaimed. "I think both teams were evenly matched but we were lucky to score a quick first goal to throw Dynamo off their stride."

Steaua, back in Europe's premier club competition after a 10-year absence, made a flying start with Ghionea heading in at the far post in the third minute. Dynamo equalised 13 minutes later when Rebrov beat Steaua's Portuguese keeper Carlos Fernandes with a rising shot into the near corner after a neat interchange with Brazilian Diogo Rincon.

But the visitors quickly regained the lead with Badea's diving header hitting the post and trickling over the goal line in the 24th minute.

Dica made it 3-1 two minutes before the interval, surprising Ukraine keeper Olexander Shovkovsky with a great curving free kick from 30 metres. The home side wasted a number of chances in the second half before Dica added his second against the run of play in the 79th minute to seal the emphatic win for the 1986 European champions.

Dynamo compounded their misery when Rebrov limped off the pitch late in the game with a knee injury. Coach Anatoly Demyanenko, however, was philosophical in defeat. "There's no panic in our team right now," he said. "We'll analyse the game and talk about our mistakes tomorrow morning. But I can say that our defending was really awful tonight. All their goals were scored after our bad mistakes."

DID YOU KNOW?
Sergei Rebrov, Dynamo's all-time leading scorer, notched his 30th goal in European competition in the 16th minute of this game

STATE OF PLAY   GROUP E

	P	W	D	L	F	A	Pts
STEAUA BUCHAREST	1	1	0	0	4	1	3
LYON	1	1	0	0	2	0	3
REAL MADRID	1	0	0	1	0	2	0
DYNAMO KIEV	1	0	0	1	1	4	0

AC MILAN 3 v AEK ATHENS 0

Referee
Mike Riley (ENG)

Assistant Referee
Glenn Turner (ENG) David Bryan (ENG)

Fourth Official
Mark Clattenburg (ENG)

Scorers

17'	Inzaghi
41'	Gourcuff
76'	Kaká (pen)

Teams

AC Milan		AEK Athens	
01	Dida	Sorrentino	28
02	Cafu	Cirillo	05
19	Favalli	Dellas	55
03	Maldini	Moras	04
17	Simic	Pautasso	13
32	Brocchi	Tziortziopoulos	14
08	Gattuso	Emerson	25
20	Gourcuff	Julio Cezar	99
22	Kaká	Delibasic	09
09	Inzaghi	Kapetanos	35
07	Oliveira	Liberopoulos	33

Substitutes

70' > 10 Seedorf < 07 Oliveira		19 Lagos > 35 Kapetanos <	45'
75' > 23 Ambrosini < 32 Brocchi		17 Ivic > 55 Dellas <	55'
79' > 18 Jankulovski < 19 Favalli		88 Tozser > 25 Emerson <	70'

Discipline

22'	Maldini	Cirillo	27'
		Moras	64'

8	Shots on goal	3
5	Shots wide	3
17	Fouls committed	17
7	Corners	3
6	Offsides	0
39' 28"	Ball. Poss. (time)	30' 33"
57%	Ball. Poss. (%)	43%

AC Milan 3 v AEK Athens 0
Group H
San Siro
Attendance: 70,000

Inzaghi nets Milan's opener

Milan's Yoann Gourcuff – the young French midfielder dubbed 'the new Zinedine Zidane' – scored the second goal as his side won 3-0 against AEK Athens.

Milan were in charge of the game throughout and, although the Greek side tested Milan keeper Dida on occasions, they never managed to truly compete with the Italians in midfield.

Both sides had early chances with Gennaro Gattuso bringing AEK Athens' Italian keeper Stefano Sorrentino into action with a 12th minute shot and then at the other end Dida did well to save Andrija Delibasic's close-range header.

Brazilian Ricardo Oliveira, making his first start for Milan, flashed a header wide in the 16th minute before the six-times European champions grabbed the lead. Captain Paolo Maldini made a short burst down the left flank and whipped over a cross which Filippo Inzaghi met with an expertly angled header.

Milan, who left out Italian World Cup winners Alessandro Nesta and Andrea Pirlo, who had both looked tired in the opening day league win over Lazio, had a comfortable grip on the midfield exchanges and Carlo Ancelotti's side doubled their lead four minute before the break when Kaká ran down the right flank and put over a cross to the back post which close-season French signing Gourcuff met with a firm header to make it 2-0.

Gourcuff made an fine first impression in the Champions League and Ancelotti singled the 20-year-old out for praise, saying "It is great to see a player of his age play with such authority and confidence, he was an excellent signing by the club."

AEK did not give up the fight with Brazilian Julio Cesar testing his compatriot Dida with a fierce strike on the stroke of half-time. Nikos Liberopoulos tried his luck with a low, testing long-range effort four minutes after the restart which had Dida scrambling.

But the game was securely in Milan's hands in the 77th minute when Inzaghi was ruled to have been pulled down by AEK defender Evangelos Moras and Kaká converted the spot-kick.

AEK's Spanish coach Lorenzo Serra Ferrer declined to criticise his side for their display. "Against a team like Milan, with all their experience and their famous ability to keep possession it is not just about what you can do. I didn't think we coped badly. At this level you have to remember the quality of opposition you are up against," he said.

Anderlecht 1 v Lille 1
Group H
Constant Vanden Stock Stadium
Attendance: 21,107

Anderlecht's Nicolas Pareja (2nd L) celebrates his goal against Lille

ANDERLECHT 1	v	LILLE 1

Referee
Stuart Dougal (SCO)
Assistant Referee
Martin Cryans (SCO) Francis Andrews (SCO)
Fourth Official
Calum Murray (SCO)

Scorers			
41'	Pareja	Fauvergue	80'

Teams			
01	Zitka	Sylva	01
03	Descacht	Chalmé	21
26	Pareja	Plestan	25
06	van Damme	Schmitz	05
37	vanden Borre	Tafforeau	20
05	Biglia	Bastos	08
11	Boussoufa	Bodmer	12
14	Goor	Cabaye	07
10	Hassan	Makoun	17
04	Vanderhaeghe	Keita	23
07	Tchite	Odemwingie	14

Substitutes

68'	> 23 Juhasz < 05 Biglia	11 Youla > 08 Bastos <	60'
80'	> 22 O'Shea < 18 Scholes	13 Fauvergue > 07 Cabaye <	60'
86'	> 23 Richardson < 08 Rooney	26 Lichtsteiner > 14 Odemwingie <	88'

Discipline

54'	Boussoufa	Boruc	23'
83'	Goor	Youla	68'

5	Shots on goal	8
7	Shots wide	12
14	Fouls committed	13
6	Corners	5
4	Offsides	0
26' 53"	Ball. Poss. (time)	24' 48"
52%	Ball. Poss. (%)	48%

A late equaliser by substitute Nicolas Fauvergue earned Lille a 1-1 draw at Anderlecht.

The French under-21 international pounced 10 minutes from time to deny Anderlecht their first home win in seven outings in the group stages of Europe's elite competition.

The Belgian champions had opened the scoring four minutes before half-time when Argentine defender Nicolas Pareja rose highest to head home a Mbark Boussoufa corner. But after extensive pressure in the second half, Lille finally levelled when Fauvergue latched on to a low cross on the left from Nigerian forward Peter Odemwingie.

Anderlecht had plenty of possession, but the French side had the better chances, striking the woodwork twice. Yohan Cabaye unleashed a low drive which clipped the foot of and post halfway through the first half, while Kader Keiter went even closer when his right-foot shot rebounded off the junction of the post and crossbar. The visitors, playing in the UEFA Champions League for only a second successive season, went close to taking the lead on the half-hour when former Anderlecht player Odemwingie had a deflected shot smothered by the Anderlecht keeper.

Just five minutes before the break, the home crowd were angered when Boussoufa squandered a gilt-edged chance by shooting straight at Sylva with only the keeper the beat. But their anger soon turned to joy when, from the resulting Boussoufa corner, Pareja headed his side in front.

Lille pushed hard for an equaliser straight from the re-start and went close in the 55th minute, but Mathieu Bodmer's 20-metre effort flew just wide of the upright. They were rewarded in the 80th minute when Fauvergue found the net.

Anderlecht coach Frank Vercauteren blamed second-half nerves for his side squandering their lead. "We were not used to being ahead at this level and it got to the players in the second half. But we didn't lose, we created some chances and I was very happy with the first-half performance."

STATE OF PLAY	GROUP H						
	P	W	D	L	F	A	Pts
AC MILAN	1	1	0	0	3	0	3
ANDERLECHT	1	0	1	0	1	1	1
LILLE	1	0	1	0	1	1	1
AEK ATHENS	1	0	0	1	0	3	0

DID YOU KNOW?
This was just Anderlecht's third point from a total of 14 UEFA Champions League group matches

Match Day 2
Tuesday 26 September 2006

Treble Chance

Didier Drogba scores the first Chelsea hat-trick in Europe for almost a decade

Crouch at the Double

The beanpole striker bags a wonderfully athletic brace to hand Liverpool a vital win

Spot On

Gunners beat Porto 2-0 to keep up their 100% record in this season's UEFA Champions League

"I hope one day when I am not here I will be able to look back with pride."

Arsène Wenger, Arsenal manager

Arsenal 2 v Porto 0
Group G
Emirates Stadium
Attendance: 59,861

Thierry Henry glances a rare header into the net to put Arsenal 1-0 ahead

Thierry Henry, with post-World Cup fatigue forgotten and injury healed, showed his old, lethal self, breaking the deadlock against Porto with his 50th goal in European competition over the span of his career at three clubs.

As if to enhance the event with novelty he claimed it with a confident header and stranger still it was his second headed goal in a row, having registered another in Saturday's first league win at the Emirates Stadium over Sheffield United.

"A player who has been here for seven years can learn and show you another part of their game," said an admiring Arsène Wenger.

The 38th minute opener came when another of Wenger's many discoveries, Emmanuel Eboué, burst down the right wing and swerved a deep cross over Pepe for Henry to head back across the goalkeeper and into the net.

Nothing could distract the Gunners, not even the recurrence of Johan Djourou's foot injury in the warm-up that meant Justin Hoyte had to be upgraded to left-back with Gallas switching to central defence.

Beforehand Wenger had talked about the need to control the fixture rather than indulge in a headlong chase after goals. The inclusion of Robin van Persie instead of Emmanuel Adebayor gave him a forward with a natural inclination to drop deep and become a fifth midfielder.

Arsenal could still have gone ahead in the fourth minute had a linesman not deemed that the ball had gone behind before Cesc Fábregas cut it back for Kolo Touré to finish.

Helder Postiga, the former Spurs striker, made no impact before being replaced. The rejigged Porto had no time to settle before Arsenal had put themselves in a comfortable position. On 48 minutes Gallas went on a run across the pitch, stopping only to let Henry deliver the final ball that freed Hleb on the right. His finish for his first European goal was low and efficient.

The manager's 10th anniversary had coincided with coverage of Tony

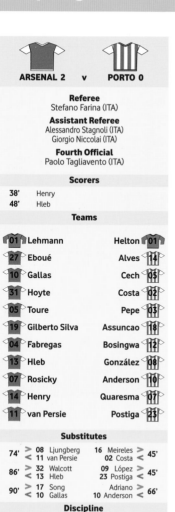

ARSENAL 2 v PORTO 0

Referee
Stefano Farina (ITA)

Assistant Referee
Alessandro Stagnoli (ITA)
Giorgio Niccolai (ITA)

Fourth Official
Paolo Tagliavento (ITA)

Scorers

38'	Henry
48'	Hleb

Teams

Arsenal	Porto
01 Lehmann	Helton 01
27 Eboué	Alves 14
10 Gallas	Cech 05
31 Hoyte	Costa 02
05 Toure	Pepe 03
19 Gilberto Silva	Assuncao 18
04 Fabregas	Bosingwa 12
13 Hleb	González 08
07 Rosicky	Anderson 10
14 Henry	Quaresma 07
11 van Persie	Postiga 23

Substitutes

74'	> 08 Ljungberg < 11 van Persie	16 Meireles > 02 Costa <	45'
86'	> 32 Walcott < 13 Hleb	09 López > 23 Postiga <	45'
90'	> 17 Song < 10 Gallas	Adriano > 10 Anderson <	66'

Discipline

64'	Rosicky	Costa	32'
88'	Gilberto Silva		

Arsenal		Porto
2	Yellow cards	1
0	Red cards	0
6	Shots on target	4
6	Shots off target	3
15	Fouls committed	9
9	Corners	7
1	Offsides	8
32' 31"	Ball. Poss. (time)	31' 33"
51%	Ball. Poss. (%)	49%

Arsène Wenger directs operations from the touchline

Blair's valedictory Labour Party conference and caused Wenger to comment, "I listened to Tony Blair saying, 'Ten years ago I started all this.' I thought, 'Is he speaking about me or not?'" Wenger joked. "He said how the world has changed and I must say our world here has changed as well. I hope one day when I am not here I will be able to look back with pride."

STATE OF PLAY					GROUP G		
	P	W	D	L	F	A	Pts
ARSENAL	2	2	0	0	4	1	6
CSKA MOSCOW	2	1	1	0	1	0	4
PORTO	2	0	1	1	0	2	1
HAMBURG	2	0	0	2	1	3	0

DID YOU KNOW?
Porto have never won on English soil, a 1-1 draw at Manchester United in 2003/04 being the only time they have avoided defeat in seven visits

CSKA Moscow 1 v Hamburg 0
Group G
Olympic Stadium
Attendance: 26,000

CSKA MOSCOW 1 v HAMBURG 0

Referee
Jan W. Wegereef (NED)
Assistant Referee
Jantinus Meints (NED)
Roger Geutjes (NED)
Fourth Official
Hendrikus S.H. (Bas) Nijhuis (NED)

Scorers
59' Dudu

Teams

CSKA Moscow		Hamburg	
35	Akinfeev	Wächter	01
06	Berezoutski	Kompany	10
24	Berezoutski	Mathijsen	05
04	Ignashevitc	Reinhardt	04
02	Semberas	Sorin	02
07	Carvalho	de Jong	28
25	Rahimic	Jarolim	14
20	Dudu	Mahdavikia	07
18	Zhirkov	Wicky	06
11	Vagner Love	Ljuboja	38
09	Olic	Sanogo	17

Substitutes

45'	> 17 Krasic < 02 Semberas	09 Guerrero > 02 Sorin <	70'
76'	> 22 Aldonin < 09 Olic	15 Trochowski > 28 de Jong <	70'
84'	> 10 Jô < 07 Carvalho	11 Lauth > 38 Ljuboja <	80'

Discipline

61'	Vagner Love	Sorin	33'
		Mathijsen	54'
		Lauth	85'
		Jarolim	86'

1	Yellow cards	3
0	Red cards	1
3	Shots on target	2
4	Shots off target	8
15	Fouls committed	17
8	Corners	3
0	Offsides	1
29' 16"	Ball. Poss. (time)	31' 46"
48%	Ball. Poss. (%)	52%

Jubilant CSKA fans acclaim victory

A second-half header by Brazil midfielder Dudu gave Russian champions CSKA Moscow a 1-0 win over Hamburg.

Dudu outjumped Boubacar Sanogo and beat goalkeeper Stefan Wachter with a strong header from 10 yards in the 59th minute after a corner by fellow Brazil international Daniel Carvalho.

Carvalho could have added a second just a few minutes later when his free kick ricocheted off the head of Hamburg's Iranian defender Mehdi Mahdavikia, but Wachter stopped the ball on the line.

Wachter, playing in place of suspended first-choice keeper Sascha Kirschstein, made another great reflex save with his feet to deny Ivica Olic in the 14th minute when the Croatia striker fired a low shot from close range after evading three defenders in the box.

CSKA dominated in the first half but had trouble breaking down a tight German defence without their top striker Jo. The 19-year-old Brazilian, the Russian premier league's leading scorer, had not fully recovered from a knee injury and was left on the bench. But the Russians came alive after the break, creating a string of chances before Dudu's goal.

The Germans moved forward late in the game in search of an equaliser. Substitute striker Jose Guerrero just missed the near post with a powerful shot from the edge of the box and Sanogo wasted another chance after a goalmouth scramble.

Hamburg's misery was compounded four minutes from time when substitute Benjamin Lauth was shown a straight red card by Dutch referee Jan Wegereef for elbowing winger Yuri Zhirkov.

DID YOU KNOW?
This was the first time that these two clubs had met in European competition. Indeed CSKA had never before met German opposition

STATE OF PLAY

GROUP G

	P	W	D	L	F	A	Pts
ARSENAL	2	2	0	0	4	1	6
CSKA MOSCOW	2	1	1	0	1	0	4
PORTO	2	0	1	1	0	2	1
HAMBURG	2	0	0	2	1	3	0

BENFICA 0 v **MAN UNITED 1**

Referee
Frank De Bleeckere (BEL)

Assistant Referee
Peter Hermans (BEL) Walter Vromans (BEL)

Fourth Official
Stéphane Breda (BEL)

Scorers
Saha   60'

Teams

12	Quim	van der Sar	01
13	Alcides	Neville	02
03	Anderson	Heinze	04
05	Leo	Ferdinand	05
04	da Silva	O'Shea	22
26	Karagounis	Vidic	15
08	Katsouranis	Carrick	16
06	Petit	Ronaldo	07
20	Simao	Scholes	18
21	Gomes	Rooney	08
15	Jorge Alves	Saha	09

Substitutes

63'	> 25 Assis < 26 Karagounis	14 Smith > 09 Saha <	85'
65'	> 30 Miccoli < 15 Jorge Alves	24 Fletcher > 08 Rooney <	85'
82'	> 09 Mantorras < 03 Anderson		

Discipline

26'	Katsouranis	Carrick	07'
86'	Petit	Scholes	10'
		Heinze	66'

2	Yellow cards	3
0	Red cards	0
4	Shots on target	7
6	Shots off target	5
19	Fouls committed	20
4	Corners	0
2	Offsides	0
32' 4"	Ball. Poss. (time)	24' 47"
57%	Ball. Poss. (%)	43%

Benfica 0 v Manchester United 1
Group F
Stadium of Light
Attendance: 61,000

Cristiano Ronaldo celebrates setting up Saha for the only goal of the game

Louis Saha's second-half strike allowed Manchester United to avenge last season's nightmare in Lisbon as they beat Benfica 1-0.

Rarely convincing against a side responsible for their embarrassingly early European exit 12 months ago, United nevertheless carved out a triumph based on grit, determination and the flair provided by Cristiano Ronaldo.

If the one-fingered gesture he produced as he left the Stadium of Light last year saw him depart in disgrace, Ronaldo could have got away with another on this occasion, signalling the margin of victory.

Though Saha took the glory with his third goal in two Champions League games, it was Ronaldo who threatened more, especially in the latter stages as the visitors looked to exploit the gaps left by a Benfica side desperate to force a deserved equaliser.

The victory cemented United's position at the top of Group F, although concern still lingers about the form of Wayne Rooney, who worked hard without looking like ending a barren streak in this competition that now extended to 11 matches. He had been shifted to the left wing because Ferguson had reverted to the 4-5-1 system that he often favours in Europe

Carlos Queiroz and Sir Alex Ferguson plot the downfall of the Portuguese giants

and for long spells Rooney was a peripheral figure.

For a player of such supposed high calibre, Michael Carrick gave the ball away far too often. It was central defender Nemanja Vidic, though, who gifted possession to Paulo Jorge and presented Benfica with the best opportunity of the opening period. Jorge quickly found Nuno Gomes, who took aim from 20 yards, only for Edwin van der Sar to make a good save.

The Dutchman was certainly one of United's most effective performers, along with Gabriel Heinze, who marked his first European outing since rupturing cruciate ligaments in Villarreal last season with typical tenacity.

Cristiano Ronaldo too rose above average, leaving Georgios Karagounis for dead with a smart turn before letting fly with a stinging 25-yard shot that proved too much for Quim to hold.

Had Saha's luck been in, he might have been presented with a tap-in. As it was, the ball bounced up awkwardly as the Frenchman rushed in, struck him on the chest and bobbled wide.

Benfica have a formidable record at home, so United were entitled to be invigorated by the manner in which they quelled one of Europe's more boisterous crowds whose abuse accompanied Ronaldo's every touch. Yet, in a Portugal shirt he is a hero on this ground. Fittingly, it was the Portuguese who instigated the move for the goal. Saha took Ronaldo's visionary pass, cut inside from the right and unleashed a powerful left-foot drive that took a slight but decisive deflection off Anderson on its way into the net.

The goal gave the game a totally different complexion and it took a remarkable triple save from Quim, who denied Ronaldo, Fletcher and Carrick a

minute from time, to prevent United doubling their margin of victory.

The United manager was well pleased with his side's victory. "Unlike last time," said a satisfied Ferguson, "we were prepared to defend properly."

DID YOU KNOW?
This was United's first UEFA Champions League away win in three years

CELTIC 1 v FC COPEN'N 0

Referee
Florian Meyer (GER)

Assistant Referee
Carsten Kadach (GER)
Holger Henschel (GER)

Fourth Official
Babak Rafati (GER)

Scorers
36   Miller (pen)

Teams

01	Boruc	Christiansen 01
05	Caldwell	Bergdølmo 15
46	McGeady	Gravgaard 14
03	Naylor	Hangeland 05
02	Telfer	Jacobsen 02
16	Gravesen	Hutchinson 13
18	Lennon	Linderoth 06
44	McManus	Nørregaard 04
25	Nakamura	Silberbauer 08
09	Miller	Allbäck 11
07	Zurawski	Berglund 09

Substitutes

74'	> 37 Beattie < 07 Zurawski	23 Kvist > 09 Berglund < 56'
56'	> 29 Maloney < 09 Miller	16 Thomasen > 20 Bergdølmo < 75'
88'	> 11 Pearson < 46 McGeady	

Discipline

0	Yellow cards	0
0	Red cards	0
3	Shots on target	2
2	Shots off target	2
15	Fouls committed	23
4	Corners	1
5	Offsides	3
30' 50"	Ball. Poss. (time)	24' 16"
56%	Ball. Poss. (%)	44%

STATE OF PLAY						GROUP F	
	P	W	D	L	F	A	Pts
MAN UNITED	2	2	0	0	4	2	6
CELTIC	2	1	0	1	3	3	3
BENFICA	2	0	1	1	0	1	1
COPENHAGEN	2	0	1	1	0	1	1

Celtic 1 v FC Copenhagen 0
Group F
Parkhead
Attendance: 57,598

Kenny Miller goes close with a header

Celtic bolstered their hopes of progressing from Group F thanks to a hard won victory over FC Copenhagen.

A 36th minute Kenny Miller penalty was enough in a game that Celtic made unnecessarily hard work of as Copenhagen offered little attacking threat and failed to impose their physical advantage.

Michael Gravgaard's clumsy challenge on Shunsuke Nakamura as the Japan international sought to skip past him inside the penalty area, nine minutes before the interval, was crucial in lifting the edginess beginning to descend on Parkhead. Miller made no mistake from the spot and only a brilliant point-blank save from Jesper Christiansen prevented the former Wolves striker from doubling the advantage moments later.

Celtic's pre-match optimism was tempered by the absence of their Dutch striker, Jan Vennegoor of Hesselink, who failed to recover from an ankle injury. Manager Gordon Strachan had been deeply hurt by the club's embarrassing exit at the qualifying stage the previous year and was determined to build on his apparently seamless introduction to Scottish football by achieving UEFA Champions League success.

During a low-key second period, Christiansen, the former Rangers goalkeeper, used his feet to save smartly from the ever-busy Miller, but Hjalte Norregaard reminded home fans of the slenderness of Celtic's lead when he forced Artur Boruc into action from 20 yards. The referee Florian Meyer resisted two claims from Celtic for another, clinching, penalty but Strachan's men held firm.

Strachan hailed the "excellent" news from Lisbon of Manchester United's victory over his team's next opponents, Benfica, with the former Coventry and Southampton manager hoped his former club could embark on a winning streak against Celtic's nearest challengers for qualification.

Copenhagen manager, Stale Solbakken, was not overly downhearted by his side's display ahead of successive matches against Manchester United. He said: "Celtic deserved their victory. I am a little bit disappointed with our offensive performance, but I am pleased with the way we handled the atmosphere. I am just thinking about our next game, but the group is still a very open affair."

DID YOU KNOW?
Kenny Miller had failed to score in any of his first 18 matches whilst with Celtic. His winning goal against Copenhagen now made it two in two games, following his goal against Rangers the previous weekend

Miller celebrates his winning penalty

Celtic fans in full cry

REAL MADRID 5 v DYNAMO KIEV 1

Referee
Graham Poll (ENG)
Assistant Referee
David Babski (ENG)
Shaun Procter-Green (ENG)
Fourth Official
Mike Dean (ENG)

Scorers

20'	van Nistelrooy	Milevskiy	47'
70'	van Nistelrooy (pen)		
27', 61'	Raúl		
45'	Reyes		

Teams

01	Casillas	Shovkovskiy	01
05	Cannavaro	Gavrancic	32
03	Carlos	Nesmachniy	26
24	Mejia	Sablic	06
04	Sergio Ramos	Belkevich	08
06	Diarra	Correa	07
08	Emerson	Gusev	20
19	Reyes	Rincon	15
14	Guti	Yussuf	37
07	Raul	Milevskiy	25
17	van Nistelrooy	Shatskikh	16

Substitutes

45'	23 Beckham / 19 Reyes	55 Rybka / 08 Belkevich	70'
72'	09 Ronaldo / 17 van Nistelrooy	17 Mikhalik / 07 Correa	74'
84'	10 Robinho / 07 Raul	88 Aliev / 88 Rincon	81'

Discipline

82'	Sergio Ramos	Shatskikh	66'
		Shovkovskiy	68'

1	Yellow cards	1
0	Red cards	1
15	Shots on target	4
8	Shots off target	6
18	Fouls committed	17
10	Corners	1
1	Offsides	1
28' 33"	Ball. Poss. (time)	24' 33"
54%	Ball. Poss. (%)	46%

STATE OF PLAY — **GROUP E**

	P	W	D	L	F	A	Pts
LYON	2	2	0	0	5	0	6
REAL MADRID	2	1	0	1	5	3	3
STEAUA BUCH	2	1	0	1	4	4	3
DYNAMO KIEV	2	0	0	2	2	9	0

Real Madrid 5 v Dynamo Kiev 1
Group E
Bernabeu Stadium
Attendance: 79,497

Raul celebrates his 27th minute goal

Real Madrid ran riot with a five-star attacking display against 10-man Dynamo Kiev as their hunt for a 10th European Cup finally got underway.

Fabio Capello's men put a 2-0 defeat at Lyon on matchday one behind them as Ruud van Nistelrooy celebrated becoming a father by scoring a brace, as did his strike partner Raul, with a further goal from Jose Antonio Reyes.

But the five goal display did not gloss over continuing defensive frailties. A better team than Kiev would have made Real pay for glaring defensive weaknesses with more than just Artem Milevskiy's consolation effort. On an early counter attack, Milevskiy struck the legs of the out-rushing Iker Casillas after being sent clear by Valentin Belkevich as Kiev showed they were capable of causing Real problems at the back.

But while they would have to improve in defence, Real were at times irresistible when going forward. A spin and shot from van Nistelrooy hinted at his menace and then, seconds later, he displayed all his predatory prowess, tapping home a drilled shot from Roberto Carlos that Shovkovskiy could only parry to give Real a 20th-minute lead.

The hosts' cutting edge told again when Raul added to his formidable Champions League tally by stealing in at the far post to head home Reyes' inswinging cross from the right in the 27th minute. Raul went close again before Reyes, in first-half stoppage time, made it 3-0, curling Diarra's bouncing cross past Shovkovskiy with the outside of his boot.

Kiev pulled a goal back two minutes after the restart when Milevskiy followed up a shot from Carlos Correa that Casillas failed to hold. David Beckham, on for Reyes, bent a cross onto the head of his former Manchester United team-mate van Nistelrooy, who almost found the bottom corner.

But the Ukrainians were the architects of their own downfall in the 61st minute when, after a poor back pass from Goran Gavrancic, Raul pounced with the sharpness of old to round the keeper and slot home. Van Nistelrooy was then hauled down by Shovkovskiy, who was red-carded, when clean through and he dusted himself down and tucked the resultant penalty past substitute keeper Olexandr Rybka in the 70th minute.

STEAUA BUCH. 0 v **LYON 3**

Referee
Howard Webb (ENG)
Assistant Referee
Philip Sharp (ENG) David Bryan (ENG)
Fourth Official
Martin Atkinson (ENG)

Scorers

	Fred	43'
	Tiago	55'
	Benzema	89'

Teams

13	Fernandes	Coupet	01
24	Ghionea	Abidal	20
03	Goian	Clerc	02
18	Marin	Cris	03
15	Nesu	Müller	04
11	Bostina	Malouda	10
10	Dica	Juninho	08
20	Lovin	Tiago	21
16	Nicolita	Toulalan	28
22	Paraschiv	Fred	11
09	Badea	Wiltord	22

Substitutes

55'	> 07 Oprita< 11 Bostina	12 Reveillere >20 Abidal <	76'
58'	> 08 Petre< 22 Paraschiv	06 Kallstrom >21 Tiago <	83'
76'	> 21 Thereau< 20 Lovin	19 Benzema >11 Fred <	85'

Discipline

68'	Oprita	Toulalan	78'
76'	Nicolita		
90'	Petre		

0	Yellow cards	1
0	Red cards	0
2	Shots on target	7
9	Shots off target	4
16	Fouls committed	19
5	Corners	7
4	Offsides	3
24' 44"	Ball. Poss. (time)	23' 2"
51%	Ball. Poss. (%)	49%

Steaua Bucharest 0 v Lyon 3
Group E
Ghencea Stadium
Attendance: 25,000

Steaua Bucharest's goalkeeper Carlos Fernandes takes his towel from the net after handing Fred the opening goal on a plate

Goals from Fred, Tiago and substitute Karim Benzema gave Olympique Lyonnais an impressive 3-0 away win over Steaua Bucharest.

The win took France's five-times-in-a-row champions to six points after their opening victory over Real Madrid but

rocked Steaua, whose hopes had risen after their 4-1 first round away win over Dynamo Kiev.

Lyon came out firing with Tiago and Juninho always a threat. Steaua's Portuguese goalkeeper Carlos then made a spectacular save to keep out a 30-metre missile by Jeremy Toulalan, prompting the home fans to hope for a

LILLE 0 v AC MILAN 0

Referee
Manuel Enrique Mejuto Gonzalez (ESP)
Assistant Referee
Pedro Medina Hernandez (ESP)
Javier Hugo Novoa Robles (ESP)
Fourth Official
David Fernandez Borbalan (ESP)

Teams

01	Sylva	Dida	01
21	Chalmé	Cafu	02
25	Plestan	Kaladze	04
20	Tafforeau	Nesta	13
04	Tavlaridis	Ambrosini	23
22	Vitakic	Gattuso	08
12	Bodmer	Kaká	22
17	Makoun	Jankulovski	18
13	Fauvergue	Pirlo	21
23	Keita	Seedorf	10
14	Odemwingie	Gilardino	11

Substitutes

62'	> 07 Cabaye < 13 Fauvergue	09 Inzaghi > 11 Gilardino <	76'
85'	> 05 Schmitz < 04 Tavlaridis		

Discipline

90'	Cabaye	Jankulovski	88'

1	Yellow cards	1
0	Red cards	0
9	Shots on target	6
5	Shots off target	9
22	Fouls committed	9
4	Corners	5
2	Offsides	4
27' 35"	Ball. Poss. (time)	33' 34"
45%	Ball. Poss. (%)	55%

repeat of his vintage performance against Kiev two weeks ago.

However, this time it was a Carlos error that opened the door for Lyon when he dropped a straightforward catch to leave Fred with a simple task in front of goal five minutes from the break.

Tiago rose above Steaua's defence to score with a powerful header from a Juninho corner 10 minutes into the second half and substitute Benzema got the third in the last minute after a neat Juninho backheel.

"We are halfway to qualifying," said Lyon coach Gérard Houllier. "We prepared very well for this match because we were warned of Steaua's threat after their result in Kiev."

"Lyon gave us few chances," said Steaua coach Cosmin Olaroiu while skipper Sorin Paraschiv described the visitors as "the strongest team we have ever met."

Lille 0 v AC Milan 0
Group H
Stade Félix-Bollaert, Lens
Attendance: 22,500

AC Milan's Kaká rounds Tony Sylva, but his shot from a tight angle was saved by the Lille goalkeeper

Lille and AC Milan missed a glut of chances between them as they fought out an entertaining goalless draw in their Group H clash.

Clarence Seedorf saw a second-half effort disallowed for the away side and although there was no lack of enthusiasm, each team will be ruing a lack of ruthlessness in the final third.

Milan had a hat-trick of great chances in the last five minutes of the first half and will be wondering how they failed to breach a nervy Lille defence.

The first, after 40 minutes, occurred when Andrea Pirlo played Kaká in with a 30-yard pass, giving the Brazilian a one-on-one with Tony Sylva in the home goal. Kaká took the ball past Sylva but his touch was a fraction heavy and he left himself with a tight angle, allowing the keeper to nudge the ball wide of the near post when the shot arrived.

Then Marek Jankulovski drilled the ball high over the bar and just three minutes before the interval, Gennaro Gattuso's incisive slide-rule pass was collected by Alberto Gilardino, who proceeded to drag the ball wide of the far post eight yards from goal, while Dutch midfielder Seedorf ended a surging run into the penalty area, only for him to completely mis-hit his shot from six yards.

Nicolas Fauvergue also had a handful of chances for the home side and although his movement was a constant problem for the Rossoneri, he disappointed with his final touch. Lille continued to create chances, but Dida remained unbeaten, with Keita blazing over from the edge of the box and Gregory Tafforeau drawing three saves from him in the space of 20 second-half minutes.

AEK Athens 1 v Anderlecht 1
Group H
Spiros Louis Stadium
Attendance: 35,618

AEK Athens' Julio Cesar celebrates with his team-mates Daniel Tozser (L) and Perparim Hetemaj (R) after scoring the equaliser against Anderlecht

AEK Athens suffered yet another night of UEFA Champions League frustration when they were held to a 1-1 draw by Belgian team Anderlecht, leaving them bottom of the group.

AEK coach Lorenzo Serra Ferrer, already missing injured midfielder Emerson, sprung a surprise by dropping his most experienced striker Nikos Liberopoulos to the bench along with Vassilis Lakis and Martin Pautasso.

Akis Zikos, a finalist with Monaco two years ago, was also missing from the team after straining his thigh in the warm-up.

There was little to applaud in the opening 25 minutes but the opening goal, a simple tap-in for Frutos after good work by Mbark Boussoufa down the left, served to increase the tempo.

AEK immediately hit back when Finland under-21 midfielder Perparim Hetemaj, who had a fine game, found Julio Cesar on the edge of the Anderlecht area and the Brazilian coolly fired past goalkeeper Daniel Zitka.

Although they created the better chances the Greek side failed to score a second goal.

Liberopoulos duly appeared at half-time and ought to have put AEK ahead on the hour when his close range effort just squeezed wide. From the resulting corner Evangelos Moras found room for a free header but put it over the bar. Shortly after, Frutos was within a whisker of getting on to the end of Cristian Leiva's cross. AEK continued to create opportunities, but were frustrated by some solid defending and their own profligate finishing.

AEK ATHENS 1 v ANDERLECHT 1

Referee
Claus Bo Larsen (DEN)

Assistant Referee
Anders Norrestrand (DEN)
Palle Udsen (DEN

Fourth Official
Anders Hermansen (DEN)

Scorers
| 28' | Júlio César | Frutos | 25' |

Teams
28	Sorrentino	Zitka	01
05	Cirillo	Descacht	03
31	Georgeas	Pareja	26
04	Moras	van Damme	06
24	Udeze	vanden Borre	37
56	Hetemaj	Biglia	05
07	Kiriakidis	Boussoufa	11
19	Lagos	Goor	14
88	Tozser	Leiva	08
99	Cezar	Frutos	29
35	Kapetanos	Tchite	07

Substitutes
45'	> 33 Lyberopoulos < 35 Kapetanos	36 Lagaer > 11 Boussoufa <	81'
55'	> 23 Lakis < 99 Cezar		
70'	> 09 Delibasic < 56 Hetemaj		

Discipline
03'	Cezar	Vanden Borre	31'
62'	Cirillo	Goor	67'
		Tchite	78'

2	Yellow cards	3
0	Red cards	0
1	Shots on target	2
10	Shots off target	0
10	Fouls committed	22
5	Corners	2
4	Offsides	6
27' 0"	Ball. Poss. (time)	22' 22"
55%	Ball. Poss. (%)	45%

STATE OF PLAY — GROUP H
	P	W	D	L	F	A	Pts
AC MILAN	2	1	1	0	3	0	4
ANDERLECHT	2	0	2	0	2	2	2
LILLE	2	0	2	0	1	1	2
AEK ATHENS	2	0	1	1	1	4	1

Match Day 2
Wednesday 27 September 2006

"Six consecutive victories, top of our league in England and top of our group in the Champions League."
Jose Mourinho

Levski Sofia 1 v Chelsea 3
Group A
Vasil Levski National Stadium
Attendance: 27,950

Didier Drogba celebrates his second goal

Didier Drogba continued his excellent form with a superb hat-trick in Sofia to give Chelsea a second successive win.

Drogba steered the ball over the line in the 69th minute to complete his first Chelsea hat-trick and take his season's tally to seven.

Before a capacity crowd in their first ever home UEFA Champions League group game, Levski attacked with pace and movement. Initially Chelsea seemed to miss the rested Claude Makelele and had difficulty controlling Levski's wide players, with Wayne Bridge standing in for Ashley Cole.

Again it was not spectacular Chelsea, but Jose Mourinho made it clear he cared little for style over substance. A first Champions League away victory since November 2005 and a run of six consecutive wins left his squad ready for Barcelona.

Drogba's contribution contrasted with another quiet display from Andriy Shevchenko, who put one well-hit shot not far over. Meanwhile Drogba was prospering alongside a striker who commands such attention from defenders that space opens for others.

Mourinho was reluctant to heap praise on Drogba. "It's nice for him. He's playing well and scoring goals and it's good, but the most important thing is six consecutive victories, top of our league in England and top of our group in the Champions League

Even Roman Abramovich seems pleased, which was unusual at this time of frosty relations between owner and manager

Drogba nets his third

Jose Mourinho is all smiles after a comprehensive win

LEVSKI SOFIA 1 v **CHELSEA 3**

Referee
Laurent Duhamel (FRA)

Assistant Referee
Vincent Texier (FRA)
Stéphane Duhamel (FRA)

Fourth Official
Bruno Coue (FRA)

Scorers		
89'	Ognyanov	Drogba 52', 59', 68'

Teams

	Levski Sofia	Chelsea	
01	Petkov	Cech	01
20	Angelov	Bridge	18
03	Milanov	Ricardo Carvalho	06
04	Tomasic	Ferreira	20
11	Topuzakov	Terry	26
07	Borimirov	Ballack	13
06	Eromoigbe	Essien	05
21	Telkiyski	Lampard	08
25	Wagner	Mikel	12
27	Bardon	Drogba	11
10	Yovov	Shevchenko	07

Substitutes

67'	> 09 G Ivanov < 21 Telkiyski	21 Kalou > 12 Mikel <	63'
71'	> 16 Ognyanov < 27 Bardon	16 Robben > 11 Drogba <	71'
86'	> 77 Koprivarov < 07 Borimirov	24 Wright-Phillips > 07 Shevchenko <	83'

Discipline

60'	Angelov	Mikel	54'

1	Yellow cards	1
0	Red cards	0
7	Shots on target	7
3	Shots off target	6
10	Fouls committed	15
8	Corners	3
1	Offsides	3
35' 46"	Ball. Poss. (time)	34' 3"
51%	Ball. Poss. (%)	49%

and still not playing very, very well. Playing well enough but still not very, very well. We need to work and improve and put the players at the top of their form."

There were bright moments from Jon Obi Mikel before the interval on his first start. Cech was impressive, but most of his action came with the game effectively over. He made a sharp triple save, and two other stops, to deny Levski at 3-0 before the Bulgarians got a late consolation.

Drogba hit the bar before getting his first goal and deserved the fortune that saw him steer in a Lampard shot to complete his hat-trick. He'd had to wait more than half an hour for his opener, turning in a loose ball after Georgi Petkov saved well from Mikel.

Chelsea extended their lead soon after the break when Bridge's long, diagonal pass from inside his own half picked out Drogba, who used his chest and strength to turn away from Elin Topuzakov and hit a low shot that Petkov got a hand to but could not stop.

Any doubt ended when Drogba rolled the ball over the line after Lampard's shot had been going well wide. "The hat-trick meant a lot to me because I have been looking for it since I came here," Drogba said.

It scarcely mattered that Mariyan Ognyanov burst through to pull a goal back.

DID YOU KNOW?
Drogba's hat-trick was the first in Europe by a Chelsea player since Gianluca Vialli in 1997 against Tromso in the Cup Winners' Cup

STATE OF PLAY			GROUP A				
	P	W	D	L	F	A	Pts
CHELSEA	2	2	0	0	5	1	6
BARCELONA	2	1	1	0	6	1	4
WERDER BREMEN	2	0	1	1	1	3	1
LEVSKI SOFIA	2	0	0	2	1	8	0

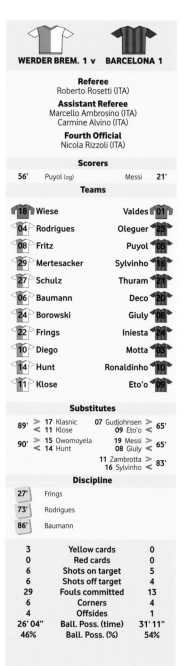

WERDER BREM. 1 v BARCELONA 1

Referee
Roberto Rosetti (ITA)

Assistant Referee
Marcello Ambrosino (ITA)
Carmine Alvino (ITA)

Fourth Official
Nicola Rizzoli (ITA)

Scorers

| 56' | Puyol (og) | | |
| | | Messi | 21' |

Teams

18	Wiese	Valdes	01
04	Rodrigues	Oleguer	23
08	Fritz	Puyol	05
29	Mertesacker	Sylvinho	16
27	Schulz	Thuram	21
06	Baumann	Deco	20
24	Borowski	Giuly	08
22	Frings	Iniesta	24
10	Diego	Motta	03
14	Hunt	Ronaldinho	10
11	Klose	Eto'o	09

Substitutes

89'	> 17 Klasnic < 11 Klose	07 Gudjohnsen > 09 Eto'o <	65'
90'	> 15 Owomoyela < 14 Hunt	19 Messi > 08 Giuly <	65'
		11 Zambrotta > 16 Sylvinho <	83'

Discipline

27'	Frings
73'	Rodrigues
86'	Baumann

3	Yellow cards	0
0	Red cards	0
6	Shots on target	5
6	Shots off target	4
29	Fouls committed	13
6	Corners	4
4	Offsides	1
26' 04"	Ball. Poss. (time)	31' 11"
46%	Ball. Poss. (%)	54%

STATE OF PLAY **GROUP A**

	P	W	D	L	F	A	Pts
CHELSEA	2	2	0	0	5	1	6
BARCELONA	2	1	1	0	6	1	4
WERDER BREMEN	2	0	1	1	1	3	1
LEVSKI SOFIA	2	0	0	2	1	8	0

Werder Bremen 1 v Barcelona 1
Group A
Weserstadion
Attendance: 41,256

Werder Bremen coach Thomas Schaaf implores his team to hang on to their slender lead in the closing stages, but Lionel Messi's late equaliser sent Barca home happy

Lionel Messi netted a last-gasp equaliser for Barcelona after Carles Puyol's own goal looked to have gifted Werder Bremen a priceless victory.

Puyol's blushes were spared when substitute Messi finished neatly in the 89th minute after the Germans had held their advantage for much of the second period.

Having lost twice to the Catalans in last season's Champions League group stages, Bremen were in no mood to fold easily this time around and they carved out an opportunity as early as the second minute. Aaron Hunt latched onto an inviting through-ball from Tim Borowski, but his weak finish landed comfortably in the arms of Victor Valdes in the Barcelona goal.

As Werder continued to buzz, Frings found an inch of space in a crowded penalty box and hit a dangerous swerving shot on the half-volley which only narrowly missed Valdes' right-hand post.

Hunt was creating the bulk of the German side's chances and he tested Valdes again on the half-hour mark with an effort from just outside the box which the Barca keeper had to get down low to his left to catch.

Barcelona started the second-half with renewed purpose and a Ronaldinho corner straight after the break should have been converted. A teasing ball into the danger area was missed by three orange shirts, with Ludovic Giuly most culpable.

Bremen's breakthrough was not far away, however, and in the 56th minute a fully-stretched Puyol, under pressure from Borowski, guided an inswinging Hunt cross into his own goal.

Barca's luck was to worsen five minutes later when Eto'o was stretchered-off following an innocuous looking fall. He was replaced by Eidur Gudjohnsen, while Messi also entered the fray in place of Giuly.

With 15 minutes remaining only a fantastic save from Wiese kept out Messi after the Argentinian had jinked his way expertly into the box.

But there was no stopping Messi a second time and after tidy link-up play with Deco on the edge of the Bremen box, the youngster ran on to plant a killer finish past Wiese and clinch what could prove to be a crucial Group A point.

Liverpool 3 v Galatasaray 2
Group C
Anfield
Attendance: 41,976

Luis Garcia scores to make it 2-0

LIVERPOOL 3 v **GALATASARAY 2**

Referee
Luis Medina Cantalejo (ESP)

Assistant Referee
Victoriano Carrasco (ESP) Luis Perez (ESP)

Fourth Official
Rafael Dominguez (ESP)

Scorers

9', 52'	Crouch	Ümit Karan	59', 65'
14'	Luis García		

Teams

Liverpool		Galatasaray	
25	Reina	Mondragon	01
05	Agger	Ak	05
12	Aurelio	Song	04
23	Carragher	Tomas	02
03	Finnan	Akman	18
14	Alonso	Haspolatli	19
08	Gerrard	Ilic	22
10	Luis Garcia	Sarioglu	55
16	Pennant	Topal	14
15	Crouch	Turan	66
18	Kuyt	Sukur	09

Substitutes

65' > 11 Gonzalez < 18 Kuyt		99 Karan > 19 Haspolatli <	45'
78' > 22 Sissoko < 16 Pennant		11 Hasan Sas > 14 Topal <	45'
90' > 17 Bellamy < 15 Crouch		16 Carrusca > 66 Turan <	86'

Discipline

83'	Alonso	Akman	35'
88'	Finnan	Hasan Sas	84'

2	Yellow cards	2
0	Red cards	0
8	Shots on target	6
6	Shots off target	3
16	Fouls committed	18
8	Corners	3
0	Offsides	0
25'34"	Ball. Poss. (time)	27'59"
48%	Ball. Poss. (%)	52%

Completely dominant following Peter Crouch's stunning second goal, lashed with an elastic right-footed scissor-kick seven minutes into the second period to give the hosts a three goal lead, Liverpool came close to late capitulation.

So spirited was Galatasaray's revival in the last half-hour that the hosts were desperate for the final whistle. Had Sasa Ilic and Hakan Sukur not fluffed late chances, this could have been a night of humiliation, not celebration.

"It shouldn't have been that close because we were comfortable, but if you step back against Galatasaray they'll come at you," conceded Crouch, though few could have envisaged the 2005 winners clinging to a slender lead after their early flourishes. For almost an hour, refreshed by the manager's rotation policy, it was a stroll.

Steven Gerrard, beginning in a central berth for the first time in over a month, zipped a fine ninth-minute pass to the flank where Fabio Aurelio collected and conjured a glorious cross which veered into the six-yard box. Crouch, enjoying a first start in five matches, eased gleefully in front of Orhan Ak at the far post to volley beyond Faryd Mondragon. Five minutes later, Cihan Haspolatli sliced a clearance which was gathered by Jermaine Pennant, another fresh face running riot, bursting between Arda Turan and Orhan. The watching Steve McClaren's England squad was impressed by the pinpoint cross which an unmarked Luis García nodded into an unguarded net.

DID YOU KNOW?
This was the 94th Liverpool game in succession that manager Benitez had made changes to his starting line-up

STATE OF PLAY — GROUP C

	P	W	D	L	F	A	Pts
LIVERPOOL	2	1	1	0	3	2	4
PSV EINDHOVEN	2	1	1	0	1	0	4
GALATASARAY	2	0	1	1	2	3	1
BORDEAUX	2	0	1	1	0	1	1

Crouch leaps into orbit to lash home a splendid strike to put Liverpool 3-0 ahead

"We forgot to play football in the first half," said the visiting coach, Erik Gerets, when Mondragon should have conceded also to Dirk Kuyt and Gerrard. His pummelling was not complete, even if there was no disgrace in stumbling to the majesty of Crouch's second goal.

Pennant and Steve Finnan dispossessed Ayhan on the right touchline with the full-back's centre met by the back-flipping Crouch with an overhead kick to defy belief. It was his 10th goal in eight starts for club and country, though he will never score a better. "It was amazing, showing all the quality Peter has but, from then on in, it became so difficult for us," said Benítez. "They just went for it after that and we had problems in wide areas, especially with the second ball, and needed more control in the middle."

Arda and Sabri provided the centres nodded beyond the exposed Reina by Karan to prompt memories of Milan's implosion in Istanbul. Liverpool were rocking.

Had either of the late chances been converted, Liverpool would have experienced the Italians' misery. As it is, from the top of the group, they can breathe easier.

Umit Karan scores to put Liverpool nerves on edge

Crouch's robo dance makes an appearance after his bicycle kick wonder-goal

Bordeaux 0 v PSV Eindhoven 1
Group C
Stade Chaban-Delmas
Attendance: 23,587

BORDEAUX 0   v   PSV EINDHO'N. 1

Referee
Olegario Benquerença (POR)
Assistant Referee
Paulo Ribeiro (POR) Joao Dos Santos (POR)
Fourth Official
Augusto Duarte (POR)

Scorers
Väyrynen   65'

Teams

16 Ramé	Gomes	01
03 Henrique	Alex	04
13 Jemmali	Kromkamp	02
06 Jurietti	Lamey	19
18 Faubert	Salcido	23
24 Mavuba	Afelley	20
05 Menegazzo	Mendez	11
14 Micoud	Simons	06
17 Wendel	Väyrynen	07
09 Darcheville	Koné	10
21 Enakarhire	Tardelli	26

Substitutes

45'	29 Chamakh / 14 Micoud	16 Aisatti / 20 Afelley	72'
74'	20 Dalmat / 06 Jurietti	18 Addo / 07 Väyrynen	79'
89'	07 Laslandes / 13 Jemmali	33 Beerens / 26 Tardelli	85'

Discipline

Kromkamp	22'
Salcido	60'
Väyrynen	65'
Lamey	85'

Mika Vaeyrynen scored a magnificent goal to clinch the points in a tight match

A superb second-half goal by Mika Vaeyrynen gave PSV Eindhoven a 1-0 win at Girondins Bordeaux in a lacklustre match.

The Finnish forward struck from inside the box to beat Bordeaux goalkeeper Ullrich Ramé following a fine one-two with Ivory Coast winger Arouna Kone in the 65th minute.

Bordeaux posed little threat before the interval as playmaker Johan Micoud, lacking inspiration on the ball, struggled to get the French side going.

Coach Ricardo replaced Micoud with forward Marouane Chamakh at half-time, but Bordeaux were too goal shy and naive to break down their opponents. The hosts had to wait until the 81st minute to create their first clear chance when a close-range volley from defender David Jemmali was cleared by PSV keeper Gomes.

The Dutch side finished with 10 men after defender Michael Lamey was sent off for a foul on Chamakh in the 86th minute. In the dying minutes, Bordeaux tried everything, but PSV, using all their Champions League experience, managed to hang on.

PSV coach Ronald Koeman said "This is a good step on our way to the second round as we knew we had to win a match away from home."

"We're really disappointed," added Bordeaux midfielder Rio Mavuba. "We failed to up the pace in the match. PSV played the way they wanted to. Now, we have very little choice but to try win the return match if we want to keep our hopes alive."

0	Yellow cards ·	3
0	Red cards	1
4	Shots on target	3
10	Shots off target	0
10	Fouls committed	25
4	Corners	4
0	Offsides	1
27' 58"	Ball. Poss. (time)	25' 24"
52%	Ball. Poss. (%)	48%

"This is a good step on our way to the second round."
Ronald Koeman

STATE OF PLAY   GROUP C

	P	W	D	L	F	A	Pts
LIVERPOOL	2	1	1	0	3	2	4
PSV EINDHOVEN	2	1	1	0	1	0	4
GALATASARAY	2	0	1	1	2	3	1
BORDEAUX	2	0	1	1	0	1	1

INTER MILAN 0 v **BAYERN MUN. 2**

Referee
Steve Bennett (ENG)

Assistant Referee
Glenn Turner (ENG) Kevin Pike (ENG)

Fourth Official
Rob Styles (ENG)

Scorers

	Pizarro	81'
	Podolski	90'

Teams

12	Julio César	Kahn	01
02	Cordoba	da Silva	03
11	Grosso	Lahm	21
13	Maicon	Sagnol	02
23	Materazzi	van Buyten	05
04	Zanetti	Ottl	39
15	Dacourt	Salihamidzic	20
07	Figo	Schweinsteiger	31
05	Stankovic	van Bommel	17
18	Crespo	Makaay	10
08	Ibrahimovic	Pizarro	14

Substitutes

67'	> 91 Gonzalez < 07 Figo	07 Scholl > 20 Salihamidzic <	70'
77'	> 21 Solari < 05 Stankovic	24 Santa Cruz > 10 Makaay <	82'
77'	> 10 Adriano < 18 Crespo	11 Podolski > 14 Pizarro <	89'

Discipline

41'	Ibrahimovic	Ottl	35'
54'	Materazzi	Sagnol	40'
58'	Ibrahimovic	Scholl	76'
85'	Grosso		

3	Yellow cards	3
2	Red cards	0
4	Shots on target	15
5	Shots off target	9
17	Fouls committed	17
8	Corners	3
8	Offsides	0
25' 55"	Ball. Poss. (time)	32' 45"
42%	Ball. Poss. (%)	58%

Inter Milan 0 v Bayern Munich 2

Group B
San Siro
Attendance: 79,000

Bayern Munich forward Claudio Pizarro (obscured) scores the first goal past Inter Milan goalkeeper Julio Cesar

Bayern Munich continued their perfect start to Group B of the Champions League with a win at the San Siro that gave nine-man Inter Milan a mountain to climb to reach the second stage.

In a tense first half Bayern's offside trap prevented Hernan Crespo from breaking through on two occasions, but Ibrahimovic showed better timing to latch onto Dejan Stankovic's through-ball. With just Oliver Kahn to beat, the Swede's final touch deserted him, allowing the Bayern goalkeeper to bear down on the ball and block the eventual shot.

Daniel van Buyten and Ibrahimovic were involved in a couple of tussles with the Inter player claiming a penalty as the Belgian defender held his ground to allow Kahn to collect a ball he was never favourite to reach.

Ibrahimovic's patience boiled over just before the break as he deliberately barged van Buyten out of the way as Lucio cleared danger, but the booking for the Swede was to have ramifications. Just over 10 minutes into the second half, he was shown a second yellow card for a foul on Bastian Schweinsteiger and departed for an early bath.

By this time, Bayern were already beginning to gain the upper hand with Ottl and Mark van Bommel making more of an impression.

Roy Makaay fired a 10-yard shot into the ground and straight at Julio Cesar with just over an hour played as the game finally began to open up.

As the Bayern fans began to call for a goal, Pizarro duly obliged. Substitute Mehmet Scholl was involved in the build-up, but it was the Peruvian's strength which enabled him to hold off Ivan Cordoba and, somehow, dig out a shot which bounced almost in slow motion past Cesar.

As frustration set in, Inter full-back Grosso sent Willy Sagnol flying, with an elbow, near the touchline and referee Steve Bennett didn't hesitate in showing the red card a second time. There was still time for Podolski to grab his first Champions League goal just seconds after coming in, placing his shot into the top corner after breaking clear of a non-existent Inter defence following a mistake by Cordoba to send the travelling fans and Munich players and management team wild.

Bayern Munich defender Willy Sagnol leaps past Inter Milan defender Fabio Grosso. The pair would later be involved in the incident which saw Grosso red carded

DID YOU KNOW?
Bayern Munich had lost on their six previous visits to Italy, most recently a 4-1 humbling in the San Siro by AC Milan in the 2005/06 first knockout round

Bayern Munich coach Felix Magath embraces forward Roy Makaay after a magnificent victory in the San Siro

SPARTAK MOS. 1 v SPORTING LIS. 1

Referee
Martin Hansson (SWE)
Assistant Referee
Henrik Andren (SWE) Joakim Flink (SWE)
Fourth Official
Martin Ingvarsson (SWE)

Scorers

5'	Boyarintsev	Nani	59'

Teams

30	Kowalewski	Ricardo	01
02	Géder	Caneira	12
13	Jiránek	Garcia	15
15	Kovac	Polga	04
49	Shishkin	Souza	13
03	Stranzl	Veloso	24
23	Bistrov	da Cunha	18
07	Boyarintsev	Moutinho	28
24	Mozart	Tello	11
09	Titov	Liedson	31
10	Pavlyuchenko	Yannick	20

Substitutes

80'	21 Owusu-Abeyie 10 Pavlyuchenko	19 Alecsandro 15 Garcia		45'
80'	39 Rebko 24 Mozart	76 Paredes 13 Souza		58'
		34 Alves 20 Yannick		82'

Discipline

79'	Stranzl	Souza	10'
		Veloso	19'

1	Yellow cards	2
0	Red cards	0
6	Shots on target	3
11	Shots off target	6
15	Fouls committed	19
9	Corners	5
3	Offsides	3
26' 7"	Ball. Poss. (time)	26' 43"
50%	Ball. Poss. (%)	50%

Spartak Moscow 1 v Sporting Lisbon 1
Group B
Luzhniki Stadium
Attendance: 75,101

Nani goes aerial after his goal against Spartak Moscow

At the Luzhniki Stadium in Moscow, Sporting Lisbon recovered from an early goal to earn a vital away point.

Denis Boyarinstev opened the scoring for the hosts after just five minutes.

Spartak Moscow paid the price for failing to turn first-half dominance into goals when Luís Almeida da Cunha (otherwise known as Nani) equalized on the hour.

Spartak had the upper hand for the entirety of the first period, but scored just once through Boyarintsev's early stunner. He struck after just four minutes when he capitalised on Sporting's inability to clear Yegor Titov's right-wing free-kick. With the away team hovering, Boyarintsev powered his way into position before unleashing a soaring effort which raced beyond Ricardo to make it 1-0.

Lisbon fought back and nearly found an equaliser when the lively Nani chipped a free-kick towards goal as Wojciech Kowalewski was organising the home wall. The Polish keeper reacted quickly enough and back-tracked six yards before palming the ball over the crossbar.

At half-time Angelo Miguel Garcia was replaced by Felisbino Alecsandro as Sporting attempted to get back into the game and in the first five minutes after the interval the hosts went close.

Bystrov, again getting the better of his man, then fired in a near-post cross which Pavluchenko met firmly only for Ricardo to produce a reaction save of the highest calibre.

Then, against the run of play Sporting produced a brisk but perfectly executed counter-attack which culminated in Nani dragging the ball into the area at pace to give himself a one-on-

one with Kowalewski. He touched the ball past the keeper and rolled it in from a tight angle to punish the hosts and claim a point.

Both sides could have won it but Kowalewski punched to safety when Nani made another well-timed run into the box and Boyarintsev missed at the other end, failing to connect with the ball with a wonderful last-minute chance.

VALENCIA 2   v   ROMA 1

Referee
Herbert Fandel (GER)
Assistant Referee
Volker Wezel (GER)
Sönke Glindemann (GER)
Fourth Official
Lutz Wagner (GER)

Scorers

13'	Angulo	Totti (pen)	18'
29'	Villa		

Teams

01	Canizares	Doni 32
04	Ayala	Cassetti 77
02	Miguel	Chivu 13
24	Moretti	Ferrari 21
06	Albelda	Panucci 02
20	Albiol	Aquilani 08
22	Edu	De Rossi 16
14	Vicente	Perrotta 20
10	Angulo	Pizarro 07
09	Morientes	Tonetto 22
07	Villa	Totti 10

Substitutes

72'	21 Silva / 07 Villa	09 Montella / 08 Aquilani	45'
87'	11 Regueiro / 09 Morientes	35 OKaká Chuka / 77 Cassetti	65'
90'	19 Martínez / 14 Vicente		

Discipline

18'	Ayala	Ferrari	74'
35'	Albelda	De Rossi	80'
90'	Pizarro		

3	Yellow cards	2
0	Red cards	0
7	Shots on target	3
5	Shots off target	4
17	Fouls committed	18
8	Corners	3
4	Offsides	5
29' 53"	Ball. Poss. (time)	27' 10"
52%	Ball. Poss. (%)	48%

Valencia 2 v Roma 1
Group D
Mestalla Stadium
Attendance: 48,000

Valencia's Fernando Morientes (R) is challenged by Roma's Matteo Ferrari

Goals from Miguel Angel Angulo and David Villa ensured maximum points for Valencia as they treated Roma's Francesco Totti to a disappointing 30th birthday.

The Italian forward scored his side's only goal from the penalty spot as they crashed to a 2-1 defeat at the Mestalla to leave Valencia three points clear at the top of Group D.

The game got off to a brisk start and Valencia had a corner within the first minute of play. Vicente delivered the ball into the middle where centre-half

Roberto Ayala, up for an early foray in the opposing box, met the cross, which was saved by Matteo Ferrari.

Within two minutes Roma had a chance, Simone Perotta – supplementing lone striker Totti from midfield – glancing wide from Christian Panucci's cross.

Perotta was again involved in the 12th minute, but his header lacked the power to trouble Santiago Canizares. Within seconds the ball was at the other end of the pitch where Villa found enough space to tee up Angulo, who volleyed smartly past Alexander Doni to strike a blow for the hosts.

David Villa stuns Roma with the winning goal for Valencia

> **"It has been a great night for Valencia. We worked hard and never lost belief in ourselves."**
> Miguel Angel Angulo, Valencia

The lead lasted only seven minutes. Max Tonetto fired a cross into the Valencia box and Emiliano Moretti hauled down Marco Cassetti, giving away a penalty. Ayala received a caution in the aftermath and Totti placed the ball on the spot before sending it past Canizares and into the bottom left-hand corner of the net.

It was not long before the Spanish side reasserted themselves and after seeing Fernando Morientes caught offside they got the formula right in the 28th minute. Moretti made up for his earlier indiscretion and turned provider when he took advantage of a David Albelda free-kick to play in Villa from the left. Villa was first to meet the ball and lashed in a right-footed effort from outside the area.

David Pizarro saw his long-range effort parried by Canizares two minutes later as the visitors chased a second equaliser and Villa tried his luck from distance in the 43rd minute, but neither side could find another opening before the break.

Roma boss Luciano Spalletti took action at the interval, bringing on Vincenzo Montella, surprisingly dropped after an eye-catching performance in Sunday's 4-0 rout of Parma, in place of Alberto Aquilani to give Totti a genuine attacking foil. But Montella struggled and the second period began with a series of fouls. Roma found it hard to carve out any obvious chances with the game stopping and restarting at regular intervals and Valencia seemed happy to slow the pace of the game, killing it off.

Shakhtar Donetsk 2 v Olympiakos 2
Group D
Olympic Stadium
Attendance: 20,000

The emotion all got a bit much for this Donetsk fan during his team's turbulent game against Olympiakos

SHAKHTAR DN. 2 v OLYMPIAKOS 2

Referee
Eric Braamhaar (NED)

Assistant Referee
Patrick Gerritsen (NED)
Wijnand Rutgers (NED)

Fourth Official
Kevin (Bernie Raymond) Blom (NED)

Scorers

34'	Matuzalem	M Konstantinou	24'
70'	Marica	Castillo	68'

Teams

35	Shust	Nikopolidis	71
03	Hubschman	Julio César	55
04	Tymoschuk	Anatolakis	32
36	Elano	Kostoulas	19
07	Fernandinho	Pantos	30
18	Lewandowski	Nery Castillo	07
09	Matuzalem	Djordjevic	11
26	Rat	Georgatos	21
33	Srna	Maric	08
25	Brandao	Stoltidis	06
29	Marica	Konstantinou	23

Substitutes

76'	11 Vorobey / 25 Brandao	02 Patsatzoglou / 32 Anatolakis	45'
76'	38 Jadson / 36 Elano	10 Rivaldo / 30 Pantos	85'
89'	17 Aghahowa / 29 C Marica	09 Okkas / 23 Konstantinou	90'

Discipline

35'	Lewandowski	Maric	33'
72'	Hubschman	Pantos	65'
90'	Tymoschuk		

3	Yellow cards	2
0	Red cards	0
12	Shots on target	6
7	Shots off target	6
22	Fouls committed	16
10	Corners	2
3	Offsides	1
29' 8"	Ball. Poss. (time)	20' 32"
59%	Ball. Poss. (%)	41%

Shakhtar Donetsk twice came from behind to draw 2-2 with Olympiakos in a lively Champions League Group D match as the Greek side extended their dismal away record.

Olympiakos opened the scoring when Nery Castillo evaded three Ukrainian players and fed the ball through for striker Michalis Konstantinou to fire home from close range in the 24th minute.

Shakhtar levelled nine minutes later through Brazilian midfielder Matuzalem but were behind again in the 68th minute when Castillo found the target.

Two minutes later, Romanian striker Ciprian Marica fired the second equaliser for the hosts. Shakhtar dominated from then on but could not snatch the winner.

STATE OF PLAY   GROUP D

	P	W	D	L	F	A	Pts
VALENCIA	2	2	0	0	6	3	6
ROMA	2	1	0	1	5	2	3
OLYMPIAKOS	2	0	1	1	4	6	1
SHAKHTAR DON	2	0	1	1	2	6	1

DID YOU KNOW?
Olympiakos had now failed to muster a win in 28 UEFA Champions League away games

Match Day 3
Tuesday 17 October 2006

Van The Man Hits 50

Ruud van Nistelrooy nets his 50th Champions League goal as Madrid win big in Bucharest

You Cannot Be Serious

Arsenal can't believe a disallowed goal and defeat in Moscow

Chelsea Win The Battle Of The Giants

Didier Drogba's wonder strike sends Chelsea into orbit and Barca into the mire

"Russia's a football country and they have as much money now as everywhere else and they are producing good teams."

Arsène Wenger

CSKA Moscow 1 v Arsenal 0
Group G
Olympic Stadium
Attendance: 36,500

Daniel Carvalho smashes the winning goal past Arsenal's Jens Lehmann

CSKA MOSCOW 1 v   ARSENAL 0

Referee
Manuel Enrique Mejuto Gonzalez (Spain)

Scorers
24'	Carvalho

Teams

CSKA Moscow	Arsenal
35 Akinfeev	Lehmann 01
06 Berezoutski	Djourou 20
24 Berezoutski	Gallas 10
04 Ignashevitch	Hoyte 31
02 Semberas	Toure 05
22 Aldonin	Gilberto Silva 19
07 Carvalho	Fabregas 04
25 Rahimic	Hleb 13
20 Dudu	Rosicky 07
18 Zhirkov	Henry 14
11 Vagner Love	van Persie 11

Substitutes

85'	> 09 Olic < 11 Vagner Love	25 Adebayor > 11 van Persie <	68'
89'	> 39 Taranov < 07 Carvalho	22 Clichy > 20 Djourou <	75'
90'	> 17 Krasic < 22 Aldonin	32 Walcott > 07 Rosicky <	80'

Discipline

61'	Rahimic	Henry	86'
83'	Ignashevitch		
85'	Vagner Love		

CSKA		Arsenal
3	Yellow cards	1
0	Red cards	0
4	Shots on target	1
4	Shots off target	6
17	Fouls committed	12
10	Corners	4
5	Offsides	7
22'57"	Ball. Poss. (time)	39'02"
37%	Ball. Poss. (%)	63%

Arsenal lost their six-game unbeaten record in Moscow as Arsène Wenger complained that the referee, Mejuto González, repeatedly gave decisions to the home side amid a searing atmosphere at the Lokomotiv Stadium.

But he already had cause for criticism the moment he walked out on to the torn pitch before the Group G clash. "It was a very intense game and we battled back in difficult circumstances, one of which was the quality of the pitch," said Wenger. "This was an October pitch in Russia. UEFA has to look into that because it is not acceptable to play on pitches like that in the Champions League. CSKA are a good side. They deserve a better pitch as well because then they would be even better."

Wenger was concerned at the number of key decisions that went against his side, notably Thierry Henry's late disallowed goal, but also the foul from which Moscow took their lead. Daniel Carvalho slammed home a well-worked free-kick after Kolo Touré was adjudged to have shoved Dudu over 19 yards out. Yet the Spanish referee had allowed the home side a shot before calling back play for the foul. "At first he didn't give a free-kick and let play go on a long time," said a tetchy Wenger. "Then he gave the free-kick and that was very surprising. The minimum you can say is that important decisions in the game have gone for them and against us."

He was surely referring to the moment his team thought they had eualised as Henry collected Touré's long, high pass and swept a fine shot past the goalkeeper Igor Akinfeev, but before he had wheeled away to celebrate the Arsenal captain was called

STATE OF PLAY   GROUP G

	P	W	D	L	F	A	Pts
CSKA MOSCOW	3	2	1	0	2	0	7
ARSENAL	3	2	0	1	4	2	6
PORTO	3	1	1	1	4	3	4
HAMBURG	3	0	0	3	2	7	0

Thierry Henry's late 'goal' was disallowed controversially for handball

Henry leads the protests as Arsenal lick their wounds following defeat in Moscow

The Russian champions and league leaders played with a certain assuredness. Part-financed by the £5.4m-a-year sponsorship from Roman Abramovich's oil giant Sibneft, and with Brazilian talent, the east have a potential challenger to the wests domination.

Forwards Dudu, Vagner Love and Daniel Carvalho combined to often outpace and outwit the Gunners. Their movement drew Touré's foul on Dudu 19 yards out, giving CSKA the perfect chance to execute a training-ground set play. A back-heel from Sergei Ignashevich confused Arsenal; Carvalho unleashed a drive of such ferocity that the 19 year-old defender Johan Djourou, who had been charging down the shot, turned his back and he ball flashed past the unsighted Jens Lehmann.

Five minutes later the German was called into an acrobatic save, tipping Carvalho's dipping drive over. From the resulting corner he had to gather Dudu's header. CSKA seemed to have doubled their lead on 35 minutes only for the linesman's flag to deny them. Again Carvalho delivered from the left and Vagner Love headed in, but from an offside position.

Emmanuel Adebayor was called off the bench, providing an outlet for an aerial assault. Only then could Arsenal come back into the game. The Gunners, now with Gaël Clichy and Theo Walcott also on the pitch, threw bodies forward in search of the point. Arsenal then had another late goal ruled out. The ball was in CSKA's net as Touré met Adebayor's flick from Fábregas's cross, but it was disallowed for offside.

Wenger recognised that his team had been inferior. "Until it was 1-0 Moscow were sharper than us and winning more fights than us. They got what they deserved. But we didn't underestimate them. Maybe they overestimated us."

Despite their travails, this was the first time Arsenal had lost an away match in this competition since Bayern Munich in February 2005 and their first defeat of any description since August.

back and booked for handball. As Henry left the pitch he harangued the officials, claiming the ball had hit his stomach. Wenger was equally flabbergasted. "The referee hasn't seen anything; it was a goal. You have to accept that a referee gives goals because he doesn't see things, but this is a new thing; the referee has cancelled it because he sees things that didn't exist. It is a new problem that they have raised." Henry was more vexed than his manager. "I'm more than angry. If you look at the replay you'll see it's not a handball. I was shocked that the referee gave me a yellow card. It was a good goal. Do you think that if the keeper had seen a handball he would not have reacted and appealed?"

Porto 4 v Hamburg 1
Group G
Estadio do Dragão
Attendance: 37,500

PORTO 4	v	HAMBURG 1

Referee
Alain Hamer (Luxembourg)

Scorers

15', 81'	López	Trochowski	89'
45'	Luis González (pen)		
69'	Postiga		

Teams

01	Helton	Kirschstein 12
14	Alves	Atouba 03
05	Cech	Mathijsen 05
13	Fucile	Sorin 02
03	Pepe	Benjamin 30
08	González	de Jong 28
16	Meireles	Mahdavikia 07
10	Anderson	Trochowski 15
07	Quaresma	Wicky 06
09	López	Ljuboja 38
23	Postiga	Sanogo 17

Substitutes

43'	> 20 Jorginho < Oliveira	13 Fillinger > 30 Benjamin <	45'
75'	> 29 Moraes < 23 Postiga	16 Klingbeil > 06 Wicky <	54'
80'	> 17 De Freitas < 07 Quaresma	09 Guerrero > 03 Atouba <	68'

Discipline

22'	Quaresma	Ljuboja	26'
30'	Fucile	Mahdavikia	31'
		de Jong	86'

2	Yellow cards	3
0	Red cards	0
8	Shots on target	5
1	Shots off target	10
19	Fouls committed	19
5	Corners	5
3	Offsides	2
28' 37"	Ball. Poss. (time)	28' 37"
50%	Ball. Poss. (%)	50%

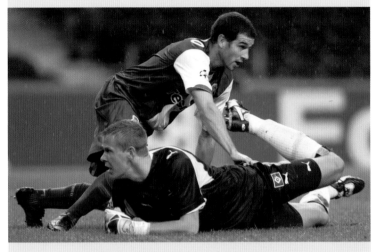

Porto's Lisandro Lopez celebrates prodding his first goal past Hamburg goalkeeper Sascha Kirchstein

In Portugal, Porto hammered Hamburg 4-1 with Argentine striker Lisandro Lopez scoring twice to put Porto right back into the running for qualification.

Lopez opened the scoring in the 14th minute when he tapped in a cross from the left by Brazilian teenager Anderson and added his second nine minutes from time.

It wasn't all one way traffic, as Hamburg had an equaliser disallowed for a foul by striker Danijel Lljuboja on goalkeeper Helton after 38 minutes.

Porto doubled their lead with a penalty by another Argentinian, Luis Gonzalez, in first half stoppage time, the midfielder sending a low shot inside the right post of goalkeeper Sascha Kirschstein after a handball by Lljuboja.

Despite losing winger Anderson to an injured thigh just before the break, Lopez's strike partner Helder Postiga scored the third in the 69th minute and Piotr Trochowski hit the German team's consolation goal one minute from the end.

Winger Quaresma believed the team had what it takes to finish in the last 16, adding "from now on we have to play like we did tonight."

> "It was a fair result,
> I thought it was a shame that we let
> in one goal almost at the end."
> Jesualdo Ferreira, Porto coach

STATE OF PLAY   GROUP G

	P	W	D	L	F	A	Pts
CSKA MOSCOW	3	2	1	0	2	0	7
ARSENAL	3	2	0	1	4	2	6
PORTO	3	1	1	1	4	3	4
HAMBURG	3	0	0	3	2	7	0

CELTIC 3 v **BENFICA 0**

Referee
E Braamhaar (Holland)

Scorers
56', 66'	Miller
90'	Pearson

Teams
01	Boruc	Quim	12
05	Caldwell	Alcides	13
03	Naylor	Leo	05
02	Telfer	da Silva	04
18	Lennon	Rocha	33
44	McManus	Assis	25
25	Nakamura	Katsouranis	08
15	Sno	Petit	06
29	Maloney	Simao	20
09	Miller	Gomes	21
07	Zurawski	Miccoli	30

Substitutes
84'	> 20 Jarosik < 07 Zurawski		22 Nélson > 08 Katsouranis <	72'
88'	> 11 Pearson < 15 Sno		17 Fonseca > 21 Gomes <	78'

Discipline
69'	Sno	Katsouranis	63'

1	Yellow cards	1
0	Red cards	0
5	Shots on target	1
8	Shots off target	14
13	Fouls committed	23
6	Corners	4
1	Offsides	2
35' 12"	Ball. Poss. (time)	28' 48"
55%	Ball. Poss. (%)	45%

Celtic 3 v Benfica 0
Group F
Parkhead
Attendance: 58,313

Kenny Miller takes on Benfica's Leo

A comprehensive victory over Benfica left Celtic with the realistic opportunity of reaching the next phase of the competition for the first time since the metamorphosis of the European Cup into the Champions League, and with Manchester United yet to travel to Glasgow, Celtic remained in with a shout of winning the group, let alone qualifying for the knockout stages for the first time.

Kenny Miller tucked away two chances in the space of 10 minutes early in the second half to take his total to three in this season's competition. In the 90th minute, with Benfica beaten, Miller was involved again as the substitute Stephen Pearson bounced in the third.

It was an exhilarating night at Parkhead, as the stadium crackled. With three key men, Thomas Gravesen, Aiden McGeady and Jan Vennegoor of Hesselink missing, Gordon Strachan pulled off one of Celtic's greatest European successes. The absence of Hesselink in particular worried Celtic, but 19 year-old Evander Sno, signed from Feyenoord for £250,000 in the summer, and named after the heavyweight boxer, Holyfield, put on a dazzling display.

Nuno Assis struck the Celtic crossbar in the 58th minute, but that was to be the closest Benfica came to a goal and the significance of the timing was that it came less than two minutes after Miller's opener. Sno started the move. One of a series of swift, short passes from him found Maloney and from there the ball was ferried to the overlapping Lee Naylor. Naylor's cross was low and hard and Shunsuke Nakamura sliced it, but conveniently for Celtic it

Stephen Pearson notches Celtic's third goal

getting more and more confident," gleamed Strachan. "You are guaranteed his work-rate, all that was missing was goals. When he wasn't scoring goals, he was a good team-mate and when you are a good team-mate while not at your most productive, other players will respond to that."

The significance of a victory over Celtic's nearest challengers for second place in Group F was not lost on the manager. "This win was a big step, no doubt about it," he added.

ran to Miller, who stabbed it instinctively past Quim. The stadium erupted, only to then gasp at Nuno Assis's shot, and there was more audible concern when from Benfica's third corner – it took them 55 minutes to win their first – the imposing Luisao charged in. A combination of green and white hoops smothered the big defender's effort and relief turned to expectancy as Miller and Maloney led a breakaway. Some 70 yards later, Miller and Maloney exchanged passes and Miller coolly steered his second around Quim.

That was it for Benfica, with play slowing until the late introduction of Pearson. When Quim parried a Nakamura snapshot, the substitute bundled in the third to produce a repeat of the 1969 score between the teams in their only previous meeting at Parkhead. Celtic went on to reach the final that season, even though Benfica won the return 3-0 and lost out on the toss of a coin.

Afterwards Strachan paid tribute to the resurgent form of his striker. Miller's early season goal drought, which had seen him go eight competitive games without finding the net, was a distant memory thanks to three goals in two Champions League matches. "Kenny is

> **"This win was a big step, no doubt about it."**
> Gordon Strachan, Celtic manager

Celtic fans revel in the atmosphere of a big European night

Kenny Miller scores Celtic's second goal

MAN UTD 3 v **COPENHAGEN 0**

Referee
Jan Wegereef (Netherlands)

Scorers

39'	Scholes
46'	O'Shea
83'	Richardson

Teams

01	van der Sar	Christiansen	01
06	Brown	Gravgaard	14
03	Evra	Hangeland	05
22	O'Shea	Jacobsen	02
15	Vidic	Wendt	17
16	Carrick	Hutchinson	13
24	Fletcher	Linderoth	06
07	Ronaldo	Nørregaard	04
18	Scholes	Silberbauer	08
08	Rooney	Allbäck	11
09	Saha	Berglund	09

Substitutes

60'	> 14 Smith < 09 Saha	20 Pimpong > 09 Berglund <	57'
61'	> 20 Solskjaer < 16 Carrick	23 Kvist > 04 Nørregaard <	57'
77'	> 23 Richardson < 18 Scholes	28 Bergvold > 08 Silberbauer <	81'

Discipline

51'	Patrice Evra

1	Yellow cards	0
0	Red cards	0
10	Shots on target	3
10	Shots off target	7
16	Fouls committed	14
6	Corners	1
6	Offsides	4
38' 28"	Ball. Poss. (time)	27' 45"
58%	Ball. Poss. (%)	42%

Manchester United 3 v FC Copenhagen 0
Group F
Old Trafford
Attendance: 72,020

Paul Scholes lashes in the opening goal

Wayne Rooney's promotion to captain could not bring him his first UEFA Champions League goal for two years, but he wore the armband with distinction. With three successive victories, United's significant improvement in Europe meant they looked set to become one of the first teams to reach the next phase.

The latest triumph was accomplished courtesy of a splendid goal by Paul Scholes and fortuitous ones from John O'Shea and substitute Kieran Richardson, though the margin of victory could have been far more handsome had United not been so 'gratuitous', to use Ferguson's description.

Alan Smith, in particular, will wonder how he missed an opportunity to score after coming off the bench for the latest stage in his rehabilitation from the broken leg against Liverpool in February. Yet, Ferguson spoke about a 'good attacking performance', indicating that the team are being driven by their failure to qualify from a moderate group last season. "They have grown up," he said. "They don't want any more embarrassments like last season, and they're playing good football into the bargain."

Ferguson was particularly entitled to be satisfied given that he was forced to reconfigure his team on two occasions in quick succession, Ryan Giggs complaining of feeling unwell in the warm-up and asking to be put on the bench, followed by Rio Ferdinand pulling out with a cricked neck. In came Darren Fletcher and Wes Brown, with Rooney made captain a week before his 21st birthday. "Some players, like Paul Scholes, don't want to be captain, so it was an easy choice," said Ferguson. "And Wayne did fantastically, as I expected."

Ferguson described the shot with which Scholes gave United the lead as 'sensational', although the same could not be said of the second and third goals. O'Shea's instinctive reaction was to flick the ball goalward with his right boot after Cristiano Ronaldo's corner flew into his path 38 seconds into the second half. Instead the ball struck his standing foot and ricocheted off his heel into the goal. Seven minutes from the end, Richardson's ambitious long range straight shot somehow squirmed under the goalkeeper Jesper Christiansen, hitherto the Danes' best player.

United's evening was tarnished only by the resignations of Nick Humby and Andy Anson, both of whom attained jobs elsewhere after becoming increasingly marginalised and disillusioned under the Glazers. David Gill, the chief executive, described himself as "very disappointed".

John O'Shea tangles with Markus Allback

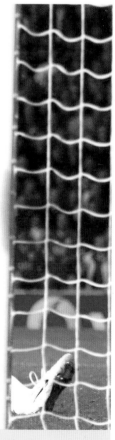

Captain Wayne Rooney could not end his European goal drought, just failing to convert this Ronaldo cross

STEAUA BUCH 1 v REAL MADRID 4

Referee
Roberto Rosetti (Italy)

Scorers

64'	Badea	Sergio Ramos	9'
		Raul	34'
		Robinho	56'
		van Nistelrooy	76'

Teams

13	Fernandes	Casillas	01
24	Ghionea	Cannavaro	05
03	Goian	Roberto Carlos	03
18	Marin	Helguera	21
23	Saban	Sergio Ramos	04
11	Bostina	Diarra	06
10	Dica	Emerson	08
20	Lovin	Robinho	10
16	Nicolita	Guti	14
22	Paraschiv	Raul	07
09	Badea	van Nistelrooy	17

Substitutes

59'	21 Thereau / 23 Saban	23 Beckham / 14 Guti	71'
62'	08 Petre / 20 Lovin	09 Ronaldo / 17 van Nistelrooy	78'
78'	07 Oprita / 22 Paraschiv		

Discipline

28'	Dica
75'	Goian

2	Yellow cards	0
0	Red cards	0
3	Shots on target	10
10	Shots off target	10
20	Fouls committed	10
5	Corners	3
1	Offsides	1
24' 58"	Ball. Poss. (time)	33' 06"
43%	Ball. Poss. (%)	57%

Steaua Bucharest 1 v Real Madrid 4
Group E
Stadionul Stadium
Attendance: 20,000

Sergio Ramos celebrates his opening goal

Comprehensive wins away from home for both Real Madrid and group leaders Lyon seemed to have ended Group E as a competition even by the halfway point of the fixtures.

Madrid triumphed 4-1 in Bucharest on a special night for striker Ruud van Nistelrooy, who netted his 50th European Cup goal with a superb lob to complete the scoring.

Sergio Ramos opened the scoring from a 10th minute corner and Raul made it 2-0 after the Steaua goalkeeper parried a shot from van Nistelrooy. Robinho hit the third from a pacy counter-attack before Valentin Badea pulled one back for the home side as substitute Cyril Thereau provided the pass for Badea to score from close range. But van Nistelrooy slammed the door shut on the home side 14 minutes from the end.

Robinho, Sergio Ramos, substitute Ronaldo and Raul all wasted good opportunitites to add to Real's score while Badea and Nicolae Dica missed chances to reduce the gap.

Los Merengues bounced back from a woeful 1-0 defeat at Madrid minnows Getafe in the league. Van Nistelrooy said, "Everything has improved. All of the game against Getafe was very bad and after the match we spoke so that this would never happen again. Our intention was to demonstrate here that we are Real Madrid. We have a lot of quality and now the important thing is to continue in this way."

David Beckham concurred. "(Against Steaua) the attitude has been right and there is more commitment," he said, "The meeting after the game against Getafe was used for this. We are very happy because we have done what we had to do."

"We lost to a much better team," Steaua Bucharest skipper Sorin Paraschiv said. "We just hope to qualify for UEFA Cup."

Real Madrid's captain Raul Gonzalez (L) fights for the ball with Steaua Bucharest's Daniel Oprita

DYNAMO KIEV 0 v **LYON 3**

Referee
Domencio Messina (Italy)

Scorers
	Juninho	31'
	Kallstrom	38'
	Malouda	51'

Teams
21	Lutsenko	Vercoutre	30
04	Rodolfo	Abidal	20
30	El Kaddouri	Clerc	02
32	Gavrancic	Cris	03
81	Markovic	Squillaci	29
07	Correa	Diarra	15
17	Mikhalik	Kallstrom	06
15	Rincon	Malouda	10
37	Yussuf	Juninho	08
25	Milevskiy	Fred	11
05	Rebrov	Wiltord	22

Substitutes
45'	> 16 Shatskikh < 05 Rebrov	28 Toulalan > 08 Juninho <	58'
45'	> 20 Gusev < 07 C Correa	12 Reveillere > 20 Abidal <	69'
85'	> 09 Kleber < 25 A Milevskiy	21 Tiago > 15 Diarra <	80'

Discipline
65'	Yussuf	Kallstrom	67'
82'	Milevskiy	Malouda	70'

2	Yellow cards	2
0	Red cards	0
4	Shots on target	4
8	Shots off target	9
18	Fouls committed	18
6	Corners	2
6	Offsides	1
31' 04"	Ball. Poss. (time)	30' 40"
51%	Ball. Poss. (%)	49%

STATE OF PLAY — GROUP E
	P	W	D	L	F	A	Pts
LYON	3	3	0	0	8	0	9
REAL MADRID	3	2	0	1	9	4	6
STEAUA BUCH	3	1	0	2	5	8	3
DYNAMO KIEV	3	0	0	3	2	12	0

Dynamo Kiev 0 v Lyon 3
Group E
Valery Lobanovsky Stadium
Attendance: 24,000

Lyon players celebrate Juninho's opening goal

Lyon had one foot in the knock-out round after Brazilian play-maker Juninho steered them to a 3-0 victory at Dynamo Kiev.

Juninho opened the scoring with a trademark free-kick, which soared up before dipping wickedly into the top right corner in the 31st minute. Seven minutes later Swedish midfielder Kim Kallstrom put the French side in the driving seat with a fine solo goal, which saw him collect the ball on the right side of the box and rifle home from a tight angle after a neat run.

Winger Florent Malouda completed the scoring in the 50th minute, heading Juninho's floated corner in off the underside of the bar. The goals kept the Lyon firmly at the top of the group with a maximum nine points from three games.

Dynamo's already faint hopes of progressing were all but dashed by their third consecutive defeat. The hosts missed out on a consolation goal when a bullet header by Ayila Yussuf from a corner was tipped over the bar by the impressive Remy Vercoutre, deputising between the posts.

They were out of luck again in a late goalmouth melée following a poor backpass on a miserable night for the Ukrainian side.

Fans at the Olympic Stadium had begun the evening by providing plenty of vocal support for Ukraine's most popular club. But many started leaving after the first goal, until only about half were left by the end of the game.

Lyon coach Gérard Houllier was well-pleased with the French champions' performance, telling a news conference: "They were first-class — all of the team and not just one particular player. And they deserved their victory. I am very pleased by the teamwork...the team played 'total football'."

Juninho's free-kick crashes into the back of the Kiev net

"I am very pleased by the teamwork... the team played 'total football'."
Gérard Houllier, Lyon coach

Dynamo Coach Demyanenko ponders a third heavy defeat in the group stage

"Lyon are, in my view, one of the best teams in Europe today... and their victory was logical."
Anatoliy Demyanenko, Dynamo coach

LILLE 3 v **AEK ATHENS 1**

Referee
Florian Meyer (Germany)

Scorers

68'	Mathieu Robail	Ivic	68'
82'	Gygax		
90'	Makoun		

Teams

01	Sylva	Sorrentino	28
21	Chalmé	Cirillo	05
25	Plestan	Georgeas	31
20	Tafforeau	Papastrathopoulos	15
04	Tavlaridis	Udeze	24
12	Bodmer	Emerson	25
07	Cabaye	Lakis	23
17	Makoun	Tozser	88
18	Robail	Zikos	16
23	Keita	Julio Cezar	99
14	Odemwingie	Lyberopoulos	33

Substitutes

64'	27 Mirallas > / 07 Cabaye <	17 Ivic > / 88 Tozser <	56'
78'	11 Youla > / 18 Robail <	09 Delibasic > / 23 Lakis <	71'
78'	10 Gygax > / 14 Odemwingie <	07 Kiriakidis > / 17 Ivic <	77'

Discipline

45'	Plestan	Boruc	11'
57'	Tavlaridis	Papastrathopoulos	38'
61'	Robail	Julio Cezar	43'
73'	Keita	Lyberopoulos	62'
		Emerson	70'

4	Yellow cards	5
0	Red cards	0
7	Shots on target	4
6	Shots off target	4
30	Fouls committed	24
6	Corners	5
2	Offsides	2
31' 52"	Ball. Poss. (time)	30' 20"
52%	Ball. Poss. (%)	48%

Lille 3 v AEK Athens 1
Group H
Stade Felix-Bollaert, Lens
Attendance: 15,000

Lille's Matthieu Robail (R) takes on AEK Athens Nikos Georgas

In Group H another French contender, Lille, laid down a strong marker that they would challenge AEK Athens all the way for second place in the group behind Milan with a 3-1 victory in their temporary home of Lens.

The win came courtesy of two late goals. Daniel Gygax put the French side 2-1 up with eight minutes remaining before midfielder Jean Makoun wrapped up victory in injury time.

Young striker Mathieu Robail had opened the scoring for Lille after 64 minutes, but the visitors levelled four minutes later through substitute Vladimir Ivic.

Lille dictated the pace from the kick-off and created a great chance on 28 minutes with a header from close range by midfielder Mathieu Bodmer which AEK's Italian goalkeeper Stefano Sorrentino managed to block.

Relying on counter-attacks, the visitors threatened a few minutes later with a long-range effort from Brazilian forward Julio Cesar that required a brilliant save from spectacular Lille and Senegal goalkeeper Tony Sylva.

The home side soon resumed their forward march and came close again when Robail hit the side netting from close range just before half-time.

In the second half of a scrappy match featuring nine yellow cards, Lille appeared to run out of steam of ideas until Robail put them ahead, giving the signal for an exciting finale.

This was Lille's first victory in the group stage of the Champions League.

"We fought hard for this victory, showing character and pride," said Lille coach Claude Puel. "This will give us a lot of confidence," he added. "We are improving, we have more experience but it's still too early to talk about qualifying."

Anderlecht 0 v AC Milan 1
Group H
Constant Vanden Stock Stadium
Attendance: 20,129

Anderlecht keeper Daniel Zitka reflects on Milan's goal

ANDERLECHT 0 v AC MILAN 1

Referee
Luis Medina Cantalejo (Spain)

Scorers
Kaka 58'

Teams

Anderlecht		AC Milan	
01	Zitka	Dida	01
03	Descacht	Bonera	25
23	Juhasz	Kaladze	04
37	Vanden Borre	Nesta	13
05	Biglia	Gattuso	08
11	Boussoufa	Kaká	22
31	De Man	Jankulovski	18
14	Goor	Pirlo	21
04	Vanderhaeghe	Seedorf	10
29	Frutos	Inzaghi	09
07	Tchite	Oliveira	07

Substitutes

70'	> 10 Hassan < 04 Vanderhaeghe	02 Cafu > 07 Oliveira <	50'
84'	> 24 Akin < 11 Boussoufa	11 Gilardino > 09 Inzaghi <	72'
84'	> 36 Lagaer < 37 Vanden Borre	32 Brocchi > 10 Seedorf <	81'

Discipline

07'	Vanden Borre		
		Kaladze	25'
		Bonera	32'
		Bonera	48'

Anderlecht		AC Milan
1	Yellow cards	2
0	Red cards	1
2	Shots on target	6
9	Shots off target	12
15	Fouls committed	10
5	Corners	6
3	Offsides	2
24' 20"	Ball. Poss. (time)	30' 58"
41%	Ball. Poss. (%)	52%

A second-half strike from Kaká helped 10-man AC Milan squeeze past Anderlecht. The Brazilian midfielder popped up in the 58th minute to rifle home from 25 yards to save Milan's blushes and keep his side top of the group with seven points from three outings.

But victory came at a price. Milan played most of the second half with 10 men after Daniele Bonera was sent off following a second booking after he kicked the ball away in anger when disputing a decision by the referee.

The crucial away victory arrived thanks to a goal from the increasingly influential Kaka. The Brazilian midfielder

STATE OF PLAY — GROUP H

	P	W	D	L	F	A	Pts
AC MILAN	3	2	1	0	4	0	7
LILLE	3	1	2	0	4	2	5
ANDERLECHT	3	0	2	1	2	3	2
AEK ATHENS	3	0	1	2	2	7	1

It's hard work being a Champions League manager: Anderlecht coach Frank Vercauteren in animated encouragement of his players

"We were very patient and disciplined throughout and didn't allow the red card to get to us."
Carlo Ancelotti, AC Milan coach

popped up in the 58th minute to rifle home superbly from 25 metres from Clarence Seedorf's pass.

Milan went close to doubling their lead two minutes later, but Zitka managed to parry away Cafu's close range shot.

Anderlecht had the better of the opening period of the first half, but despite dominating it was the home goalkeeper Daniel Zitka who was threatened the most. After 10 minutes, Zitka got down well to deny Filippo Inzaghi with a volley and he was called upon to make a crucial save 20 minutes later from Brazilian striker Oliveira's well-directed header.

Anderlecht's only real chance of the opening 45 minutes fell to captain Bart Goor, whose long-range drive whistled past Dida's left-hand post.

After the goal Milan sat back and goalkeeper Dida saved smartly at the feet of Mohamed Tchite as Anderlecht swept forward, before defender Roland Juhasz struck the crossbar with a header with just three minutes remaining.

Anderlecht coach Frank Vercauteren blamed poor defending for his side's defeat. "It's clear to me that there was no marking for their goal. We defended badly and that cost us the game," he said. "But we had chances to equalise and should have equalised."

"We defended badly and that cost us the game."
Frank Vercauteren, Anderlecht coach

Match Day 3
Wednesday 18 October 2006

Chelsea 1 v Barcelona 0
Group A
Stamford Bridge
Attendance: 45,999

Drogba's shot hits the back of the net sparking incredible scenes of celebration

Goal hero Didier Drogba and Jose Mourinho dedicated their landmark victory over Barcelona to Victoria Buchanan, who worked at Stamford Bridge, but died in a road smash the day before the game. An emotional Drogba commented, "Maybe we should forget the victory. I dedicate my goal to her and her family."

Their thoughts also went out to stricken keepers Petr Cech and Carlo Cudicini who had both been hospitalised after suffering sickening head injuries at Reading. Mourinho added: "Petr is at the heart of all of us. It's not something we even need to think of. Every one of my players knows his situation. But also we know we had to win this match for Chelsea and for the team. It was a great victory; not just the three points, but the way we got them. The team was simply magnificent. We showed just unbelievable commitment. It was 11 against 11

and Chelsea was the best team and deserved to win. Even the most fanatical Spanish supporter – if they want to be honest – has to say Chelsea was the best team."

The Blues strode five points clear at the top of Group A and Mourinho added: "It's not about eliminating Barcelona, it's about winning the group. For us, the goal is simple – to take the points and make sure we come in first place."

Barca superstar Ronaldinho was left crestfallen and coach Frank Rijkaard admitted: "In this match, Chelsea were better. But if you saw us last season you'd know we lose games and don't always play well so this is no big surprise. The strike from Drogba was the difference. Apart from that, there was not too much between the teams."

Rijkaard laughed off suggestions that Barcelona will struggle even to qualify for the latter stages, saying "We have to qualify however we can but we still have the confidence to do that. We

> ## Even the most fanatical Spanish supporter – if they want to be honest – has to say Chelsea was the best team."
> ## Jose Mourinho

CHELSEA 1 v **BARCELONA 0**

Referee
Frank De Bleeckere (Belgium)

Scorers
36' Drogba

Teams

40	Hilário	Valdes	01
09	Boulahrouz	Marquez	04
06	Ricardo Carvalho	Puyol	05
03	A Cole	van Bronckhorst	12
26	Terry	Zambrotta	11
13	Ballack	Deco	20
05	Essien	Edmilson	15
08	Lampard	Xavi	06
04	Makelele	Ronaldinho	10
11	Drogba	Gudjohnsen	07
07	Shevchenko	Messi	19

Substitutes

77'	16 Robben > / 07 Shevchenko <	24 Iniesta > / 12 van Br'horst <	56'
90'	21 Kalou > / 11 Drogba <	08 Giuly > / 07 Gudjohnsen <	60'
		23 Oleguer > / 05 Puyol <	74'

Discipline

53'	Lampard	van Bronckhorst	45'
		Xavi	66'
		Deco	86'

1	Yellow cards	3
0	Red cards	0
5	Shots on target	5
9	Shots off target	9
19	Fouls committed	18
5	Corners	3
0	Offsides	1
20' 31"	Ball. Poss. (time)	34' 59"
37%	Ball. Poss. (%)	63%

STATE OF PLAY — GROUP A

	P	W	D	L	F	A	Pts
CHELSEA	3	3	0	0	6	1	9
BARCELONA	3	1	1	1	6	2	4
WERDER BREMEN	3	1	1	1	3	3	4
LEVSKI SOFIA	3	0	0	3	1	10	0

Stand-in keeper Hilario celebrates his clean sheet

have just got to accept the group standings. It doesn't mean we are out of it."

Drogba controlled a pass from Cole, turned Carles Puyol and unleashed a fierce drive past Valdes in the first minute of the second half and reflected on his excellent winner by saying he had been waiting for such a moment for years. It was easy to understand what he was getting at. Sent off in the Camp Nou that began the sequence, he was forced to watch Chelsea's victory in the return from the stands. The following season he came on as a substitute at Stamford Bridge and was withdrawn in the return. At that time his place in the team was far from guaranteed, but Drogba looked irreplaceable now. This splendidly taken goal, combining the strength and touch characterising, continued the striker's impressive run. At the end he threw his shirt into the crowd and waved a large Chelsea flag. "I was waiting for this for two years now because it was difficult for me to play against Barcelona and not score in four games," Drogba said. "The first game I

was sent off. I was happy because my team won [that tie], and last year was very difficult for me because I was on the bench and supporting my partners and they were unlucky not to win. Today we played as a team and with good spirit."

Drogba said the team had been desperate to win for Cech and Cudicini, and as a tribute to Victoria Buchanan. The 28 year-old worked for Chelsea Pitch Owners Association; she was cycling to work and was killed in an accident involving a lorry. "Chelsea is a big family," Drogba said.

There could be none of the wild exultation with which each victor club has marked success over the other in the knockout phase during the past two seasons, but the victors' happiness will be prolonged. Drogba decided the game, but there was as much satisfaction for the team in seeing their system restrict Barcelona to very few chances as Hilario, third choice keeper, stepping into the breach in the absence of Cech and Cudicini, kept a

Contrasting reactions between Barcelona coach Frank Rijkaard and Chelsea's rampant fans to Drogba's goal

clean sheet without being unduly exerted. Edmilson's highly ambitious 45-yarder suggested the European champions planned to test Chelsea's new keeper on his debut and Hilario saved Lionel Messi's angled drive in the 24th minute and turned a low shot from Xavi around the post on the half-hour. But very little else came his way.

Despite talk of Ronaldinho's return to form, Boulahrouz, at right-back, forced him deep and when he attempted to slip into the middle where he was stepping into congestion and eager challenges. More than that, Chelsea's win would have been more comfortable had Shevchenko's finishing not continued to desert him.

Andrei Shevchenko's travails continued as he failed to find the net once again

WERDER BRE. 2 v LEVSKI SOFIA 0

Referee
Paul Allaerts (Belgium)

Scorers
45'	Naldo
73'	Diego

Teams
18	Wiese	Petkov	01
04	Rodrigues	Angelov	20
08	Fritz	Tomasic	04
29	Mertesacker	Topuzakov	11
27	Schulz	Borimirov	07
05	Wome	Eromoigbe	06
22	Frings	Telkiyski	21
10	Diego	Wagner	25
07	Vranjes	Bardon	27
14	Hunt	Domovchijski	17
11	Klose	Yovov	10

Substitutes
45'	> 17 Klasnic < 05 Wome	18 Ivanov > 17 Domovchijski <	64'
73'	> 16 Andreasen < 07 Vranjes	24 Dimitrov > 10 Yovov <	79'
82'	> 23 Almeida < 11 Klose	77 Koprivarov > 21 Telkiyski <	79'

Discipline
38'	Fritz	Tomasic	40'
		Borimirov	45'

1	Yellow cards	2
0	Red cards	0
5	Shots on target	0
11	Shots off target	4
15	Fouls committed	19
5	Corners	3
3	Offsides	3
34' 06"	Ball. Poss. (time)	27' 54"
55%	Ball. Poss. (%)	45%

Werder Bremen 2 v Levski Sofia 0
Group A
Weserstadion
Attendance: 36,000

Werder Bremen's Brazilian defender Naldo (R) scores his team's first goal from a free-kick past Levski Sofia's goalkeeper Georgi Petkov

A goal on the stroke of half-time from Naldo followed by a second-half strike by Diego helped Werder Bremen to a victory that effectively ended the qualification hopes of Levski Sofia.

The result further turned the heat on reigning European champions Barcelona following defeat by Chelsea.

Bremen were the better team throughout. Miroslav Klose narrowly missed for the Germans after just four minutes and next it was the turn of Aaron Hunt to be wayward with his finishing as Bremen started well.

Hristo Yoyov showed that Levski were not there to make up the numbes when he went close to scoring, but there was no mistaking

Werder Bremen's Per Mertesacker (C) jumps for the ball with Levski goalkeeper Georgi Petkov, Igor Tomasic (3rdR) and Daniel Borimirov (R)

that the hosts were enjoying the better of the chances.

Naldo had his first chance from a free-kick after 35 minutes but his shot was saved by Georgi Petkov. It looked as if the first half would be goalless but as the period went into stoppage time, Bremen took the lead. It was another free-kick, awarded by Belgian referee Paul Allaerts for a foul on Hunt by Daniel Borimirov and Naldo's shot from more than 30 yards went in off the left-hand post of Petkov.

The side from Sofia started the second half well, clearly intent on getting themselves back on terms with Bremen. Valeri Domovchiyski was wide

with an effort in the first minute of the second period, but Bremen still looked a potent attacking force as Schulz, Clemens Fritz and Hunt all missed chances to extend the lead held by Thomas Schaaf's side.

The Germans were getting better and better but must have been relieved when they got their second goal of the night after 73 minutes. Klasnic fed the ball to Diego and the former Porto player did well to escape the attention of his marker and score.

The game was all over bar the shouting and Hugo Almeida had a shot saved as Bremen went close to further extending their lead.

BORDEAUX 0 v **LIVERPOOL 1**

Referee
Tom Henning Ovrebo (Norway)

Scorers
	Crouch	58'

Teams
Bordeaux		Liverpool	
16	Ramé	Reina	25
03	Henrique	Carragher	23
13	Jemmali	Finnan	03
06	Jurietti	Hyypia	04
08	Alonso	Riise	06
24	Mavuba	Alonso	14
05	Menegazzo	Gonzalez	11
14	Micoud	Luis Garcia	10
17	Wendel	Zenden	32
09	Darcheville	Bellamy	17
07	Laslandes	Crouch	15

Substitutes
63'	29 Chamakh > 07 Laslandes <	18 Kuyt > 15 Crouch <	65'
63'	22 Faubert > 08 Alonso <	22 Sissoko > 11 Gonzalez <	69'
71'	12 Perea > 09 Darcheville <	28 Warnock > 17 Bellamy <	87'

Discipline
22'	Jurietti	Zenden	26'
42'	Ramé	Kuyt	86'

2	Yellow cards	2
0	Red cards	0
1	Shots on target	6
17	Shots off target	7
8	Fouls committed	21
8	Corners	6
3	Offsides	4
37' 11"	Ball. Poss. (time)	21' 51"
63%	Ball. Poss. (%)	37%

Bordeaux 0 v Liverpool 1
Group C
Parc Lescure
Attendance: 33,000

Rafa Benitez begins to feel the pressure as Liverpool absorb a bombardment by Bordeaux

Rafa Benitez paid tribute to Peter Crouch as Liverpool put one foot in the UEFA Champions League knockout stages.

Liverpool's 6ft 7in striker bounced back from a glaring first-half miss to nod the 58th-minute winner in Bordeaux from Craig Bellamy's corner. It was Crouch's 11th goal of the season and it kept the

Reds on top of Group C with their first away win of the campaign.

Benitez said: "For a striker to keep going when they miss chances is very important. They know they've got to keep at it if they are eventually going to take one. It's really good for them to score goals because when they are doing that and playing well it's important for everyone."

STATE OF PLAY **GROUP C**

	P	W	D	L	F	A	Pts
LIVERPOOL	3	2	1	0	4	2	7
PSV EINDHOVEN	3	2	1	0	3	1	7
GALATASARAY	3	0	1	2	3	5	1
BORDEAUX	3	0	1	2	0	2	1

Bordeaux fans get behind their team

A close range header from Peter Crouch finds the back of the Bordeaux net

Crouch celebrates a classic single goal away win

This was a classic Benitez smash-and-grab raid. Liverpool soaked up pressure, sometimes with considerable trouble. One clever push through Riise's legs by Alejandro Alonso created a chance for a driven cross that Jamie Carragher was forced to dive full-length to head away. Fernando Menegazzo tested goalkeeper Jose Reina with a snap shot a minute into the second half, the French side having had 65% of the opening period possession to underline the problems Liverpool were creating for themselves.

Lilian Laslandes and Jean-Claude Darcheville – players who have had time in the English leagues – were beginning to cause growing danger with their movement and pace.

Crouch had missed two easier chances in the first half, but his header gave keeper Ulrich Ramé no chance.

Bordeaux came close to an equaliser when Chamakh sent a flashing header from a cross inches wide with eight minutes left. Then Menegazzo saw a low header go wide from Jurietti's cross.

Stand-in skipper Jamie Carragher defended Benitez's rotation system, which had seen Momo Sissoko and Dirk Kuyt left on the bench despite the team lacking the injured Steven Gerrard: "The manager has a big squad and he believes all players are capable of doing the job – and we've proved that tonight."

Benítez looked a relieved man at the final whistle when he indulged in unusually extravagant celebrations. "The final score is the most important thing for me, but I also felt the performance of the team was good," he said. "The players worked really hard to control the game and it's difficult to do that. We now need to win against Bordeaux at home, but football's not always that easy. Winning away was important for us, especially in the Champions League, but the clean sheet was also a big thing. But because we couldn't score the second goal and Bordeaux carried on going forward it was difficult right to the end. The group depends on the next game so let's wait and see, but this will give the players lots of confidence."

GALATASARAY 1 v PSV EINDHO'N 2

Referee
Yuri Baskakov (Russia)

Scorers

19'	Ilic	Kromkamp	59'
		Kone	72'

Teams

01	Mondragon	Gomes	01
05	Ak	Alex	04
04	Song	Kromkamp	02
02	Tomas	Reiziger	03
18	Akman	Salcido	23
22	Ilic	Cocu	08
23	Inamoto	Culina	15
55	Sarioglu	Mendez	11
66	Turan	Simons	06
26	Yylmaz	Farfan	17
99	Karan	Arouna Koné	10

Substitutes

67'	> 19 Haspolatli < 26 A Yylmaz	07 Väyrynen > 11 Mendez <	62'
70'	> 19 Ates < 22 Ilic	16 Aisatti > 15 Culina <	90'
70'	> 09 Sukur < 99 Ü Karan		

Discipline

32'	Ak	Salcido	04'
34'	Akman		
89'	Tomas		

3	Yellow cards	1
0	Red cards	0
4	Shots on target	5
4	Shots off target	6
16	Fouls committed	21
11	Corners	4
2	Offsides	4
28' 05"	Ball. Poss. (time)	26' 56"
51%	Ball. Poss. (%)	49%

Galatasaray 1 v PSV Eindhoven 2
Group C
Atatürk Stadium
Attendance: 22,000

PSV Eindhoven players celebrate Jan Kromkamp's equaliser against Galatasaray

PSV Eindhoven came from a goal down to beat Galatasaray 2-1 with two second-half strikes in their Group C clash, putting the Dutch club in a strong position.

PSV were now level with group leaders Liverpool on seven points, while Galatasaray and Girondins Bordeaux face an uphill struggle with just one point apiece.

Riot police deal quickly and effectively with an irate Galatasaray fan

STATE OF PLAY — GROUP C

	P	W	D	L	F	A	Pts
LIVERPOOL	3	2	1	0	4	2	7
PSV EINDHOVEN	3	2	1	0	3	1	7
GALATASARAY	3	0	1	2	3	5	1
BORDEAUX	3	0	1	2	0	2	1

The Istanbul side dominated the first half and Serbian midfielder Sasa Ilic put them ahead after 19 minutes, picking up a pass from Umit Karan and firing home a deflected shot.

Galatasaray kept up the pressure through much of the first half and PSV only managed a few speculative efforts on goal, hardly troubling goalkeeper Farid Mondragon.

"The match started as we feared," PSV coach Ronald Koeman told NOS-TV afterwards, "We had hardly any possession of the ball, and we were not able to come out and play properly and then we conceded the early goal. But when we did escape their pressure we came back into the match. At half-time we knew we had a possibility of winning the match. Overall, I think we were the better side and deserved to win."

The Dutch team picked up the pace after half-time and the Colombian keeper was at fault when PSV equalised in the 59th minute. Defender Jan Kromkamp sprinted into the penalty area from the right and drove in a shot which slipped through Mondragon's hands.

Buoyed by the goal, the Dutch side enjoyed a sustained period of pressure on the Galatasaray goalmouth.

Ivorian striker Arouna Kone sealed the win for the Dutch side in the 72nd minute. Left clear with only Mondragon to beat, he knocked the ball past him into the right-hand corner of the goal. The goal sparked a pitch incursion by a Turkish fan, who was dragged away by police for his trouble.

Necati Ates almost earned a last-gasp equaliser for Galatasaray with a powerful close-range strike which forced a good save from Brazilian goalkeeper Gomes.

"I think in first half we showed how good we are, but that changed when they scored," said Galatasaray coach Erik Gerets.

> "Overall, I think we were the better side and deserved to win."
> Ronald Koeman, PSV coach

Sporting Lisbon 0 v Bayern Munich 1
Group B
Jose Alvalade Stadium
Attendance: 48,000

Another Sporting miss, this time by Yannick Djalo

> "Without a doubt Bayern are a great team."
> Paulo Bento, Sporting Lisbon coach

A brilliant performance by goalkeeper Oliver Kahn helped 10-man Bayern Munich secure a 1-0 win over Sporting Lisbon and preserve their 100 per cent start in Group B.

Midfielder Bastian Schweinsteiger scored an outstanding goal after 19 minutes which proved decisive, but he turned from hero to villain just after half-time when he was sent off for a second yellow card, picked up for a foul on substitute Yannick.

SPORTING LIS. 0 v BAYERN MUN. 1

Referee
Terje Hauge (Norway)

Scorers
Schweinsteiger 19'

Teams

Sporting Lisbon	Bayern Munich
01 Ricardo	Kahn 01
12 Caneira	da Silva 03
04 Polga	Lahm 21
13 Souza	Sagnol 02
24 Veloso	van Buyten 05
18 da Cunha	Ottl 39
10 Martins	Schweinsteiger 31
28 Moutinho	van Bommel 17
11 Tello	Pizarro 14
19 Alecsandro	Podolski 11
31 Liedson	Santa Cruz 24

Substitutes

45'	> 20 Yannick < 10 Martins	06 Demichelis > 39 Ottl <	45'
57'	> 80 Bueno < 19 Alecsandro	20 Salihamidzic > 24 Santa Cruz <	50'
70'	> 76 Paredes < 24 Veloso	19 dos Santos > 11 Podolski <	65'

Discipline

45'	Tello	Schweinsteiger	25'
49'	Liedson	Ottl	28'
68'	Veloso	Schweinsteiger	46'
		van Bommel	75'
		dos Santos	84'

Sporting		Bayern
3	Yellow cards	5
0	Red cards	1
5	Shots on target	4
20	Shots off target	8
17	Fouls committed	20
10	Corners	2
1	Offsides	2
29' 16"	Ball. Poss. (time)	29' 16"
50%	Ball. Poss. (%)	50%

Goalkeeper Oliver Kahn acknowledges the final whistle and a clean sheet thanks to his own wonderful performance

Bayern, who had a first-half penalty appeal waved away by Norwegian referee Terje Hauge, could even have won by a bigger margin. Two minutes after their goal, midfielder Santa Cruz squandered a good chance to double the score when his header went wide.

Sporting poured forward in search of an equaliser and created several good chances, but could find no way past Kahn. When he was finally beaten after 58 minutes by Brazilian defender Polga, his right-hand post came to his rescue.

"Without a doubt Bayern are a great team," Sporting coach Paulo Bento told reporters. "In the second half we failed to score in spite of our numerical advantage. Sporting didn't start the game well and it was then that we gave away a goal. Afterwards, when we reacted, we didn't have any luck."

Bayern now have the maximum nine points, five points ahead of Sporting on four.

STATE OF PLAY   GROUP B

	P	W	D	L	F	A	Pts
BAYERN MUNICH	3	3	0	0	7	0	9
SPORTING LISBON	3	1	1	1	2	2	4
INTER MILAN	3	1	0	2	2	4	3
SPARTAK MOSCOW	3	0	1	2	2	7	1

Bayern's players salute their travelling supporters

Inter Milan 2 v Spartak Moscow 1
Group B
San Siro
Attendance: 40,000

INTER MILAN 2 v **SPARTAK MOS. 1**

Referee
Bertrand Layec (France)

Scorers

02', 09' Cruz	Pavluchenko	54'

Teams

Inter Milan		Spartak Moscow	
12	Julio César	Kowalewski	30
02	Cordoba	Géder	02
13	Maicon	Jiránek	13
23	Materazzi	Kovac	15
04	Zanetti	Rodriguez	17
15	Dacourt	Shishkin	49
07	Figo	Bistrov	23
05	Stankovic	Boyarinstev	07
14	Vieira	Mozart	24
09	Cruz	Titov	09
20	Recoba	Pavlyuchenko	10

Substitutes

58'	> 16 Burdisso < 20 Recoba	21 Owusu-Abeyie > 12 Mozart <	45'
69'	> 10 Adriano < 07 Figo	25 Kalinichenko > 20 Bistrov <	75'
90'	> 25 Samuel < 09 Cruz		

Discipline

33'	Figo	Rodriguez	32'
		Kalinichenko	82'

Inter		Spartak
1	Yellow cards	2
0	Red cards	0
8	Shots on target	4
6	Shots off target	6
22	Fouls committed	18
4	Corners	3
3	Offsides	4
32' 45"	Ball. Poss. (time)	30' 15"
52%	Ball. Poss. (%)	48%

Inter Milan's Julio Cruz celebrates with team-mate Alvaro Recoba after scoring the second goal against Spartak Moscow

Inter Milan made life hard for themselves, but held on to defeat Spartak Moscow to earn their first points of the Champions League group stage.

It seemed like it was going to be an easy night for Roberto Mancini's side when Julio Cruz struck twice in the first nine minutes, but Spartak didn't go down without a fight and Roman Pavlyuchenko's goal in the 54th minute brought them right back in it.

Dejan Stankovic had a goal disallowed while Spartak had a chance to equalise late on, but goalkeeper Julio Cesar ensured Inter kept hold of the full three points to finally get their UEFA Champions League campaign up and running.

Despite having made a dreadful start, Inter coach Roberto Mancini appeared to be taking their crucial tie with Spartak lightly as he left Hernan Crespo on the bench, preferring instead to hand Julio Cruz a rare start. The Argentinian was keen to take his chance, however, and slammed a close-range effort in after just two minutes. Alvaro Recoba's free-kick was inadvertently played into the path of Cruz by Patrick Vieira, and Cruz accepted the gift to fire in off the underside of the crossbar.

Recoba and Cruz combined again to double the home side's advantage before 10 minutes had even been played. The Uruguayan, benefiting from the suspension to Zlatan Ibrahimovic to earn a place in the starting XI, lofted his cross from the left onto the head of Cruz, who couldn't miss from six yards out.

Inter appeared too comfortable with a two-goal cushion and allowed Spartak to slowly find a way back into the game. Although the Russians rarely posed a threat to Julio Cesar in the Inter goal, their increased possession was looking ominous. Just 10 minutes into the second half, Spartak

A Spartak fan urges his side on against the odds at the San Siro

Inter Milan's Javier Zanetti (L) tackles Spartak Moscow's Vladimir Bystrov

deservedly pulled a goal back with Pavlyuchenko converting Denis Boyarintsev's low cross.

Inter reacted and thought they had regained their two-goal advantage when Dejan Stankovic slotted the ball in, but referee Bertrand Layec had spotted an earlier foul by the Serbian and ruled the goal out.

Cruz went close to completing his hat-trick, but the lead remained just one goal and the home side almost paid the ultimate price at the end.

Julio Cesar reacted well to palm Boyarintsev's shot away to safety as Spartak threatened a late equalizer, which would have dealt a near-fatal blow to Inter's qualification hopes. Inter held on, however, to record their first win in Europe this season and give themselves a realistic hope of making it through to the second round.

Valencia 2 v Shakhtar Donetsk 0
Group D
Mestalla
Attendance: 45,000

Valencia's Mario Regueiro (R) fights for the ball with Shakhtar's Vyacheslav Sviderskiy

VALENCIA 2 v **SHAKHTAR D. 0**

Referee
Mike Riley (ENG)

Scorers
30', 45' Villa

Teams

Valencia		Shakhtar	
01	Canizares	Pletikosa	01
02	Miguel	Chigrynskiy	27
24	Moretti	Leonardo	08
17	Navarro	Sviderskiy	32
06	Albelda	Tymoschuk	04
20	Albiol	Fernandinho	07
22	Edu	Matuzalem	09
15	Joaquin	Rat	26
11	Regueiro	Jadson	38
09	Morientes	Aghahowa	17
07	Villa	Marica	29

Substitutes

	In / Out	In / Out	
52'	18 Lopez / 22 Edu	03 Hubschman / 17 Aghahowa	45'
64'	19 Gavilán Martínez / 11 Regueiro	25 Brandao / 17 Aghahowa	46'
77'	21 Silva / 07 Villa	11 Vorobey / 07 Fernandinho	84'

Discipline

42'	Albelda	Sviderskiy	01'
		Tymoschuk	33'
		Marica	58'
		Brandao	62'
		Sviderskiy	76'

1	Yellow cards	5
0	Red cards	1
6	Shots on target	2
13	Shots off target	5
15	Fouls committed	20
6	Corners	3
1	Offsides	4
31' 16"	Ball. Poss. (time)	30' 06"
52%	Ball. Poss. (%)	48%

A David Villa brace gave Valencia victory over 10-man Shakhtar Donetsk, but they could have had many more in a match they dominated.

Villa got both goals in the first half before Viacheslav Sviderskiy saw red for Donestk midway through the second period.

With La Liga leaders Valencia looking to bounce back from their first defeat of the season, a 3-2 reverse at Celta Vigo, the match got off to a rough start with Sviderskiy earning a yellow card – one that would come back to haunt him – after just 26 seconds for a foul on Edu.

The first chance on goal took a while longer to come, and when it did, Joaquin Sanchez's sixth-minute shot was easily blocked by Shakhtar goalkeeper Stipe Pletikosa. Shakhtar's first chance came in the 11th minute when Francelino Matuzalem tried his luck from range, but sent the ball wide of the target.

Valencia began to dominate. Edu drilled a shot goalwards from 20 yards, but it was charged down by Luis Fernandinho. David Villa was then fouled by Jose Leonardo and dusted himself off to force Pletikosa into a save from a 25-yard free-kick.

The next clear-cut chance became the goal when Villa got the ball inside the area and finished with left-footed shot from close range.

Valencia continued to push, with Joaquin seeing his effort blocked by Pletikosa in the 42nd minute before Villa plundered the second goal just before half-time. Joaquin was the provider, crossing from the right for Villa to head home from six yards.

Valencia's dominance carried over into the second half, and they had some superb opportunities to add to their lead in the opening minutes of the period. David Navarro sent a powerful volley narrowly wide before Villa's right-footed shot had to be tipped over by Pletikosa. Regueiro headed over from Villa's corner before the Villa himself missed the target with a free-kick from the edge of the area.

Sviderskiy was then required to get in a block when substitute Jaime

STATE OF PLAY — GROUP D

	P	W	D	L	F	A	Pts
VALENCIA	3	3	0	0	8	3	9
ROMA	3	2	0	1	6	2	6
OLYMPIAKOS	3	0	1	2	4	7	1
SHAKHTAR DON.	3	0	1	2	2	8	1

Gavilan shot goalwards. It was to be Sviderskiy's last meaningful contribution before he earned himself an early bath with a foul on Emiliano Moretti, referee Mike Riley deeming it worthy of a second yellow card.

Valencia continued to seek a third goal that just would not come. David Albelda volleyed over from long-range, while Pletikosa fumbled David Silva's shot from 20 yards, but got away with it. Valencia took the hint and settled for a 2-0 win that kept them three points clear in Group D.

Valencia celebrate Villa's second goal

DID YOU KNOW?
This victory meant Valencia had won 12 of their 15 games at the Mestalla

Shakhtar Donetsk coach Mircea Lucescu speaks during the post-match news conference at the Mestalla Stadium in Valencia

DID YOU KNOW?
Valencia's Mestalla Stadium is the fifth largest in Spain with 53,000 seats. But the club are due to move to the 75,000 seat Nou Mestalla in 2009

Olympiakos 0 v AS Roma 1

Group D
Spiros Louis Stadium
Attendance: 30,000

Roma players celebrate Perrotta's winning goal

OLYMPIAKOS 0	v	AS ROMA 1

Referee
Graham Poll (ENG)

Scorers
	Perrotta 76'

Teams

Olympiakos		Roma
71 Nikopolidis		Doni 32
55 Julio César		Cassetti 77
32 Anatolakis		Chivu 13
14 Zewlakow		Ferrari 21
07 Nery Castillo		Panucci 02
11 Djordjevic		De Rossi 16
21 Georgatos		Faty 14
01 Kafes		Perrotta 20
06 Stoltidis		Taddei 11
23 Konstantinou		Tonetto 22
10 Rivaldo		Totti 10

Substitutes

61'	> 08 Maric < 01 Kafes	28 Rosi > 77 Cassetti <	66'
71'	> 09 Okkas < 11 Djordjevic	08 Aquilani > 14 Faty <	78'
86'	> 18 Borja < 10 Rivaldo	19 Defendi > 11 Taddei <	90'

Discipline
	Max Tonetto 03'

Olympiakos		Roma
0	Yellow cards	1
0	Red cards	0
2	Shots on target	2
9	Shots off target	6
19	Fouls committed	18
2	Corners	4
1	Offsides	6
27' 36"	Ball. Poss. (time)	29' 54"
48%	Ball. Poss. (%)	52%

Midfielder Simone Perrotta's first goal in the UEFA Champions League was enough to give AS Roma a scrappy, but valuable 1-0 win at Olympiakos, which left second-placed Roma with six points in Group D, three points behind leaders Valencia, but with a five-point cushion over Olympiakos and Shakhtar Donetsk.

Olympiakos had plenty of possession, but were made to rue missed chances with Michalis Konstantinou going close twice. Cyprus international Konstantinou thought he had put them ahead after 28 minutes, but his header was ruled out because team-mate Giorgios Anatolakis had simultaneously barged Roma goalkeeper Doni into the back of the net. Twelve minutes later, Konstantinou rose above the Roma defence to meet a Rivaldo free-kick, but his header hit the bar and went over.

Roma, who were wearing black armbands to commemorate a metro crash in Rome the previous day, stole the points when Italy's Perrotta slid in at the near post in the 76th minute to turn in a cross from second half substitute Aleandro Rosi.

Uruguayan Nery Alberto Castillo, who had been linked with Chelsea and Manchester United, drifted inside two defenders and shot from the edge of the area. Doni dived to his right to make a good save.

Roma, playing very deep and seemingly looking for a draw, came more into the game in the second half with Francesco Totti firing over and Cristian Chivu producing a good save from Antonis Nikopolidis in the the Olympiakos goal. Totti opened up the Olympiakos defence with a telling pass that freed Rosi down the right to set up Perrotta's goal.

He could have finished things off himself in injury time when he latched on to a poor back pass from Grigoris Georgatos, but pushed his shot wide.

STATE OF PLAY — GROUP D

	P	W	D	L	F	A	Pts
VALENCIA	3	3	0	0	8	3	9
ROMA	3	2	0	1	6	2	6
OLYMPIAKOS	3	0	1	2	4	7	1
SHAKHTAR DON.	3	0	1	2	2	8	1

Match Day 4
Tuesday 31 October 2006

Chelsea Dagger

The Blues strike a killer blow to holders Barecelona thanks to Drogba's last ditch equaliser in the Nou Camp

Three Up For Brazilian Genius

Kaká nets a superb hat-trick as Milan move up a gear and are just a point away from qualification

British Nightmare

Liverpool seal their place in the last 16, but the rest of the British clubs have a collective nightmare. Fergie, for one, is not happy

"There's no margin for error now."
Frank Rijkaard

Barcelona 2 v Chelsea 2
Group A
Nou Camp
Attendance: 98,000

Chelsea's players are cock-a-hoop after Didier Drogba's late, late equaliser

BARCELONA 2 v **CHELSEA 2**

Referee
Stefano Farina (Italy)

Assistant Referee
Alessandro Griselli (Italy)
Giuseppe De Santis (Italy)

Fourth Official
Oscar Girardi (Italy)

Scorers

| 03' | Deco | Lampard | 52' |
| 58' | Gudjonsen | Drogba | 90' |

Teams

01	Valdes	Hilário	40
04	Marquez	Boulahrouz	09
05	Puyol	Ricardo Carvalho	06
12	van Bronckhorst	A Cole	03
11	Zambrotta	Terry	26
20	Deco	Ballack	13
03	Motta	Essien	05
06	Xavi	Lampard	08
10	Ronaldinho	Makelele	04
07	Gudjohnsen	Robben	16
19	Messi	Drogba	11

Substitutes

57'	> 15 Edmilson < 03 Motta	21 Kalou > 16 Robben <	73'
77'	> 08 Giuly < 07 Gudjohnsen	10 J Cole > 09 Boulahrouz <	75'
84'	> 24 Iniesta < 06 Xavi	20 Ferreira > 13 Ballack <	90'

Discipline

38'	Messi	Lampard	27'
42'	Motta	Robben	29'
64'	Gudjohnsen	A Cole	37'
65'	Edmilson	J Cole	81'
		Terry	87'
		Essien	89'

4	Yellow cards	6
0	Red cards	0
3	Shots on target	5
7	Shots off target	6
15	Fouls committed	31
3	Corners	4
2	Offsides	1
40' 15"	Ball. Poss. (time)	25' 46"
61%	Ball. Poss. (%)	39%

Chelsea pegged back Barca in injury time through a dramatic Didier Drogba goal to claim a 2-2 draw at the Nou Camp and provoke elaborate touchline celebrations from their manager.

Barca had looked on course to claim only their second win in Group A, and gain revenge for their 1-0 defeat at Stamford Bridge, as they held a 2-1 advantage heading into injury-time. But Drogba's goal seriously dented Barca's hopes of making it through to the next phase. Equally Chelsea's stunning equaliser virtually ensured the club's passage to the knockout stage, in yet another thriller between the giants of European football.

Having fallen 2-1 behind to a goal from Gudjohnsen, the precious point was salvaged with a composed move. Michael Essien crossed deep, the advanced John Terry headed back and Drogba, on the run, took the ball on his chest and surged past Rafael Márquez to shoot home at the near post. Mourinho said: "I was thinking there was still a chance to do it and how unfair it would be to lose a game

where we were the best team by far. The goal came in the last minute but it was more than deserved. It would have been very, very unfair to go home without a point.'"

Deco's stunning opener in the third minute illustrated how steep the cost of a mistake can be in the Champions League. Khalid Boulahrouz, the master of Ronaldinho a fortnight earlier, lost possession to him and the Portuguese midfielder weaved his way down the left before cutting inside to drive low past Hilario from 20 yards with his right foot. Chelsea reacted badly. Drogba barged into Thiago Motta before then being shoved over by Márquez. The game had plenty of controversy. Márquez brought his studs down on Essien's groin. Equally, a high challenge by Ricardo Carvalho on Deco in the final moments was reckless.

Misunderstanding heightened the problem when Rijkaard's players, shortly before the interval, demanded a red card for Ashley Cole's expulsion for a second booking when it turned out that it was actually Lampard who had been shown an earlier yellow card.

STATE OF PLAY					GROUP A		
	P	W	D	L	F	A	Pts
CHELSEA	4	3	1	0	8	3	10
WERDER BREMEN	4	2	1	1	6	3	7
BARCELONA	4	1	2	1	8	4	5
LEVSKI SOFIA	4	0	0	4	1	13	0

Deco celebrates the opening goal

Xavi shoots at goal as Barcelona push Chelsea back early in the second half

over from the edge of the six-yard box. A goal did arrive within seconds. With Barcelona appealing for offside against Drogba, Lampard at first mis-controlled a Claude Makelele pass, but chased after it, caught up with the ball near the byline and turned to whirl a shot over Valdés from that tight angle. It was an uncanny strike, with the goalkeeper shocked to be beaten from such a position. If he meant it, Lampard scored a goal Ronaldinho would have been proud of. But did he intend a cross?

Barcelona regained the lead sleekly after 57 minutes. Boulahrouz was foolish to lunge at Ronaldinho and the Brazilian, taming a crossfield pass, beat him with a single flick before rolling the ideal delivery from the left with the outside of his right foot. Gudjohnsen, in the middle, converted it easily.

But then came the last seconds drama and the sight of the hirsute Chelsea manager sliding down the touchline on his knees like a celebrating teenager.

Barcelona playmaker Deco declared that Drogba's goal left him feeling as though they had lost the match. Deco said: "I think that after leading 1-0 and they draw level, and then you score again to make it 2-1 and continue playing well, and they return again to draw, it is almost like a defeat. I believe that the attitude of the team has been good. We have been able to pressure them, but we have failed in some aspects."

Barca captain Carles Puyol felt his team should have secured three points: "We deserved a better result. Some good play by them and the good control of Drogba has inflicted much damage on us. I was very angry because we have played a good game. We had the result in our favour and we had to be intelligent. We had control of the game and we had chances to score some more goals."

Midfielder Edmilson added on Barca's official website: "Chelsea did not deserve to win. We deserved to. We must raise our heads. We depend on ourselves. We must be strong in our home games."

DID YOU KNOW?
Hours before the game against Barcelona, Chelsea notified UEFA of a change of kit; instead of all black, they had decided to wear the all white of Barcelona's hated rivals Real Madrid

Barcelona could have struck again in the ninth minute as Lionel Messi, linking with Deco, got past Cole and Lampard before putting his cutback in the path of Ronaldinho 12 yards out, but the Brazilian's finish went high. In the 21st minute Ronaldinho fed Xavi perfectly and Hilario did well to touch the shot round the post.

Chelsea fought back. In the 33rd minute Víctor Valdés saved an Essien header from Drogba's cross and, at the resultant corner, the keeper needed to turn behind an angled shot from Arjen Robben. Robben ought to have scored after receiving a fine ball from Lampard in the 51st minute, but fired

Mourinho's celebration was in part a response to the fact that the Chelsea manager – who had whipped up a storm about diving before this match, accusing Eidur Gudjohnsen and Lionel Messi of liking to take a plunge – had been taunted all night by the Nou Camp crowd, who sang "Mourinho, go to the theatre", mocking his claims that Barca playmaker Messi is an "actor". Frank Rijkaard said: "I was surprised by his reaction. Obviously he was happy. It makes no sense for me to comment on him. I think the crowd were fair enough. It shows a good sense of humour. There was no abuse. I think that's fun."

Post-match Mourinho, continuing his theme from earlier rounds of games, criticised Barca's players for intimidating referee Farina by exaggerating fouls and trying to force him into showing cards. Farina booked 10 players, including six from Chelsea, sparking a UEFA investigation.

Carles Puyol was quick to respond to the Chelsea manager's comments, claimed Chelsea started the diving. "I think you will find it was them that did

John Terry receives a card from referee Farina as things get tetchy

that first," Puyol said. "If you watch it again in the television you will be able to see that quite clearly. I think it was Drogba and someone else – I can't remember – who threw themselves on the floor. I don't know if they were looking for cards, but we certainly weren't. I don't care what Mourinho says."

Frank Rijkaard had plenty to say about the referee too. He stormed onto the pitch after the final whistle to confront referee Stefano Farina. The Dutch coach had to be dragged away by Puyol and then spat angrily on the grass. He was fuming because Farina called for six minutes of stoppage-

Eidur Gudjohnsen scores against his old club

Drogba strikes the last second equalizer to send Mourinho to his knees

Lampard salutes the travelling fans after his equaliser. But did he mean it?

Rijkaard confronts referee Farina

Chelsea and two behind Werder Bremen meaning the reigning European champions can ill afford any more slip-ups in their final two games if they are to avoid an embarrassing early exit from the competition. Rijkaard said: "There's no margin for error now. We have to beat both teams and win our last two games. We just have to do it."

Mourinho described his team's display as "...brilliant. Physically very strong, mentally very strong, tactically always under control against a very difficult team," he said. Frank Lampard, one of those booked and consequently suspended from the next match in Bremen, agreed that the new-look Chelsea proved their self-belief and resilience with their gutsy fightback in the Nou Camp. Lampard said: "Maybe we would have lost the game in the past. When you come to these places, it's such an arena and they have such big names – but we have big names too and you have to realise that."

time and only played five. Rijkaard said: "He blew up one minute before he should have done, but I'm not blaming that for the result. It was a battle on the pitch and it was interesting during the game and I went on because I wanted to thank the referee for his participation."

The draw left Barca third in Group A after four games, five points behind

Levski Sofia 0 v Werder Bremen 3
Group A
Vasil Levski Stadium
Attendance: 25,368

Teenage goalkeeper Nikolay Mihaylov is stunned by Bremen's blitz of three goals in six minutes

LEVSKI SOFIA 0 v WERDER BRE. 3

Referee
Matteo Trefoloni (Italy)
Assistant Referee
Marco Ivaldi (Italy) Stefano Papi (Italy)
Fourth Official
Antonio Giannocarro (Italy)

Scorers

Mihajlov og	33'
Baumann	35'
Frings	37'

Teams

Levski Sofia		Werder Bremen	
88	Mihajlov	Wisse	18
20	S Angelov	Rodrigues	04
03	Milanov	Fritz	08
04	Tomasic	Mertesacker	29
11	Topuzakov	Wome	05
07	Borimirov	Baumann	06
06	Eromoigbe	Frings	22
21	Telkiyski	Diego	10
25	Wagner	Vranjes	07
27	Bardon	Hunt	14
10	Yovov	Klose	11

Substitutes

45'	> 12 Mitrev< 88 Mihajlov		17 Klasnic >14 Hunt <	74'
57'	> 28 E Angelov< 04 Tomasic		16 Andreasen >06 Baumann <	78'
69'	> 24 Dimitrov< 21 Telkiyski		03 Pasanen >05 Wome <	85'

Discipline

87'	Wagner	Wome	20'
		Vranjes	69'

1	Yellow cards	2
0	Red cards	0
2	Shots on target	4
8	Shots off target	4
9	Fouls committed	17
13	Corners	2
4	Offsides	1
29'35"	Ball. Poss. (time)	28'26"
51%	Ball. Poss. (%)	49%

Werber Bremen moved two points ahead of European Champions Barcelona in their bid to emerge from Group A alongside Chelsea, thanks to a 3-0 away win at Levski Sofia.

The German side scored three in three minutes as first Levski Champions League debutant 18 year-old goalkeeper Nikolay Mihaylov was credited with an own goal in the 34th minute, captain Frank Baumann added a quickfire second and Torsten Frings got number three.

"It was shocking," said Levski Sofia coach Stanimir Stoilov. "We conceded the goal and then we were knocked out in the quickest possible way. Unfortunately, the big teams waste no time in punishing such mistakes."

Stoilov gave his backing to teenage goalkeeper. Mihaylov — son of Bulgarian Football Union president Borislav 'Bobby' Mihaylov — who failed to gather the ball from a Lucio Vagner's back pass in the 33rd minute to concede an own goal. "I thought he (Mihaylov) was playing very well until that happened," Stoilov said. "We don't have to write off young players just because they are making errors. He will continue to be part of the team, but now he'll have to be much more responsible, to work much harder and to wait for his revenge. Such a mistake happens once in 10 years."

Mihaylov, whose father was keeper for the Bulgarian team that reached the semi-finals at the 1994 World Cup, had only pulled on the gloves because of Georgi Petkov's finger injury. Mihaylov suffered the wrath of Levski supporters, who started booing him every time he touched the ball, and it was no surprise when he was substituted at half-time. His place between the posts was filled by 19 year-old Bozhidar Mitrev, making his senior debut.

Levski had made a bright enough start at Vasil Levski stadium with Nigerian midfielder Richard Eromoigbe and Croatian-born defender Igor Tomasic coming close to scoring midway through the first half. "It was a pity as Werder got their opener when we looked like the better side," Stoilov said. "But we are lacking experience and self confidence."

STATE OF PLAY   GROUP A

	P	W	D	L	F	A	Pts
CHELSEA	4	3	1	0	8	3	10
WERDER BREMEN	4	2	1	1	6	3	7
BARCELONA	4	1	2	1	8	4	5
LEVSKI SOFIA	4	0	0	4	1	13	0

Levski striker Hristo Yovov said there was little his team could do against such a strong opposition. "It was a good lesson for us," he said. "The Germans were the better side and they deserved to win. It's obvious that we're still not strong enough to compete in the Champions League. We've lost any chances of progressing, but we'll have to show some good football in the remaining matches."

Levski are bottom of Group A with no points from their four matches. They have now scored just once while conceding 13 goals.

"Such a mistake happens once in 10 years."
Stanimir Stoilov, Levski Sofia coach

Torsten Frings celebrates his goal against Levski

Werder Bremen's Miroslav Klose (R) challenges Levski Sofia's Richard Eromoigbe

Liverpool 3 v Bordeaux 0
Group C
Anfield
Attendance: 41,978

Benitez shocked everyone by not tinkering with his starting line-up for the first time in 99 matches

LIVERPOOL 3 v **BORDEAUX 0**

Referee
Markus Merk (Germany)

Assistant Referee
Heiner Müller (Germany)
Jan-Hendrik Salver (Germany)

Fourth Official
Manuel Graefe (Germany)

Scorers
23', 76'	Luis Garcia
71'	Gerrard

Teams
Liverpool		Bordeaux	
25	Reina	Ramé	16
23	Carragher	Cid	25
03	Finnan	Jemmali	13
04	Hyypia	Marange	23
06	Riise	Ducasse	19
14	Alonso	Faubert	18
08	Gerrard	Menegazzo	05
10	Luis Garcia	Micoud	14
22	Sissoko	Wendel	17
15	Crouch	Chamakh	29
18	Kuyt	Darcheville	09

Substitutes
58'	> 32 Zenden < 14 Alonso	12 Perea > 29 Chamakh <	12'
73'	> 16 Pennant < 15 Crouch	26 Obertan > 09 Darcheville <	59'
78'	> 09 Fowler < 10 Luis Garcia	24 Mavuba > 14 Micoud <	75'

Discipline
55'	Sissoko	Menegazzo	67'

Liverpool		Bordeaux
1	Yellow cards	0
0	Red cards	1
9	Shots on target	3
11	Shots off target	10
14	Fouls committed	18
2	Corners	2
4	Offsides	1
38' 07"	Ball. Poss. (time)	21' 59"
65%	Ball. Poss. (%)	35%

Rafa Benitez booked Liverpool's place in the last 16 and laid the controversy which had surrounded the club to rest in one fell swoop.

Benitez caused a shock...by naming an unchanged team for the first time in 99 games. He picked the 11 who beat Aston Villa on Saturday and Steven Gerrard admitted: "We were told the side an hour before kick-off and the lads looked round in astonishment when he kept the same team!"

Liverpool went ahead through Luis Garcia's 23rd-minute strike. Garcia has a habit of scoring in the UEFA Champions League and he was there just beyond the far post to meet a Gerrard cross with a left-foot volley which bounced away from Ulrich Ramé into the far corner. After that Liverpool absorbed constant pressure from the visiting side, but controversy reigned after Brazilian

Bordeaux's Fernando Menegazzo departs after being shown a red card

Momo Sissoko fires in a shot

about Riise's behaviour. "I thought English football was about fair play," he grumbled. "Just before the sending off we put the ball into the stands and Liverpool were supposed to give it to us back, but they didn't. They tried to score a goal instead and I was disappointed with that. Liverpool should not need to resort to that. I felt it was a turning point in the game. It's not the only reason why we lost but it was a key moment."

Liverpool quickly added two more goals. Steven Gerrard notched his first of the season and Garcia wrapped it up. Gerrard skipped on to Boudewijn Zenden's pass to steer his first club goal of the season beyond the exposed Ulrich Ramé to relieve the tension. Benitez said: "Steven has been searching for that goal. When you have scored 23 one season and it takes a long time in the next campaign to get off the mark, then you do get worried."

David Jemmali's horrible error presented Luis García with his second goal – his 10th in the Champions League in 23 appearances – five minutes later, with the substitute Robbie Fowler unfortunate not to score amid a succession of late chances.

As for the controversy, the Liverpool director who launched an anonymous attack on Benitez quit hours before the big game. Former chairman Noel White had stunned fellow boardroom members when he had anonymously blasted Benitez's rotation policy a week earlier.

White was sorry to be leaving, but accepted he had no choice. "For the 21 years I have had the privilege of being a director of this great institution my guiding principle has been to act in the best interests of the club," he said. "In view of the controversy caused by comments in a national newspaper, attributed to an anonymous director, and the effect this has had on the chairman, my fellow directors, the manager and many supporters, I feel the honourable course is to resign."

Liverpool chairman David Moores called for everyone at Anfield to pull together in the wake of White's resignation. Moores warned there was no place for taking the club's business outside the walls of Anfield. "This is very sad for both the club and Mr White, who has

midfielder Fernando Menegazzo's brutal headbutt on John Arne Riise.

Liverpool's Norwegian defender had blood pouring from a wound above his left eye after the 67th-minute incident. Benitez said: "It was a headbutt and you could see the blood. You do not like to see things like that on the pitch. You want to see goals and good football played rather than this kind of thing. But it made a difference because after the sending off there was more space for us to play in."

With Liverpool leading 1-0, Bordeaux's Menegazzo lost his cool over a disputed throw-in. Menegazzo, enraged by Riise failing to return the ball after Bordeaux pumped the ball into touch with a team-mate on the turf, thrust his head into the Norwegian's face. The Brazilian was dismissed, departing with a scowl, and Bordeaux's hopes went with him.

Bordeaux coach Ricardo Gomes offered no excuses for Menegazzo's conduct, though he was just as scathing

Steven Gerrard bigs up the celebrations after his first goal of the campaign

Luis Garcia enjoys his second, and Liverpool's third, goal

"We were told the side an hour before kick-off and the lads looked round in astonishment when he kept the same team!"
Steve Gerrard, Liverpool captain

been a valuable member of the board for 21 years," said Moores. "However, the board considers that the statements made do not reflect its own views and that this is not the Liverpool way of doing business. It is vital that we pull together at all times whether on the field or off it."

Benítez reflected on the resignation of White, whose public criticism of the management team had not been shared by the chairman or fellow board members. "It is a pity, I have not had a bad relationship with Noel White and I am sorry this has happened. Now, though, I would prefer to look to the future."

Benítez then turned to his side's victory, which puts them in the knock-out stage with two games to spare, "This is important for us, and it gives us the chance now to go on and win the group in our next match here against PSV Eindhoven. Then we can maybe make changes for the last game and give young players European experience."

PSV EINDHO'N 2 v GALATASARAY 0

Referee
Martin Hansson (Sweden)

Assistant Referee
Stefan Wittberg (Sweden)
Henrik Andren (Sweden)

Fourth Official
Hakan Jonasson (Sweden)

Scorers

59'	Simons
84'	A Koné

Teams

01	Gomes	Mondragon	01
14	Da Costa	Ak	05
04	Alex	Song	04
02	Kromkamp	Tomas	02
23	Salcido	Akman	18
20	Afelley	Ilic	22
08	Cocu	Inamoto	23
11	Mendez	Sarioglu	55
06	Simons	Hasan Sas	11
17	Farfan	Turan	66
10	A Koné	Karan	99

Substitutes

45'	> 15 Culina < 02 Kromkamp	19 Haspolatli > 66 Turan <	67'
76'	> 07 Väyrynen < 20 Afelley	10 Ates > 22 Ilic <	70'
86'	> 16 Aisatti < 10 A Koné	09 Hakan Sukur > 99 Karan <	79'

Discipline

	Turan	27'
	Tomas	38'
	Haspolatli	73'
	Inamoto	88'

0	Yellow cards	3
0	Red cards	1
7	Shots on target	1
14	Shots off target	2
11	Fouls committed	13
8	Corners	3
66	Offsides	0
31' 40"	Ball. Poss. (time)	28' 20"
55%	Ball. Poss. (%)	45%

PSV Eindhoven 2 v Galatasaray 0
Group C
Philips Stadion
Attendance: 35,000

PSV Eindhoven's Timmy Simons scores against Galatasaray

PSV Eindhoven ensured their place in the last 16 alongside Liverpool.

The Dutch side moved on to 10 points with a 2-0 win over Galatasaray at the Philips Stadion. Belgium midfielder Timmy Simons netted the first for the Dutch in the 59th minute and Ivory Coast striker Arouna Kone (84) made sure of the win. Galatasaray, who had been in control for much of the first half, had been reduced to 10 men after 38 minutes when Croatian defender Stjepan Tomas saw red after wrestling Farfan to the ground as he bore down on goal.

After the dismissal Koeman's men started to pass the ball around and attempted to take advantage of the

*Galatasaray's Stepjan Tomas departs after receiving a red card
from Sweden's referee Martin Hansson*

Eindhoven coach Ronald Koeman encourages his team into the last 16

dismissal, but ultimately it was a comfortable night for PSV.

PSV coach Ronald Koeman was surprised by his team's progress after they reached the last 16 of the Champions League with two group games to spare. PSV, who drew their opening match against Liverpool, secured their spot among Europe's finest after four matches. Ajax, the 1995 champions, had always needed at least five matches to qualify for the next stage.

"It is strange to see the group standings right now," Koeman observed. "It is surprising what we did in only four matches, but despite some changes we had we have a real team already. The new boys adjusted perfectly and the squad understands there is more in it. We have to see where it ends."

It is the third year in succession the Dutch champions have reached the last 16, but Koeman was targeting a big finish for the group stage. "With two matches left we want to get a maximum result," he said. A score draw at Anfield and a win over Bordeaux would be enough to top Group C.

"This is luxury and we didn't expect it after the draw, because we thought it was a tough group," midfielder Simons said. "We are getting better every week also because our performances in the Dutch league give us more confidence. We have a tight team that rarely gives away any chances, while our offence always is dangerous."

extra space created by their man advantage, and they took the lead after 59 minutes. Farfan's free-kick from the right was headed towards goal by Philip Cocu and Mondragon could only palm the ball into the air, leaving Simons to nod it in at the far post.

Now Farfan was rampant. The Galatasaray defence could not contain him, and he provided PSV with a wonderful chance to double their lead after 65 minutes, but Kone – unmarked – headed wide of an open goal from the Peruvian's inch-perfect cross after good work down the right wing.

Galatasaray coach Eric Gerets brought Hakan Sukur on for the last ten minutes in a final attempt to get something out of the game. The veteran striker had come off the bench to score on Saturday, but he could not repeat the trick here and PSV sealed their place in the last 16 with a second after 84 minutes. Kone beat Junichi Inamoto and, though he was pushed away from goal as he took the ball around Mondragon and managed to wrap his foot around the ball to hammer it into the empty net.

It was tough on Galatasaray who had looked impressive before Thomas's

BAYERN MUN. 0 v SPORTING LIS. 0

Referee
Massimo Busacca (Switzerland)

Assistant Referee
Stéphane Cuhat (Switzerland)
Francesco Buragina (Switzerland)

Fourth Official
Martin Salm (Switzerland)

Teams

01	Kahn	Ricardo	01
21	Lahm	Caneira	12
30	Lell	Polga	04
02	Sagnol	Souza	13
05	van Buyten	de Castro	27
06	Demichelis	Martins	10
39	Ottl	Moutinho	28
20	Salihamidzic	Paredes	76
10	Makaay	Tello	11
14	Pizarro	Liedson	31
24	Santa Cruz	Yannick	20

Substitutes

45'	> 19 dos Santos		18 da Cunha >		45'
	< 30 Lell		10 Martins <		
79'	> 08 Karimi		21 Farnerud >		52'
	< 24 Santa Cruz		76 Paredes <		
			19 Alecsandro >		78'
			20 Yannick <		

Discipline

50'	van Buyten	de Castro	80'
57'	Demichelis	da Cunha	88'

2	Yellow cards	2
0	Red cards	0
5	Shots on target	1
11	Shots off target	16
13	Fouls committed	12
6	Corners	4
0	Offsides	2
35' 58"	Ball. Poss. (time)	26' 03"
58%	Ball. Poss. (%)	42%

Bayern Munich 0 v Sporting Lisbon 0
Group B
Allianz Arena
Attendance: 66,000

Oliver Kahn applauds his fans after Bayern clinch their place in the last 16

Bayern Munich went through to the last 16 following a goalless draw at home to Sporting Lisbon.

With Mark van Bommel, Owen Hargreaves and Bastian Schweinsteiger all unavailable, Bayern coach Felix Magath selected full-back Willy Sagnol to play in midfield and promoted the rarely used Christian Lell to occupy his place at right-back. The reshuffle barely worked. It was hard to remember Bayern looking less comfortable in a home match than they did in the first 45 minutes against the Portuguese side.

Amid jeers from a full house at the Allianz Arena, Magath made amends at half-time, taking off Lell, putting Sagnol back in his usual place and bringing on the Paraguayan Julio Dos Santos.

Bayern looked more secure as a result and with better finishing from Roy Makaay they would have made it four wins out of four. Bayern really should have taken the lead 10 minutes later when Makaay reached Martin Demichelis' through-ball, but he fired over from close range. Just to prove it was not going to be the Dutchman's night, he then missed the best opportunity of the game, firing at Ricardo with Sagnol once again the provider.

First place, however, is still in their grasp. Magath was quick to own up to his mistake. "The starting side was clearly not the ideal formation," Magath conceded. "I thought that Sagnol could make up for the absence of van Bommel in midfield but it didn't work out. The good thing is that we kept

> ## "If that free-kick had gone in we would have been in trouble."
> ### Oliver Kahn, Bayern Munich

Roy Makaay fails to find a way past Sporting Lisbon's goalkeeper Ricardo

another clean sheet and it still looks very good in terms of finishing as group winners. There's no reason now why we shouldn't go and win in Moscow to make sure."

Sporting bamboozled the Bayern midfield with their neat passing and sharp running in the first half, but they rarely found the right final ball and Oliver Kahn, in fact, had few saves to make. The closest they came was a free-kick from wonderkid Joao Moutinho that hit the bar. Kahn also made an excellent save from Custodio's shot, which took a deflection off the heal of Martin Demichelis, but was saved by the diving Bayern number one.

Kahn recognised Bayern had been lucky to escape. "It really wasn't easy against such mobile opponents," Kahn admitted. "If that free-kick had gone in we would have been in trouble."

Bayern Munich's French defender Willy Sagnol (2ndL) and Peruvian forward Claudio Pizarro (3rdL) challenge Sporting Lisbon's midfielder Carlos Martins (L)

SPARTAK MOS. 0 v **INTER MILAN 1**

Referee
Claus Bo Larsen (Denmark)

Assistant Referee
Bill René Hansen (Denmark)
Henrik Sonderby (Denmark)

Fourth Official
Peter Rasmussen (Denmark)

Scorers
Cruz 01'

Teams

30	Kowalewski	Julio César	12
13	Jiránek	Burdisso	16
15	Kovac	Cordoba	02
17	Rodriguez	Maicon	13
49	Shishkin	Materazzi	23
03	Stranzl	Zanetti	04
23	Bistrov	Dacourt	15
07	Boyarinstev	Figo	07
24	Mozart	Stankovic	05
09	Titov	Cruz	09
10	Pavlyuchenko	Ibrahimovic	08

Substitutes

45'	> 19 Cavenaghi < 17 Rodriguez	11 Grosso > 07 Figo <	72'
52'	> 27 Covaliciuc < 23 Bistrov	21 Solari > 09 Cruz <	84'

Discipline

0	Yellow cards	0
0	Red cards	0
3	Shots on target	6
10	Shots off target	6
12	Fouls committed	15
6	Corners	1
4	Offsides	1
31' 52"	Ball. Poss. (time)	25' 02"
56%	Ball. Poss. (%)	44%

Spartak Moscow 0 v Inter Milan 1
Group B
Luzhniki Stadium
Attendance: 40,000

Inter Milan's Julio Cruz (R) celebrates with team-mate Luis Figo after scoring in the first minute against Spartak Moscow

Julio Cruz scored the only goal for Inter in the first minute to secure a 1-0 win away at Spartak Moscow and move Inter Milan up to second in Group B, ahead of Sporting Lisbon.

The Spartak players almost missed the start of the game after being stuck in traffic on their way to the Luzhniki Olympic stadium and had to use Moscow underground to the ground. They were consequently slow starters and a couple of defensive howlers allowed Zlatan Ibrahimovic to break clear down the right and cross for the Argentinian forward to slot home.

As the temperature dropped well below zero, the Italians were content to sit back and rely on counter-attacks. Cruz had a good chance to double the lead late in the first half but missed the far post from the edge of the box after being left unmarked on the left.

Inter's Dejan Stankovic (L) and Spartak's Vladimir Bystrov fight for the ball

Spartak's coach Vladimir Fedotov calls time on his side's UEFA Champions League ambitions

Spartak rarely threatened the Inter goal before the break, Brazilian midfielder Mozart testing Julio Cesar with a long-range effort for their only real scoring chance.

The second half began in a similar fashion as Ibrahimovic wasted a great chance to make it 2-0 in the first minute after the re-start only to head wide from point-blank range. Spartak defender Roman Shishkin hit the crossbar with a powerful blast from 30 metres late in the match as the Russians pressed for an equalizer, but the visitors withstood the treat.

Dejan Stankovic could have added a second for Inter in injury time, but failed to lob the ball over onrushing Woiciech Kowalewski after going one-on-one with the Spartak keeper.

Inter Milan boss Roberto Mancini remarked, "It was important to win. Spartak are an excellent team and we had many worrying moments. We were tired and wasted a lot of scoring chances. We are very satisfied now. We won, we won away, and we won on artificial turf."

"You just can't afford to give a goal away to a team like Inter in the first minute."
Yegor Titov, Spartak captain

SHAKHTAR D. 2 v VALENCIA 2

Referee
Peter Fröjdfeldt (Sweden)
Assistant Referee
Fredrik Nilsson (Sweden)
Kenneth Petersson (Sweden)
Fourth Official
Åke Andreasson (Sweden)

Scorers

02'	Jadson	Morientes	18'
28'	Fernandinho	Ayala	68'

Teams

35	Shust	Canizares	01
27	Chigrynskiy	Ayala	04
03	Hubschman	Miguel	02
07	Fernandinho	Moretti	24
18	Lewandowski	Navarro	17
09	Matuzalem	Albiol	20
26	Rat	Edu	22
38	Jadson	Silva	21
33	Srna	Angulo	10
17	Aghahowa	Morientes	09
25	Brandao	Villa	07

Substitutes

75'	> 29 Marica < 25 Brandao	15 Joaquin > 09 Morientes <	77'
80'	> 06 Duljaj < 07 Fernandinho	16 Hugo Viana > 17 Navarro <	87'
		11 Regueiro > 07 Villa <	90'

Discipline

47'	Brandao	Villa	55'
53'	Hubschman	Angulo	90'
66'	Srna		
75'	Lewandowski		
84'	Matuzalem		

5	Yellow cards	2
0	Red cards	0
10	Shots on target	5
9	Shots off target	5
20	Fouls committed	9
4	Corners	5
1	Offsides	2
29' 09"	Ball. Poss. (time)	25' 49"
53%	Ball. Poss. (%)	47%

STATE OF PLAY — GROUP D

	P	W	D	L	F	A	Pts
VALENCIA	4	3	1	0	10	5	10
ROMA	4	2	1	1	7	3	7
OLYMPIAKOS	4	0	2	2	5	8	2
SHAKHTAR DON.	4	0	2	2	4	10	2

Shakhtar Donetsk 2 v Valencia 2
Group D
Shakhtar Stadium
Attendance: 25,000

Qualification sparks mass celebrations amongst the Valencia players

Valencia qualified for the knock-out stages after twice coming from behind to secure a 2-2 draw away to Shakhtar Donetsk.

In a see-saw match, Donetsk relied on their Brazilian imports, with Jadson drawing first blood two minutes into the game by curling a free-kick over the wall. Shakhtar had more opportunities soon after, with Brazilian Matuzalem hitting a post in the ninth minute and Julius Aghahowa denied by Valencia keeper Santiago Canizares four minutes later. Fernando Morientes evened the score at the 18 minute mark when he reacted sharply to a loose ball as the Shakhtar defence failed to clear a free-kick to net his fourth goal in the group stages.

Fernandinho put the home side ahead again after 28 minutes when he fired in a drive from more than 20 metres that eluded Canizares. The visitors roared back in the 67th minute when an unmarked Robert Ayala easily headed home a corner. Shakhtar pressed in the late stages, but had few real scoring opportunities.

Valencia's David Navarro was carried off on a stretcher after suffering a serious nose injury in a collision involving several players in his own area.

Jadson celebrates the opening goal from a curling free-kick

DID YOU KNOW?
Both Jadson and Fernandinho scored their first Champions League goals against Valencia

Goalscorer Fernandinho (R) of Shakhtar Donetsk fights for the ball with Valencia's David Silva

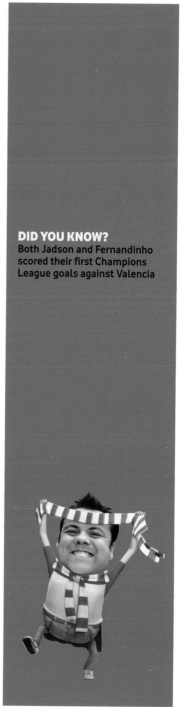

AS ROMA 1 v **OLYMPIAKOS 1**

Referee
Olegário Benquerença (Portugal)

Assistant Referee
José Cardinal (Portugal)
Bertino Miranda (Portugal)

Fourth Official
Paulo Pereira (Portugal)

Scorers

66'	Totti	
	Júlio César	19'

Teams

32	Doni	Nikopolidois 71
13	Chivu	Julio César 55
21	Ferrari	Domi 03
05	Mexes	Kostoulas 19
02	Panucci	Patsatzoglou 02
08	Aquilani	Zewlakow 14
16	De Rossi	Djordjevic 11
07	Pizarro	Maric 08
11	Taddei	Stoltidis 06
22	Tonetto	Konstantinou 23
10	Totti	Rivaldo 10

Substitutes

45'	> 20 Perrotta < 21 Ferrari	32 Anatolakis > 02 Patsatzoglou <	65'
63'	> 23 Vucinic < 08 Aquilani	18 Borja > 11 Djordjevic <	86'
		01 Kafes > 08 Maric <	90'

Discipline

90'	Totti	Kostoulas	26'
90'	Pizarro	Julio César	31'
		Konstantinou	47'
		Djordjevic	79'

2	Yellow cards	4
0	Red cards	0
7	Shots on target	4
9	Shots off target	4
16	Fouls committed	17
5	Corners	4
9	Offsides	2
33' 56"	Ball. Poss. (time)	25' 10"
58%	Ball. Poss. (%)	43%

AS Roma 1 v Olympiakos 1
Group D
Stadio Olimpico
Attendance: 40,000

Olympiakos' Julio Cesar (R) celebrates with his team mates Christos Patsatzoglou (C) and Milos Maric after scoring against AS Roma

Roma look best placed to join Valencia in the last 16 following a 1-1 draw against Olympiakos in the Stadio Olimpico.

Francesco Totti turned from villain to hero after his penalty kick shortly after the half-hour mark was saved by Olympiakos goalkeeper Antonios Nikopolidis as he scored a vital equaliser in the second half.

The Greek side were searching for a much-needed victory in the Group D showdown and began in confident fashion earning two corners in the opening minutes. They almost broke the deadlock with Christian Chivu's poor clearance proving an assist for Rivaldo, whose right-footed effort forced Roma goal-keeper Alexander Doni to dive to his left to clear.

STATE OF PLAY — GROUP D

	P	W	D	L	F	A	Pts
VALENCIA	4	3	1	0	10	5	10
ROMA	4	2	1	1	7	3	7
OLYMPIAKOS	4	0	2	2	5	8	2
SHAKHTAR DON.	4	0	2	2	4	10	2

Even Rivaldo's presence couldn't secure the three points for Olympiakos

Just when Roma started to come to life, Olympiakos struck. Julio Cesar latched onto a corner kick and got in ahead of Daniele De Rossi and Matteo Ferrari inside the box to head past Doni.

Midway through the first half, the Roma fans demanded a penalty after an apparent handball by Michal Zewlakow from Tonetto's cross but the referee waved play on. The Italians continued to press forward and should have equalised shortly after but Christian Panucci failed to apply the finishing touch after Nikopolidis had been unable to hold onto Totti's powerful free-kick.

Roma were given a helping hand when the referee did point to the spot after Julio Cesar brought down Rodrigo Taddei inside the area. But Totti saw his penalty saved by Nikopolidis. The miss seemed to spur Roma on and Aquilani's right-footed effort from outside the area went wide.

Substitute Simone Perrotta tried his luck from outside the area early in the second half, but his effort went wide and, on the hour mark, the Italy international had a goal disallowed for a clear offside. Coach Spalletti made his second substitution shortly after, with Mirko Vucinic taking Aquilani's place upfront. Vucinic made an impact straight away, with his close-range effort towards the far post forcing Nikopolidis to fully stretch to clear.

Roma's prayers were finally answered with Taddei serving Totti inside the area, who controlled the ball before firing past Nikopolidis. The goal inspired the hosts, who surged forward determined to take the lead.

Olympiakos survived several late scares with David Pizarro and Vucinic going close for Roma, but Nikopolidis made sure his team took home a point that keeps them in the competition.

DID YOU KNOW?
Trond Sollied's Olympiakos were trying to make club history by winning a game on the road for the first time in Europe's elite competition, but for the 30th time they were denied

Match Day 4
Wednesday 1 November 2006

Copenhagen 1 v Manchester United 0
Group F
Parken Stadion
Attendance: 40,000

Marcus Allback slams home the winning goal to send makeshift Manchester United to defeat in Copenhagen

Manchester United's progress to the knockout stages stalled on a night of sub-zero temperatures and sub-standard performances as Marcus Allback, a striker who managed only six goals in two years at Aston Villa, stabbed in the decisive goal 73 minutes to ruin United's immaculate record in Group F.

The Premiership leaders were desperately short of their best form, taking the gloss off Sir Alex's 20th-anniversary commemorations over the next week. Ferguson was justified in complaining about the effects of a Bruce Springsteen concert the previous weekend on the pitch. Downpours throughout the afternoon of the game and even the odd blizzard exacerbated the rutting of the surface. "The pitch was very difficult and that's why it was the game it was," said Ferguson. "There wasn't a lot of football. It wasn't an easy pitch and it took us 20 minutes just to get any rhythm."

Ferguson was stretching the truth when he said United had been "in control of the match" and insisted he was happy with the number of chances they created as well as making several disparaging remarks about Copenhagen, effectively portraying their tactics as no more refined than the 80s Wimbledon and sniping that "what football there was came from us. We knew they would play a lot of long balls into our area and I felt we defended very well apart from the one instance and it cost us the game."

Yet his team selection had hinted at a feeling that all United had to do was turn up and a win would be theirs against the Champions League newcomers. With Ryan Giggs, Louis Saha and Gary Neville injured, he picked only five first-team certs, making six changes from his side that had torn Bolton apart 4-0 at the weekend.

Rooney and Ronaldo were strangely peripheral while Ole Gunnar Solskjaer eventually left the pitch with a hamstring strain. An injury to Nemanja Vidic reinforced a hugely disappointing night.

FC Copenhagen's goalkeeper Jesper Christiansen saves a typically cheeky Paul Scholes lob

Rooney heads for goal

COPENHAGEN 1 v **MAN UNITED 0**

Referee
Wolfgang Stark (Germany)
Assistant Referee
Harry Ehing (Germany)
Christian Dingert (Germany)
Fourth Official
Günter Perl (Germany)

Scorers

73'   Allbäck

Teams

01	Christiansen	van der Sar	01
14	Gravgaard	Brown	06
05	Hangeland	Heinze	04
02	Jacobsen	O'Shea	22
17	Wendt	Silvestre	27
28	Bergvold	Vidic	15
13	Hutchinson	Carrick	16
06	Linderoth	Fletcher	24
04	Nørregaard	Ronaldo	07
08	Silberbauer	Rooney	08
11	Allbäck	Solskjaer	20

Substitutes

68'	> 09 Berglund < 28 Bergvold	05 Ferdinand > 15 Vidic <	45'
71'	> 23 Kvist < 08 Silberbauer	18 Scholes > 24 Fletcher <	71'
89'	> 16 Thomasen < 11 Allbäck	03 Evra > 04 Heinze <	80'

Discipline

28'	Hangeland	Ronaldo	82'

1	Yellow cards	1
0	Red cards	0
3	Shots on target	4
4	Shots off target	9
15	Fouls committed	14
7	Corners	2
5	Offsides	6
24' 42"	Ball. Poss. (time)	34' 56"
41%	Ball. Poss. (%)	59%

STATE OF PLAY					GROUP F		
	P	W	D	L	F	A	Pts
MAN UNITED	4	3	0	1	7	3	9
CELTIC	4	2	0	2	6	6	6
BENFICA	4	1	1	2	3	4	4
COPENHAGEN	4	1	1	2	1	4	4

Rooney trudges off after a 17th consecutive European match without scoring

O'Shea squandered their most inviting opportunity, 10 minutes after the interval, and it was to be a costly miss.

Heinze failed to clear as Atiba Hutchinson headed down a left-wing cross for Allback inside the six-yard area who poked the ball past the hopelessly exposed van der Sar. "It was a bad goal for us to lose because we knew their danger was from set pieces," Ferguson said. "Until then our defending had been very good and they had never looked like scoring."

Scholes, a substitute, had a late chance to salvage a draw, but the goalkeeper Jesper Christiansen charged down his attempted lob. Then Ronaldo turned in Rooney's stoppage-time cross only for the effort to be disallowed because he was offside. The linesman's flag means United's qualification will have to wait until, at least, the visit to Celtic in 19 days.

If the defeat was not bad enough for United, reminiscent of a far more costly loss against Lille last season which saw United crash out of the competition, Ferguson must also do without veteran striker Solskjaer for the foreseeable future after he limped off with a hamstring injury in the final minute when United had already used their three allotted substitutes.

Jesper Christiansen and Brede Hangeland celebrate defeating Manchester United

> **"There wasn't a lot of football. It wasn't an easy pitch and it took us 20 minutes just to get any rhythm."**
> **Sir Alex Ferguson**

Benfica 3 v Celtic 0
Group F
Stadium of Light
Attendance: 49,000

BENFICA 3 v **CELTIC 0**

Referee
Kyros Vassaras (Greece)
Assistant Referee
Dimitrios Bozatzidis (Greece)
Dimitris Saraidaris (Greece)
Fourth Official
Christoforos Zografos (Greece)

Scorers

10'	Caldwell og
22'	Nuno Gomes
76'	Karyaka

Teams

12	Quim	Boruc 01
05	Leo	Caldwell 05
04	da Silva	Naylor 03
22	Nélson	Telfer 02
33	Rocha	Lennon 18
25	Assis	McManus 44
08	Katsouranis	Nakamura 25
06	Petit	Pearson 11
20	Simao	Sno 15
21	Gomes	Maloney 29
30	Miccoli	Miller 09

Substitutes

33'	> 19 Karyaka < 30 Miccoli	46 McGeady > 29 Maloney <	65'
84'	> 16 Beto < 06 Petit	07 Zurawski > 15 Sno <	72'
89'	> 09 Mantorras < 21 Gomes		

Discipline

28'	Rocha	Sno	05'
54'	Leo	Maloney	55'
		Pearson	87'

2	Yellow cards	3
0	Red cards	0
4	Shots on target	1
12	Shots off target	4
18	Fouls committed	15
6	Corners	3
8	Offsides	4
29' 32"	Ball. Poss. (time)	29' 31"
50%	Ball. Poss. (%)	50%

Celtic's Lisbon Lions receive a standing ovation from the entire crowd, but their feat of winning the European Cup in 1967 could not be matched by their modern day counterparts

Celtic's previous two trips to Lisbon had been indelibly etched in the minds of their supporters and the lions of Lisbon were there to relive past glories. But defender Gary Caldwell will want to erase memories of this game after scoring an own-goal and being at fault for Benfica's second as Celtic's dismal run away from home in the Champions League continued.

Gordon Strachan's side, with nine defeats and one draw in their past 10 away games in the tournament, were comprehensively defeated after Nuno Gomes and Andrei Karyaka added to Caldwell's own goal.

The competition's head-to-head rule means this result cancels out his side's victory by the same scoreline over Benfica in Glasgow, and United's defeat in Copenhagen ensures there will be no charity from Sir Alex at Parkhead on November 21. "That was a poor performance by the group, including myself," Strachan said. "We now have to analyse it and be honest about it. It's a learning process. There

Nuno Gomes sends the Stadium of Light wild with the second goal

STATE OF PLAY — GROUP F

	P	W	D	L	F	A	Pts
MAN UNITED	4	3	0	1	7	3	9
CELTIC	4	2	0	2	6	6	6
BENFICA	4	1	1	2	3	4	4
COPENHAGEN	4	1	1	2	1	4	4

Gary Caldwell, on ground, has just put the ball past goalkeeper Artur Boruc for an own goal

are three teams going for second place now."

The Scottish champions lifted the European Cup in Lisbon in 1967 and won a tie against Benfica two years later on the toss of a coin, but Celtic began this match nervously and Caldwell had

Celtic's Shaun Maloney in full flight

already been fortunate not to concede a penalty after a tackle on Fabrizio Miccoli before he turned a tantalising cross from Nelson beyond Artur Boruc. Then, after 22 minutes, he inexplicably failed to deal with a routine ball from the home goalkeeper, Quim, and as the ball rebounded

from the defender's face, Nuno Gomes was on hand to strike home a well-deserved second goal.

A warm reception for the surviving members of Celtic's 1967 side, especially from the 8,000 Celtic fans inside the Stadium of Light, during the half-time break was welcome relief for the travelling fans, but the class of 2006 failed to improve their mood. Karyaka, a Benfica substitute, finished the contest as he side-footed past Boruc from 18 yards after a pass from the out-standing Nelson.

Celtic's chances were few and far between. Caldwell almost made amends for his earlier mistakes when his hooked shot from 12 yards was saved on the line by Quim before the ball was eventually cleared to safety and in the dying seconds, a Nakamura free-kick from 25 yards was well-saved by Quim.

"The group is much more open now," said Benfica's manager Fernando Santos. "The 3-0 result in Glasgow a fortnight ago was not fair. We believed we could rectify that result and we did that tonight."

Andrei Karyaka scores to make it 3-0

Gordon Strachan contemplates the tough task of qualifying after a comprehensive defeat

"The group is much more open now."
Fernando Santos, Benfica manager

ARSENAL 0 v **CSKA MOSCOW 0**

Referee
Lubos Michel (Slovakia)
Assistant Referee
Roman Csabay (Slovakia)
Marián Ruzbarsky (Slovakia)
Fourth Official
Richard Havrilla (Slovakia)

Teams

01	Lehmann	Akinfeev	35
22	Clichy	Berezoutski	06
10	Gallas	Berezoutski	24
31	Hoyte	Ignashevitch	04
05	Toure	Semberas	02
19	Gilberto Silva	Carvalho	07
04	Fabregas	Krasic	17
13	Hleb	Rahimic	25
07	Rosicky	Dudu	20
14	Henry	Zhirkov	18
11	van Persie	Vagner Love	11

Substitutes

71'	> 32 Walcott < 13 Hleb	22 Aldonin > 17 Krasic <	40'
82'	> 30 Aliadiere < 11 van Persie	09 Olic > 11 Vagner Love <	85'
89'	> 16 Flamini < 04 Fabregas	39 Taranov > 07 Carvalho <	90'

Discipline

02'	Henry	Berezoutski	45'
53'	Hleb	Semberas	90'

2	Yellow cards	2
0	Red cards	0
5	Shots on target	1
18	Shots off target	4
18	Fouls committed	15
4	Corners	4
7	Offsides	3
42' 28"	Ball. Poss. (time)	23' 54"
64%	Ball. Poss. (%)	36%

STATE OF PLAY — GROUP G

	P	W	D	L	F	A	Pts
CSKA MOSCOW	4	2	2	0	2	0	8
ARSENAL	4	2	1	1	4	2	7
PORTO	4	2	1	1	7	4	7
HAMBURG	4	0	0	4	3	10	0

Arsenal 0 v CSKA Moscow 0
Group G
Emirates Stadium
Attendance: 60,003

A disbelieving Wenger pleads for a goal, but one was not forthcoming

Arsenal squandered an incredible host of chances in as one-sided a goalless draw has ever been seen, to the utter frustration of their manager.

"The normal score in this game is 7-0, maybe 7-1 because they had a chance as well," said Arsène Wenger, and the assessment was no overstatement. "We created nine clear-cut chances to win the game without scoring. There was a division between the teams."

Thierry Henry had complained in his programme notes about the groans with which Arsenal fans had greeted their team's failure to put Everton to the sword on Saturday, but the Arsenal captain was twice one-on-one with Igor Akinfeev and both times he uncharacteristically sent the ball narrowly when goals might have seemed easier outcomes. Van Persie also wasted several golden chances before being replaced by Jérémie Aliadière.

The misses became more incredulous by the minute. Following a slick build-up involving Alexander Hleb, striker van Persie snatched at his shot when the ball fell for him on the penalty spot, driving it high into the stands.

Then, after 12 minutes, the Dutchman flashed an effort just wide of the far post from 20 yards. Rosicky then fed Gilberto down the right and his low centre picked out the on-rushing Henry who nipped in front of his marker to reach the ball ahead of diving keeper Igor Akinfeev six yards out but could only guide it the wrong side of the near post. A quick one-two with Rosicky sent Cesc Fabregas clear and he rounded the keeper but hit the side-netting from a tight angle.

After 35 minutes Hleb slipped a pass through to van Persie, who beat the offside trap. However, to do so, the Dutchman was at full stretch and so could only stab the ball past the post.

There was another good chance for Henry in the closing moments of the first half, when he timed his run to perfection and latched on to Rosicky's sweeping pass. However, while the Arsenal captain's deft touch with the outside of his boot guided the ball past

Akinfeev it also drifted just the wrong side of the post.

Henry then returned the favour, cutting the ball back to the Czech midfielder from the left byline. However, two yards out and with the net at his mercy Rosicky could only stab his shot straight at the CSKA keeper, who was already on the ground.

After 65 minutes Henry skipped into the left side of the area and chipped the ball back across goal where van Persie just failed to connect at the far post. Next van Persie, just six yards out, headed wide following a deep cross from the right when it looked easier to score.

CSKA did offer some threat. A 50-yard pass gave Vagner Love a race with William Gallas and it required Jens Lehmann, after being a virtual spectator for much of the match, to deny the Brazilian.

Indeed it could so easily have been worse. Late on, when Henry was the first to unwittingly connect with a

> **"How the shot from Tomas [Rosicky] did not go in, I still ask myself – but sometimes football is a bit weird."**
> Thierry Henry

Thierry Henry falls to his knees after another chance goes begging

Cesc Fabregas wishes the ground would open up and swallow him after a glaring miss

DID YOU KNOW?
Arsenal had 28 shots at goal, of which only 5 were on target in this game

Tomas Rosicky misses an open goal

corner it hit the outside of his own post, to avoid an embarrassing own goal.

Wenger concluded, "I feel this team has great potential and how we mature will determine whether we win a trophy. We were not playing for a trophy tonight but we were playing for qualification. There is nothing mystical about our not scoring, it is simpler than that – we just need to put the ball in the net."

Henry remained ever confident Arsenal were a side about to 'explode' into greatness. He declared: "In a game like that you, are closer to exploding into a great team than not heading in the right direction. When I went in to the dressing room, I said to the guys that we lost the same kind of game against Man City. It is difficult to have a go at the team with the way we played against Moscow. Although I know there is frustration that the result was not there, we are still in a good position to qualify."

Henry admits none of the Arsenal players could believe just how they failed to record a comfortable victory given a performance which Wenger described as the best he had overseen in the UEFA Champions League. The Gunners skipper reflected: "We have won games in Europe during my time when I did not know how we won. Against Moscow, I do not know how we did not. As the skipper, when I walked back into the dressing room I could not say anything to the team. We had the right aggressiveness, the right attitude and played good football. We created chances once again and did not put the ball in the back of the net... Cesc had one, Robin [van Persie] had three. We had so many opportunities. How the shot from Tomas [Rosicky] did not go in, I still ask myself – but sometimes football is a bit weird."

Henry believed the crowd in the new stadium can very much act as a twelfth man. The Arsenal captain said: "They were brilliant – geeing us up when we were missing chances. They were right behind us. I did not have any doubt about it. Right from the start the fans had the right attitude."

Hamburg 1 v Porto 3
Group G
AOL Arena
Attendance: 51,00

Porto's Lisandro Lopez celebrates scoring the second goal past Hamburg's goalkeeper Sascha Kirschstein

HAMBURG 1 v **PORTO 3**

Referee
Laurent Duhamel (France)

Assistant Referee
Vincent Texier (France)
Stéphane Duhamel (France)

Fourth Official
Damien Ledentu (France)

Scorers

62'	van der Vaart	González	44'
		López	61'
		Bruno Moraes	87'

Teams

12	Kirschstein	Helton 01
03	Atouba	Alves 14
10	Kompany	Fucile 13
05	Mathijsen	Pepe 03
02	Sorin	Assuncao 18
07	Mahdavikia	Bosingwa 12
15	Trochowski	González 08
23	van der Vaart	Meireles 16
33	Feilhaber	Quaresma 07
38	Ljuboja	López 09
17	Sanogo	Postiga 23

Substitutes

58'	> 09 Guerrero < 38 Ljuboja		29 Moraes > 23 Postiga <	70'
65'	> 22 Berisha < 03 Atouba		20 Jorginho > 09 López <	82'
71'	> 16 Klingbeil < 10 Kompany		05 Cech > 16 Meireles <	90'

Discipline

60'	van der Vaart	Meireles	64'
		Moraes	77'

1	Yellow cards	2
0	Red cards	0
5	Shots on target	5
17	Shots off target	12
20	Fouls committed	24
7	Corners	2
1	Offsides	0
32' 15"	Ball. Poss. (time)	26' 20"
55%	Ball. Poss. (%)	45%

While Arsenal were being held at home, Porto increased the pressure on them by winning 3-1 in Hamburg.

Porto coach Manuel Ferreira sang the praises of striker Lucho Gonzalez who scored a sublime first goal. Gonzalez, lurking 25 metres out, accepted a weak defensive header in the 44th minute and beat Sascha Kirschstein with a shot that whistled into the top left-hand corner.

"It was a fantastic, fabulous goal," said Ferreira. "It also came at an important time at the end of the first half and I think it was decisive. We have every chance to go on now in the next two games and qualify." Hamburg's meek exit from the Champions League let down German football as well as the club and their fans, according to coach Thomas Doll. Hamburg, the 1983 European champions, saw their faint hopes of progress from Group G extinguished as they had now lost four out of four games. "We represented German football very badly in the Champions League," Doll told reporters after the

players were booed from the pitch at the end of their latest defeat. "We lacked the necessary aggression and the players will have to look at themselves and think about whether they really put everything they had into their performances."

It was only after Porto had increased their lead in the 61st minute through Lisandro Lopez that the home side showed signs of life. Rafael van der Vaart, making his first appearance in the group phase after a long injury lay-off, headed in powerfully from Piotr Trochowski's cross and Hamburg had chances to equalise before substitute Bruno Moraes made the game safe for Porto, cutting in from the right to shoot inside the far post three minutes from time.

"It's simply not good enough to start playing only after you've gone one or two goals down," Doll said. "I can totally understand why the crowd were whistling the players." Hamburg had rotten luck with injuries during the group phase and Doll was hardly helped by the club's decision to sell defenders Khalid Boulahrouz and

STATE OF PLAY — GROUP G

	P	W	D	L	F	A	Pts
CSKA MOSCOW	4	2	2	0	2	0	8
ARSENAL	4	2	1	1	4	2	7
PORTO	4	2	1	1	7	4	7
HAMBURG	4	0	0	4	3	10	0

Daniel van Buyten before the start of the group stage. The team have played poorly in domestic competition, too: they are already out of the German Cup and with nine games played in the Bundesliga they have managed just one win. Doll said he was satisfied he had sufficient quality in the squad, however, and promised a recovery in the Bundesliga. "The quality is there and the players have the right character," he said. "They just have to show it. We now have to concentrate on the Bundesliga and I'm convinced we can come back."

"It is not good enough to start playing only when we are one or two goals down."
Thomas Doll, Hamburg coach

Porto's Bruno Moraes and Raul Meireles (L) celebrate Moraes's clinching third goal against Hamburg

Hamburg coach Thomas Doll watches his side slump to yet another defeat and out of the UEFA Champions League

AC Milan 4 v Anderlecht 1
Group H
San Siro
Attendance: 42,300

Kaká soaks up the plaudits after his hat-trick goal

AC MILAN 4 v **ANDERLECHT 1**

Referee
Herbert Fandel (Germany)

Assistant Referee
Volker Wezel (Germany)
Mike Pickel (Germany)

Fourth Official
Jochen Drees (Germany)

Scorers

06', 22', 56' Kaká	Juhász	61'
88' Gilardino		

Teams

	AC Milan	Anderlecht	
01	Dida	Zitka	01
03	Maldini	Descacht	03
13	Nesta	Juhasz	23
17	Simic	Vanden Borre	37
32	Brocchi	Biglia	05
20	Gourcuff	Boussoufa	11
22	Kaká	De Man	31
18	Jankulovski	Goor	14
10	Seedorf	Hassan	10
11	Gilardino	Vanderhaeghe	04
07	Oliveira	Arouna Kone	10

Substitutes

19'	> 02 Cafu < 13 Nesta	24 Akin > 04 Vanderhaeghe <	40'
66'	> 08 Gattuso < 20 Gourcuff	09 Mpenza > 11 Boussoufa <	80'
72'	> 21 Pirlo < 07 Oliveira	36 Lagaer > 37 Vanden Borre <	85'

Discipline

74'	Gattuso	Biglia	58'
88'	Gilardino	Hassan	83'

2	Yellow cards	2
0	Red cards	0
7	Shots on target	9
12	Shots off target	11
21	Fouls committed	4
6	Corners	3
2	Offsides	2
30' 41"	Ball. Poss. (time)	28' 16"
52%	Ball. Poss. (%)	48%

The win gave the six-times European champions 10 points, five ahead of second-placed Lille with two games to play.

AC Milan coach Carlo Ancelotti described playmaker Kaká as the best in the world, "There are lots of great players in circulation, but nobody is worth as much as him," Ancelotti was quoted as saying in Corriere dello Sport. "Nobody has more determination or is capable of making such a difference in a match. He is better than Ronaldinho."

The 24 year-old put the hosts ahead from the penalty spot in the seventh minute, after Roland Juhasz tripped Alberto Gilardino, then scored once more in each half before Juhasz pulled one back for the visitors just after the hour mark.

Any lingering hopes Anderlecht's players might have harboured about fighting their way back into the contest were blown away, however, when Alberto Gilardino restored Milan's three-goal cushion late on after breaking the offside and thumping the ball home.

His second goal – a lovely, curling shot into the top corner after a one-two with Cafu – followed near misses by team-mates Ricardo Oliveira and Dario Simic.

Anderlecht played more aggressively after the break. Congolese striker Mohamed Tchite got in a couple of snapshots, though neither was on target. After Kaka's third, though, the odds were heavily stacked against an Anderlecht comeback. Once again the goal came out of a solo run by the Brazilian but this time, instead of running directly at the opposition, he cut round a defender on the edge of the area before angling a right-footed shot past keeper Daniel Zitka.

When Juhasz headed Anderlecht's consolation goal from a corner, Milan briefly looked rattled. Left-back Marek Jankulovski almost complicated what should have been a trouble-free night when he botched a clearance and the ball skewed off the post, while Tchite fired in a dangerous ball from close range that Dida managed to smother on his line.

The Brazilian's hat-trick took his tally in the UEFA Champions league this season to five – the same as Chelsea's Didier Drogba. He has scored 16 goals in the competition since joining Milan from Brazilian club Sao Paolo as an unknown 21 year-old in July 2003. According to Ancelotti, it was not only his ability to score that marked Kaká out from his peers. "Ricky has always scored goals, he's an excellent finisher. But he was not always so good at setting up his team-mates," said Ancelotti. "Now, however, he has improved even that aspect of his game. With Kaká in this kind of form, I'm looking forward to seeing who they award the Golden Ball to."

The Golden Ball is the annual prize awarded to the best player in the European leagues. "Certainly, I would like

> ## "Kaká is better than Ronaldinho."
> ### Carlo Ancelloti

AC Milan's Yoann Gourcuff flies into the sky after being tackled by Anderlecht's Juhasz Roland

Kaka's third goal is on its way

to win it very much, but I can only do my duty, then hope that I'm rewarded for the results," Kaká said. "For now, though, I want to play as well as I can for Milan and my national team. I don't feel that I've fulfilled my potential yet. There's always something I can improve on."

DID YOU KNOW?
Perhaps the most appropriately named player in the 2006/07 UEFA Champions League was Anderlecht's Mark De Man. However it would have been even better if he was a defender rather than a midfield player!

AC Milan's Alessandro Nesta (L) fights for the ball with Anderlecht's Mbark Boussoufa

AEK ATHENS 1 v **LILLE 0**

Referee
Steve Bennett (England)

Assistant Referee
David Babski (England)
Peter Kirkup (England)

Fourth Official
Mark Clattenburg (England)

Scorers
74' Liberopoulos

Teams

28	Sorrentino	Sylva	01
05	Cirillo	Chalmé	21
55	Dellas	Plestan	25
31	Georgeas	Tafforeau	20
04	Moras	Tavlaridis	04
25	Emerson	Bodmer	12
56	Hetemaj	Cabaye	07
88	Tozser	Makoun	17
16	Zikos	Robail	18
99	Julio Cezar	Kader Keita	23
33	Lyberopoulos	Odemwingie	14

Substitutes

47'	35 Kapetanos / 25 Emerson	02 Debuchy / 18 Robail	57'
58'	11 Manduca / 99 Cezar	11 Youla / 14 Odemwingie	57'
88'	07 Kiriakidis / 56 Hetemaj	13 Fauvergue / 17 Makoun	77'

Discipline

37'	Dellas	Tavlaridis	03'
71'	Kapetanos	Tavlaridis	22'
		Makoun	36'
		Kader Keita	45'
		Cabaye	76'

2	Yellow cards	5
0	Red cards	0
3	Shots on target	3
9	Shots off target	11
10	Fouls committed	16
5	Corners	3
2	Offsides	0
31' 16"	Ball. Poss. (time)	22' 39"
58%	Ball. Poss. (%)	42%

STATE OF PLAY — GROUP H

	P	W	D	L	F	A	Pts
AC MILAN	4	3	1	0	8	1	10
LILLE	4	1	2	1	4	3	5
AEK ATHENS	4	1	1	2	3	7	4
ANDERLECHT	4	0	2	2	3	7	2

AEK Athens 1 v Lille 0
Group H
Spiros Louis Stadium
Attendance: 14,373

AEK Athens' Nikos Liberopoulos celebrates after scoring the winning goal against Lille

AEK Athens enjoyed their first ever UEFA Champions League win, beating 10-man Lille 1-0. Nikos Liberopoulos scored the only goal.

The Greece striker struck in the 74th minute when he stepped inside Jean Makoun and drilled the ball past the goalkeeper Tony Sylva.

AEK were helped by the dismissal of Lille's Greek defender Efstathios Tavlaridis, who succeeded in collecting two yellow cards in the first 22 minutes. His first came in the third minute when he brought down Liberopoulos outside the penalty area. He was given a let-off by referee Steve Bennett for a crude challenge soon after, but the Englishman could not ignore another clumsy tackle on Perparim Hetemaj and the Greek was sent off.

Lille's response was to defend from deep inside their own half although Mathieu Bodmer forced a good save from Stefano Sorrentino in the AEK goal. AEK, who started with three front men, brought on another striker at half-time as Pantelis Kapetanos replaced Emerson at the interval.

The pressure grew on the Lille defence and after several wasted attempts, AEK finally made the breakthrough 15 minutes from the end.

Lille coach Claude Puel paid tribute to his players. "After the sending off of Tavlaridis, my team kept competing and played well," he said. "But AEK were patient and waited for their opening. We made it hard for them to break us down and I thought we deserved a share of the honours."

AEK coach, Lorenzo Serra Ferrer, could not contain his glee: "Tonight's win is a starting point for us so we can grow as a team and it will also mean a great deal for future of the club."

DID YOU KNOW?
Nikos Liberopoulos's goal allowed AEK Athens to record their first ever win in a Champions League group game at their 22nd attempt

AEK Athens' Pantelis Kapetanos (L) fights for the ball with Lille's Mathieu Debuchy

AEK Athens' Julio Cesar is tackled by Lille's Mathieu Chalme

"Tonight's win is a starting point for us so we can grow as a team and it will also mean a great deal for future of the club."
Lorenzo Serra Ferrer, AEK coach

REAL MADRID 1 v STEAUA BUCH. 0

Referee
Konrad Plautz (Austria)

Assistant Referee
Markus Mayr (Austria)
Egon Bereuter (Austria)

Fourth Official
Bernhard Brugger (Austria)

Scorers

70' Nicolita og

Teams

01	Casillas	Cernea	12
05	Cannavaro	Ghionea	24
03	Roberto Carlos	Goian	03
21	Helguera	Marin	18
04	Sergio Ramos	Stancu	27
06	Diarra	Dica	10
08	Emerson	Nicolita	16
14	Guti	Paraschiv	22
10	Robinho	Petre	08
07	Raul	Badea	09
17	van Nistelrooy	Oprita	07

Substitutes

59'	> 23 Beckham < 06 Diarra	20 F Lovin > 12 Badea <	79'
74'	> 09 Ronaldo < 17 van Nistelrooy	21 Thereau > 20 Paraschiv <	79'
87'	> 19 Reyes < 10 Robinho	28 Coman > 46 Oprita <	85'

Discipline

Petre	18'
Nicolita	37'
Cernea	73'
Goian	75'

0	Yellow cards	4
0	Red cards	0
4	Shots on target	2
12	Shots off target	8
15	Fouls committed	31
5	Corners	3
4	Offsides	4
37' 51"	Ball. Poss. (time)	24' 12"
61%	Ball. Poss. (%)	39%

STATE OF PLAY — GROUP E

	P	W	D	L	F	A	Pts
LYON	4	4	0	0	9	0	12
REAL MADRID	4	3	0	1	10	4	9
STEAUA BUCH.	4	1	0	3	5	9	3
DYNAMO KIEV	4	0	0	4	2	13	0

Real Madrid 1 v Steaua Bucharest 0

Group E
Santiago Bernabeau Stadium
Attendance: 69,000

Beckham's introduction changed Real's fortunes.
Will it make all the difference to their Champions League challenge?

Forgotten man David Beckham came off the bench to inspire a lethargic Real Madrid through to the Champions' League knockout stages and increase his chances of a first-team recall after a week of non-stop speculation about his future.

Beckham was a 59th-minute substitute against Steaua Bucharest and Real scored the decisive goal shortly after his introduction. The former England captain was a constant threat down the right and on 61 minutes his free-kick was headed just wide by the Real defender Sergio Ramos. The pressure finally paid off on 70 minutes when the Steaua defender Banel Nicolita inexplicably put a back pass wide of his own keeper and into his own net with no Real Madrid player anywhere near him.

Real striker Ruud van Nistelrooy spurned the chance to extend his side's lead two minutes later when he blasted a penalty over the bar after he had been brought down by Cernea as he bore down on the goal.

Real had to suffer several nervous moments. Petre Marin forced a sharp save from Iker Casillas with a curling shot from the left and fellow midfielder Daniel Oprita skewed a close-range effort over the bar moments later.

Steve McManaman was revealed as Beckham's unexpected inspiration as he aimed to prove himself a success, despite his lack of apparent favour with coach Fabio Capello, with Real. Macca emerged from the Real Madrid benches to score a wonder goal in the 2000 European Cup final, and end up with two UEFA Champions League winners medals. Beckham was similarly seeking glory in the Champions League to prove himself as one of English football successful exports. The former Liverpool star initially failed to make an impact with Real, but hung on and refused to be forced out and it paid off as he scored in the Final and teamed up for England duty on a high.

A close friend of Beckham's revealed: "Remember what happened to McManaman. He started a quarter of the games in the season he scored in the European Cup Final. David is a big game player, so he was unhappy at not starting major games such as Barcelona and Athletico Madrid, but at this point no-one is panicking. He has started a fifth of the games this season and has come off the bench each time he hasn't started. He only missed one game last week, through injury."

Beckham made it clear that suggestions that he could be sold in January for a cut price fee is way off the mark. In the build up to the Champions League tie he said: "I am happy here. My family are happy here. At the moment I play for Real Madrid. Let's hope it carries on. If it gets to January, nothing changes. I am not leaving. I am not going anywhere in January. I want to stay because I believe we can win something this season."

Beckham also said would be patient as he tries to get back into the Madrid starting line up. But the situation has

Ruud van Nistelrooy celebrates the only goal of the game scored by Steaua's Nicolita, but two minutes later missed a penalty

Raul and Steaua's Petre Martin contest a header

alerted clubs around the world, including Los Angeles Galaxy, Celtic and Tottenham, who have all been linked with a move for the 31 year-old midfielder.

But club President Ramon Calderon insisted all was well in the world of the Galacticos. "I think David Beckham is happy in Madrid and Madrid are happy

Under pressure coach Fabio Capello earned some breathing space with this victory

with David Beckham," said Calderon. "Logic dictates we will continue together. We are a marriage that is working well." A new contract had been agreed with the old regime where Beckham's entourage had won important concessions on image rights. Calderon is not so keen to give up such a big slice to Beckham. Becks and Posh's newly launched perfume has been getting the big sell in Spain; it was everywhere — on TV, billboards, magazines, and hoardings. Brand Beckham has usually been associated with leading companies such as "Police" sun-glasses; Adidas boots, Pepsi soft drinks, but the personal brand of perfume takes it to a new level. It was an incredible turnaround as a year ago Posh was known to want her hubby home in Hertfordshire. Now the Beckhams were not so keen to quit Madrid where they are both enjoying the sweet smell of success off the field and the former England captain still dreams of European Cup success on it.

The result at least guaranteed Real second place at least in Group E with nine points from four games, three behind leaders Olympique Lyon and six ahead of Steaua, with two games left. But it was by no means a vintage performance. Poor finishing, including a missed penalty from van Nistelrooy, meant that all that separated the sides at the end was the visiting midfielder's second-half own goal. "Obviously we didn't put on much of a spectacle, scoring lots of goals, but we controlled the game and they didn't have many sights of our goal," Real goalkeeper Iker Casillas said. "We created enough chances to have won without their gift. We can't be playing that badly because we are near the top in the league, are in the next stage of the Champions League and in the King's Cup."

While the players celebrated the effectiveness of their side's performance, it was Real President Calderon who reminded them of the need to provide some entertainment for the fans. "Let's hope we can score more goals against Celta Vigo in the league on Sunday so that the fans can enjoy themselves a little more," he said.

Lyon 1 v Dynamo Kiev 0
Group E
Stade de Gerland
Attendance: 41,000

LYON 1 v **DYNAMO KIEV 0**

Referee
Pieter Vink (Netherlands)
Assistant Referee
Jantinus Meints (Netherlands)
Adriaan Inia (Netherlands)
Fourth Official
Bjorn Kuipers (Netherlands)

Scorers
14'	Benzema

Teams
	Lyon		Dynamo Kiev	
01	Coupet	Shovkovskiy	01	
20	Abidal	Rodolfo	04	
02	Clerc	El Kaddouri	30	
03	Cris	Gavrancic	32	
29	Squillaci	Cernat	10	
10	Malouda	Gusev	20	
08	Juninho	Mikhalik	17	
21	Tiago	Yussuf	37	
28	Toulalan	Kleber	09	
19	Benzema	Milevskiy	25	
14	Govou	Rebrov	05	

Substitutes
75'	22	Wiltord	44	Rodrigo		45'
	19	Benzema	12	Gavrancic		
79'	06	Kallstrom	16	Shatskikh		66'
	08	Juninho	20	Rebrov		
87'	15	Diarra	08	Belkevich		77'
	14	Govou	46	Cernat		

Discipline
62'	Malouda	El Kaddouri	35'
		Gusev	68'

1	Yellow cards	2
0	Red cards	0
4	Shots on target	2
11	Shots off target	4
25	Fouls committed	21
6	Corners	1
3	Offsides	4
37' 21"	Ball. Poss. (time)	22' 53"
62%	Ball. Poss. (%)	38%

Lyon's Karim Benzema (L) is congratulated by team-mate Juninho after scoring against Dynamo Kiev

In the other Group E game, Lyon beat Dynamo Kiev 1-0 to book their place in the last 16. Karim Benzema scored the first-half winner for the French champions, who had won all four of their games thus far.

With Lyon's number nine Fred out of action until the winter break because of a strained thigh muscle, Gérard Houllier banked on Benzema instead of the towering John Carew. The French under-21 striker proved a reliable replacement as he slotted home from

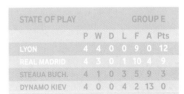

STATE OF PLAY			GROUP E			
	P	W	D	L	F	A	Pts
LYON	4	4	0	0	9	0	12
REAL MADRID	4	3	0	1	10	4	9
STEAUA BUCH.	4	1	0	3	5	9	3
DYNAMO KIEV	4	0	0	4	2	13	0

Dynamo Kiev's Oleg Gusev (L) tangles with Lyon's Florent Malouda

close range after winger Sidney Govou outmanoeuvred two defenders to set him up in the 14th minute.

Govou had a chance to double the lead, but blasted over with goalkeeper Olexander Shovkovsky beaten on the half-hour mark.

Kiev, who are a much better side than their results suggest, responded through striker Kleber but he missed their best chance in the first half when he shot wide from outside the box. Soon after the break Benzema, nicely set up by midfielder Tiago, had an opportunity to shine again but his right-foot shot missed the target.

Minutes later, Benzema squandered another chance to put the result beyond doubt but his volley was too weak to find the net. The rest of the half was more balanced and Kiev came close to equalising through Artem Milevsky who skimmed the post.

Lyon keeper Gregory Coupet, back from a hand injury, preserved their lead when he kept out a close-range

> **"I'm happy with the qualification, but what makes me really pleased is that we have not conceded a goal in this UEFA Champions League so far."**
> Gérard Houllier, Lyon coach

"**Tonight we lost to one of the best sides in Europe.**"
Anatoly Demyanenko, Kiev coach

header by number nine Kleber with 10 minutes to go.

"We were a bit too shy and nervous in the first half," said Kiev coach Anatoly Demyanenko. "Tonight we lost to one of the best sides in Europe. We have learned a lot and we are going to try qualify for the UEFA Cup."

"It's a shame there were not more goals tonight," said Houllier. "The result should have been something like 3-1 or 4-1 as 1-0 hardly shows what a superb game it was. I was particularly impressed by Kiev tonight."

DID YOU KNOW?
Lyon's 1-0 victory over Kiev was their 14th successive victory in all competitions

Lyon keeper Gregory Coupet and coach Gérard Houllier celebrate qualification

Match Day 5
Tuesday 21 November 2006

Hoop La

Shunsuke Nakamura attains legendary status by scoring the goal which defeats mighty Manchester United and sends Celtic through the knockout stage for the first time

Arsenal On The Brink

Despite a much needed 3-1 win Arsène Wenger's men aren't quite over the finishing line yet

Shakh Attack

Shakhtar Donetsk defeat the golden boys of Roma to give themselves a shock chance of knocking out the Italian stallions

"I'll go to sleep tonight, check Teletext in the morning and if it says there that we have qualified, I'll finally believe it."

Gordon Strachan, Celtic manager

Celtic 1 v Manchester United 0
Group F
Parkhead
Attendance: 60,632

CELTIC 1 v **MAN UNITED 0**

Celtic's bench goes ballistic as Nakamura's free-kick finds its mark

Referee
Manuel Mejuto González (Spain)
Assistant Referee
Pedro Medina Hernández (Spain)
Javier Hugo Novoa Robles (Spain)
Fourth Official
Alfonso Álvarez Izquierdo (Spain)

Scorers
81' Nakamura

Teams

Celtic	Man United
01 Boruc	van der Sar 01
06 Balde	Neville 02
03 Naylor	Heinze 04
02 Telfer	Ferdinand 05
16 Gravesen	Vidic 15
18 Lennon	Carrick 16
44 McManus	Giggs 11
25 Nakamura	Ronaldo 07
15 Sno	Scholes 18
10 Vennegoor of Hesselink	Rooney 08
07 Zurawski	Saha 09

Substitutes

45' > 29 Maloney < 15 Sno		03 Evra > 12 Heinze < 87'	
45' > 20 Jarosik < 07 Zurawski		22 O'Shea > 20 Carrick < 87'	
85' > 09 Miller < 25 Nakamura			

Discipline

33'	McManus	Scholes	49'
89'	Maloney		
89'	Lennon		

3	Yellow cards	1
0	Red cards	0
3	Shots on target	4
3	Shots off target	12
16	Fouls committed	10
1	Corners	7
3	Offsides	3
26' 23"	Ball. Poss. (time)	37' 59"
41%	Ball. Poss. (%)	59%

Gordon Strachan struggled to take in the enormity of defeating Manchester United and progression to the last 16 of the Champions League for the first time in Celtic's history. "We are tired now, it has been an emotional day," he conceded. "I'll go to sleep tonight, check Teletext in the morning and if it says there that we have qualified, I'll finally believe it."

The Celtic captain, Neil Lennon, was shocked, but ecstatic to learn that his side had qualified for the Champions League knockout stages after their dramatic victory. When congratulated on reaching the next round, Lennon told a television reporter: "Have we? If that really is true then it is the best result of my whole career. Just to beat Manchester United alone is enough. I can't speak highly enough of the players."

Victory came as Nakamura scored a beauty of a free-kick in a comparable manner to the one he lodged into the net at Old Trafford. This time Nemanja Vidic fouled Jiri Jarosik and the Japanese midfielder piloted the dead ball high past the left-hand of Edwin van der Sar from 30 yards. A picture perfect goal that sent Parkhead into paroxysms.

Sir Alex Ferguson was livid as Manchester United squandered territorial dominance. "We are disappointed," Ferguson lamented. "We threw it away, there is no question of that. You need to score goals to win football matches and we didn't have enough in the last third of the field to do that. We had some good opportunities but the finishing was disappointing."

Celtic entered uncharted territory as Sir Alex's team fashioned few opportunities,

STATE OF PLAY GROUP F

	P	W	D	L	F	A	Pts
CELTIC	5	3	0	2	7	6	9
MAN UNITED	5	3	0	2	7	4	9
BENFICA	5	2	1	2	6	5	7
COPENHAGEN	5	1	1	3	2	7	4

Thomas Graveson winds up to unleash a vicious shot

Typical Celtic humour 'welcomes' Manchester United to Glasgow

Louis Saha sees his penalty saved by Artur Boruc in the Celtic goal

"The best result of my whole career."
Neil Lennon, Celtic captain

despite an overwhelming superiority in technique. Soon after they had fallen behind to that exquisite Nakamura free-kick in the 81st minute, Saha paused fatally when sent clear because of a mistaken belief that he was offside.

And yet that was not Saha and United's best opportunity. That came from the penalty spot when referee Rafael Mejuto González had been cruel to rule that Shaun Maloney, half-turning in the defensive wall, was guilty of intent as Cristiano Ronaldo's free-kick rebounded from his arm. Boruc dived smartly to his right to parry Saha's effort from the

spot. By preserving the lead he guaranteed that Celtic would stand above United even if the clubs finish level on points. The advantage came from the two away goals in the loss at Old Trafford.

Ferguson had endured a similar outcome three weeks earlier when United lost 1-0 in Copenhagen after having the bulk of possession. "We had terrific chances in Copenhagen and didn't take them," he said. "We didn't have as many clear-cut ones tonight, but we had good openings."

Ferguson was upbeat, though, on the possibility of his team lifting themselves

Parkhead celebrates a famous victory

for virtually a knockout tie against Benfica to decide who qualifies from Group F alongside Celtic. "Historically, we do things the hard way," he said. "We are going to have to do it the hard way again and get a point against Benfica. It's a home match, and of course we will try to win. Our home form is very good, we have no worries on that score, but we want to have a better edge to our game."

Ferguson refused to blame French striker Saha for the defeat. "Louis is disappointed, he has missed a penalty kick in an important match," he said. "But the players will help him, we will all help him. He'll probably miss another penalty in his career. Understandably, the players are disappointed. We have five days to lift them now but if we want to win the league we have to show character and I am sure that we will."

Ferguson also claimed Saha "heard the [referee's] whistle" when he missed the first chance and the goalkeeper's penalty save owed much to time-wasting by Celtic players, particularly Neil Lennon, which tested Saha's temperament further.

Saha's penalty miss came as no surpise to Celtic captain Lennon – he had an inside line from his Manchester United counterpart. Lennon revealed that Gary Neville had predicted Saha would not score from the spot. "Gary Neville actually came across and said to me about Saha: "His head has gone, he's going to miss this."" Saha stepped up and Artur Boruc duly palmed his shot away.

United's players are unsure what to do with themselves after the final whistle

SHUNSUKE NAKAMURA

Shunsuke Nakamura had already been dubbed the 'Beckham of the Far East', but after scoring the goal which defeated Manchester United, Gordon Strachan believed the Celtic player can stand scrutiny with the original. How ironic that Sir Alex should be the one to suffer from Nakamura's ability to bend it like Beckham as 60,000 watched the playmaker curl the 28 yard free-kick over the Manchester United wall and beyond van der Sar. The goal prompted an explosion of noise that shook the east end of Glasgow, raising Nakamura to the kind of cult status reserved for true Celtic legends.

"Shunsuke is world class," Strachan said. "To be able to do that, in that pressure situation, is something few people can do. David Beckham delivered two great corners in a minute in the UEFA Champions League final in 1999 and that brought Manchester United the European Cup."

For Strachan it was the ultimate payback for risking his own reputation on the 28 year-old. When the Celtic manager paid Reggina of Italy £2.8 million for the midfield player in August 2005, it was felt that Nakamura was too frail for the rigours of Scotland and after a calamitous appearance weeks later in the Old Firm derby against Rangers, that impression was justified. However, Nakamura vindicated Strachan. He works out every day after training at the gym in the corner of the stadium to build up his upper body strength. After matches he sits around in his kit politely discussing the game with the legion of Japanese reporters who have been camped in Glasgow for 16 months and follow his every move.

"It was the best goal of my life," Nakamura said. "Van der Sar is one of the best goalkeepers in the world and now I have beaten him twice. The free-kick at Old Trafford was good, but this was better. There are a lot of young players outside Japan now and this has, hopefully, proved that they can be at this level."

Nakamura enjoys Glasgow far more than Italy, recommending two sushi restaurants and the city's shops. Best of all, he says, are the fans. "They cheer you for the slightest thing and the European nights have been amazing." Born and raised in the port city of Yokohama, Nakamura began playing soccer competitively at the age of five, playing with the local youth club side, Misono FC, until he entered junior high school. In fifth grade, he was selected for Yokohama's city all-star team's tour of the former Soviet Union, even though the team was only meant to include sixth graders.

In 1997, 19 year-old Nakamura joined Yokohama Marinos of the J League and made such an impact over five years that in 2002 Nakamura left Marinos to join Reggina of Serie A, when the clubs agreed to a £1.8 million transfer fee after a six-month loan period.

Steve Perryman, the former Tottenham Hotspur player and manager of J League clubs Shimizu S-Pulse and Kashiwa Reysol, once remarked that Nakamura was so good, he "could open a tin of beans with his left foot". Zico, the national coach of Japan at the 2006 World Cup, lauded Nakamura's improvement, especially his physical development, stating, "He is the soul of our midfield."

An immediate effect of Nakamura's goal was that Celtic's shares soared by 15 per cent overnight. "The shares are up because of the win," Stan Lock, an analyst for Brewin Dolphin, said. "There are a few million pounds involved and the further you go the bigger it gets." The rise in the share price added about £4 million to the value of the club — a fair return indeed!

"He's so good he could open a tin of beans with his left foot." – Steve Perryman

Benfica 3 v Copenhagen 1
Group F
Stadium of Light
Attendance: 47,500

Benfica celebrate a vital, if comfortable win

Italian winger Fabrizio Miccoli scored twice as Benfica defeated FC Copenhagen 3-1 to stay in the race to qualify from Group F. Benfica would secure their place in the knockout stage with a win in their last game; a result which would knock Manchester United out.

Three first-half goals gave Benfica a comfortable 3-1 victory. Marcus Allback snatched a consolation for Copenhagen, but the Danish side are now out of contention in their first UEFA Champions League campaign.

Benfica dominated from the start and opened the scoring through Brazilian defender Leo who netted with an acutely angled shot from the right after 14 minutes. Two minutes later, Miccoli doubled the lead with a shot from just outside the box after a good exchange with Nuno Gomes.

Miccoli scored the third goal after 37 minutes when Copenhagen goalkeeper Jesper Christiansen failed to hold the ball.

Benfica's Leonardo Lourenco "Leo" of Brazil celebrates his opening goal against FC Copenhagen

BENFICA 3 v **COPENHAGEN 1**

Referee
Roberto Rosetti (Italy)
Assistant Referee
Paolo Calcagno (Italy) Marco Ivaldi (Italy)
Fourth Official
Gianluca Rocchi (Italy)

Scorers

14'	Leo	Allbäck	89'
16', 37'	Miccoli		

Teams

	Benfica	Copenhagen	
12	Quim	Christiansen	01
03	Anderson	Gravgaard	14
05	Leo	Hangeland	05
22	Nélson	Jacobsen	02
33	Ricardo Rocha	Wendt	17
25	Assis	Gronkjaer	10
08	Katsouranis	Hutchinson	13
06	Petit	Linderoth	06
20	Simao	Nørregaard	04
21	Nuno Gomes	Silberbauer	08
30	Miccoli	Allbäck	11

Substitutes

70'	19 Karyaka / 30 Miccoli	09 Berglund / 04 Nørregaard	59'
80'	26 Karagounis / 25 Assis	23 Kvist / 08 Silberbauer	59'
86'	09 Mantorras / 08 Katsouranis	28 Bergvold / 17 Wendt	83'

Discipline

27'	Miccoli	Linderoth	24'
90'	Nélson	Silberbauer	27'

2	Yellow cards	2
0	Red cards	0
10	Shots on target	4
5	Shots off target	11
21	Fouls committed	12
4	Corners	4
10	Offsides	3
32' 30"	Ball. Poss. (time)	32' 32"
50%	Ball. Poss. (%)	40%

STATE OF PLAY — GROUP F

	P	W	D	L	F	A	Pts
CELTIC	5	3	0	2	7	6	9
MAN UNITED	5	3	0	2	7	4	9
BENFICA	5	2	1	2	6	5	7
COPENHAGEN	5	1	1	3	2	7	4

ARSENAL 3 v **HAMBURG 1**

Referee
Claus Bo Larsen (Denmark)

Assistant Referee
Bill René Hansen (Denmark)
Anders Nørrestrand (Denmark)

Fourth Official
Peter Rasmussen (Denmark)

Scorers

52'	van Persie	van der Vaart	04'
82'	Eboué		
88'	Baptista		

Teams

01	Lehmann	Wächter	01
22	Clichy	Atouba	03
27	Eboué	Mathijsen	05
06	Senderos	Reinhardt	04
05	Toure	Benjamin	30
04	Fabregas	Fillinger	13
16	Flamini	Mahdavikia	07
13	Hleb	Trochowski	15
08	Ljungberg	van der Vaart	23
14	Henry	Wicky	06
11	van Persie	Sanogo	17

Substitutes

70'	> 25 Adebayor < 11 van Persie	33 Feilhaber 07 Mahdavikia	<	45'
75'	> 32 Walcott < 08 Ljungberg	38 Ljuboja 03 Atouba	<	67'
81'	> 09 Baptista < 13 Hleb	11 Lauth 06 Wicky	<	87'

Discipline

19'	Senderos	Benjamin	27'
41'	Hleb	van der Vaart	32'
53'	Henry	Sanogo	47'
57'	Clichy		

4	Yellow cards	3
0	Red cards	0
4	Shots on target	3
8	Shots off target	7
14	Fouls committed	25
7	Corners	3
1	Offsides	3
56' 26"	Ball. Poss. (time)	21' 24"
63%	Ball. Poss. (%)	37%

Arsenal 3 v Hamburg 1
Group G
Emirates Stadium
Attendance: 59,962

Arsène Wenger and Pat Rice rejoice after the key second goal hits the back of the Hamburg net

Huge relief at the Emirates where Theo Walcott inspired a better second half performance and a 3-1 victory over whipping boys Hamburg.

But Arsenal now had to travel to Porto for the final group match without their captain after Thierry Henry received an unnecessary caution for dissent. The Arsenal skipper had another frustrating night, capped by a needless second-half booking for a confrontation with Joris Mathijsen.

The Frenchman had already rued the booking that had followed the annulment of his equalising goal in Moscow, Arsenal's last away match, but its cost continued to bite as this second yellow resulted in a one-match ban. Although CSKA Moscow's slip at home to Porto made Arsenal favourites to top Group G, the fixture in Portugal was now significant.

"It's a blow because we wanted Thierry in Porto," said Arsène Wenger of Henry's. "We will have to do it without him. We want to win so much that I am

Thierry Henry and Joris Mathilsen continue their running battle

"Theo was
an injection
of power
and pace."
Arsène Wenger

Henry dives to meet a Walcott cross, but the chance went begging

Rafael van der Vaart leaps into orbit after scoring a belter in just the fourth minute

confident we'll make it. I could see Thierry was frustrated. He was held back by his shirt being pulled on quite a few occasions. "

A draw with Porto would probably be enough to see Arsenal win the group and, like Arsenal, Porto would also progress on a better head-to-head against CSKA Moscow. Wenger noted that conspiracists had made up their minds about the final match in the group. "If it finishes as a draw, no-one is disappointed," he said, with a smile. There would be a danger of complacency however. A Porto victory combined with CSKA winning in Hamburg would deposit Arsenal alongside Tottenham in the UEFA Cup.

Wenger admitted, though, that Arsenal's promising position would not have been possible without the influence of their 17 year-old winger Walcott. The Gunners were facing another embarrassing home draw, against a team with nothing at all to show for their four previous matches in the group, when the England international made his entrance on 75 minutes. Eight minutes later, Arsenal were ahead after Emmanuel Eboué collected Walcott's dabbed centre to fire his goal in off Stefan Wächter; two minutes from time and the kid's hoisted cross provided Julio Baptista with the headed goal that gave the scoreline some sparkle. "Theo was an injection of

DID YOU KNOW?
This was the first occasion at the Emirates that Arsenal have come from a goal behind to win a match

power and pace," said Wenger. "He is at the moment in a mental state where he knows he can affect the game when he comes on and he has the physical ingredients to do that. I first of all put him on the right and you could see straight away when he went to the right that he made a big difference. I involve him a lot. He has played a few games already and I am watching him closely. He'll soon get a start. I feel he learns by being in touch with a team that is under pressure for winning the game."

Last season's Champions League finalists were drifting during a disjointed first half. "I felt we tried very hard in the first half, but the game was too sideways and not enough forwards," he said. "Our game was more direct in the second half. We played with two central strikers and were more direct. The team refused to accept defeat and never, at any time, felt sorry for themselves after going behind and then hitting the bar and post."

Seven minutes away from a result that Wenger might have considered even worse than a disaster, Arsenal suddenly, belatedly found the pace, power and luck to scramble past the Germans. When substitute Baptista added a quickfire third, Wenger's side jumped from third to first in the group.

On for Freddie Ljungberg, Walcott displayed a level of penetration, particularly for the third goal, that had been

missing earlier. Hamburg had had a dream start. Hit by injuries, their formation was designed to soak up pressure by coach Thomas Doll, but after just four minutes the lone striker Boubacar Sanogo won a 50-50 challenge 20 yards from Jens Lehmann's goalline. The ball ran to Mehdi Mahdavikia, who switched it back inside to Rafael van der Vaart. With Mathieu Flamini flustered and Kolo Touré sent the wrong way by van der Vaart's shimmy, his shot curled over and beyond Lehmann.

It was not until the introduction of Emmanuel Adebayor, Walcott and Baptista that Arsenal bucked their ideas up.

Part of Arsenal's problem was Henry's preoccupation with his running battle with Mathijsen. There were several angry exchanges, but the Hamburg player was baffled as to why Henry suddenly snapped when he knew the consequences. "If he knew he would be suspended with another booking then that is a stupid thing if he

takes a yellow card like that," said Mathijsen. "It was a yellow card – he was too late in the challenge. The ball had been gone for two or three seconds."

Mathijsen had refused to be overawed by the confrontation with Henry. If you show too much respect, he scores. We had a good battle. We talked during the game and he said he would do anything to win for his team – and I said I'd do the same for mine. But at the end he was laughing and we shook hands."

Henry admitted that he only had himself to blame for missing Arsenal's crucial Champions League game in Porto, cautioned for the third time in three consecutive group games when he clattered into Dutch defender Joris Mathijsen. He will now be suspended for a match in which Arsenal must avoid defeat to guarantee a place in the knockout stages. Henry admitted: "I concede that the booking I picked up wasn't very clever. It was the result of frustration, but I'm not making excuses – I deserved the yellow card."

> "I'm not making excuses – I deserved the yellow card."
> Thierry Henry

Emmanuel Eboué celebrates his goal with provider Theo Walcott and Cesc Fabregas

CSKA Moscow 0 v Porto 2
Group G
Lokomotiv Stadium
Attendance: 35,000

Porto's players celebrate victory in Moscow

CSKA MOSCOW 0 v   **PORTO 2**

Referee
Kyros Vassaras (Greece)

Assistant Referee
Dimitrios Bozatzidis (Greece)
Konstantinos Dalas (Greece)

Fourth Official
Ioannis Tsachilidis (Greece)

Scorers

Quaresma	02'
González	61'

Teams

35	Akinfeev	Helton	01
06	Berezoutski	Alves	14
24	Berezoutski	Fucile	15
02	Semberas	Pepe	03
22	Aldonin	Assuncao	18
07	Carvalho	Bosingwa	12
17	Krasic	González	08
25	Rahimic	Meireles	16
20	Dudu	Quaresma	07
18	Zhirkov	López	09
11	Vagner Love	Postiga	23

Substitutes

27'	37 Kochubey / 20 Dudu	20 Jorginho / 16 Meireles	70'
66'	09 Olic / 17 Krasic	29 Moraes / 23 Postiga	76'
		02 Costa / 07 Quaresma	88'

Discipline

46'	Vagner Love	Assuncao	07'
67'	Kochubey	Pepe	19'
73'	Rahimic	Alves	38'
90'	Zhirkov		

4	Yellow cards	3
0	Red cards	0
2	Shots on target	6
8	Shots off target	5
12	Fouls committed	24
10	Corners	10
2	Offsides	5
32' 32"	Ball. Poss. (time)	28' 51"
53%	Ball. Poss. (%)	47%

Porto threw Arsenal's group wide open with an impressive 2-0 win at CSKA Moscow as goals by Ricardo Quaresma and Lucho Gonzalez powered the Portuguese champions to victory.

Quaresma struck just 80 seconds into the game and Gonzalez added a second on the hour as Porto overtook the Russians in Group G. The Russian champions were completely outplayed in their first defeat in European competition this season.

The visitors scored their first before the home side could settle. Porto captain Gonzalez started the move on the right before Lisandro Lopez found Quaresma unmarked at the far post and the Portugal striker fired home from close range.

CSKA's worries intensified midway through the first half when their Brazilian international Dudu was forced to leave the pitch with a hamstring injury.

Porto totally dominated the first half, wasting several good chances to add to their tally. However, Gonzalez made no mistake in the 61st minute when he drove a low shot from the edge of the box into the far corner.

Porto coach Jesualdo Ferreira praised his team's effort. "The early goal

Porto's Alan leaves CSKA Moscow's Yuri Zhirkov for dead

Bruno Alves is ecstatic at the final whistle

> **"Porto deserved their victory."**
> Valery Gazzayev, CSKA Moscow coach

> **"The early goal gave our young team a lot of confidence."**
> Jesualdo Ferreira, Porto coach

gave our young team a lot of confidence and in the second half we made timely substitutions to maintain our flow," he told reporters. "Today we played well individually and also showed great team spirit. Now we have a good chance to qualify for the last 16 as we only need a draw in our last match at home to Arsenal."

CSKA's misery was compounded after the interval when their Brazilian striker Vagner Love and Bosnian midfielder Elver Rahimic received yellow cards, forcing them to miss their team's last group match against Hamburg through suspension.

CSKA coach Valery Gazzayev blamed his side's poor play on a heavy schedule and their 15,000-km round trip through seven time zones to the eastern port city of Vladivostok the previous weekend. "We're still feeling the effects of our trip to Vladivostok. Nevertheless, Porto deserved their victory," said Gazzayev, who took charge of the team despite the death of his younger brother, who was killed in a car crash on Saturday.

CSKA had only two days to prepare for the match after landing in Moscow in the early hours of Sunday. They had crushed Luch 4-0 in Vladivostok on Saturday to clinch their second consecutive league title.

A draw in the last match at their Estadio do Dragão will see both Porto and Arsenal qualify at the expense of Moscow, who had until this result been favourites to go through alongside the Gunners.

DID YOU KNOW?
Porto also beat CSKA 1-0 in a group tie on their only previous visit to the Russian capital two years ago when they reached the next round at the expense of the army side

DID YOU KNOW?
Ricardo Quaresma's second minute opener was the first goal conceded by CSKA in their seventh game of this season's competition, including their two qualifying round matches

AEK Athens 1 v AC Milan 0
Group H
Olympic Stadium
Attendance: 70,000

AEK Athens players celebrate victory over six-times European Champions Milan

AEK ATHENS 1 v **AC MILAN 0**

Referee
Eric Braamhaar (Netherlands)

Assistant Referee
Arie Brink (Netherlands)
Wilco Lobbert (Netherlands)

Fourth Official
Bjorn Kuipers (Netherlands)

Scorers

32'	Julio Cezar

Teams

28	Sorrentino	Dida	01
05	Cirillo	Bonera	25
55	Dellas	Costacurta	05
15	Papastrathopoulos	Maldini	03
14	Tziortziopoulos	Brocchi	32
25	Emerson	Gourcuff	20
88	Tozser	Kaká	22
16	Zikos	Pirlo	21
99	Julio Cezar	Seedorf	10
33	Lyberopoulos	Inzaghi	09
11	Manduca	Oliveira	07

Substitutes

66'	> 07 Kiriakidis < 88 Tozser	18 Jankulovski > 05 Costacurta <	45'
78'	> 04 Moras < 14 Tziortziopoulos	15 Borriello > 07 Oliveira <	70'
86'	> 56 Hetemaj < 99 Julio Cezar	16 Kalac > 01 Dida <	78'

Discipline

34'	Tziortziopoulos	Oliveira	45'
58'	Tozser	Seedorf	75'

2	Yellow cards	2
0	Red cards	0
7	Shots on target	7
4	Shots off target	16
20	Fouls committed	12
4	Corners	10
1	Offsides	3
20' 33"	Ball. Poss. (time)	36' 43"
36%	Ball. Poss. (%)	64%

Milan's inconsistent form continued with a 1-0 defeat at AEK Athens. The Italians, however, went through to the knockout stage as Lille could only draw with Anderlecht.

Three weeks after recording their first ever win in the group stages of the Champions League, AEK Athens posted number two when they stunned AC Milan. The victory allowed AEK to climb into second place with seven points, one ahead of Lille, and go into their last match at Anderlecht as favourites to accompany the six-times European Champions into the knockout stages for the first time.

The only goal of a hard-fought game came from a direct free-kick by Brazilian striker Julio Cesar after Milan's Clarence Seedorf had fouled Nikos Liberopoulos just outside the penalty area.

However, AEK owed their famous win just as much to a staunch defence and the heroics of their Italian goalkeeper Stefano Sorrentino who made half a dozen top-class saves.

Traianos Dellas put an early header over the bar for AEK, but for most of the first half, the Greek side were on the back foot as Sorrentino kept out good efforts from Ricardo Oliveira and Kaká and twice denied Filippo Inzaghi.

The Milan defence was rarely troubled, but the game changed in the 33rd minute when Cesar fired low into the right-hand corner of Dida's goal.

The second half produced plenty of end-to-end excitement as Milan desperately

DID YOU KNOW?
In this game AC Milan's Alessandro Costacurta – at 40 years and 211 days – become the oldest player to feature in the UEFA Champions League

STATE OF PLAY		GROUP H					
	P	W	D	L	F	A	Pts
AC MILAN	5	3	1	1	8	2	10
AEK ATHENS	5	2	1	2	4	7	7
LILLE	5	1	3	1	6	5	6
ANDERLECHT	5	0	3	2	5	9	3

Julio Cesar takes the applause of the crowd after his belting free-kick found the back of the Milan net

went in search of an equaliser with qualification at that stage not yet secured. Both Sorrentino and Dida were busy, the latter having to make an acrobatic save to prevent Julio Cesar adding a second. Dida injured himself in the process and was later replaced by Australian international keeper Zeljko Kalac.

Hard though they pushed, there was nothing that Milan could do and the 60,000 AEK fans duly celebrated in a sea of yellow and black flags. AEK coach Lorenzo Serra Ferrer said: "It was a great night for AEK fans and for Greek football. The fans kept our team spirit fresh throughout the match. AEK had never

won a match before this campaign and no-one thought it would be possible for us to finish in the top two. Now we are one of the favourites to go through."

"We had our chances to score, especially through Inzaghi, but luck turned its back on us,' said Milan coach Carlo Ancellotti.

> **"It was a great night for AEK fans and for Greek football."**
> Lorenzo Serra Ferrer, AEK Athens coach

Athens fans acclaim their victory

Lille 2 v Anderlecht 2

Group H
Stade Félix-Bollaert. Lens
Attendance: 35,000

Mbo Mpenza celebrates his second goal as Anderlecht twice hit back from behind to draw 2-2 with Lille

LILLE 2 v **ANDERLECHT 2**

Referee
Tom Henning Øvrebø (Norway)
Assistant Referee
Erik Raestad (Norway)
Geir Åge Holen (Norway)
Fourth Official
Per Ivar Staberg (Norway)

Scorers

28'	Odemwingie	Mpenza 38', 48'
47'	Fauvergue	

Teams

01	Sylva	Schollen 22
21	Chalmé	Descacht 03
25	Plestan	Pareja 26
05	Schmitz	van Damme 06
20	Tafforeau	Vanden Borre 37
12	Bodmer	Biglia 05
17	Makoun	De Man 31
18	Robail	Goor 14
13	Fauvergue	Hassan 10
23	Kader Keita	Mpenza 09
14	Odemwingie	Tchite 07

Substitutes

55'	02 Debuchy / 18 Robail	11 Boussoufa / 09 Mpenza	66'
71'	08 Bastos / 13 Fauvergue	04 Vanderhaeghe / 10 Hassan	83'
75'	27 Mirallas / 14 Odemwingie	23 Juhasz / 05 Biglia	90'

Discipline

42'	Tafforeau	van Damme	34'
		Hassan	42'
		Pareja	50'
		van Damme	88'

1	Yellow cards	4
0	Red cards	1
3	Shots on target	4
18	Shots off target	2
12	Fouls committed	6
4	Corners	3
0	Offsides	6
34' 05"	Ball. Poss. (time)	27' 05"
60%	Ball. Poss. (%)	40%

A Mbo Mpenza double dampened Lille's hopes of reaching the knockout stages for the first time when the French side were held to a 2-2 draw by Anderlecht.

Lille went ahead twice courtesy of goals by forwards Peter Odemwingie and Nicolas Fauvergue but Mpenza twice cancelled out the advantage.

The French side started brightly, with a Mathieu Bodmer free kick shaving Davy Schollen's crossbar in the 11th minute. Fauvergue then pulled the ball back to fellow striker Odemwingie, who just had to slot it home to open the scoring on 28 minutes. Anderlecht, however, hit back 10 minutes later when Mpenza scored off the far post after being set up by Ahmed Hassan.

The hosts, who play their Champions League matches in Lens's Stade Felix-Bollaert, went ahead again two minutes into the second half courtesy of a Fauvergue strike only for Mpenza to equalise a minute later. The Belgian striker scored from close range after collecting a reverse pass from Mohamed Tchite.

Anderlecht had Jelle van Damme sent off two minutes from time, but it was too late to help Lille's cause. Despite late attempts by Odemwingie and Abdulkader Keita, they failed to crack their opponents' defence again.

STATE OF PLAY				GROUP H		
	P	W	D	L	F	A	Pts
AC MILAN	5	3	1	1	8	2	10
AEK ATHENS	5	2	1	2	4	7	7
LILLE	5	1	3	1	6	5	6
ANDERLECHT	5	0	3	2	5	9	3

Real Madrid 2 v Lyon 2
Group E
Santiago Bernabeu Stadium
Attendance: 78,677

Ruud van Nistelrooy nets the late equalizer which saved Madrid's blushes

Ruud van Nistelrooy gave Manchester United a timely reminder of his capabilities when he scored a late equaliser for Real Madrid at home to Lyon, but the Dutchman then missed another penalty in the 89th minute – which meant Fabio Capello's side would finish second in the group and play one of the first-phase winners in the last 16.

Real could face Chelsea, Manchester United or Liverpool in the last 16, but they showed character in fighting back from two goals down in this game. John

Carew and Florent Malouda had given the French side a 2-0 lead, but Mahamadou Diarra, who left Lyon for Madrid in the summer, gave Real hope just before half-time and van Nistelrooy salvaged a point with seven minutes remaining. Gregory Coupet then saved the Dutchman's last-gasp penalty.

All the talk in Madrid was of Real beating Lyon by three goals to overturn the 2-0 victory suffered in France on the opening day of the competition, thus

winning group E on head-to-head goal difference. Unfortunately, someone forgot to tell Gérard Houllier's team. Rather than exact revenge on Lyon, Real were often exposed themselves, as they have been in Europe and their domestic competition this season. That Madrid should have been unable to beat the only side in the tournament with a 100 per cent record should perhaps not have come as quite such a surprise to the Spanish.

DID YOU KNOW?
This was Ruud van Nistelrooy's third penalty miss in a Madrid shirt

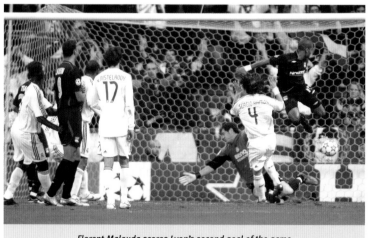

Florent Malouda scores Lyon's second goal of the game

Robinho takes on the Lyon defence

Antonio Cassano heads for goal

REAL MADRID 2 v **LYON 2**

Referee
Terje Hauge (Norway)
Assistant Referee
Arild Sundet (Norway)
Steinar Holvik (Norway)
Fourth Official
Tommy Skjerven (Norway)

Scorers

39'	Diarra	Carew	11'
83'	van Nistelrooy	Malouda	31'

Teams

01	Casillas	Coupet	01
05	Cannavaro	Abidal	20
03	Roberto Carlos	Clerc	02
21	Helguera	Cris	03
04	Sergio Ramos	Reveillere	12
06	Diarra	Squillaci	29
08	Emerson	Malouda	10
14	Guti	Juninho	08
10	Robinho	Tiago	21
07	Raul	Toulalan	28
17	van Nistelrooy	Carew	09

Substitutes

21'	> 19 Reyes < 14 Guti	15 Diarra > 28 Toulalan <	90'
76'	> 18 Cassano < 08 Emerson		

Discipline

75'	Roberto Carlos	Toulalan	19'
83'	Cannavaro	Reveillere	50'
90'	Raul	Juninho	55'
90'	Sergio Ramos	Malouda	90'

4	Yellow cards	4
0	Red cards	0
7	Shots on target	4
10	Shots off target	14
19	Fouls committed	16
5	Corners	6
5	Offsides	6
39' 34"	Ball. Poss. (time)	25' 20"
61%	Ball. Poss. (%)	39%

STATE OF PLAY — GROUP E

	P	W	D	L	F	A	Pts
LYON	5	4	1	0	11	2	13
REAL MADRID	5	3	1	1	12	6	10
STEAUA BUCH.	5	1	1	3	6	10	4
DYNAMO KIEV	5	0	1	4	3	14	1

But it was still a shock to the massed Real faithful that Lyon raced into a two-goal lead so early — and that the man expected to be crowned European Footballer of the Year should be beaten by a player who once missed out on a move to Fulham because of a failed medical. That player, Norwegian striker John Carew, magnificent all night and later to join Aston Villa, collected the ball deep and ran right through Fabio Cannavaro, held off Ivan Helguera and shot assuredly past Iker Casillas into the bottom corner early on. Lyon were two up on the half-hour. Juninho Pernambucano delivered a dipping free-kick into the Real penalty area and Florent Malouda scored from close range.

The Madrid comeback showed that there was fight in the old dog yet, but there would have to be a huge improvement if they were to seriously threaten to win the trophy.

Out of favour David Beckham and son Brooklyn watch from the stands

 STEAUA BUCH. 1 v DYNAMO KIEV 1

Referee
Jaroslav Jára (Czech Republic)

Assistant Referee
Miroslav Zlámal (Czech Republic)
Antonin Kordula (Czech Republic)

Fourth Official
Radek Kocian (Czech Republic)

Scorers

69	Dica		Cernat	29'

Teams

12	Cernea	Shovkovskiy	01
24	Ghionea	Rodolfo	04
03	Goian	El Kaddouri	30
18	Marin	Markovic	81
27	Stancu	Rodrigo	44
10	Dica	Belkevich	08
16	Nicolita	Cernat	10
22	Paraschiv	Gusev	20
08	Petre	Yussuf	37
07	Oprita	Kleber	09
21	Thereau	Shatskikh	16

Substitutes

55'	14 Cristocea > < 07 Oprita	32 Gavranic > 04 Rodolfo <	45'
66'	06 Radoi > < 22 Paraschiv	25 Milevskiy > 09 Kleber <	67'
90'	20 Lovin > < 10 Dica	15 Rincon > 10 Cernat <	78'

Discipline

30'	Oprita	Rodrigo	19'
76'	Ghionea	Kleber	26'
90'	Cernea	Yussuf	59'
		Gavranic	53'
		Rincon	67'

3	Yellow cards	5
0	Red cards	0
3	Shots on target	10
7	Shots off target	14
25	Fouls committed	13
5	Corners	3
2	Offsides	3
29' 35"	Ball. Poss. (time)	30' 57"
49%	Ball. Poss. (%)	51%

Steaua Bucharest 1 v Dynamo Kiev 1
Group E
Ghencea Stadium
Attendance: 20,000

Steaua Bucharest's Nicolae Dica celebrates after scoring the equalising goal against Dynamo Kiev

Steaua Bucharest and Dynamo Kiev drew 1-1 in a game with little meaning.

A second half goal from striker Nicolae Dica gave Steaua a consolation place in the UEFA Cup and left Kiev bottom of Group E.

Dica scored a 69th-minute equaliser with a slightly deflected shot from the edge of the area after a quick counter-attack, launched on the right by left winger Banel Nicolita. "It was a surprise when I got in front of the goal and I was lucky to score as the shot was deflected," Dica said.

Steaua secured third place with four points in the two meetings between the teams after their 4-1 away win in Kiev at the start of the competition and qualified for the UEFA Cup for the third successive season. Dynamo, who have only one point from those games, now could only finish bottom and be eliminated.

Dynamo had taken the lead after a fiercely contested opening half-an-hour when Romanian midfielder Florin Cernat scored with a clever curling free-kick.

"If you asked me whether we should have won the match, I would say 'yes', we had very good moments in the game," said Dynamo Kiev coach Anatoly Demyanenko.

Right-winger Daniel Oprita responded immediately, but failed to equalise from a one-on-one chance with the Dynamo Kiev goalkeeper Olexander Shovkovsky after a through pass from French striker Cyril Threau.

In the second half, Dynamo created chances, but Maxim Shatskikh, Oleg

STATE OF PLAY — GROUP E

	P	W	D	L	F	A	Pts
LYON	5	4	1	0	11	2	13
REAL MADRID	5	3	1	1	12	6	10
STEAUA BUCH.	5	1	1	3	6	10	4
DYNAMO KIEV	5	0	1	4	3	14	1

DID YOU KNOW?
This was Dica's third UEFA Champions League goal against Dynamo after scoring twice in Kiev in September

Gusev and Valentin Belkevich were unlucky in front of goal. Just when Steaua appeared to have run out of steam, Dica and Nicolita profited from an error in the Kiev midfield to launch the attack that led to the Steaua goal.

"I think that this [third place] is the best we could get from this group," said Steaua coach Cosmin Olaroiu. "I admit we were lucky in this match, but it paid off the lack of chances we had against Real Madrid."

Steaua Bucharest's Stelian Stancu (R) outwits Dynamo Kiev's Florin Cernat

Dynamo Kiev's coach Anatoly Demyanenko implores his players to attack after conceding a shock equalizer against the run of play

> **"I admit we were lucky in this match, but it paid off the lack of chances we had against Real Madrid."**
> **Cosmin Olaroiu, Steaua Bucharest coach**

Match Day 5
Wednesday 22 November 2006

> "It's a defeat. You are never happy with defeat. But it's a defeat that delivers us into the second stage of the competition."
> Jose Mourinho

Werder Bremen 1 v Chelsea 0
Group A
Weserstadion
Attendance: 40,000

Per Mertesacker's header hits the back of the Chelsea net for the only goal of the game

Chelsea qualified for the knock-out phase of the UEFA Champions League even though a first-half goal from Werder Bremen's Per Mertesacker condemned them to their first defeat in this season's competition.

Jose Mourinho claimed Bremen's giants had proved too much for his team to handle. "We knew the most difficult situations would be the set pieces because they have four or five players (around) 1.98 metres or two metres tall and we only two or three players strong enough in the air to cope with it," Mourinho said.

Goalscorer Per Mertesacker at 1.98-metres tall, proved Mourinho's fears correct, heading home Torsten Frings' corner.

Chelsea were well below par against a determined German side and a double injury blow compounded the agony of defeat for coach Jose Mourinho as star striker Didier Drogba and midfielder Michael Ballack both collected injuries in the second half.

Bremen looked the brighter of the two sides in the opening minutes, but Chelsea provided the first real attempt on goal when Michael Essien sent an 18-yard drive flashing past the right-hand upright in the sixth minute. Two minutes later Jon Obi Mikel squandered a fine chance to open the scoring when captain John Terry headed Geremi's free-kick back to the Nigerian youngster. But instead of making the Bundesliga side pay for some slack defending, Mikel headed high over the crossbar from the edge of the six-yard box.

Bremen, backed by their fanatical support, countered with a fine effort from Hugo Almeida which, much to

Andriy Shevchenko's free-kick was well saved by Tim Wiese

Carlo Cudicini's relief, zipped beyond an upright. In the 14th minute Cudicini was forced to dive to his left to save a 20-yard drive from Daniel Jensen and seconds later Almeida wasted a clear chance by firing wide with just the Chelsea goalkeeper to beat.

Bremen's spell of pressure eventually paid off in fine style in the 27th minute when a corner from Torsten Frings was met by the head of the unmarked Mertesacker on the edge of the six-yard box.

Chelsea should have levelled in the 32nd minute when a superb move ended with Tim Wiese denying Ballack. Mikel began the move by setting Ashley Cole free on the left-flank and the England international's subsequent pass into the feet of Drogba was despatched to Joe Cole on the left-wing with sublime accuracy by the Ivory Coast striker. Cole, making only his third start of the season, crossed perfectly for Ballack, but the German international found Wiese equal to the task.

Four minutes before the break Chelsea conjured another quick counter-attack which should have restored parity. Ballack set Mikel free and the Nigerian teenager was mature enough wait for the run of Joe Cole into the inside-left channel. The England midfielder produced a superb piece of trickery to bamboozle marker Pierre Wome, but his finish, a tame sidefooted shot, was comfortably held by Wiese.

Chelsea thought they should have had a penalty in the 47th minute when Ashley Cole was bundled over in the area, but referee Lubos Michel waved away their appeals.

A minute later a careless foul by Khalid Boulahrouz on Miroslav Klose was almost punished by Frings who brought a fine save from Cudicini when his free-kick threatened to sneak in at the near post.

In the 57th minute Mourinho made a double substitution, replacing Mikel with Arjen Robben and Drogba with Andriy Shevchenko. Drogba was helped to the dressing room after appearing to fall awkwardly on his right knee.

Chelsea were given a chance to find a way back into the game in the 68th minute when Tim Borowski handled the ball 25 yards out. But before the free-kick could be taken Ballack was helped from the field with with a large gash in his calf, but Mourinho was optimistic for his midfielder's chances of playing against Manchester United in a vital league game at the weekend. "I think it's nothing special. It is just pain because a player [Pierre Wome] put some studs on his muscle."

When the game resumed Chelsea were unlucky not to equalise with Shevchenko's free-kick bringing another fine save from the impressive Wiese. Five minutes later, Joe Cole fired in a great left-footed effort that the

WERDER BRE. 1 v CHELSEA 0

Referee
Lubos Michel (Slovakia)

Assistant Referee
Martin Balko (Slovakia)
Roman Slysko (Slovakia)

Fourth Official
Vladimír Vnuk (Slovakia)

Scorers

26'	Mertesacker

Teams

18 Wiese	Cudicini 23
04 Rodrigues	Boulahrouz 09
08 Fritz	A Cole 03
29 Mertesacker	Terry 26
05 Wome	Ballack 13
24 Borowski	J Cole 10
22 Frings	Essien 05
20 Jensen	Geremi 14
10 Diego	Makelele 04
23 Almeida	Mikel 12
11 Klose	Drogba 11

Substitutes

79'	14 Hunt / 20 Jensen	16 Robben / 12 Mikel	59'
87'	27 Schulz / 23 Almeida	07 Shevchenko / 11 Drogba	59'
90'	17 Klasnic / 11 Klose	24 Wright-Phillips / 13 Ballack	77'

Discipline

76'	Borowski	Terry	79'

1	Yellow cards	1
0	Red cards	0
4	Shots on target	4
10	Shots off target	7
21	Fouls committed	15
5	Corners	3
1	Offsides	5
28' 12"	Ball. Poss. (time)	30' 32"
48%	Ball. Poss. (%)	52%

STATE OF PLAY — GROUP A

	P	W	D	L	F	A	Pts
CHELSEA	5	3	1	1	8	4	10
WERDER BREMEN	5	3	1	1	7	3	10
BARCELONA	5	2	2	1	10	4	8
LEVSKI SOFIA	5	0	0	5	1	15	0

Bremen celebrate a famous victory

goalkeeper, at full stretch, did well to keep out. Chelsea's last chance of grabbing an equaliser came with three minutes left when Michael Essien's drive flew inches wide with Wiese beaten but Werder hung on to take a crucial three points.

In the 78th minute Terry was booked for dissent which ruled him out of their clash with Levski Sofia at Stamford Bridge, but would leave him clear of the threat of suspension in the knockout stages.

Mourinho reflected that the suspended Frank Lampard had been sorely missed. "Lampard affects the performance of everyone else in midfield." The Blues still needed a result against their final opponents, Levski Sofia, to ensure they progressed as Group A winners.

"It's a defeat. You are never happy with defeat," Mourinho said. "But it's a defeat that delivers us into the second stage of the competition. In this very difficult group to be safe in the next round, to be comfortable, to be the first in the group, to be qualified is an achievement. That's very important."

Mourinho contemplates the twin emotions of defeat and qualification for the knock out stage

DID YOU KNOW?
This was the first game of the 2006/07 season in which Chelsea had failed to score a goal

Levski Sofia 0 v Barcelona 2
Group A
Vasil Levski Stadium
Attendance: 42,000

Barca players celebrate the clinching second goal scored by Anders Iniesta

LEVSKI SOFIA 0 v BARCELONA 2

Referee
Yuri Baskakov (Russia)
Assistant Referee
Aleksei Monakhov (Russia)
Lev Antonov (Russia)
Fourth Official
Stanislav Sukhina (Russia)

Scorers

Giuly	05'
Iniesta	64'

Teams

01 Petkov	Valdes 01
20 Angelov	Marquez 04
03 Milanov	Puyol 05
04 Tomasic	Silvinho 16
11 Topuzakov	Zambrotta 11
07 Borimirov	Deco 20
06 Eromoigbe	Giuly 08
25 Wagner	Iniesta 24
27 Bardon	Motta 03
17 Domovchijski	Ronaldinho 10
10 Yovov	Gudjohnsen 07

Substitutes

57' > 21 Telkiyski		06 Xavi > 59'
< 20 Angelov		08 Giuly <
58' > 09 G Ivanov		23 Oleguer > 63'
< 17 Domovchijski		04 Marquez <
72' > 16 Ognyanov		18 Ezquerro > 81'
< 10 Yovov		24 Iniesta <

Discipline

25'	Milanov
55'	Borimirov

2	Yellow cards	0
0	Red cards	0
3	Shots on target	7
6	Shots off target	10
15	Fouls committed	10
2	Corners	9
4	Offsides	2
25' 18"	Ball. Poss. (time)	30' 54"
45%	Ball. Poss. (%)	55%

An early strike by Ludovic Giuly and a second-half goal by Andres Iniesta gave Barcelona a 2-0 win at Levski Sofia on Wednesday that kept alive their hopes of making the knockout stages of the UEFA Champions League on a night when anything less would have seen the holders crash out.

The Spanish giants got the ideal start in the fourth minute when the home side defence failed to clear Gianluca Zambrotta's right-wing cross and the unmarked Giuly's fearsome shot gave keeper Georgi Petkov no chance.

But that came after a shaky opening two minutes as Barca survived an early scare when lively Hristo Yovov was just off the target following a magnificent solo run on the left flank.

The early goal gave Barca confidence and Richard Eromoigbe fouled Eidur Gudjohnsen in a dangerous position, but Ronaldinho wasted the opportunity to double Barca's lead after his 18-metre free-kick went over the bar.

The visitors' keeper Victor Valdes was forced to show his class twice in space of a minute after a quarter of an hour saving shots from Stanislav Angelov and Yovov. Levski, however, refused to give up and the veteran Daniel Borimirov's rasping shot from 25 metres went just wide. Barcelona's left-back Silvinho then screwed his diagonal left-footer wide of the post with eight minutes remaining in the first half.

Petkov had to make two brave saves just after the interval from efforts by Gudjohnsen and Giuly. Barca doubled their lead on 65 minutes when Petkov failed to hold on to Deco's long-range shot and Iniesta made no mistake from the rebound.

The dispirited Sofia-based debutants produced little at the other end, despite the passionate support by their fans, with only French midfielder Cedric Bardon threatening a goal.

The Catalans now have to beat Werder Bremen to reach the next phase.

"We know it's going to be a difficult game, but I am very optimistic that we will come out on top and reach the last

Ludovic Giuly slots past Sofia keeper Georgi Petkov for the vital early goal

> **"The second goal was vital and took the pressure off."**
>
> Frank Rijkaard,
> Barcelona coach

16 of Europe's premier club competition," Barcelona coach Frank Rijkaard told reporters.

"We have many versatile players who are very good with the ball at their feet and capable of rising to the occasion. That's what I will ask them to do against Bremen,' he said.

Rijkaard praised Levski for a spirited performance and said a patient approach had paid off for Barcelona. "It wasn't a great game of football from us, but we were patient and got the result we needed. Levski fought back well after conceding an early goal and never made it easy for us. It is sometimes difficult to play against sides like them with the vociferous home crowd getting behind their team, but the second goal was vital and took the pressure off."

"I think we played very well until the second goal, which took the wind out of our sails. Lapses in concentration did the damage again but we were up against a great team with a wealth of experience and so many options at hand," Levski coach Stanimir Stoilov said.

DID YOU KNOW?
No European Champions have ever been eliminated at the group stage of the following season's Champions League

Liverpool 2 v PSV Eindhoven 0
Group C
Anfield
Attendance: 41,948

It's in the net! Crouch nods Liverpool's late winner

LIVERPOOL 2 v **PSV EIND'N 0**

Referee
Domenico Messina (Italy)
Assistant Referee
Marcello Ambrosino (Italy)
Fabio Comito (Italy)
Fourth Official
Massimiliano Saccani (Italy)

Scorers

65'	Gerrard
89'	Crouch

Teams

25	Reina	Gomes	10
05	Agger	Da Costa	14
23	Carragher	Alex	04
03	Finnan	Feher	22
06	Riise	Kromkamp	02
14	Alonso	Salcido	23
08	Gerrard	Afelley	20
11	Gonzalez	Mendez	11
16	Pennant	Simons	06
15	Crouch	Farfan	17
18	Kuyt	A Koné	10

Substitutes

21'	> 32 Zenden < 14 Alonso	26 Tardelli > 22 Feher <	68'
36'	> 10 Luis Garcia < 11 Gonzalez	33 Beerens > 11 Mendez <	81'
79'	> 17 Bellamy < 16 Pennant		

Discipline

0	Yellow cards	0
0	Red cards	0
3	Shots on target	3
9	Shots off target	10
6	Fouls committed	6
5	Corners	2
0	Offsides	6
29' 29"	Ball. Poss. (time)	27' 14"
52%	Ball. Poss. (%)	48%

Captain fantastic Steven Gerrard led the way as Liverpool clinched top spot in Group C.

The England midfielder, restored to his preferred central midfield role with Mohamed Sissoko sidelined, produced a goal and leadership which inspired Liverpool's victory. Gerrard broke the deadlock when he swept onto a Dirk Kuyt pass.

Liverpool's first half was one of frustration and injuries. They ended that period having seen plenty of possession and chances but without the cutting edge to go with it. Worst, though, were the losses of Xabi Alonso and Mark Gonzalez. Alonso was the victim of a fierce tackle from Csaba Feher on 14 minutes, caused really by Gonzalez's loss of the ball and a frantic lunge by both players for the loose ball. The former Real Sociedad midfielder limped on for a few minutes with an obvious ankle problem before making way for Bolo Zenden.

Soon after, Gonzalez was carried off on a stretcher after a high speed run on the left and cross at full stretch. That exertion from the Chile winger left him in agony in front of the Kop, with what was later revealed as a torn hamstring. Luis Garcia took over.

Gerrard's driving runs and hunting down of opponents – such a feature of his game – returned as he grabbed centre stage. The hosts were still on top when they took the lead in the 65th minutes. Jose Reina's ball out to Steve Finnan saw an instant pass forward from the Irish defender into Kuyt's feet. The Dutchman managed to wriggle into a yard of space before slipping the ball to Gerrard, who took a couple of strides before netting his second goal of the season – both in the Champions League.

This should have been the signal for Liverpool to impose themselves on the game, but PSV fought back, getting more men forward than at any time in the match. And it was the defiance of Jamie Carragher and growing maturity of Daniel Agger which were the key elements now for Liverpool.

Reina needed all his sharp instincts to pull down a fierce, deflected drive from Arouna Kone, as PSV sought an equalising goal. But their hopes ended in the 89th minute when Crouch headed home easily from close range,

STATE OF PLAY — GROUP C

	P	W	D	L	F	A	Pts
LIVERPOOL	5	4	1	0	9	2	13
PSV EINDHOVEN	5	3	1	1	5	3	10
BORDEAUX	5	1	1	3	3	6	4
GALATASARAY	5	0	1	4	4	10	1

Gerrard leads from the front as usual and storms past PSV's Edison Mendez

after Luis Garcia's cross from the left had been headed back across goal by Kuyt.

The visiting coach glowed about the Liverpool captain's match winning performance: "The quality of Gerrard was outstanding," Ronald Koeman said. "It was an excellent midfield performance and was something we could not match. We did not do too badly, we did not give away possession but our build-up play from the back let us down. We have dangerous players up front, but if we do not get the ball to them properly, we will not score goals. A lot of our play was really sloppy, if you do that you do not create much up front. It would have been good to have won at Anfield, but playing away to Liverpool is very different to playing Galatasaray and Bordeaux on their own grounds."

Gerrard himself had enjoyed the evening after months of being stuck out on the right hand side of Liverpool's midfield. "I've been working hard in training to get my form back, it's not altogether there yet but it's getting better," he said. "It goes without saying that I like to play in the middle. It's my favourite position and it's where I like to play. But I've got to do a job for the team and if the manager wants me to play elsewhere I will do the best I can."

> **"I've been working hard in training to get my form back, it's not altogether there yet but it's getting better."**
> **Steven Gerrard, Liverpool**

Bordeaux 3 v Galatasaray 1
Group C
Stade Chaban-Delmas
Attendance: 30,000

Bordeaux's Lilian Laslandes volleys past Galatasaray's Tolga Seyhan and Faryd Mondragon in the first minute of the second half to put Bordeaux 2-0 ahead

BORDEAUX 3 v GALATASARAY 1

Referee
Vladimír Hrinák (Slovakia)
Assistant Referee
Vladimír Medved (Slovakia)
Radomir Sluk (Slovakia)
Fourth Official
Mário Vlk (Slovakia)

Scorers

22'	Alonso	Inamoto	72'
47'	Laslandes		
50'	Faubert		

Teams

16	Ramé	Mondragon	01
21	Enakarhire	Seyhan	28
06	Jurietti	Song	04
27	Planus	Akman	18
08	Alonso	Haspolatli	19
18	Faubert	Ilic	22
24	Mavuba	Inamoto	23
14	Micoud	Sarioglu	55
17	Wendel	Hasan Sas	11
09	Darcheville	Turan	66
07	Laslandes	Hakan Sukur	09

Substitutes

45'	> 26 Obertan < 09 Darcheville	99 Karan > 22 Ilic <	45'
68'	> 19 Ducasse < 17 Wendel	14 Topal > 09 Hakan Sukur <	63'
80'	> 20 Dalmat < 14 Micoud	67 Penbe > 11 Hasan Sas <	69'

Discipline

55'	Enakarhire	Sarioglu	07'
67'	Wendel	Hasan Sas	45'
		Inamoto	50'
		Turan	59'

2	Yellow cards	4
0	Red cards	1
6	Shots on target	2
6	Shots off target	6
8	Fouls committed	21
6	Corners	5
3	Offsides	1
28' 42"	Ball. Poss. (time)	32' 23"
47%	Ball. Poss. (%)	53%

Bordeaux ensured third place in the group and a spot in the last 32 of the UEFA Cup with a 3-1 win over Galatasaray in this winner-takes-all game. The French side, who were already eliminated from the Champions League, took the chance of a consolation place in the UEFA Cup with both hands.

Bordeaux, who now had four points from five games, qualified as they were three points clear of the Turkish side and could not finish behind them as they had the better head-to-head record between the two following a goalless draw in their previous meeting in Turkey.

"It was like a final for us. Now we're going to Eindhoven for the club's honour," said veteran striker Lilian Laslandes, scorer of the second goal.

"We started brightly and scored quite early. Then we managed to keep our advantage until the break," Julien Faubert, who scored Bordeaux's third, told reporters.

The hosts were the first in action with forward Jean-Claude Darcheville just failing to slot the ball past Galatasaray's Colombian keeper Farid Mondragon from near the penalty spot in the fourth minute.

Bordeaux, the only club without a goal in the competition before kick-off, ended that unwanted record after 22 minutes when Alejandro Alonso beat Mondragon with a deflected drive from the edge of the area. Galatasaray reacted strongly, but midfielder Hasan Sas twice proved too clumsy in front of goal.

It took only 65 seconds from the start of the second half for Bordeaux to double their tally when 35 year-old

"It was like a final for us."
Lilian Laslandes, Bordeaux

> ## "Our supporters deserve a victory,"
> ## Ricardo Gomes

Alejandro Alonso on his way to scoring the second Bordeaux goal

Laslandes volleyed home a Faubert cross from the right. Three minutes later, Faubert made it three when he headed an Alonso free-kick past Mondragon.

The frustration got to the Turkish side and Arda Turan was shown a straight red card for headbutting defender Franck Jurietti just before an hour was up. Junichi Inamoto, however, scored a consolation goal 17 minutes from time with an 18-metre shot that went under Ulrich Ramé's crossbar.

"Our supporters deserve a victory," said a relieved Bordeaux coach, Brazilian Ricardo Gomes.

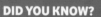

DID YOU KNOW?
Before this game Bordeaux were the only team left in Europe who had not scored a goal this season

Galatasaray's goalkeeper Faryd Mondragon shouts advice to his defence during the defeat by Bordeaux

Inter Milan 1 v Sporting Lisbon 0
Group B
San Siro
Attendance: 60,000

Goalscorer Hernan Crespo celebrates with Patrick Vieira

INTER MILAN 1 v SPORTING LIS. 0

Referee
Frank De Bleeckere (Belgium)

Assistant Referee
Mark Simons (Belgium)
Peter Hermans (Belgium)

Fourth Official
Johny Ver Eecke (Belgium)

Scorers
36'	Crespo	

Teams
12	César	Ricardo	01
02	Cordoba	Caneira	12
11	Grosso	Polga	04
13	Maicon	Souza	13
23	Materazzi	da Cunha	18
04	Zanetti	de Castro	27
15	Dacourt	Farnerud	21
05	Stankovic	Moutinho	28
14	Vieira	Paredes	76
18	Crespo	Tello	11
08	Ibrahimovic	Alecsandro	19

Substitutes
82'	> 19 Cambiasso < 11 Grosso	78 Ferreira > 12 Caneira <	15'
90'	> 16 Burdisso < 15 Dacourt	24 Veloso > 78 Ferreira <	27'
		10 Martins > 21 Farnerud <	57'

Discipline
19'	Maicon	Paredes	25'
69'	Stankovic	da Cunha	56'
		de Castro	81'

2	Yellow cards	3
0	Red cards	0
9	Shots on target	1
10	Shots off target	6
13	Fouls committed	30
4	Corners	5
2	Offsides	6
29' 53"	Ball. Poss. (time)	29' 48"
50%	Ball. Poss. (%)	50%

Incredibly, after losing their first two games, Inter Milan went through to the last 16 in the Champions League after a Hernan Crespo strike gave them a 1-0 win over Sporting Lisbon, eliminating the Portuguese side.

Nerazzuri coach Roberto Mancini opted to start with Portuguese winger Luis Figo on the bench against his former club and gave Stankovic an advanced role behind the front two.

Mancini thought his side had made a dream start in just the second minute when Swedish forward Zlatan Ibrahimovic fed strike partner Crespo, who slotted home from inside the area, but Belgian referee Frank De Bleeckere ruled the effort out for offside.

"Ibrahimovic is pure class and has all the characteristics of a great champion – he invents play, holds the ball and helps the team. He can become a true hitman too and in his third season in Italy he's learning new things," glowed Mancini in the post-match press conference.

Sporting were lively in midfield and tested Inter on the flanks, but, in a week when FIFA President Sepp Blatter caused controversy as he singled out Inter as an example of a club that "uses too many foreigners," Argentine striker

Inter's Olivier Dacourt leaves Sporting's Anderson Polga sprawling on the ground in the midfield tussle

Four minutes from the end Sporting striker Alecsandro flashed a near post header from a Tello corner just wide of the post, but with the visitors pushing forward, goalkeeper Ricardo was at full stretch to push an Ibrahimovic drive wide of the post in injury time and, although Ivan Cordoba had to produce some alert defending in the final seconds, Inter never really had to sweat as they held on to their narrow lead.

"I told you not to panic," Mancini told his supporters with a wry smile. "It's important to be qualified a round early, especially considering how the situation had panned out. Although we're sure of our place, it would give us a better draw to top the group, so we'll give it our all in Munich," he continued.

"We said it wasn't over after we lost the first two games and we have put together three positive results to qualify. Now we can go to Munich more relaxed and perhaps can even cause an upset to top the group," said Crespo.

Crespo fired Inter ahead in the 36th minute latching on to a pass over the top from Stankovic and firing past Ricardo with a confident first time shot.

While Inter looked sharp going forward, their defence coped with the neat approach play and smart touches of the Portuguese. A deflected shot from Chilean Tello, which flashed over the bar, was the nearest Sporting came to forcing a save out of Julio Cesar in the first half.

Sporting brought on attacking midfielder Carlos Martins for Pontus Farnerud early in the second half as they sought a way to get something out of the game and keep their qualification hopes alive. Inter were increasingly cautious, but went close to a second in the 75th minute when Fabio Grosso, Italy's World Cup winning left-back, burst down the flank and fired over a low cross which a sliding Crespo was just inches away from.

DID YOU KNOW?
Sporting Lisbon had lost on their last five visits to Italy

DID YOU KNOW?
This was Serie A leaders Inter's eighth consecutive victory in all competitions – a run not seen since the Gigi Simoni era

Hernan Crespo nets the winning goal

Spartak Moscow 2 v Bayern Munich 2
Group B
Luzhniki Stadium
Attendance: 25,000

SPARTAK MOS. 2 v BAYERN MUN. 2

Referee
Grzegorz Gilewski (Portugal)

Assistant Referee
Slawomir Stempniewski (Poland)
Maciej Wierzbowski (Poland)

Fourth Official
Marek Mikolajewski (Poland)

Scorers

16'	Kalinichenko	Pizarro	21', 39'
72'	Kovac		

Teams

46	Zuev	Kahn 01
02	Géder	Lell 30
13	Jiránek	Sagnol 02
15	Kovac	van Buyten 05
49	Shishkin	Demichelis 06
03	Stranzl	Ottl 39
23	Bistrov	Salihamidzic 20
25	Kalinichenko	Schweinsteiger 31
24	Mozart	van Bommel 17
09	Titov	Makaay 10
10	Pavlyuchenko	Pizarro 14

Substitutes

87'	39 Rebko	07 Scholl	83'
	02 Géder	20 Salihamidzic	

Discipline

15'	Mozart
78'	Bistrov

2	Yellow cards	0
0	Red cards	0
8	Shots on target	5
8	Shots off target	12
16	Fouls committed	22
5	Corners	4
0	Offsides	2
31' 05"	Ball. Poss. (time)	27' 34"
53%	Ball. Poss. (%)	47%

Spartak Moscow's players celebrate Radoslav Kovac's late goal, which earned them a rare UEFA Champions League point

Radoslav Kovac's second-half strike salvaged a point for Spartak Moscow as they drew 2-2 with group leaders Bayern Munich, although the German Champions have still never been beaten by any Spartak team.

The match lacked the usual Champions League intensity, with the German champions already through to the last 16. The Russians drew first blood when Ukraine international Maxim Kalinichenko wrong-footed Bayern goalkeeper Oliver Kahn with a curling free-kick into the bottom far corner from 20 metres in the 16th minute. But Claudio Pizarro quickly restored order, striking twice in the space of 17 minutes to put Bayern 2-1 ahead.

Pizarro, who also scored in the 4-0 thrashing of Spartak in their first meeting in Munich two months ago, equalised in the 22nd minute after a quickly-taken corner, flicking a header past Spartak's third-choice keeper Alexei Zuyev.

The Peru striker then beat Zuyev with a 30-metre blast into the top

"We won a point but gave up two."
Felix Magath, Bayern coach

Bayern's players mob Claudio Pizarro after his second goal in the Luzhniki Stadium

"Bayern are like a Mercedes-Benz, they never break down. Still, I'm very happy about how we fought to get that second goal. We never gave up."
Vladimir Fedotov, Spartak coach

Spartak's Geder holds of the challenge of double goalscorer Pizarro

DID YOU KNOW?
While this draw left Spartak with a slim chance of finishing third in Group B and qualifying for the UEFA Cup, it extended their winless streak to 22 matches in the competition, a UEFA Champions League record

corner in the 39th minute to put Bayern 2-1 ahead. The Germans were content to play it safe after the break but Czech Republic international Kovac secured a point for the home side, hitting the target from close range after a corner in the 72nd minute.

Spartak, bottom on two points, need to beat Sporting in a fortnight to reach the UEFA Cup by finishing third.

Spartak coach Vladimir Fedotov was pleased with the outcome, likening the opposition to a well-made German car. "We played against one of the best teams in Europe," he told reporters. "Bayern are like a Mercedes-Benz, they never break down. Still, I'm very happy about how we fought to get that second goal. We never gave up. We still have an outside chance of finishing third, thus we'll fight to the very end."

"We won a point but gave up two," said Bayern coach Felix Magath. "But it was a good game. We were very quick and passed the ball well. What we missed in the second half was that, while leading 2-1, we didn't control the ball and tried to score a third goal too quickly."

Shakhtar Donetsk 1 v AS Roma 0
Group D
Olympic Stadium
Attendance: 18,673

SHAKHTAR D. 1 v **AS ROMA 0**

Referee
Wolfgang Stark (Germany)
Assistant Referee
Harry Ehing (Germany)
Christian Dingert (Germany)
Fourth Official
Günter Perl (Germany)

Scorers
61' Marica

Teams

Shakhtar Donetsk	AS Roma
35 Shust	Doni 32
27 Chigrynskiy	Cassetti 77
05 Kucher	Ferrari 21
04 Tymoschuk	Mexes 05
06 Duljaj	Panucci 02
07 Fernandinho	Aquilani 08
26 Rat	De Rossi 16
38 Jadson	Mancini 30
33 Srna	Perrotta 20
25 Brandao	Taddei 11
29 Marica	Totti 10

Substitutes

75'	> 17 Aghahowa < 29 Marica	07 Pizarro > 21 Ferrari <	69'
80'	> 36 Elano < 38 Jadson	23 Vucinic > 30 Mancini <	78'
90'	> 19 Gay < 07 Fernandinho	09 Montella > 08 Aquilani <	78'

Discipline

Perrotta	45'
Cassetti	84'
Mexes	84'
Pizarro	89'

0	Yellow cards	4
0	Red cards	0
6	Shots on target	1
17	Shots off target	12
24	Fouls committed	20
2	Corners	2
3	Offsides	2
30' 04"	Ball. Poss. (time)	28' 53"
51%	Ball. Poss. (%)	49%

Ciprian Marica heads past Roma keeper Alexandar Doni

Ciprian Marica's 61st minute header propelled Shakhtar Donetsk to a 1-0 win over AS Roma, keeping alive the Ukrainian side's remote hopes of advancing to the next phase.

The result handed Shakhtar, under fire for mediocre play in their European campaign, a lifeline as they now had five points, two less than Roma, and could still snatch second place in the group with one game to play.

With Roma initially appearing intent on settling for a draw, Shakhtar seized control of the match after a dull first half, creating a long series of scoring chances. Romanian Marica headed home a lob from Jadson over several Roma defenders.

Jadson narrowly missed giving the home side a two-goal lead in the 75th minute, racing in on goal alone only to have the ball taken away from him by Italian keeper Doni. The midfielder was stopped by Doni again five minutes later, with fellow Brazilian Fernandinho picking up the rebound only to hit the post.

In a flurry of activity in the dying minutes, Croatia's Darijo Srna came

STATE OF PLAY — GROUP D

	P	W	D	L	F	A	Pts
VALENCIA	5	4	1	0	12	5	13
ROMA	5	2	1	2	7	4	7
SHAKHTAR DON.	5	1	2	2	5	10	5
OLYMPIAKOS	5	0	2	3	5	10	2

"The win was sweet because Roma are one of the strongest sides in Italy."

Mircea Lucascu , Shakhtar coach

roaring down the right side of the pitch, but was denied by a brilliant save from the Italian keeper.

Brandao, another of Shakhtar's Brazilian contingent, had a shot from close range parried by Doni late on. Roma's best chance came four minutes into injury time when

Vincenzo Montella, on as a substitute, took the ball after a series of passes and pushed it narrowly wide of the right post.

Shakhtar must now win their last match away to Greece's Olympiakos and hope Roma lose at home to Valencia.

Shakhtar coach Mircea Lucascu revelled in the result: "The win was sweet because Roma are one of the strongest sides in Italy," said the Romanian. "The margin of victory wasn't that big, but it still gives us revenge after the defeat we suffered in Rome," added Lucescu.

Coach Luciano Spalletti admitted he was disappointed at Roma's Ukrainian defeat and urged a massive improvement if they were to qualify against Valencia.

"The team is obviously as disappointed as I am, but we still have the opportunity to get this point and have the quality needed, so we mustn't get caught up in a panic. Clearly we must give more than we did tonight, as it was a poor performance.

Shakhtar moved the ball around quickly and with great quality, so it was difficult for us, as on the night we were never the team that we know we really are," insisted Spalletti.

DID YOU KNOW?
A week before this disappointing defeat, Roma had thrashed Catania 7-0

Roma's Daniele De Rossi argues with referee Wolfgang Stark during the unexpected defeat to Shakhtar Donetsk

Valencia 2 v Olympiakos 0
Group D
Mestalla Stadium
Attendance: 38,000

Miguel Angel Angulo drives home the first goal for Valencia

Goals either side of half-time from Miguel Angel Angulo and Fernando Morientes gave injury-ravaged Valencia a 2-0 win over Olympiakos that ensured them of first place in Group D.

Olympiakos, who had not won on the road in their previous 30 away matches in the Champions League, made a bright start at the Mestalla, but fell behind on the stroke of half-time. Then Valencia hit them again straight after the break to end the game as a contest.

Olympiakos had needed to notch up their first away win if they were to have any hope of progressing to the knockout stage and with Rivaldo at the helm they made a promising enough start. The Brazilian midfielder forced a sharp save from Santiago Canizares in the fourth minute when he unleashed a fierce half-volley from the edge of the area.

> ### "It was a good win for the team to raise the morale."
> Quique Sanchez Flores, Valencia coach

VALENCIA 2 v **OLYMPIACKOS 0**

Referee
Laurent Duhamel (France)

Assistant Referee
Vincent Texier (France)
Stéphane Duhamel (France)

Fourth Official
Stéphane Lannoy (France)

Scorers

45"	Angulo
46'	Morients

Teams

Valencia	Olympiacos
01 Canizares	Nikopolidis 71
04 Ayala	Julio César 55
23 Torres	Kostoulas 19
02 Miguel	Pantos 30
20 Albiol	Zewlakow 14
08 Baraja	Nery Castillo 07
15 Joaquin	Djordjevic 11
31 Pallardo	Stoltidis 06
21 Silva	Konstantinou 23
10 Angulo	Okkas 09
07 Villa	Rivaldo 10

Substitutes

22'	> 09 Morientes < 07 Villa	08 Maric > 23 Konstantinou <	16'
75'	> 12 Tavano < 10 Angulo	40 Babangida > 06 Stoltidis <	63'
86'	> 16 Hugo Viana < 08 Baraja	18 Borja > 07 Castillo <	70'

Discipline

45'	Pallardo	Zewlakow	30'
62'	Albiol	Maric	42'
90'	Ayala	Nery Castillo	51'
		Pantos	80'

3	Yellow cards	4
0	Red cards	0
6	Shots on target	5
6	Shots off target	6
19	Fouls committed	13
4	Corners	9
5	Offsides	4
27' 09"	Ball. Poss. (time)	26' 06"
51%	Ball. Poss. (%)	49%

Angulo celebrates his goal

Valencia's goalkeeper Santiago Canizares and Olympiakos' Felix Borja challenge for a through ball

Substitute Milos Maric, who came on for the injured Michalis Konstantinou after a quarter of an hour, was denied by another fine save from Canizares midway through the half when the Valencia keeper tipped his goalbound free-kick over the bar.

Valencia's chances of victory appeared to have suffered a major blow when striker David Villa joined the club's lengthening list of injury victims when he was forced off with what appeared to be a thigh strain in the 22nd minute.

But Quique Sanchez Flores's side rose to the challenge and Olympiakos keeper Antonis Nikopolidis had to produce a fine one-handed save to turn a diving header from Silva round post moments later.

They got the breakthrough, however, in the final minute of the half when midfielder Angulo cut inside Ieroklis Stoltidis after a neat move on the left and sent a shot curling past Nikopolidis and into the far corner.

Morientes, who had come on in place of Villa, doubled Valencia's lead, rising high above the defence to power home a fine cross from Silva at the far post. Joaquin almost added a third when he dinked a clever chip over the keeper after jinking his way into the area, but his shot was cleared off the line and he then hit the bar with a stunning free-kick taken from the right-hand touchline.

Valencia centre-back Roberto Ayala ended the game by earning himself a booking that ensured a suspension from his side's final match against Roma.

"The most important thing is that we now have two months to recover and rest before the knock-out round of games begins,"

Valencia coach Quique Sanchez Flores said. "It was a good win for the team to raise the morale."

The Greeks now had to beat third placed side Shakhtar in the final game to finish in third place and claim a UEFA Cup spot.

"It's one game, either you take it or you don't take it," Olympiakos coach Trond Sollied said. "I don't think the players are afraid to go for it."

Fernando Morientes rounds Antonis Nikopolidis to slot the second and decisive goal

Match Day 6
Tuesday 5 December 2006

Red Tide

Manchester United swept aside Benfica to qualify for the knockout stages as Ryan Giggs netted the vital second goal in a 3-1 victory

Gud-Job-Son

Barcelona avoid creating unwanted history to sneak through to the last 16

Italians Also Through

Roma defeat already qualified Valencia to make it past the group stage with Christian Panucci grabbing the all-important goal

"I think one of the British teams can win and I just hope it is us."
Sir Alex Ferguson

Barcelona 2 v Werder Bremen 0
Group A
Nou Camp
Attendance: 90,000

Ronaldinho milks the applause following his piece of genius which opened the scoring

BARCELONA 2 v WERDER BRE. 0

Referee
Massimo Busacca (SUI)

Assistant Referee
Francesco Buragina (SUI)
Matthias Arnet (SUI)

Fourth Official
Claudio Circhetta (SUI)

Scorers

13'	Ronaldinho
18'	Gudjohnsen

Teams

01	Valdés	Wiese 18
04	Márquez	Rodrigues 04
05	Puyol	Fritz 08
12	van Bronckhorst	Mertesacker 29
11	Zambrotta	Wome 05
20	Deco	Borowski 24
24	Iniesta	Torsten Frings 22
08	Ludovic	Jensen 20
03	Motta	Diego 10
10	Ronaldinho	Almeida 23
07	Gudjohnsen	Klose 11

Substitutes

62'	21 Thuram / 03 Motta	17 Klasnic / 23 Almeida	71'
73'	06 Hernández / 24 Iniesta	14 Hunt / 05 Wome	80'
85'	18 Ezquerro / 08 Ludovic		

Discipline

48'	Puyol	Wome	74'
52'	Motta	Frings	77'
		Diego	90'

2	Yellow cards	3
0	Red cards	0
5	Shots on target	3
7	Shots off target	17
19	Fouls committed	20
5	Corners	4
4	Offsides	2
25' 01"	Ball. Poss. (time)	31' 52"
44%	Ball. Poss. (%)	56%

Barcelona avoided the ignominy of becoming the first ever holders to exit at the group stage of the Champions League by defeating rivals Werder Bremen, condemning the Germans to the UEFA Cup.

As one Catalan paper illustrated in a diagram, Barca were older, smaller and lighter than Werder Bremen.

But they forgot about Ronaldinho.

The skilful Brazilian demonstrated why he had become arguably the best footballer on the planet since Zinedine Zidane's retirement, as he returned to his dazzling best. Ronaldinho eased Barcelona nerves and their passage into the last 16 with a swooning opening 20 minutes during which he scored the first, started the second, for Eidur Gudjohnsen, and performed a pass – deliberately – with the back of his head.

"That gives us a lot of tranquillity," Rijkaard said after the game. "The players put in a lot of effort in the first half to get it done."

With tension in the air, Ronaldinho set a confident tone immediately.

Watching Rafael Marquez's sweeping 40-yard pass hurtle towards him, Ronaldinho swivelled at the last instant and nodded the ball infield to Deco with the back of his head. There was a collective gasp around the Nou Camp.

His goal came after another piece of magic. Ronaldinho, swaying on the edge of the Bremen area, was fouled by Pierre Wome. Werder lined up their tall men and as Ronaldinho was about to strike the free-kick, three jumped. Ronaldinho swept his shot under them and into the corner. Barcelona were on their way.

Five minutes later Ronaldinho seized possession 40 yards out and drilled a diagonal pass over Wome to find Giuly, whose first touch took him into Wiese's area and his second teed up Gudjohnsen, who could not miss. There were 72 minutes left, but the contest was over.

Bremen had arrived with the dream of a sensational point which would consign the holders to the UEFA Cup, but it was over before they could get started. It was one way traffic. Gudjohnsen collected the ball

Ronaldinho sweeps his free-kick under the leaping Werder Bremen wall to open the scoring

near the 'D' after Deco had steamed his way upfield from a Bremen corner, and the striker drilled past three defenders before seeing his shot come back off the post. The ricochet fell to Giuly, but somehow he failed to find an empty net.

Bremen's players contemplate defeat

Only belatedly did Bremen come to life. A Daniel Jensen cross hit the bar and in the last minute it required substitute Lilian Thuram to block last-ditch as Klasnic was about to score.

Barcelona, despite taking qualification for the next phase to the wire, were alive and well in the Champions League. And, Samuel Eto'o and Lionel Messi were yet to return from injury, while Ronaldinho was in such form that Eidur Gudjohnsen left the Nou Camp saying: "One of these days he will make the ball talk."

Even by Ronaldinho's standards his was an exceptional performance, capped by a goal that had his colleagues talking animatedly about an hour after the final whistle. "It is fantastic how clever the guy is," Gudjohnsen said of Ronaldinho. "He seems ready for every situation and the bigger the game, the more he can handle it. He saw that they were going to jump. What he said in the dressing room afterwards was the two really big guys in the wall wouldn't jump, so he put it under the smaller ones. He's a great player and I guess that makes him psychic. When you play with him and see what he does with a ball, nothing surprises me any more."

Giovanni van Bronckhorst was equally enthusiastic about the Brazilian: "He knew exactly what he was doing. It was all pre-meditated although I have never seen him try it before, in training or matches. He thought what the wall would do and he pulled it off. It's amazing, but that's what you get from the best player in the world."

Gudjohnsen was not about to name his new club as favourites, especially as he knew how that remark would go down at his old one. "I am sure that Chelsea anticipated us going through," Gudjohnsen said. "I don't know who are favourites at this point. We are just glad to get through and we will worry about that when we see the draw. Before the game, the manager just said to enjoy it. What happens, happens but he said to imagine the people who dream of playing in front of 100,000 fans and to experience a fantastic night like this. For me, playing for Barcelona has been everything I dreamed of and more. You can understand why every footballer in the world dreams of playing for Barcelona. Everything about the club, the stadium, the fans, the build-up – and the best player in the world."

Chelsea 2 v Levski Sofia 0
Group A
Stamford Bridge
Attendance: 33,358

Didier Drogba gets a shot in at the Sofia goal

CHELSEA 2 v **LEVSKI SOFIA 0**

Referee
Alain Hamer (Luxembourg)

Assistant Referee
Francis Crelo (Luxembourg)
Alberto Castellani (Italy)

Fourth Official
Philippe Kalt (France)

Scorers

26'	Shevchenko
83'	Wright-Phillips

Teams

40	Hilário	Mitrev 12
09	Boulahrouz	Angelov 20
18	Bridge	Milanov 03
06	Ricardo Carvalho	Tomasic 04
20	Ferreira	Topuzakov 11
13	Ballack	Borimirov 07
05	Essien	Eromoigbe 06
08	Lampard	Bardon 27
16	Robben	Dimitrov 24
11	Drogba	Domovchijski 17
07	Shevchenko	Yovov 10

Substitutes

58'	> 19 Diarra < 20 Ferreira	30 Baltanov 24 Dimitrov	> < 59'	
68'	> 24 Wright-Phillips < 16 Robben	77 Koprivarov 10 Yovov	> < 70'	
69'	> 21 Kalou < 07 Shevchenko	09 G Ivanov 17 Domovchijski	> < 76'	

Discipline

0	Yellow cards	0
0	Red cards	0
8	Shots on target	3
18	Shots off target	8
14	Fouls committed	10
9	Corners	3
2	Offsides	2
27' 28"	Ball. Poss. (time)	25' 20"
52%	Ball. Poss. (%)	48%

Chelsea went through to the knockout phase of this competition as Group A winners thanks to a 2-0 victory over Levski Sofia.

Jose Mourinho, medicated after a heavy migraine on Sunday night that required hospital observation, found it impossible to celebrate. "My health is not very good," he said. "It is because of the medication; it is nothing special but I am not used to it. It's migraines. I don't normally have them. But I've had this one two or three days and this medication is making me down."

For two men this match was a landmark in their Chelsea careers.

Andriy Shevchenko's goal relieved some of the growing pressure on the Ukrainian striker and recalled more prolific times in his illustrious career. Arjen Robben stabbed a simple pass to Frank Lampard, whose ball was played across to the Ukrainian. His first touch took him beyond Zhivko Milanov, his next, executed with the outside of his right boot, planted the ball deftly against the inside netting of Bozhidar Mitrev's goal.

Shaun Wright-Phillips produced a far more modest achievement. The winger's goal, 14 minutes after his second-half introduction, was his first in 52 appearances since his move from

> ## "I give 100 per cent all the time and I am hungry for success with Chelsea."
> ### Andriy Shevchenko

STATE OF PLAY   GROUP A

	P	W	D	L	F	A	Pts
CHELSEA	6	4	1	1	10	4	13
BARCELONA	6	3	2	1	12	4	11
WERDER BREMEN	6	3	1	2	7	5	10
LEVSKI SOFIA	6	0	0	6	1	17	0

Shevchenko celebrates breaking his Champions League duck for Chelsea

DID YOU KNOW?
Andriy Shevchenko's goal was his first in the UEFA Champions League since he became a £30.8 million Chelsea player but it was his 44th in the tournament and his 57th in Europe overall, making him the second-highest goalscorer in the history of continental club competition, as he climbed above Eusebio in the all-time list of scorers, behind only Gerd Müller

Manchester City. It prompted Mourinho to say that, contrary to the declarations of the chief executive, Peter Kenyon, who had said negotiations with West Ham would begin over Wright-Phillips, he could not afford to lose the player from his "short" squad.

Having replaced Robben with 22 minutes left, SWP played a thrusting one-two with Ricardo Carvalho before scoring with a drive from 25 yards. By Mourinho's admission, it needed a player with his hunger to inject some desire into Chelsea's distracted performance. "We knew the result in Barcelona at half-time," he said, talking of Werder Bremen's 2-0 defeat, which meant Chelsea needed only a draw to top the group. "At 1-0 up, when we have a big month in front of us, we just controlled the game."

Claude Makelele was rested along with Ashley Cole, while John Terry was missing through suspension. Michael Essien switched to right-back as Lassana Diarra came on to play the holding role.

Levski had threatened briefly. Bardon tried his luck with an early free-kick which Hilario, playing because of an injury sustained by Carlo Cudicini earlier in the day, had to punch clear. But once Chelsea scored Levski's threat was over.

Chelsea were moved to deny comments attributed to Shevchenko in a Russian newspaper in which the striker was quoted as questioning his future at Stamford Bridge.

After a turbulent start to life in England amid much speculation as to his happiness, the Blues' record signing insisted he had given only one interview in recent weeks to a Russian magazine called ProSport and he reiterated his commitment to the club. "I give 100 per cent all the time and I am hungry for success with Chelsea," the 30 year-old said. "I have total respect for the Chelsea club and fans as well as for football in England and the culture of the country. There are always good and not so good moments in sport, that's normal. If that means there is opinion and criticism, I respect that."

Shaun Wright-Phillips shoots and then acclaims his long-range goal

GALATASARAY 3 v **LIVERPOOL 2**

Referee
Olegário Benquerença (Portugal)

Assistant Referee
João Ferreira dos Santos (Portugal)
José Cardinal (Portugal)

Fourth Official
Paulo Batista (Portugal)

Scorers

24'	Ates	Fowler	22', 90'
28'	Buruk		
79'	Ilic		

Teams

01	Mondragon	Dudek	01
21	Asik	Agger	05
02	Tomas	Carragher	23
07	Buruk	Paletta	29
16	Carrusca	Riise	06
19	Haspolatli	Alonso	14
23	Inamoto	Guthrie	35
67	Penbe	Peltier	37
55	Sarioglu	Pennant	16
10	Ates	Bellamy	17
99	Karan	Fowler	09

Substitutes

45'	> 22 Ilic < 10 Ates	10 Garcia > 35 Guthrie <	66'
45'	> 28 Seyhan < 21 Asik	15 Crouch > 17 Bellamy <	75'
75'	> 24 Güven < 16 Carrusca	34 Roque > 14 Alonso <	84'

Discipline

58'	Inamoto	Pennant	86'

1	Yellow cards	1
0	Red cards	0
8	Shots on target	6
12	Shots off target	10
15	Fouls committed	21
3	Corners	6
5	Offsides	2
33'35"	Ball. Poss. (time)	28'34"
54%	Ball. Poss. (%)	46%

Galatasaray 3 v Liverpool 2
Group C
Ataturk Stadium
Attendance: 45,000

Craig Bellamy hares after the ball with Galatasaray defenders in hot pursuit

A successful group campaign ended with an irrelevant defeat for Liverpool.

Three goals in six frantic minutes was as close as their return came to reliving that heady evening against Milan 19 months earlier in this same stadium, though this time they were not all scored by Liverpool, as they had been then, to retrieve a deficit.

Rafa Benítez bemoaned the naivety of his inexperienced defence, whose errors gave the Turks the consolation win, although they still ended the group in last place.

The inadequacies of this virtual second string was evidence that Liverpool need to add more strength in depth, now possible as Dubai International Capital were expected to complete a £450m takeover. The City financiers JP Morgan were scrutinising Liverpool's books on behalf of DIC as the state-owned private equity firm prepares a bid for the club. UEFA expressed concern that a takeover might end up widening the chasm between football's haves and have-nots. "That is the immediate threat which, in the long term, might lead to inflation in wages and transfer fees and a concentration of power that could destroy the game," said their spokesman William Gaillard.

Benítez had already been purchasing with the future in mind. Daniel Agger and Gabriel Paletta, his two young centre-halves, were let down by those around them. "My players tried and worked hard," added Benitez, "but we paid for our mistakes."

Qualification to the knockout phase was secured some time ago, but now a potential second-round contest with

DID YOU KNOW?
Robbie Fowler's brace against Galatasay were the 31 year-old's first goals in the UEFA Champions League proper

Real Madrid, Barcelona, Internazionale or Roma awaited in the draw a week on Friday.

Liverpool's defending was at times reminiscent of the ramshackle display which facilitated Milan's 3-0 half-time lead on their last visit. Xabi Alonso's horribly misplaced pass split his own defence after 24 minutes for Necati Ates to shoot beyond Jerzy Dudek. Four minutes later, Paletta headed Marcelo Carrusca's corner high into the air and Okan Buruk, 25 yards out, volleyed into the corner with the Pole, enduring a torrid return, sprawling hopelessly. Mehmet Guven then raced past John Arne Riise and his pull-back was poked home by Sasa Ilic.

Much earlier Robbie Fowler had given his team the lead, bundling in Craig Bellamy's cross, and he capped a fine personal display by nodding Jermaine Pennant's centre into an unguarded net in the 89th minute.

Bellamy departed stroppily, unimpressed at his replacement by Peter Crouch. "I'm sure he wanted to play 90 minutes, but I was thinking about other things," said the equally unimpressed-sounding Benítez.

> "My players tried and worked hard, but we paid for our mistakes."
> Rafa Benitez

Robbie Fowler opens the scoring for Liverpool

Sasa Ilic nets Galatasaray's third and decisive goal

Galatasaray's fans enjoy a small moment of glory in a disappointing Champions League campaign

PSV EINDHO'N 1 v **BORDEAUX 3**

Referee
Eduardo Iturralde Gonzalez (Spain)

Assistant Referee
Rafael Guerrero Alonso (Spain)
Roberto Díaz Pérez del Palomar (Spain)

Fourth Official
Javier Turienzo Alvarez (Spain)

Scorers

87'	Alex		
		Faubert	07'
		Dalmat	25'
		Darcheville	37'

Teams

01	Gomes	Ramé	16
18	Addo	Cid	25
04	Alex	Enakarhire	21
02	Kromkamp	Jemmali	13
03	Reiziger	Marange	23
16	Aisatti	Dalmat	20
08	Cocu	Ducasse	19
11	Mendez	Faubert	18
06	Simons	Mavuba	24
17	Farfan	Darcheville	09
26	Tardelli	Laslandes	07

Substitutes

45'	> 09 Kluivert < 26 Tardelli	12 Aisatti > 09 Darcheville <	71'
45'	> 10 A Koné < 18 Addo	26 Obertan > 20 Dalmat <	80'
63'	> 15 Culina < 16 Aisatti		

Discipline

| 21' | Mendez | Faubert | 53' |
| | | Darcheville | 70' |

1	Yellow cards	2
0	Red cards	0
4	Shots on target	4
19	Shots off target	1
12	Fouls committed	14
10	Corners	0
4	Offsides	1
37' 55"	Ball. Poss. (time)	21' 30"
64%	Ball. Poss. (%)	36%

PSV Eindhoven 1 v Bordeaux 3
Group C
Philips Stadion
Attendance: 45,500

Stephane Dalmat celebrates his goal in the 3-1 win at PSV Eindhoven

PSV, already guaranteed the runners-up spot in Group C, slumped 3-1 at home to a Bordeaux side headed for the UEFA Cup.

Julien Faubert, Stephane Dalmat and the former Nottingham Forest striker Jean-Claude Darcheville put the result beyond doubt by half-time.

"Tonight we played a good match, but I still believe that we only belong in third place in the group," Bordeaux coach Ricardo told reporters. "The first three matches we were not there, while PSV and Liverpool were ready from the

> "The first three matches we were not there, while PSV and Liverpool were ready from the beginning because they play at this level every year and we don't."
> Ricardo, Bordeaux coach

beginning because they play at this level every year and we don't."

The visitors gave PSV their first warning after three minutes when goal-keeper Gomes had to stretch to save a close range header from Darcheville. Three minutes later Bordeaux opened the scoring after Philip Cocu lost the ball and Darcheville played in Faubert, who fired past the hesitant Gomes.

Bordeaux, who had secured third place two weeks ago with a 3-1 win over Galatasaray, made it 2-0 with a superb lob from Dalmat after 24 minutes before Darcheville added a third 12 minutes later.

In between the French side's dangerous counter attacks PSV created just one chance in the first half, but Diego Tardelli missed the target from close range after some fine combination football from Alex and Jefferson Farfan.

PSV coach Ronald Koeman tried to turn the match by bringing on Patrick Kluivert and Arouna Kone up front, but, despite an effort from defender Alex that was ruled out for offside, Bordeaux had nothing to fear from a toothless Dutch offence.

It was only three minutes before time that Brazilian defender Alex hammered home a 20-metre free-kick as a late consolation for PSV. "Our first half performance was unworthy of PSV," coach Ronald Koeman told reporters. "You wonder how this can happen because so many things went wrong. This team can be excellent when everyone is 100 percent focussed. On a domestic level, matches like these are not always punished, but Bordeaux appeared four times before our goal and scored three times and that annoys me."

> **Our first half performance was unworthy of PSV. You wonder how this can happen because so many things went wrong.**
> Ronald Koeman, PSV Eindhoven coach

PSV Eindhoven's Ismail Aissati (C) challenges Bordeaux's Lilian Laslandes and Timmy Simons

AS ROMA 1 v **VALENCIA 0**

Referee
Konrad Plautz (Austria)

Assistant Referee
Markus Mayr (Austria)
Wojciech Gorgon (Austria)

Fourth Official
Dietmar Drabek (Austria)

Scorers
13' Pannuci

Teams

32	Doni	Butelle 25
77	Cassetti	Torres 23
13	Chivu	Cerrajería 26
05	Mexes	Navarro 17
02	Panucci	Albiol 20
16	De Rossi	López 18
30	Mancini	Joaquín 15
11	Taddei	Pallardó 31
22	Tonetto	Viana 16
18	Virga	Aarón 30
23	Vucinic	Tavano 12

Substitutes

75' > 20 Perrotta < 16 De Rossi	38 Romero > 18 López <	75'
83' > 28 Rosi < 18 Virga	29 Córcoles > 31 Pallardó <	90'
90' > 35 Okáká Chuka < 23 Vucinic		

Discipline
Cerrajería 79'

0	Yellow cards	1
0	Red cards	0
3	Shots on target	1
3	Shots off target	5
18	Fouls committed	19
3	Corners	3
6	Offsides	0
22' 57"	Ball. Poss. (time)	39' 02"
53%	Ball. Poss. (%)	47%

STATE OF PLAY — GROUP D

	P	W	D	L	F	A	Pts
VALENCIA	6	4	1	1	12	6	13
ROMA	6	3	1	2	8	4	10
SHAKHTAR DON.	6	1	3	2	6	11	6
OLYMPIAKOS	6	0	3	3	6	11	3

AS Roma 1 v Valencia 0
Group D
Stadio Olympico
Attendance: 40,000

Valencia's Aaron Niguez keeps his eye on the ball, but Valencia took their collective ones off their game as they went down in the Stadio Olympico

Roma ensured their progress to the knock-out stage by beating the Group D winners Valencia, who were in the grip of an acute injury crisis and had five players starting a Champions League game for the first time.

Defender Christian Panucci scored the only goal to put Roma through at the expense of surprise package Shakhtar Donetsk. Panucci struck in the 13th minute when he nodded in from close range after Valencia had failed to clear a free-kick to ensure Roma, European Cup finalists in 1984, finished second in Group D with 10 points, three behind Valencia and four ahead of third-placed Shakhtar Donetsk.

"It wasn't a beautiful game, but the result and getting through to the next stage were the important things," Roma coach Luciano Spalletti said. "The team prepared well, and showed a lot of maturity tonight. To be honest, once we went ahead I was never really frightened that the game was going to slip away from us."

The Italian team, who needed at least a draw to guarantee a place in the last 16, made a lively start with striker Mirko Vucinic muscling into the area to angle a shot directly at visiting keeper Ludovic Butelle. It was 33 year-old defender Panucci, however, who showed a finisher's instincts to put them ahead.

Playmaker Rodrigo Taddei drifted a free-kick to the far post, Philippe Mexes headed the ball back across the face of the goal and Panucci, who had slipped his marker inside the box, nodded it into the net.

Falling behind did not seem to trouble Valencia, who travelled to the Italian capital with a squad decimated by illness and injury and showed little of the dynamism of their previous games having already secured top place in the group. For most of the first half, the contest was tangled up in the middle of the pitch. Valencia finally mustered their first meaningful attempt on goal a minute before half-time when midfielder Joaquin jinked round Cristian Chivu on the edge of the

> **The problem was, there were a lot of injuries. It was like a curse."**
> Francisco Escriba, Valencia assistant coach

Roma area and unleashed a shot that fizzed over the bar.

The Spanish side looked more threatening in the second half. On the hour mark, Jorge Lopez cut round Marco Cassetti near the corner flag and whipped in a low cross to the near post, but substitute striker Nacho Insa failed to control the ball giving Roma's defence time to clear their lines.

In the end, though, it was Roma who went closer to hitting the target again four minutes from the end when winger Mancini broke forward and fired in a low, skidding drive that Butelle scooped behind for a corner.

Valencia assistant coach Francisco Escriba defended his side's disappointing performance. "It wasn't just a training run. It was a real match that we took seriously and played with all our usual determination. It made no difference that we were already qualified. We prepared for it as we would for any important European match.

The problem was, there were a lot of injuries. It was like a curse."

> **"It wasn't a beautiful game, but the result and getting through to the next stage were the important things."**
> Luciano Spalletti, Roma coach

Roma players celebrate qualification

OLYMPIAKOS 1 v SHAKHTAR DN. 1

Referee
Steve Bennett (England)

Assistant Referee
David Babski (England)
Kevin Pike (England)

Fourth Official
Martin Atkinson (England)

Scorers

54'	Castillo	Matuzalem	27'

Teams

71	Nikopolidois	Shust	35
55	Julio César	Chigrynskiy	27
03	Domi	Kucher	05
30	Pantos	Tymoschuk	04
14	Zewlakow	Fernandinho	07
07	Castillo	Matuzalem	09
11	Djordjevic	Rat	26
08	Maric	Jadson	38
06	Stoltidis	Srna	33
40	Babangida	Brandao	25
10	Rivaldo	Marica	29

Substitutes

75'	> 23 Konstantinou < 30 Pantos	17 Aghahowa > 29 Marica <	66'
83'	> 21 Georgatos < 03 Domi	06 Duljaj > 09 Matuzalem <	77'
83'	> 18 Borja < 40 Babangida	36 Elano > 07 Fernandinho <	81'

Discipline

27'	Silvestre	Brandao	13'
		Kucher	38'
		Shust	58'
		Rat	82'
		Rat	90'

1	Yellow cards	5
0	Red cards	1
5	Shots on target	5
17	Shots off target	7
11	Fouls committed	25
7	Corners	8
0	Offsides	3
34' 26"	Ball. Poss. (time)	23' 57"
59%	Ball. Poss. (%)	41%

STATE OF PLAY — GROUP D

	P	W	D	L	F	A	Pts
VALENCIA	6	4	1	1	12	6	13
ROMA	6	3	1	2	8	4	10
SHAKHTAR DON.	6	1	3	2	6	11	6
OLYMPIAKOS	6	0	3	3	6	11	3

Olympiakos 1 v Shakhtar Donetsk 1
Group D
Georgios Karaiskákis Stadium
Attendance: 33,000

Matuzalem has scored for Shakhtar, but it wasn't enough to progress

Ukrainian side Shakhtar Donetsk could only manage a draw in their final Champions League Group D game against Olympiakos, which meant they didn't challenge Roma for second place, but it was enough to guarantee them another bite of European soccer in the new year.

Their 1-1 draw, coupled with Roma's 1-0 win over Valencia in Italy, meant they missed out on second place in the group and the knockout phase of the UEFA Champions League, but the last 32 of the UEFA Cup beckons.

"It was a very good result for us. I am very happy to be playing European football in the spring," said Shakhtar coach Mircea Lucescu.

"It is not a good feeling but we tried our best," said Olympiakos coach Trond Sollied. "I said before the competition that it was a very tight group and we could either come top or fourth. Unfortunately, we came fourth. I think we deserved more than that."

The Greek champions, who had to win to claim third spot, made most of the early running with Predrag Djordjevic and Nery Alberto Castillo both going close from long range. In the 27th minute, however, the Ukrainians took the lead. Andonis Nikopolidis did well to save a close range header from Fernandinho, but

> "It was a very good result for us. I am very happy to be playing European football in the spring."
> **Mircea Lucescu, Shakhtar coach**

when the ensuing corner came over, the unmarked Matuzalem powered his header into the net.

Olympiakos fought back after the break and levelled in the 54th minute when Rivaldo, playing his last UEFA Champions League match, laid the ball back into the path of Castillo who fired past Shakhtar goalkeeper Bohdan Shust.

Chances followed at both ends as first Shakhtar's Brandao failed to make the most of a good cross and headed wide and then Shust was made to dive full-length to tip away shots from Milos Maric and Rivaldo.

Right at the end Nikopolidis made a superb reflex save to keep out Julius Aghahowa and, with the ball still bouncing dangerously, Julio Cesar swept it out for the corner. The one black mark for Shakhtar was the late dismissal of Razvan Rat who collected two yellow cards in the final six minutes.

Shakhtar Donetsk goalkeeper Shust (R) fights for the ball against Olympiakos' Julio Cesar

DID YOU KNOW?
Olympiakos, who have now failed to qualify for the last 16 of the UEFA Champions League for eight years running, finished bottom of their group for the second year in succession

DID YOU KNOW?
This was the great Brazilian playmaker Rivaldo's last ever Champions League appearance before retirement

Shakhtar Donetsk's Dmytro Chygrynskiy (L) jumps for the ball against Olympiakos' Haruna Babangida

BAYERN MUN. 1 v INTER MILAN 1

Referee
Luis Medina Cantalejo (Spain)

Assistant Referee
Juan Carlos Yuste Jiménez (Spain)
Luis Alberto Gutierrez Perez (Spain)

Fourth Official
César Muniz Fernandez (Spain)

Scorers

62'	Makaay	Vieira	90'

Teams

01	Kahn	Toldo	01
03	da Silva	Andreolli	77
21	Lahm	Maxwell	06
02	Sagnol	Maicon	13
05	van Buyten	Samuel	25
39	Ottl	Zanetti	04
20	Salihamidzic	Figo	07
31	Schweinsteiger	Gonzalez	91
17	van Bommel	Solari	21
10	Makaay	Vieira	14
14	Pizarro	Ibrahimovic	08

Substitutes

72'	> 06 Demichelis < 17 van Bommel	18 Crespo > 08 Ibrahimovic <	45'
79'	> 26 Deisle < 20 Salihamidzic	20 Recoba > 07 Figo <	70'
83'	> 24 Santa Cruz < 10 Makaay	11 Grosso > 21 Solari <	84'

Discipline

61'	van Bommel	Samuel	68'

1	Yellow cards	1
0	Red cards	0
2	Shots on target	2
10	Shots off target	5
18	Fouls committed	14
9	Corners	3
1	Offsides	3
32' 25"	Ball. Poss. (time)	25' 29"
56%	Ball. Poss. (%)	44%

Bayern Munich 1 v Inter Milan 1
Group B
Allianz Arena
Attendance: 66,000

Inter Milan's Maicon takes on Munich's Roy Makaay

In Munich, Bayern clinched top spot in Group B when they drew 1-1 with second placed Inter Milan. Dutch international striker Roy Makaay put Bayern ahead just after the hour mark, but the former Arsenal captain Patrick Vieira equalised in the last minute.

Both teams were already assured of qualification going into the final match and Inter, needing a win to leapfrog the Germans, seemed satisfied with runners-up spot.

Makaay controlled a long ball forward and beat Francesco Toldo with a great strike just inside the post to put Bayern ahead in the 62nd minute. The Italians, minus a bunch of first team regulars, grabbed a point when Patrick Vieira blasted the ball into the roof of the net with seconds remaining.

"I had a hunch it could end up as a draw," Bayern coach Felix Magath told reporters. "But that's no reason to detract from our performance in the group phase. We passed with flying colours."

Inter coach Roberto Mancini surprisingly chose to leave a clutch of first-team regulars on the bench, including goalkeeper Julio Cesar and midfielder Dejan Stankovic. But they were still good enough to keep Bayern at arm's length for most of the first half, although Makaay did get one clear sight on goal in the 40th minute,

DID YOU KNOW?
This was legendary German goalkeeper Oliver Kahn's 100th UEFA Champions League appearance, making him only the fourth player to reach that milestone

Roy Makaay scores Bayern's goal

Patrick Vieira scores Inter's last gasp equaliser

flashing a shot just wide form Claudio Pizarro's pass.

Bayern goalkeeper Oliver Kahn was left rooted to the spot when Mariano Gonzalez struck the bar with a stinging drive from over 25 metres just before the end of the first half. At the age of 37, Kahn is still in excellent shape and brought cheers from a 66,000 full house when he tipped over a Walter Samuel header from Luis Figo's 50th minute free-kick.

That was the signal for a much livelier second half. Mark van Bommel was a fraction wide with a 25-yard strike after almost an hour as Bayern pressed. Then Hasan Salihamidzic smacked a long ball into the path of Makaay, who

showed excellent control to hold off Marco Andreolli before beating Toldo to his right.

The goal brought a burst of effort from Inter, but they rarely got close to the Bayern penalty area. The home side, threatening on the break as time ran out, almost added a second from Pizarro's long-range shot in the 87th minute. Inter then finally found a way past Kahn in added time. The keeper pushed away a shot from substitute Fabio Grosso on the right, but Vieira was unmarked to smash in the equaliser.

"It was an even game between two sides who wanted to win," said Mancini. "I'm delighted that the players who don't often feature did well tonight."

SPORTING LIS. 1 v SPARTAK MOS. 3

Referee
Nicolai Vollquartz (Denmark)

Assistant Referee
Bo Abildgaard (Denmark)
Torben Jensen (Denmark)

Fourth Official
Peter Rasmussen (Denmark)

Scorers

31'	Bueno	Pavlyuchenko	08'
		Kalinichenko	16'
		Boyarinstev	89'

Teams

01	Ricardo	Zuev	46
08	Ronny	Géder	02
15	Garcia	Jiránek	13
04	Polga	Kovac	15
13	Souza	Shishkin	49
28	Moutinho	Stranzl	03
76	Paredes	Bistrov	23
11	Tello	Kalinichenko	25
80	Bueno	Mozart	24
31	Liedson	Titov	09
20	Yannick	Pavlyuchenko	10

Substitutes

28'	> 24 Veloso < 15 Garcia	07 Boyarinstev > 25 Kalinichenko <	65'
60'	> 18 da Cunha < 76 Paredes	21 Owusu-Abeyie > 10 Pavlyuchenko <	74'
68'	> 19 Alecsandro < 80 Bueno	40 Dzuba > 23 Bistrov <	90'

Discipline

21'	Polga	Zuev	44'
		Géder	48'

1	Yellow cards	2
0	Red cards	0
7	Shots on target	7
10	Shots off target	10
12	Fouls committed	14
4	Corners	5
4	Offsides	2
36' 08"	Ball. Poss. (time)	25' 06"
59%	Ball. Poss. (%)	41%

Sporting Lisbon 1 v Spartak Moscow 3
Group B
Estádio José Alvalade
Attendance: 30,000

Spartak Moscow's players are delighted with their 3-1 victory in Lisbon

Spartak Moscow gained their first win in 23 UEFA Champions League games by beating Sporting 3-1 in Lisbon to seal a UEFA Cup spot.

Roman Pavlyuchenko and Maksim Kalinichenko put the visitors in early control and although Carlos Bueno pulled a goal back in the 31st minute, Denis Boyarintsev wrapped up the three points in the 89th minute.

The roof caved in on Sporting's challenge after the heady days of that opening victory over Inter Milan to the extent that they finished bottom of the group, allowing the Russian side to progress to the UEFA Cup. The Lisbon side had started the match three points ahead of Spartak, needing only a draw to secure the UEFA Cup berth, but were surprised by two Russian goals in the opening quarter of an hour.

Spartak went ahead in the seventh minute through striker Roman Pavlyuchenko after Egor Titov hit the bar. They then doubled the lead when Maksim Kalinichenko headed home a right cross from Vladimir Bystrov after 16 minutes.

Sporting, who have now lost five of their last six European home matches, scored a consolation goal after 31 minutes when striker Carlos Bueno headed home a long cross from the left by defender Ronny.

One minute from the end, Spartak made sure of the win with a third goal by substitute Denis Boyarintsev, who tapped in a neat cross from the right by Titov.

"I am very content with the team's game, with the players' efforts and the right choice of tactics," Spartak coach Vladimir Fedotov told reporters.

Sporting coach Paulo Bento said his side were going through a patch

DID YOU KNOW?
This was Spartak Moscow's first win in 23 Champions League matches after they last registered a victory in the competition when they beat Arsenal 4-1 at home in November 2000

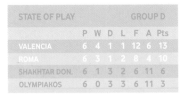

> **"We didn't have the capacity to control the game at this difficult moment that the team is going through."**
> Paulo Bento, Sporting coach

of poor form. "This was a decisive game. We didn't have the capacity to control the game at this difficult moment that the team is going through," Bento said.

"I think we started out lacking concentration, we let two goals in early on," said Sporting's substitute defender Miguel Veloso.

Spartak kept Sporting under pressure in the second half and the Lisbon side squandered several chances. Brazilian striker Liedson had a goal disallowed after 77 minutes.

> **"I am very content with the team's game, with the players' efforts and the right choice of tactics."**
> Vladimir Fedotov, Spartak coach

Portuguese wonderkid Joao Moutinho slumps to his knees after his side finish bottom of their group

Spartak Moscow's Maxym Kalynychenko and team-mate Roman Pavlyuchenko (top) celebrate the second goal against Sporting

Match Day 6
Wednesday 6 December 2006

Manchester United 3 v Benfica 1
Group F
Old Trafford
Attendance: 74,955

Wayne Rooney drives into the heart of the Benfica defence

Manchester United manager Sir Alex Ferguson said he believed a British club could win the Champions League this season as the Red Devils joined Liverpool, Arsenal, Chelsea and Celtic in the knockout stages after a 3-1 victory over Benfica at Old Trafford in their final group match. "It is fantastic for British football,' said Ferguson. "I think one of the British teams can win and I just hope it is us."

After a one-year sabbatical, United booked their customary place in the second stage with a win over Benfica.

Ryan Giggs was convinced the high and mighty of European football would live in fear of being drawn against Manchester United in the Champions League knockout phase. "There are a lot of massive teams in the next round

but if we are still in the same form when the knockout stages are played as we are at the moment, no-one will want to play against us," said the veteran Welshman.

Giggs was one of the inspirations behind United's win, netting the all-important second with a looping header after Cristiano Ronaldo had provided a sensational cross from the right.

Benfica full-back Marcos Nelson's wonderful 25-yard strike midway through the first half gave sparked a surprisingly slow-starting United into life and ignited a sterling and impressive comeback.

But three headed goals from Nemanja Vidic, Giggs and Louis Saha allowed United erased the memory of a chastening defeat in the Estadio Da Luz against Benfica 12 months earlier, which had sent them packing out of Europe. More importantly, United secured their place in the knockout

*Nelson celebrates his fantiastic strike to put Benfica
1-0 up and send shivers down United's spines*

Benfica goalkeeper Quim saves in unorthodox fashion from Louis Saha

MAN UTD 3   v   **BENFICA 1**

Referee
Herbert Fandel (Germany)

Assistant Referee
Carsten Kadach (Germany)
Volker Wezel (Germany)

Fourth Official
Lutz Wagner (Germany)

Scorers

45'	Vidic	Nelson	27'
61'	Giggs		
75'	Saha		

Teams

01	van der Sar	Quim	12
02	Neville	Nélson	22
03	Evra	Leo	05
05	Ferdinand	da Silva	04
15	Vidic	Rocha	33
16	Carrick	Assis	25
11	Giggs	Katsouranis	08
07	Ronaldo	Petit	06
18	Scholes	Simao	20
08	Rooney	Nuno Gomes	21
09	Saha	Miccoli	30

Substitutes

68'	> 04 Heinze < 03 Evra	15 Alves > 30 Miccoli <	64'
74'	> 24 Fletcher < 11 Giggs	26 Karagounis > 25 Assis <	56'
79'	> 20 Solskjaer < 18 Scholes		

Discipline

42'	Rooney	Rocha	34'
78'	Fletcher		

2	Yellow cards	1
0	Red cards	0
8	Shots on target	2
13	Shots off target	5
15	Fouls committed	11
9	Corners	2
2	Offsides	1
31' 59"	Ball. Poss. (time)	26' 09"
55%	Ball. Poss. (%)	45%

STATE OF PLAY **GROUP F**

	P	W	D	L	F	A	Pts
MAN UNITED	6	4	0	2	10	5	12
CELTIC	6	3	0	3	8	9	9
BENFICA	6	2	1	3	7	8	7
COPENHAGEN	6	2	1	3	5	8	7

phase, winning the group courtesy of Celtic's slip-up in Copenhagen.

Sir Alex Ferguson knew the outcome might have been very different after a timid opening period. "I thought the game was too slow to begin with," Ferguson said. "I don't think we play our best when we play with too much patience. There's a difference between being patient with speed and being patient with no speed and we were the latter. I think we can thank Mr Nelson for the goal because it wakened everyone up, the supporters

and the players, and we saw the real Manchester United: speed, tenacity and determination."

Vidic climbed impressively to nod Giggs's free-kick beyond Quim to equalise. It was a setback from which Benfica never recovered. "We got a break right on half-time with Vidic's goal," admitted Ferguson. "In the second half we controlled the game, it was a very good performance from us bearing in mind we had gone a goal down."

United's second goal was created by Cristiano Ronaldo, the Portuguese

Nemanja Vidic restores parity with a vital goal just before half-time

DID YOU KNOW?
Every English team in this season's Champions League topped their group

impressing in the wake of the furore that followed his display at Middlesbrough when he was accused of diving. His superb cross was headed in by Giggs.

For 18 nerve-shredding minutes Manchester United though, suffered, and it all seemed unreal after Sir Alex's team won their first three Champions League ties of the season. They were losing to a goal of stunning audacity and in danger of making a pig's ear of qualification before the three aerial goals allowed nerves to settle.

Ferguson described it as "torture" but, he was able to laugh and joke about United's tendency to make success feel like such an ordeal. His mood was not even spoiled when informed that Barcelona, Real Madrid and Inter Milan were among the clutch of second-placed teams who could be lying in wait.

Benfica coach Fernando Santos admitted conceding the goal to Vidic cost them dearly. "The goal they scored at the end of the first half caused us a lot of problems,' he said. "We started well and although we had difficulty in

possession from defence to attack we were controlling the game. Then United had four or five minutes of possession (at the end of the first half) and the goal changed the game. In the second half United were too strong for us."

United winger Cristiano Ronaldo took the opportunity to reaffirm his commitment to the club after another week of controversy. "I`m very happy at Old Trafford," he insisted "Things are running well. We are at the top of table, we are winning games. But in football you never know what is going to happen next." Recent allegations of diving made by Middlesbrough manager Gareth Southgate had only motivated him ahead of the game. He added: "I`m already used to it. The more they criticise me the better I play. Those critics do not affect me any longer."

Manchester United skipper Gary Neville did not believe booking a place in the knockout phase should be any cause for celebration at Old Trafford. After embarrassingly missing out on a place in the last 16 a year ago, and then putting their spot in the second stage at risk this season with successive defeats

DID YOU KNOW?
Since that famous night in Barcelona seven seasons ago, United had won just one of their seven knockout ties, losing to the likes of Bayer Leverkusen and FC Porto

"I'm very happy at Old Trafford."
Cristiano Ronaldo, Manchester United

to Copenhagen and Celtic, Neville, having been involved in so many of United's glory nights over the past decade, including the 1999 UEFA Champions League success, said "In terms of the Champions League, what has happened is nothing special," he said. "It was not a fantastic night for Manchester United. It was a night we would have expected and one, for 10 years, we have taken for granted. What happened last season was unacceptable and if we had not qualified, it would have been stupid and ridiculous."

United fans went home happy after the 3-1 victory

COPENHAGEN 3 v **CELTIC 1**

Referee
Bertrand Layec (France)
Assistant Referee
Bruno Faye (France) Franck Leloup (France)
Fourth Official
Olivier Thual (France)

Scorers

02'	Hutchinson	Jarosik	75'
27'	Gronkjaer		
57'	Allbäck		

Teams

01	Christiansen	Boruc	01
14	Gravgaard	Balde	06
05	Hangeland	McGeady	46
02	Jacobsen	Naylor	03
17	Wendt	Wilson	12
10	Gronkjaer	Gravesen	16
13	Hutchinson	Jarosik	20
23	Kvist	Lennon	18
06	Linderoth	McManus	44
08	Silberbauer	Miller	09
11	Allbäck	Zurawski	07

Substitutes

56'	> 04 Nørregaard < 02 Jacobsen	25 Nakamura > 16 Gravesen <	69'
81'	> 28 Bergvold < 11 Allbäck	11 Pearson > 46 McGeady <	69'
90'	> 09 Berglund < 10 Gronkjaer	48 O'Dea > 44 McManus <	73'

Discipline

55'	Gronkjaer	Miller	25'
		Jarosik	29'
		McManus	39'

1	Yellow cards	3
0	Red cards	0
5	Shots on target	4
10	Shots off target	10
21	Fouls committed	15
5	Corners	5
2	Offsides	2
26' 49"	Ball. Poss. (time)	35' 33"
43%	Ball. Poss. (%)	57%

Copenhagen 3 v Celtic 1
Group F
Parken Stadion
Attendance: 40,000

Marcus Allback volleys Copenhagen's third goal

Gordon Strachan had no illusions over the task he still faced to make Celtic a realistic force in Europe as their woeful away run continued with comprehensive defeat in Copenhagen. It cost the Scottish champions the opportunity of progressing to the last 16 as winners of Group F. Instead they finished as runners-up to Manchester United.

FC Copenhagen dismantled Celtic, with Atiba Hutchinson and former Chelsea winger Jesper Gronkjaer putting the Danes two up early on before the outstanding Marcus Allback made it three. Jiri Jarosik's late goal was immaterial. "I know the problems and I'll sort them out, don't worry about that," said the Celtic manager. "We should have been celebrating with the fans here but defeat wipes that thought away. I know how to make the team better and I'll do it, but the sense of disappointment is overwhelming just now."

With only 90 seconds played Hutchinson played a one-two with Allback on the edge of the penalty area before dancing through a weak Celtic rearguard and slotting under Artur Boruc.

Copenhagen, seeking to finish their first season in the group phase on a high, punished the wastefulness of Kenny Miller, who passed up two chances to equalise, as Gronkjaer fired home from six yards after Celtic failed to deal with one of many dangerous plays by Linderoth. Allback's third finished the contest in the 57th minute. Strachan lost Stephen McManus due to a groin injury before Jarosik arrived at the back post to convert Shunsuke Nakamura's free-kick.

That goal arrived as Celtic looked more hungry in the second half following

STATE OF PLAY

GROUP F

	P	W	D	L	F	A	Pts
MAN UNITED	6	4	0	2	10	5	12
CELTIC	6	3	0	3	8	9	9
BENFICA	6	2	1	3	7	8	7
COPENHAGEN	6	2	1	3	5	8	7

DID YOU KNOW?
Celtic had by now failed to win in 12 consecutive trips away from Parkhead in the UEFA Champions League

Jesper Gronkjaer celebrates the second goal

Dejected Celtic players at least had qualification to ease the wounds of the 3-0 defeat

"If Celtic can go through to the last 16, there is no reason why a Danish team cannot do the same."
Stale Solbakken, FC Copenhagen manager

"I know the problems and I'll sort them out, don't worry about that."
Gordon Strachan, Celtic manager

complete domination by Copenhagen in the first.

Strachan said his midfield had struggled in the first half with Copenhagen were strong on set pieces and having played with high intensity. "Both sides had a lot of chances, the biggest difference was that they were more clinical than us," he said, adding that it made no difference to him to finish second.

FC Copenhagen manager Stale Solbakken praised winger Jesper Gronkjaer and said he was satisfied with his side's performance, although he acknowledged Celtic had little to play for. "If Celtic can go through to the last 16, there is no reason why a Danish team cannot do the same," said the Copenhagen manager, Stale Solbakken. "There is very little between the teams."

PORTO 0 v ARSENAL 0

Referee
Markus Merk (Germany)

Assistant Referee
Christian Schräer (Germany)
Heiner Müller (Germany)

Fourth Official
Jochen Drees (Germany)

Teams

01	Helton	Lehmann 01
14	Alves	Clichy 22
13	Fucile	Djourou 20
03	Pepe	Eboué 27
18	Assuncao	Toure 05
12	Bosingwa	Gilberto Silva 19
08	González	Fabregas 04
16	Meireles	Flamini 16
07	Quaresma	Hleb 13
09	López	Ljungberg 08
23	Postiga	Adebayor 25

Substitutes

81'	> 29 Moraes	11 van Persie	>	79'
	< 23 Postiga	25 Adebayor	<	
80'	> 06 Ibson			
	< 16 Meireles			

Discipline

0	Yellow cards	0
0	Red cards	0
2	Shots on target	1
10	Shots off target	3
9	Fouls committed	13
5	Corners	4
2	Offsides	1
25' 44"	Ball. Poss. (time)	34' 06"
43%	Ball. Poss. (%)	57%

STATE OF PLAY — GROUP G

	P	W	D	L	F	A	Pts
ARSENAL	6	3	2	1	7	3	11
PORTO	6	3	2	1	9	4	11
CSKA MOSCOW	6	2	2	2	4	5	8
HAMBURG	6	1	0	5	7	15	3

Porto 0 v Arsenal 0
Group G
Estadio do Dragão
Attendance: 35,000

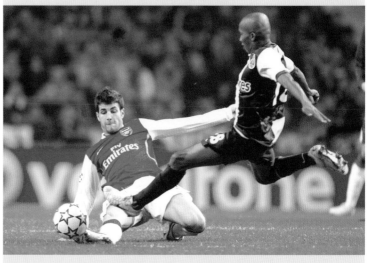

Cesc Fabregas tackles Porto's Luis Gonzalez

Arsène Wenger admitted Arsenal had been over-cautious and nervous against Porto after they progressed to the knockout stage without looking like scoring and having registered only one shot on target from a tame Cesc Fábregas free-kick.

"I must say we suffered," Wenger said. "Porto played well and they looked to have improved since our first game. I feel as well we were a bit flat physically and a little bit over-cautious. When we won the ball we didn't go forward enough and give enough support to Adebayor. The good thing is we didn't make a stupid mistake with a young defence.

Defensively we were quite sound even if we were lucky once or twice with the post. It was a little bit a nervous performance because we knew to go out would be a massive disappointment when we have been in the final last year."

The manager promised a return to more free-flowing and dynamic ways when the knock-out stage began in February.

Goalless draws had been a feature of Arsenal's path to the final in season 2005/06, including at home to Real Madrid and at Juventus and Villarreal.

Wenger's team, though, knew a draw would suffice and played with that at the forefront of their minds. The game lacked intensity and excitement as Porto, too, knew a point would take them out of the group.

It all finished with the unedifying sight of both teams making no attempt to score, accepting a stalemate that saw them both qualify. There was not even the pretence of trying to break the deadlock. It was not a positive for football. "I think that happened only in the last five minutes," said Wenger, "and the game was very fair. Both teams tried and Porto even until the 85th minute tried very hard to beat us. Overall I felt it was normal in the last three or four minutes that the teams didn't gamble any more because any counterattack or goal you concede at that stage and you are out."

Lacking the injured Henry, Wenger played Adebayor as a lone striker and kept Robin van Persie on the bench until the 79th minute, with Mathieu Flamini's inclusion a sign of Arsenal's relative lack of ambition. Still Wenger was pleased to have won the group. "It means we play the second game at home, and in a direct knockout situation it has an importance."

Arsenal did have to live on their nerves when word came through that CSKA Moscow had gone 2-1 in front against Hamburg. Had the German side not fought back to win, neither Arsenal nor their opponents could have afforded to lose this game, so the clubs ended the night by passing innocuously to close out the draw.

That made Arsenal's two lucky escapes early in the second half all the more important. The first saw a terrible error by teenage Swiss defender Joohan Djourou allow Ricardo Quaresma to strike for goal with a shot which hit the woodwork.

The Estadio do Dragão, despite its 50,000 capacity, created an unreal atmosphere. A long-range drive by Paulo Assuncao in the 41st minute was off-target, yet it got a roar from spectators glad to have their attention engaged. However, the bookies had known the score from the off, as they had odds for the draw of 5-4 on.

> "Both teams tried and Porto even until the 85th minute tried very hard to beat us."
> Arsène Wenger, Arsenal manager

Two of Arsenal's young defensive stars, Johan Djourou and Emmanuel Eboué celebrate a clean sheet and qualification as Group winners

Theo Walcott throws his shirt to the travelling fans in celebration

HAMBURG 3 v **CSKA MOSCOW 2**

Referee
Stefano Farina (Italy)
Assistant Referee
Alessandro Stagnoli (Italy)
Alessandro Griselli (Italy)
Fourth Official
Paolo Tagliavento (Italy)

Scorers

28'	Berisha	Ivica Olic (pen)	23'
84'	van der Vaart	Zhirkov	65'
90'	Sanogo		

Teams

01	Wächter	Akinfeev	35
03	Atouba	Berezoutski	06
05	Mathijsen	Berezoutski	24
04	Reinhardt	Semberas	02
14	Jarolim	Aldonin	22
27	Laas	Carvalho	07
07	Mahdavikia	Krasic	17
15	Trochowski	Dudu	20
23	van der Vaart	Zhirkov	18
22	Berisha	Olic	09
38	Ljuboja	Taranov	39

Substitutes

69'	> 33 Feilhaber < 03 Atouba		50 Grigoriev > 20 Dudu <	09'
75'	> 09 Guerrero < 38 Ljuboja		15 Odiah > 39 Taranov <	77'
83'	> 17 Sanogo < 14 Jarolim		37 Kochubey > 15 Odiah <	87'

Discipline

49'	Atouba	Dudu	31'
69'	Atouba	Berezoutski	82'

1	Yellow cards	2
1	Red cards	0
4	Shots on target	1
4	Shots off target	6
17	Fouls committed	12
10	Corners	4
5	Offsides	7
22' 57"	Ball. Poss. (time)	39' 02"
37%	Ball. Poss. (%)	63%

STATE OF PLAY — GROUP G

	P	W	D	L	F	A	Pts
ARSENAL	6	3	2	1	7	3	11
PORTO	6	3	2	1	9	4	11
CSKA MOSCOW	6	2	2	2	4	5	8
HAMBURG	6	1	0	5	7	15	3

Hamburg 3 v CSKA Moscow 2
Group G
AOL Arena
Attendance: 49,699

Hamburg supporters declare that their side had restored some 'ehre' (honour) after the 3-2 victory

Hamburg ended CSKA Moscow's Champions League qualification hopes, and regained some semblance of pride for themselves, when they struck twice in the last six minutes to snatch a 3-2 victory in their quest to make the knockout phase.

CSKA Moscow had twice taken the lead, but Rafael van der Vaart, whose equaliser the previous month gave Holland a draw against England, made it 2-2 with six minutes left and Boubacar Sanogo secured late victory.

Moscow, needing a win in Group G to stand a chance of going through, took the lead with a penalty from Ivica Olic in the 23rd minute. Milos Krasic took the ball into the area on the right and pushed it past Timothy Atouba, who was adjudged to have brought him down. Olic sent Stefan Wächter the wrong way from the spot.

Danijel Ljuboja forced a full-length save from Igor Akinfeev with a 30-yard shot and from the ensuing corner Atouba flicked on for Berisha to turn in at the far post. Yuri Zhirkov scored a fabulous solo goal to restore the Moscow lead in the 65th. Zhirkov hooked the ball over a defender's head just inside the Hamburg half and went on a long, slaloming run before beating Stefan Waechter and putting his side back ahead.

Hamburg were heading for a sixth defeat from six matches before van der Vaart smacked in a weak headed clearance from the edge of the area and the Germans kept pushing, they were rewarded when Boubacar Sanogo crashed the Dutchman's chipped pass into the roof of the net in the final minute.

Moscow finish third behind Arsenal and Porto and will go on to play in the UEFA Cup. However, there was a sour note to Hamburg's victory, as Thimothee Atouba reacted to jeering from the crowd following his substitution. The Cameroon defender, who had given away the penalty, made a series of offensive hand gestures to the fans and received a red card from the referee after he had left the field.

"That was a good match in which we played very well from the first

Hamburg players celebrate a goal with coach Thomas Doll

minute," said Hamburg coach Thomas Doll. "My players did everything I told them to and the tactics worked, but they also reacted marvellously at the end to pull it back. We always believed in ourselves and were rewarded for that at the end. The victory has no bearing on the group but it certainly does for the confidence of my players. We gave a fantastic farewell to Europe."

Valeriy Gazzaev, CSKA coach was sanguine in defeat. "I'm happy with the way my players performed but in the end it wasn't enough. We gave it our best shot and played with total effort. I am convinced my team will continue to evolve and improve step by step over the coming years. I can also promise that we will take our partition in the UEFA Cup very seriously."

Besart Berisha enjoys his goal against CSKA

AC MILAN 0 v **LILLE 2**

Referee
Graham Poll (England)

Assistant Referee
Peter Kirkup (England)
Darren Cann (England)

Fourth Official
Mike Dean (England)

Scorers
Odemwingie	07'
Kader Keita	67'

Teams

16	Kalac	Malicki	16
25	Bonera	Chalmé	21
04	Kaladze	Plestan	25
17	Simic	Tafforeau	20
23	Ambrosini	Tavlaridis	04
32	Brocchi	Bodmer	12
20	Gourcuff	Cabaye	07
18	Jankulovski	Debuchy	02
21	Pirlo	Makoun	17
15	Borriello	Kader Keita	23
09	Inzaghi	Odemwingie	14

Substitutes

45' > 10 Seedorf < 32 Brocchi	18 Robail > 14 Odemwingie < 72'
54' > 22 Kaká < 23 Ambrosini	11 Youla > 23 Keita < 83'
72' > 07 Oliveira < 15 Borriello	13 Fauvergue > 12 Bodmer < 88'

Discipline

	Kader Keita	58'

0	Yellow cards	1
0	Red cards	0
4	Shots on target	1
4	Shots off target	6
17	Fouls committed	12
10	Corners	4
5	Offsides	7
22' 57"	Ball. Poss. (time)	39' 02"
37%	Ball. Poss. (%)	63%

STATE OF PLAY — GROUP H

	P	W	D	L	F	A	Pts
AC MILAN	6	3	1	2	8	4	10
LILLE	6	2	3	1	8	5	9
AEK ATHENS	6	2	2	2	6	9	8
ANDERLECHT	6	0	4	2	7	11	4

AC Milan 0 v Lille 2
Group H
San Siro
Attendance: 37,000

Lille's Efstathios Tavlaridis celebrates after winning at AC Milan

Injury hit Milan lost at the San Siro to inspired Lille, who joined their hosts in the knock-out phase thanks to goals by Peter Odemwingie and Kader Keita.

Claude Puel's side were made to sweat until the last minute as AEK Athens almost spoiled the party for them in the other group game. However, the Greeks' 2-2 draw at Anderlecht handed Lille their first ever place in the last 16.

Despite having the support of a 37,000 crowd at the San Siro, Milan, already Group winners, mustered little threat, and a Filippo Inzaghi header that rebounded off the crossbar on the hour mark was the best they had to offer.

Lille sent their first warning early on, with Odemwingie's right-footed strike from the edge of the area forcing goalkeeper Zeljko Kalac to make his first save and it was not long before the visitors broke the deadlock. Kalac failed to hold on to Mathieu Bodmer's long range strike and Odemwingie reacted quickly to drive home the loose ball.

The hosts reacted with Andrea Pirlo's direct free-kick towards the far post, saved by goalkeeper Gregory Malicki. But midway through the first half, Lille could have extended their advantage after Dario Simic gave the ball away to Odemwingie, whose close-range effort forced Kalac to fully stretch to clear.

The home fans demanded a penalty after Marco Borriello was brought down inside the area by Gregory Tafforeau, but referee Graham Poll waved the appeals away. Kalac was then forced to make an acrobatic save to palm Kabaye's powerful free-kick over the crossbar. One minute before the break, Malicki had to make a rapid dash from his line to prevent Borriello from capitalising on a Pirlo pass.

Shortly after the restart, Odemwingie missed a golden chance to make it 2-0 after a fast counter-attack by Lille left the Nigerian forward with only Kalac to beat but his close-range effort was straight at the goalkeeper.

Ancelotti brought on Kaká in the hope his team would find the equaliser and they almost succeeded with Inzaghi's header from from Yohann Gourcuff's corner smacking against the crossbar. It proved costly for the hosts as Lille scored a second minutes later. Keita played a one-two with Bodmer before firing past Kalac.

Milan were fortunate not to concede their third three minutes later, with Kabaye's powerful right-footed strike beating Kalac, but coming back off the crossbar. The visitors held on and as news arrived of the final result in Belgium, Lille players began their celebrations. Milan's skulked off to receive a flea in their ear from enraged boss Carlo Ancelotti. "We may have won the group but losing in this manner is unacceptable," Milan coach Carlo Ancelotti said. "We have to be angry with ourselves. It hurts to lose at home and we didn't play well."

Goalscorer Peter Odemwingie wasn't surprised at Lille's astounding win.. "I could see the whole team was really confident before the game," he said. "We were really motivated and we have our coach to thank for that. Straight after our 2-2 draw last time he told us we were going to go to Milan and qualify. We believed we could do it, we worked hard and we're delighted with the result."

"It felt great to score," Odemwingie said. "It was a quick goal, which was exactly what we needed. I'm a striker and I haven't been scoring lately so to score against Milan was very satisfying."

Lille's Kader Keita celebrates with team-mate Peter Odemwingie after scoring the second goal against AC Milan

> **"We may have won the group but losing in this manner is unacceptable."**
> Carlo Ancelotti, Milan coach

DID YOU KNOW?
This was the first time that Lille have ever qualified for the knockout stages of the UEFA Champions League

DID YOU KNOW?
This was Lille's 10th consecutive match without defeat

Lille's Mathieu Bodmer is tackled by AC Milan's Kakha Kaladse (L) as Dario Simic watches

ANDERLECHT 2 v **AEK ATHENS 2**

Referee
Peter Fröjdfeldt (Sweden)

Assistant Referee
Fredrik Nilsson (Sweden)
Stefan Wittberg (Sweden)

Fourth Official
Martin Ingvarsson (Sweden)

Scorers

37'	Vanden Borre	Lakis	75'
63'	Frutos	Cirillo	81'

Teams

01	Zitka	Sorrentino	28
03	Descacht	Cirillo	05
23	Juhasz	Georgeas	31
26	Pareja	Papastathopoulos	15
37	Vanden Borre	Pautasso	13
05	Biglia	Kiriakidis	07
31	De Man	Tozser	88
14	Goor	Zikos	16
10	Hassan	Julio Cezar	99
29	Frutos	Lyberopoulos	33
07	Tchite	Manduca	11

Substitutes

65'	> 11 Boussoufa < 11 Hassan	23 Lakis > 07 Kiriakidis <	50'
80'	> 36 Lagaer < 29 Frutos	56 Hetemaj > 99 Cezar <	58'
		09 Delibasic > 11 Manduca <	58'

Discipline

0	Yellow cards	0
0	Red cards	0
7	Shots on target	6
10	Shots off target	8
9	Fouls committed	10
4	Corners	8
6	Offsides	3
28' 36"	Ball. Poss. (time)	34' 59"
45%	Ball. Poss. (%)	55%

Anderlecht 2 v AEK Athens 2
Group H
Constant Vanden Stock Stadium
Attendance: 20,000

AEK Athens' Bruno Cirillo celebrates after scoring against Anderlecht

Anderlecht squandered a 2-0 lead, and with it the chance of their only group win, when Vassilis Lakis and Bruno Cirillo struck in the last 14 minutes to earn AEK Athens a 2-2 draw in Brussels. But Athens could not find the win which would have seen them qualify for the last 16.

AEK had to settle for a UEFA Cup spot following the draw and Lille's surprise 2-0 win at AC Milan. "It's heartbreaking, but I am proud of the way my players fought back and kept going until the end," AEK coach Lorenzo Serra Ferrer told reporters. "But it could have been worse considering the way we went behind. We could have missed the UEFA Cup."

There was disappointment on both sides as the Belgian side let slip their chance of reaching the UEFA Cup. "Tonight was the story of our

> ## "Tonight was the story of our Champions League campaign. We have given away a lot of late and silly goals."
> ### Daniel Zitka, Anderlecht

STATE OF PLAY — GROUP H

	P	W	D	L	F	A	Pts
AC MILAN	6	3	1	2	8	4	10
LILLE	6	2	3	1	8	5	9
AEK ATHENS	6	2	2	2	6	9	8
ANDERLECHT	6	0	4	2	7	11	4

Anderlecht's Nicolas Frutos (L) celebrates with team-mate Bart Goor after scoring against AEK Athens

Champions League campaign. We have given away a lot of late and silly goals," said Anderlecht goalkeeper Daniel Zitka. "We are still learning at this level and our biggest lesson is that the game is 90 minutes, not 75."

Anthony vanden Borre put Anderlecht in front after 38 minutes when he toe-poked home his first Champions League goal following a goalmouth scramble. Nicolas Frutos doubled the home team's lead in the 63rd with a powerful strike after AEK keeper Stefano Sorrentino parried away a Mohamed Tchite shot.

The Belgian champions looked on course for their first Group H victory until the visitors struck back 15 minutes from the end with a header from substitute Vassilios Lakis. Bruno Cirillo grabbed a dramatic equaliser with a volley in the 81st to set up a pulsating finish, but the Greek team were unable to grab a vital winner and must settle for a place in Europe's second-tier competition.

AEK Athens' Nikos Liberopoulos and Akis Zikos (R) look down at the end of the game

DID YOU KNOW?
Since the Group Stages were introduced to the competition AEK Athens have never qualified for the knockout stages of the UEFA Champions League

DYNAMO KIEV 2 v REAL MADRID 2

Referee
Mike Riley (England)

Assistant Referee
Philip Sharp (England)
Glenn Turner (England)

Fourth Official
Howard Webb (England)

Scorers
13', 27' Shatskikh   Ronaldo (1 pen)   86', 88'

Teams

Dynamo Kiev		Real Madrid	
01	Shovkovskiy	Lopez	13
04	Rodolfo	Roberto Carlos	03
81	Markovic	Mejia	24
26	Nesmachniy	Salgado	02
44	Rodrigo	Gómez	38
08	Belkevich	Beckham	23
20	Gusev	De la Red	27
17	Mikhalik	Diarra	06
37	Yussuf	Nieto	36
25	Milevskiy	Cassano	18
16	Shatskikh	Ronaldo	09

Substitutes

34'	> 29 Mandzyuk < 04 Rodolfo	26 Garcia > 27 De la Red <	70'
85'	> 14 Rotan < 25 Milevskiy	30 Valero > 36 Nieto <	74'

Discipline

29'	Rodrigo	Ronaldo	37'

1	Yellow cards	1
0	Red cards	0
5	Shots on target	6
6	Shots off target	12
12	Fouls committed	32
3	Corners	7
3	Offsides	1
26' 16"	Ball. Poss. (time)	32' 05"
45%	Ball. Poss. (%)	55%

Dynamo Kiev 2 v Real Madrid 2
Group E
Valery Lobanovsky Stadium
Attendance: 30,000

Ronaldo burst into life, scoring two goals in the last four minutes in Kiev

Forgotten man Ronaldo scored two goals in the last four minutes to earn Real Madrid a 2-2 draw against Dynamo Kiev in their final UEFA Champions League Group E match.

The Ukrainians had been cruising to their first Champions League victory of the season following a first-half double by Uzbek striker Maxim Shatskikh before Ronaldo fired the first from close range following a David Beckham corner in the 86th minute, then added the second with an 88th-minute penalty.

The match, played in a nearly empty 83,000-seat stadium, lacked the usual Champions League intensity with both teams already assured of their finishing places in the group.

Real coach Fabio Capello rested several first-choice players, including captain Raul, centre-back Fabio Cannavaro and midfielder Emerson, while leaving number one goalkeeper

Iker Casillas and strikers Robinho and Ruud van Nistelrooy on the bench.

Despite playing only for pride, Capello said he was determined to get the result. "No coach in the world wants to lose and I would never go into a match looking to lose," the Italian told Reuters. "That's why I had a big talk at half-time to fire up the team as we were lacking some intensity in the first half."

Shatskikh fired Dynamo ahead in the 13th minute, beating Real's second-choice keeper Diego Lopez with a crisp volley after a Valentin Belkevich cross from the right. He doubled the lead by slotting home past the onrushing

Hardy Dynamo Kiev fans show their support for their team

"Ronaldo is a world-class striker, that's why you can never count him out."
Fabio Capello, Real Madrid coach

Madrid coach Fabio Capello directs operations

DAVID BECKHAM

Despite being consigned to the reserves for much of the season under new coach Fabio Capello, Real Madrid President Ramon Calderon insisted he wanted David Beckham to stay at the club for the rest of his career.

Beckham enjoyed the rarity of a full run-out in the absence of midfield regulars Emerson and Raul as Real drew 2-2 with Dynamo Kiev on Matchday 6. The 31 year-old hit the post in the second half, and Calderon admitted he had been very impressed by the former England captain's attitude as he battled to get back into the first team. "Beckham is an exceptional player on and off the pitch. I would like him to sign on for the rest of his career," Calderon said on his club's website. "He has never complained about being benched and his charm and caring attitude always shine through."

Beckham's four-year contract was set to run out in the summer of 2008, and he would be free to negotiate with other clubs from January 2007. The rumour already abounded that he had his eyes set on a move either back to the Premiership, possibly with Arsenal, or to the United States. He and his wife, Victoria, had struck up a close friendship with A list movie star Tom Cruise and new wife Katie Holmes and the Cruises were spotted at Madrid games over the second half of the season.

Beckham's return to the Madrid starting line-up coincided with the Galacticos pushing hard for the title, which was eventually won on the final day thanks to a stirring comeback against Real Mallorca. By then Beckham had signed a deal worth over $32 million with Los Angeles Galaxy in the Major League Soccer competition in the States and Brand Beckham had begun its all out assault on winning the hearts, minds and wallets of the America public.

Tim Leiweke, chief executive of the Anschutz Entertainment Group which owns the Galaxy, said that Beckham's presence could be worth $1 billion to the team and by the time he had arrived in California in mid-July, the Galaxy had already sold 250,000 shirts. Beckham-mania had arrived Stateside.

"Beckham is an exceptional player on and off the pitch."
Roman Calderon, Real Madrid President

Dynamo Kiev's Maksim Shatskikh celebrates his second goal against Real Madrid

Lopez after a great through ball by Artem Milevsky 14 minutes later.

The visitors also had their chances in the opening half, but first striker Antonio Cassano wasted a great chance after going one-on-one with Dynamo keeper Olexander Shovkovsky, then full back Michel Salgado missed another opportunity by shooting just wide of the post.

Shatskikh missed a good chance for a hat-trick shortly after the break when he failed to finish another fine pass from the right. At the other end, Beckham was unlucky not to find the target midway through the second half when his shot hit the post, while Shovkovsky stopped Roberto Carlos's powerful drive several minutes later, setting the stage for Ronaldo's heroics.

Capello praised the Brazilian, saying: "Ronaldo is a world-class striker, that's why you can never count him out. It is very important for us that Ronaldo is getting back into his top form after a long injury break."

Dynamo coach Anatoly Demyanenko was left to rue missed chances. "We played a good game, had many chances to score a few more, but once again paid the price for our mistakes," he said. "Overall, of course, I'm very disappointed with our Champions League showing this year."

> **"Overall, of course, I'm very disappointed with our Champions League showing this year."**
> Anatoly Demyanenko, Dynamo coach

DID YOU KNOW?
This was the 10th meeting between the two sides in Europe's premier club competition, with the Spanish giants holding a sizable edge with four wins against just one for Dynamo seven-and-a-half years ago

LYON 1 v **STEAUA BUCH. 1**

Referee
Darko Ceferin (Slovenia)

Assistant Referee
Andrej Kokolj (Slovenia)
Milan Kogej (Slovenia)

Fourth Official
Robert Krajnc (Slovenia)

Scorers

12'	Diarra	Dica	02'

Teams

	Lyon	Steaua	
01	Coupet	Cernea	12
23	Berthod	Ghionea	24
05	Cacapa	Goian	03
04	Müller	Marin	18
12	Reveillere	Radoi	06
15	Diarra	Stancu	27
06	Kallstrom	Cristocea	14
21	Tiago	Dica	10
18	Ben Arfa	Nicolita	16
09	Carew	Paraschiv	22
14	Govou	Thereau	21

Substitutes

64'	> 22 Wiltord < 09 Carew		09 Badea > 21 Thereau <	73'
65'	> 28 Toulalan < 21 Tiago		08 Petre > 06 Radoi <	78'
80'	> 34 Remy < 14 Govou		07 Oprita > 14 Cristocea <	82'

Discipline

61'	Cacapa	Dica	30'
		Paraschiv	35'
		Radoi	66'

1	Yellow cards	3
0	Red cards	0
3	Shots on target	2
9	Shots off target	8
12	Fouls committed	20
6	Corners	2
2	Offsides	2
30' 47"	Ball. Poss. (time)	25' 10"
55%	Ball. Poss. (%)	45%

Lyon 1 v Steaua Bucharest 1
Group E
Stade de Gerland
Attendance: 40,000

Lyon's Hatem Ben Arfa is tackled by Steaua Bucharest's Dorin Goian

Group E winners Lyon were held to a dull 1-1 draw by Steaua Bucharest.

Steaua were already sure to finish third behind second-placed Real Madrid, who drew 2-2 at Dynamo Kiev, and go into the last 32 of the UEFA Cup.

Lyon were caught off guard after two minutes when playmaker Nicolae Dica chested the ball down from a Sorin Paraschiv cross before volleying it past Gregory Coupet to open the scoring.

The Ligue 1 leaders, who were without several key players, struck back 10 minutes later when France midfielder Alou Diarra headed home a Kim Kallstrom cross from the left. "We knew they were playing well away from home so we had to perform well," said Lyon coach Gérard Houllier. Diarra said: "I am happy as it is my first goal in the Champions League. We knew nothing was at stake, but it was important to play well because a lot of us usual substitutes were on the field."

> **"I am happy as it is my first goal in the Champions League."**
> **Alou Diarra, Lyon**

Houllier had decided to rest defender Cris and Eric Abidal as well as influential midfielder Juninho while first choice strikers Karim Benzema and Fred were injured. The former Liverpool manager's tactics resulted in Lyon playing poor football at times, allowing Steaua to create several chances.

Steaua Bucharest's Nicolae Dica (L) nets the opening goal

DID YOU KNOW?
Nicolae Dica's goal was the first that Lyon had conceded on home turf in the UEFA Champions League this season

DID YOU KNOW?
Lyon have yet to make it past the quarter-finals in the UEFA Champions League

Alou Diarra celebrates his first goal in the Champions League

Champions League Legend

During the 2006/07 season, European football said goodbye to one of its greatest ever heroes. Ferenc Puskás was a sublime player, blessed with skill, flashing ingenuity and a rapier like left foot. But Puskás stood out to most fans of his era because he simply did not look like a footballer. In fact that very fact often lulled his opponents into a false sense of security.

"Look at that little fat chap. We'll murder this lot." Few judgments have been wider of the mark. "Fat and little" were as close as those remarks, from an England player, got to anything resembling the truth as he sized up the opposition.

Ninety minutes later Hungary had slaughtered England 6-3. They were the first continental foreign team to inflict defeat on England at Wembley. And what a defeat. It wasn't just the score. The style of football played by the Magnificent Magyars might as well have come from another planet. England, self-styled masters of the game, were humiliated.

That "little fat chap" was Ferenc Puskás, the Hungarian captain. Indeed, he was an odd looking footballer. He was short, stocky, barrel-chested, overweight, couldn't head and only used one foot.

Yet no one in Britain had seen ball skills like his as he inspired a performance that completely demolished England's reputation as a world football power.

Puskás was known as the 'Galloping Major', a reference to the fact that he was an army officer playing for an army team. Later, when he was exiled in Spain, he became known as the 'Little Canon' ('Canoncito Pum'). For that one foot, his left, packed such a thunderbolt shot that he scored 83 goals in 84 internationals and he remains the only player to have scored four goals in a European Cup Final.

FERENC PUSKÁS
Born: 2 April, 1927 Budapest, Hungary

International Caps	◆	Hungary 84, Spain 4
International Goals	◆	Hungary 83
Clubs	◆	Kispest Honved, Real Madrid
Club Honours	◆	European Cup 1959, 60, 66
	◆	World Club Championship 1960
	◆	Spanish Championships 1961, 62, 63, 64, 65
	◆	Spanish Cup 1962
	◆	Hungarian Championship 1950, 52, 54, 55
	◆	Olympic Gold Medal 1952

Puskás was born in Budapest in April 1927 and had been something of a boy wonder, making his debut for his father's old team Kispest at the age of 16. At 18 he was an international, appearing for Hungary against Austria in 1945.

Hungary had been a significant soccer nation before the war, losing 4-2 to Italy in the 1938 World Cup Final. But as the Soviet Union grabbed land and colonised peoples under the Communist banner in the aftermath of war, even football was not unaffected.

Military teams, emphasising the might of the Soviet way of life, sprang up all over Eastern Europe. Hungary was no exception. Basically the authorities took the Kispest club and all their players and in 1948 turned them into Honved, the team of the Hungarian Army.

Using national service as a pretext to annexe talent, Honved became the most successful club in Europe in the days before the European Cup and that club side was to form the basis of the national team.

That first season, Puskás scored 50 goals as he won the first of his four Hungarian Championships with Honved.

Of course, Communist sports teams were technically amateurs. Consequently they could compete in the Olympic Games. Puskás was captain of his country when they took the soccer gold medal by defeating Yugoslavia in the final at Helsinki in 1952.

Visitors peruse the memorabilia on show in the National Museum, dominated by an action photograph of the great man

PUSKÁS FERENC STADION

The Hungarian National Stadium was renamed the Ferenc Puskás Stadium in 2002, a fitting tribute to one of the true greats of European football

By 1954, Hungary were the hot favourites to win the World Cup in Switzerland. They hadn't lost for four years and scored 17 goals in their first two games when the finals began.

First they beat South Korea 9-0, them handed out an 8-3 hammering to West Germany — one of the more fancied teams in the competition. However, Puskás was injured by the West German centre-half Werner Liebrich and missed the quarter-final against Brazil, a shameful match that became known as the Battle of Berne.

Apart from the ferocity of the tackling, the Brazilians invaded the Hungarian dressing room after the match claiming that Puskás, a spectator on the touchline, had attacked and wounded their centre-half Pinheiro. Fighting broke out, bottles were thrown and players hit each other with football boots. Mayhem apart, Hungary were 4-2 winners.

Puskás's damaged ankle kept him from the semi-final against Uruguay, which Hungary won 4-2 in extra time.

And so to the final — against West Germany, the team they had annihilated in the early rounds.

Captain Puskás declared himself fit, but it was a controversial decision. According to Brian Glanville in his book, The Story of the World Cup: "Puskás, clearly hampered by his ankle, was unwontedly heavy and slow."

Nonetheless, Hungary led 2-0 after just eight minutes, the second goal coming from Puskás. But their game began to go awry. Germany pulled back to 2-2, then took the lead through Rahn.

The turning point came when Puskás found a gap and slid the ball past the German keeper Turek. Welsh linesman Mervyn Griffiths had his flag up. The goal was disallowed for offside.

West Germany had won 3-2 and caused one of the football upsets of the century. Hungary, having conquered all before them, had lost the one that really mattered — the World Cup Final.

Back at Honved, Puskás became even better known in Western Europe as his club travelled abroad playing exhibition matches. In December 1954 they came to Molineux where they were beaten 3-2 by a Wolverhampton Wanderers side in its prime. The victory led the Wolves manager, Stan Cullis, to announce that his team were "champions of the world."

Changes in Eastern Europe, however, were soon to see the break-up of that great Hungarian side. They were on a par with the magnificent Brazilians who succeeded them as the world's best team. But by the next World Cup, Hungary had disintegrated and were never to achieve their rightful status as World Champions.

The cause was the Hungarian uprising of 1956, when the rebels revolted against their Soviet masters. There was bitter fighting, with tanks and bloodshed on the streets.

Puskás was with the rest of his Honved team-mates in Spain when the revolution took place. They had been playing a European Cup tie against Bilbao and Puskás, along with Kocsis and Czibor, defected to the West.

Puskás's coffin lies in state in the centre of the stadium named after him during his funeral on 9 December 2006

In one of the truly memorable matches, Real beat Eintracht Frankfurt 7-3. Di Stefano scored a hat-trick. Puskás went one better, getting four goals. Real had won the European Cup five times in a row, becoming immortal legends in the process.

Their period of supremacy was coming to an end, however. In November that year they eventually lost their first European Cup tie – going down 4-3 to deadly rivals Barcelona. It was the beginning of the end of a remarkable era.

Puskás was to play in one more European Cup Final, for Real Madrid against Benfica in 1962. Benfica won 5-3, though Puskás, aged 35, scored all three goals for Real! In 39 European matches for Real, he scored an amazing 35 goals.

The same year he was picked to play for Spain in the World Cup Finals in Chile. The team was packed with talent. Apart from Gento, there was Luis del Sol and Luis Suarez. It made little difference, Spain won just one of their three matches and finished bottom of their qualifying group.

Puskás continued to play for Real until 1966 when he retired to concentrate on coaching. He had only mediocre success until 1971 when he took the Greek Champions Panathinaikos to the European Cup Final where they lost 2-0 to Ajax at Wembley.

But perhaps the sweetest moment was in 1993 when Puskás, the star who had defected to flee the uprising, was allowed back home to became caretaker-manager of the Hungarian side during the World Cup qualifiers.

The Hungarians didn't make it to the finals in America, but a great national hero had been forgiven.

Puskás was diagnosed with Alzheimer's disease in 2000. He was admitted to a Budapest hospital in September 2006 and died on 17 November 2006 of pneumonia. In a state funeral, his coffin was moved from Stadium Puskás Ferenc to Heroes' Square for a military salute. He was laid to rest under the dome of the St Stephen's Basilica in Budapest on 9 December 2006.

A guard of honour accompanies Puskás's body

Puskás spent a year in Austria, but failed to get a playing permit. He wanted to play in Italy, but he piled on weight as he drifted aimlessly around Europe and having turned 30 he was considered too old and too fat.

He was rescued by his old Honved manager Emil Oestreicher, now in charge at Real Madrid. The famous "royals" in their all-white strip had been turned into a club that dominated Europe by the vision of their president, Santiago Bernabeu.

They had won the first European Cup in 1956 and had retained it the following year. Among their star players were centre-forward Alfredo Di Stefano, a naturalised Argentinian, and Francisco Gento, the flying winger.

In 1958, 31-year-old Puskás joined them, receiving a £10,000 signing-on fee. Overweight? Maybe. A has-been? Hardly.

The player rejected by the Italians struck up a sensational partnership with Di Stefano and was four times the leading scorer in the Spanish Championship. The climax of this outstanding Real side was the 1960 European Cup Final played before 135,000 at Hampden Park.

section
five

knockout
stage

The Draw For The Knockout Stage

The Rules

Teams who qualify from the same group could not play each other. And at the first knockout round stage, neither could teams from the same country.

The Teams

Group winners: Chelsea, Bayern Munich, Liverpool, Valencia, Lyon, Manchester United, Arsenal, Milan.

Runners-up: Barcelona, Inter Milan, PSV Eindhoven, Roma, Real Madrid, Celtic, Porto, Lille.

The Draw

FC Porto v Chelsea
Celtic v AC Milan
PSV Eindhoven v Arsenal
Lille v Manchester United
Roma v Lyon
Barcelona v Liverpool
Real Madrid v Bayern Munich
Inter Milan v Valencia

UEFA's CEO Lars-Christer Olsson selects a ball from the bowl during the draw at UEFA HQ in Nyon on 15 December

Three of the four English teams were given handsome rewards for topping their groups when the draw pitted them against opposition they would expect to beat. The unlucky club were Liverpool, who faced the reigning European champions.

Barcelona President Joan Laporta bullishly believed his club were still "the team to beat". He said after the draw, "We and Liverpool are the last two European champions and it will be an extraordinary tie between us. They will be very tough rivals and play a physical style of football. They also have players that we know very well like Luis García, who played with us, and Xabi Alonso. But we are the team to beat."

Laporta was also happy for his team to be travelling to Liverpool. "It's the city where the Beatles were born and it will be very interesting," he continued. "I really like the Beatles and I think it will be very entertaining to go to The Cavern and visit the city, it will be an added incentive in this draw."

Benítez confronted Liverpool's daunting draw by insisting his side's status as overwhelming underdogs will be "perfect", with the Spaniard hoping to exploit the holders' apparent complacency to eliminate them from the

> ## "We are the team to beat."
> ### Joan Laporta, Barcelona President

DID YOU KNOW?
The last time Liverpool met Spanish giants Barcelona they beat them 1-0 on aggregate in the semi-final on the way to winning the 2001 Uefa Cup

competition. "I received a lot of phone calls from people in Barcelona and they were all saying they wanted us," he said. "I knew before that Barça would think: 'OK, good, we're a better team than the rest of the sides involved, and especially Liverpool.' They will have confidence, and everyone sees them as one of the best sides in the world, but this is the Champions League. In these kind of games, you will see a big difference in our players who raise their levels."

Barça may have needed to beat Werder Bremen in the last group game to remain with a chance of retaining their title, but Rafael Benítez was all too aware gifted strikers Samuel Eto'o and Lionel Messi would have recovered from the injuries that had kept them out for much of the season by the time the teams met.

Manchester United were happiest with the draw after being paired with French minnows Lille, who had to contend with the drawback of having to play their home games in Lens's Stade Félix-Bollaert because their own decrepit ground is unfit for European games. But while Lille may have boasted few household names – Uzbekistan-born Nigerian striker Peter Odemwingie was perhaps their best known player – their

Rara Benítez was not daunted by the prospect of meeting the European Champions Barcelona, while his opponents' President, Joan Laporta, seemed more concerned about visiting the sights of Liverpool made famous by the Beatles than winning a football match

young side was expertly led by highly-rated manager Claude Puel and they had beaten a crisis-hit United in the group stages in 2005 before holding them to 0-0 draw at Old Trafford. "[Their] players have improved since

last year," said United club secretary Ken Merritt. "They have played all the group stages away from Lille and have still qualified – so it has not made a great impact. We need to get a good result there and then do the business against them at Old Trafford – which we did not do last time."

United's jubilation at the draw was tempered only by Sir Alex's memories of the French side being one of the dirtiest teams he had ever faced in Europe. Ferguson was incensed by Lille's "pathetic" tactics in their two previous meetings. The United manager had since complained bitterly about what he perceived to be unduly aggressive and negative tactics.

AC Milan President Silvio Berlusconi heaped more misery on former golden boy Andriy Shevchenko by blasting him as a "lap dog" to his wife. The Ukrainian striker had endured a miserable time in England netting just three Premiership goals since his summer move from the Milan giants. Jose Mourinho admitted Shevchenko was not one of his 'untouchables', prompting speculation he may return to Milan. But Berlusconi said: "In my home, I'm in charge. But when Shevchenko's wife calls for him and sends him to hide under his bed he

> **"In my home, I'm in charge. But when Shevchenko's wife calls for him and sends him to hide under his bed he runs like a little lap dog. A real Milan fan and a real man would not have behaved like he has."**
> **Silvio Berlusconi, AC Milan President**

Milan President Silvio Berlusconi (seen here with coach Carlo Ancelotti) opened a full broadside on former striker Andriy Shevchenko – calling him a "lap dog"

Celtic boss Gordon Strachan itches to be out there playing rather than on the sidelines at the mouthwatering prospect of facing AC Milan

runs like a little lap dog. A real Milan fan and a real man would not have behaved like he has."

Celtic manager Gordon Strachan was so excited about the prospect of facing six-times champions AC Milan that he wished he could trade his position as Celtic's manager for a place in the team. Strachan's only previous encounter with the Italians had come in a friendly when at Manchester United. Full-back Paolo Maldini, still playing at the age of 38, was his opponent and Strachan said: "He was a young left-back, 18 years-old, and I thought 'great, easy night'. I spent 90 minutes in reverse. That was the Milan team that had Ruud Gullit and Marco van Basten; I think we scraped a draw. This must be the only time since I packed it in that I've thought 'I wouldn't mind playing in this.' I wish I had a new hip!"

Strachan insisted that Milan's poor form in Serie A would count for little. "I looked at the odds for the tournament this morning and we were 100-1, so whoever we got in the draw we would have been underdogs."

Arsenal were paired with unfancied PSV Eindhoven, who had finished behind Liverpool in the group stages, and Jose Mourinho would have another reunion with the club he sensationally guided to the title in 2004 as Chelsea faced Porto.

Elsewhere there were some ties to savour as many people's favourites faced inconsistent Roma, while Italian champions-by-default Inter Milan were drawn against Valencia and Bayern Munich were paired with Real Madrid.

DID YOU KNOW?
Real Madrid and Barcelona both moved to deny any suggestion that they had worked with controversial Spanish doctor Eufemiano Fuentes. The doctor, who was being investigated in a judicial inquiry into doping in cycling, claimed he had worked with unnamed Primera Liga football clubs. Fuentes had told French paper Le Monde: "I have worked with Primera Liga and Segunda Division Spanish clubs, sometimes directly with the footballers themselves, sometimes sharing my knowledge with the club doctors."

Asked directly by Le Monde if he had worked with Real Madrid and Barcelona, Fuentes replied: "I cannot reply. I have been threatened with death. I have been told if I say certain things myself or my family could have severe problems. I have been threatened three times and I am not going to be threatened a fourth time.

Fuentes also revealed he had had an offer from abroad, saying: "I was given an offer by an Italian club, but I rejected it."

ALL CHANGE PLEASE

New UEFA President Michel Platini spelt out his plans for a new era in European football including a pro-posal for 'play-offs' for UEFA Champions League qualification. Platini proposed a new final qualifying round where there could be play-off-style matches, where the lowest-placed qualifiers from England, Spain, Italy, France, Germany and Portugal would play against each other.

The current system works on seeding; clubs from the major leagues usually avoid each other in the final qualifying round and have easier games against smaller teams. Platini said: "It's not about disturbing England, Italy or Spain, but about finding a good balance. My problem is that the two English, Spanish and Italian teams in the final quali-fying round do not play against each other, they play against smaller teams. Perhaps the teams from the bigger countries, who have four and three qualifying teams, should play against each other. We want to add some of the other countries to the competition and to do that we have take some of the others away. I'm not sure that the fourth clubs from Spain, Italy and England are more important than the champions of Poland, the Czech Republic and Denmark."

Reaction around Europe was mixed.

I'm not sure that the fourth clubs from Spain, Italy and England are more important than the champions of Poland, the Czech Republic and Denmark."
Michel Platini, UEFA President

1st Knockout Round
Tuesday 20 February 2007 – First Legs

Red Tidal Wave

Liverpool dispose of the reigning Champions Barcelona after Karaoke wars break out between Craig Bellamy and John Arne Riise

Mourinho in the dock

Despite a narrow victory over former club Porto, Jose Mourinho's future remains on the line

French Lesson

Roma knock out highly fancied Lyon to the delight of their hordes of travelling fans

"I was pleased to see it go in – if it hadn't I probably would have had a few words off the boss."
Ryan Giggs

Lille 0 v Manchester United 1
Stade Félix-Bollaert, Lens
Attendance: 40,000

United's players celebrate Ryan Giggs's late and controversial free-kick

LILLE 0 v **MAN UNITED 1**

Referee
Eric Braamhaar (NED)

Assistant Referee
Adriaan Inia (NED) Arie Brink (NED)

Fourth Official
Bas Nijhuis (NED

UEFA Referee Observer
Karl-Heinz Tritschler (GER)

Scorers

	Giggs	83'

Teams

	Lille	Man United	
01	Sylva	van der Sar	01
21	Chalmé	Evra	03
25	Plestan	Ferdinand	05
20	Tafforeau	Neville	02
04	Tavlaridis	Vidic	15
12	Bodmer	Carrick	16
02	Debuchy	Giggs	11
17	Makoun	Ronaldo	07
35	Obraniak	Scholes	18
13	Fauvergue	Larsson	17
14	Odemwingie	Rooney	08

Substitutes

57'	07 Cabaye 13 Fauvergue	09 Saha 07 Ronaldo	67'
75'	09 Audel 14 Odemwingie	22 O'Shea 18 Scholes	90'
84'	08 Bastos 01 Sylva		

Discipline

04'	Fauvergue	Evra	15'
27'	Debuchy	Vidic	30'

2	Yellow cards	2
0	Red cards	0
3	Shots on target	4
7	Shots off target	4
17	Fouls committed	18
5	Corners	4
0	Offsides	2
28' 52"	Ball. Poss. (time)	31' 21"
47%	Ball. Poss. (%)	53%

Ryan Giggs shot first and asked questions afterwards and his controversial free-kick winner proved decisive to the anger of Lille.

"I was not breaking the rules, so I would do it again," Giggs told the Manchester Evening News. "I asked the referee if I could I take the kick quickly and he came over and said `do you want the whistle?' and I said `no, I'll take a quick one'. I was pleased to see it go in – if it hadn't I probably would have had a few words off the boss. I was just amazed by what then happened around us; we didn't know what was going on.'"

The goal, just seven minutes from the end, sparked a furore from Lille's players, some of whom at one stage stormed off the pitch. But his manager backed his winger's quick-thinking. "The bottom line is that Ryan Giggs showed great presence of mind," said Ferguson, "and that's not cheating. I believe they should be looking at themselves rather than blaming us. It is not our fault that their goalkeeper took an inordinately long time to line up the defensive wall in front of him."

Of the walk off protest the United manager said: "We expect UEFA to come down hard on them. To leave the pitch and try to influence the officials and the outcome of the game remains a disgrace. Their saving grace, I suppose, was that their players did not actually walk down the tunnel, but five or six of their players were off the pitch. If nothing else, once you do that you have to ask for the referee's permission to come back on and that didn't happen. I have certainly never seen anything like it before and I don't ever expect to see it again."

There was more controversy off the pitch, or at least in the stands, as United fans were attacked by a police baton charge as their overfull enclosure of supporters threatened to become a problem and spill onto the pitch. Post-match the two clubs traded accusations as to who was to blame, but for certain it would not be the last time counterfeit tickets would prove to be a problem during the season.

Cristiano Ronaldo is beaten to the ball by Lille keeper Tony Sylva

Alex Ferguson makes his feelings known as Lille protest about Giggs' winner

The game itself was a patchy affair with Nicolas Fauverge wasting a good early chance for Lille before becoming one of four players to see yellow in the opening half hour. Lille were on top as the game drifted along, but a moment of magic from Wayne Rooney kick-started a period of pressure from United when he took possession in the middle of the pitch. Skipping past Nicolas Plestan with ease, Rooney chipped a delicate cross goal narrowly beyond a diving Giggs. Soon after, Ronaldo got the better of left-back Grégory Tafforeau for once and stung Sylva's gloves with a rasping drive. United were now on top.

Les Dogues then thought they had scored when Peter Odemwingie headed in Ludovic Obraniak's centre, only to be penalised for pushing

"It is not our fault that their goalkeeper took an inordinately long time to line up the defensive wall in front of him."

Sir Alex Ferguson

Vidic and the flurry of chances continued with Odemwingie curling wide before Larsson squirmed free and lobbed over.

Then came the late, controversial winner, the posturing from Lille and recriminations on both sides.

Coach Puel took solace in the fact that his side were no longer scared of playing Europe's heavyweight teams such as United. "The big difference has been the change in mentality," he said. "We were like spectators last year. This year we have more ambition

and we're more attack-minded. The players have realised they don't need to feel inhibited when they play top teams. I always want my players to impose themselves rather than worry about the opposition. That philosophy has stuck with me."

The United enclosure is clearly overfull and the off the pitch problems are about to begin

CELTIC 0 v **AC MILAN 0**

Referee
Terje Hauge (NOR)

Assistant Referee
Steinar Holvik (NOR)
Jan Petter Randen (NOR)

Fourth Official
Espen Berntsen (NOR)

UEFA Referee Observer
Michel Vautrot (FRA)

Teams

01	Boruc	Kalac	16
46	McGeady	Kaladze	04
03	Naylor	Maldini	03
48	O'Dea	Oddo	44
12	Wilson	Ambrosini	23
18	Lennon	Gattuso	08
44	McManus	Gourcuff	20
25	Nakamura	Kaká	22
15	Sno	Jankulovski	18
09	Miller	Pirlo	21
10	Vennegoor of Hesselink	Gilardino	11

Substitutes

63'	> 20 Jarosik < 09 Miller	25 Bonera > 04 Kaladze <	63'
82'	> 16 Gravesen < 18 Lennon	07 Oliveira > 11 Gilardino <	77'

Discipline

36'	Nakamura	Maldini	10'
		Gilardino	71'

1	Yellow cards	2
0	Red cards	0
3	Shots on target	6
4	Shots off target	6
14	Fouls committed	16
1	Corners	3
1	Offsides	4
32' 13"	Ball. Poss. (time)	24' 53"
56%	Ball. Poss. (%)	44%

Celtic 0 v AC Milan 0
Parkhead
Attendance: 58,785

Alberto Gilardino and Lee Naylor vie for the ball

Celtic and AC Milan fought out a tight goalless draw, but there were chances aplenty at Parkhead.

The best opportunity fell to Alberto Gilardino midway through the first half but he was denied by a superb reflex save from Celtic goalkeeper Artur Boruc, while moments earlier Jan Vennegoor of Hesselink failed to convert an opening from a Shunsuke Nakamura free-kick.

Kenny Miller tested Kalac with a low effort after being played in by Aiden McGeady, while Yoann Gourcuff – in for the injured Clarence Seedorf – got on the end of a cross from Andrea Pirlo, but headed straight at Boruc.

After half-time Milan enjoyed the bulk of possession and Gennaro Gattuso should have done better on 52 minutes when Pirlo freed him with another defence-splitting pass, but the former Rangers favourite slid his attempt the wrong side of Boruc's left-hand

> **Milan are a better team than us, but of course there now comes a point where we want to win."**
> **Gordon Strachan**

post. At the other end, left-back Lee Naylor went close with a rasping drive which rose just over the junction of post and crossbar.

Massimo Ambrosini and Gilardino passed up decent half-chances from the edge of the area, but Celtic held on under heavy late pressure.

Gordon Strachan believed the Scottish champions had a realistic chance at the San Siro. He insisted that victory was possible should they play to the best of their abilities. "It won't be a night to carry passengers," said a bullish Strachan. "Milan are a better team than us, I think we all agree on that. They

have better players. We have been lucky this season to play some world famous teams; Manchester United, Benfica, Milan — it has been fantastic. But of course there now comes a point where we want to win."

Strachan has a fondness for statistics, and needs no reminding that his

Parkhead in full cry

Alberto Gilardino reflects on a missed opportunity for Milan

side have never achieved an away victory in this competition. Yet the one time Celtic avoided defeat on their UEFA Champions League travels was Barcelona's Nou Camp.

The attacking threat of Carlo Ancelotti's men, sixth in Serie A, had been severely blunted by the sale of Andriy Shevchenko to Chelsea; their current strikers, Ricardo Oliviera, Filippo Inzaghi and Alberto Gilardino, scored only 17 goals between them in this campaign.

"Celtic are a very physical team. They play at high rhythm," said Ancelotti.

> **"Celtic are a very physical team. They play at high rhythm."**
> **Carlo Ancelotti**

PSV Eindhoven 1 v Arsenal 0
Philips Stadion
Attendance: 35,000

Cesc Fabregas gets in a shot despite the attentions of Timmy Simons

PSV EINDHO'N. 1 V   ARSENAL 0

Referee
Tom Henning Øvrebø (NOR)
Assistant Referee
Geir Age Holen (NOR) Erik Raestad (NOR)
Fourth Official
Tommy Skjerven (NOR)
UEFA Referee Observer
Günter Benkö (AUT)

Scorers

83' Mendez

Teams

PSV Eindhoven		Arsenal	
01	Gomes	Lehmann	01
14	Da Costa	Clichy	22
04	Alex	Gallas	10
02	Kromkamp	Senderos	06
23	Salcido	Toure	05
08	Cocu	Gilberto Silva	19
15	Culina	Fabregas	04
11	Mendez	Hleb	13
06	Simons	Rosicky	07
10	Arouna Koné	Adebayor	25
26	Tardelli	Henry	14

Substitutes

65'	> 28 Xiang < 14 Da Costa	09 Baptista > 13 Hleb <	76'
75'	> 07 Väyrynen < 26 Tardelli		

Discipline

	Senderos	63'

PSV		Arsenal
0	Yellow cards	1
0	Red cards	0
4	Shots on target	6
2	Shots off target	5
9	Fouls committed	8
1	Corners	9
0	Offsides	2
32' 20"	Ball. Poss. (time)	36' 36"
46%	Ball. Poss. (%)	54%

PSV Eindhoven took an important step towards reaching the quarter-finals of the Champions League for the second time in three years with a 1-0 win against Arsenal in the first leg of their last-16 tie.

PSV spent the first half on the back foot, but made Arsenal pay for yet another catalogue of missed chances when Edison Méndez drilled low past Jens Lehmann midway through the second half. The goal caused a tense finale which PSV survived thanks largely to the excellence of goalkeeper Heurelho Gomes.

Fancy dress added colour to the crescendo that greeted PSV's early attacks, despite the absence of top scorer Jefferson Farfan through injury, yet it was Arsenal who worked the first opening on 14 minutes. Henry's pass was deflected to Tomás Rosicky, whose shot crept under goalkeeper Gomes only to be hacked clear by Carlos Salcido. PSV were giving the ball away too easily and not until the 21st minute did they carve out a clear sight of goal, Lehmann blocking Méndez's snapshot from distance.

The Gunners were finding their range, and Henry and Rosicky both went close before the Frenchman spurned a terrific opportunity to put his team ahead on 43 minutes, firing straight at Gomes after turning his marker on the penalty spot.

DID YOU KNOW?
Edison Mendez's angled winner past Jens Lehmann was the first goal ever scored by an Ecuadorian in Europe's showpiece tournament. "I feel like when PSV play my whole country plays too," he said. "All of Ecuador cheered that effort against Arsenal. It was a historic achievement."

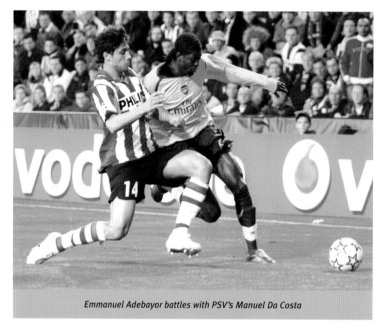

Emmanuel Adebayor battles with PSV's Manuel Da Costa

PSV pressed higher after the interval and finally got behind the Arsenal defence on 53 minutes when Phillip Cocu's raking pass picked out Arouna Koné. The Ivory Coast forward shot first time but dragged his attempt wide. He made amends eight minutes later, however, laying the ball off to Méndez who drilled low beyond Lehmann to give PSV the advantage.

Arsenal responded with further pressure. On 69 minutes, Gomes leapt spectacularly to tip over Cesc Fabregas's drive, then five minutes later dived to grasp Adebayor's header. Arsenal, though, could not find a way

Edison Mendez scores and then celebrates his goal with his team-mates

**"This was the best possible result for us and based on our second-half performance, we deserved it."
Ronald Koeman, PSV coach**

It all gets a bit much for the Arsenal manager as his team spurn yet more chances

"We lost our rhythm and didn't create anything. In the first half we had our chances, but didn't take them."
Arsène Wenger, Arsenal manager

through, with the Brazilian keeper and compatriot Alex in the heart of the defence fittingly ensuring the Carnival celebrations would carry on long into the night.

"This was the best possible result for us and based on our second-half performance, we deserved it," glowed PSV coach Ronald Koeman. "We've shown this evening nothing is impossible in football — we might have less quality than Arsenal, but if you have the right tactics and the organisation is perfect, it's possible to beat them."

Arsène Wenger looked forward to the home leg. "We played well in the first half, but a lot worse in the second. The team's level dropped and the fluency and the passing were not as good. We lost our rhythm and didn't create anything. The result is disappointing for us, but we have enough confidence to get through in the second match."

DID YOU KNOW?
Left-back Sun Xiang made his debut in this game, making him the first Chinese soccer player to play in the UEFA Champions League

DID YOU KNOW?
No nation has ever had four teams in the quarter-finals of the Champions League. The last time a country provided four clubs in the last eight of a European competition was back in 2001 when Spain's Alaves, Celta Vigo, Barcelona and Rayo Vallecano all reached the UEFA Cup quarter-finals. None of them went on to lift the trophy, though, with Liverpool beating Barcelona in the semi-final and Alaves in the final

REAL MADRID 3 v BAYERN MUN. 2

Referee
Frank De Bleeckere (BEL)

Assistant Referee
Peter Hermans (BEL) Walter Vromans (BEL)

Fourth Official
Serge Gumienny (BEL)

UEFA Referee Observer
Ken Ridden (ENG)

Scorers

10', 28'	Raul	Lucio	23'
34'	van Nistelrooy	van Bommel	88'

Teams

01	Casillas	Kahn	01
05	Cannavaro	da Silva	03
03	Roberto Carlos	Lahm	21
21	Helguera	Sagnol	02
38	Gómez	van Buyten	05
23	Beckham	Demichelis	06
16	Gago	Hargreaves	23
14	Guti	Schweinsteiger	31
07	Raúl	van Bommel	17
20	Higuaín	Makaay	10
17	van Nistelrooy	Podolski	11

Substitutes

53'	10 Robinho / 20 Higuaín	20 Salihamidzic / 06 Demichelis	45'
59'	15 Raul Bravo / 03 Roberto Carlos	14 Pizarro / 11 Podolski	61'
		07 Scholl / 31 Schweinsteiger	70'

Discipline

	Demichelis	38'
	Schweinsteiger	56'
	Hargreaves	60'

0	Yellow cards	3
0	Red cards	0
6	Shots on target	7
2	Shots off target	6
20	Fouls committed	23
2	Corners	4
2	Offsides	2
21' 57"	Ball. Poss. (time)	30' 15"
42%	Ball. Poss. (%)	58%

Real Madrid 3 v Bayern Munich 2
Bernabeu Stadium
Attendance: 80,000

Oliver Kahn can't contain his joy at Bayern's second goal at the Bernabeu

Fabio Capello, whose side went into this game having scored just two goals in their last four Primera División matches, faced further pressure after a pulsating match ended with a vital last-minute goal for Bayern.

The hosts had already launched several forays into the Bayern area by the time they went ahead in the tenth minute. Van Nistelrooy split the defence with a devastating through-ball and, although Oliver Kahn half-blocked Raúl's attempt to round him, the rebound fell perfectly for the Spanish international to roll his fourth goal of this campaign into the unguarded net

But Bayern hit back almost immediately when Willy Sagnol's free-kick from the right saw Iker Casillas stay rooted to his line to allow Lucio to head home. It was a temporary reprieve: Madrid retook the lead as easily as they had lost it. Beckham's corner reached Ivan Helguera, whose header did not seem dangerous, but it looped up in the air and dropped in just below the crossbar, being followed up by Raul who was credited with the goal.

Five minutes later, another Beckham dead ball delivery, another Helguera header, the ball going in at the same post. This time Ruud van Nistelrooy was alert to poke home the defender's header. Madrid were cruising, Beckham having a wonderful free-kick tipped

> **"I know Real are vulnerable. Our chances of progressing are better than 50 percent."**
> **Ottmar Hitzfeld, coach Bayern Munich**

over the bar in the opening moments of the second half.

Surprisingly Bayern then took control. "At 3-1 up, the fear took hold of us," said Capello. "Things have not been going well for us, maybe there was a psychological issue there. We tied up, like a tennis player whose arm goes. Teams have scored a lot of goals against us at the Bernabeu and we suffered a kind of fear."

The introduction of Claudio Pizarro, who Capello hailed as having "changed the game", tipped the balance in Bayern's favour as Madrid slipped deeper into defence. He brought one sensational save from Casillas, but just when it looked like the final whistle was to bring revival to the Bernabeu after all, their crisis was prolonged when, in the 88th minute, a loose ball fell to van Bommel on the edge of the box and the

David Beckham thanks the crowd for their support after inspiring
Real Madrid to a narrow 3-2 win over Bayern Munich

"Bayern grew in strength. They played more long, dangerous passes in the second half and psychologically we were afraid."
Fabio Capello,
coach
Real Madrid

Oliver Kahn tips over a long range shot as Real look to extend their lead

Mark van Bommel celebrates his late and vital goal to make it 3-2

Dutchman duly made no mistake to set up an enthralling second leg.

Real's plight was made worse when news came through that David Beckham would be out for six weeks after tearing a ligament in his right knee.

Bayern Munich coach Ottmar Hitzfeld criticised Real Madrid saying their defensive weaknesses would help his side's bid to overturn a 3-2 first-leg deficit. Hitzfeld told the Frankfurter Allgemeine Sonntagszeitung that even though Italy captain Fabio Cannavaro was one of the best players at last year's World Cup, the centre-half was having 'big problems' with the Spanish giants. "The (Real) coach can't sort out the defence, Fabio Capello, a master of defensive strategy," he said. "I know Real are vulnerable. Our chances of progressing are better than 50 percent. We have shown how to put (them) under pressure and how to exploit the weak points in their defence."

Madrid coach Fabio Capello said: "Bayern grew in strength. They played more long, dangerous passes in the second half and psychologically we were afraid — like when a tennis player stiffens up on a crucial point. Both teams performed better than in recent games and our supporters were also a great help to us. It was important to get a win."

First Knockout Round
Wednesday 21 February 2007 – First Legs

Barcelona 1 v Liverpool 2
Nou Camp
Attendance: 95,000

Craig Bellamy's own peculiar celebration rounded off an incredible week for himself and Liverpool

BARCELONA 1 v **LIVERPOOL 2**

Referee
Kyros Vassaras (GRE)

Assistant Referee
Dimitrios Bozatzidis (GRE)
Dimitrios Saraidaris (GRE)

Fourth Official
Ioannis Tsachilidis (GRE)

UEFA Referee Observer
Serge Muhmenthaler (SUI)

Scorers		
14'	Deco	
	Bellamy	43'
	Riise	74'

Teams		
01 Valdés	Reina	25
02 Belletti	Agger	05
04 Márquez	Arbeloa	02
05 Puyol	Carragher	23
11 Zambrotta	Finnan	03
20 Deco	Riise	06
06 Xavi	Alonso	14
03 Motta	Gerrard	08
10 Ronaldinho	Sissoko	22
19 Messi	Bellamy	17
22 Saviola	Kuyt	18

Substitutes			
54'	> 24 Iniesta / < 03 Motta	16 Pennant > / 17 Bellamy <	80'
65'	> 08 Ludovic / < 06 Xavi	32? Zenden > / 22 Sissoko <	84'
83'	> 07 Gudjohnsen / < 22 Saviola	15 Crouch > / 18 Kuyt <	90'

Discipline		
	Agger	23'
	Kuyt	35'
	Sissoko	61'
	Bellamy	77'

0	Yellow cards	4
0	Red cards	0
4	Shots on target	5
8	Shots off target	2
17	Fouls committed	29
6	Corners	2
5	Offsides	6
33' 57"	Ball. Poss. (time)	20' 14"
62%	Ball. Poss. (%)	38%

Liverpool stood on the verge of knocking out the holders after almost as spectacular a recovery as overhauling the 3-0 deficit to Milan before winning the tournament in 2005. The tie was played against the backdrop of events on the Algarve, when Liverpool's training camp had degenerated into a drunken frenzy with Craig Bellamy threatening John Arne Riise with a nine-iron golf club and earning an £80,000 fine. But, after the Welshman celebrated his equaliser in the Nou Camp with a lusty golf swing as he tore towards the corner flag, all that was left was for Bellamy to tee up Riise for the second-half winner to complete an astonishing comeback.

> ## "We've got to be realistic. We're facing the best side in Europe, a team full of world-class players, even if they're not playing at top form of late."
> ## Steven Gerrard

Barca's players celebrate Deco's early goal

> ## "It was destiny for both of us to score."
> ## John Arne Riise

Barcelona were as frail in defence as they were delicately beguiling in attack and took the lead in the 14th minute. Gerrard could not stop Zambrotta from crossing, Arbeloa, on his first start, failed to climb high enough to connect and Deco, free of Riise, headed in at the far post. Deco was soon shooting against Pepe Reina after Messi had put him through. Liverpool, though, were bright when they got a loan of the ball.

Barca laid siege to the Liverpool goal for the next 15 minutes. However, the Catalan giants did not make their dominance count. "We did not know how to score when we had the chance," said Rijkaard, who felt Bellamy's goal on the stroke of half-time was a massive psychological blow for his side. "I think their goal affected us mentally," the former AC Milan midfielder admitted. "It

was more a question of not knowing how to finish off the game than anything. It was the right moment to finish the game, because Liverpool did not look like they had the confidence that they had after they had made it 1-1. But we didn't."

It was Bellamy's late leveller which began the turnaround. On 39 minutes he had fired a warning shot after Steven Gerrard had swung a free-kick to the far post, where the unmarked striker headed into the side-netting. Barça did not heed the warning and two minutes before the break, Liverpool levelled. Finnan's cross from the right reached Bellamy, who headed goalwards and Valdés, though getting both hands on to the ball, carried it over the line. Although Dirk Kuyt put the loose ball into the net, the goal was Bellamy's.

The Nutter with the Putter had become the unlikely hero. "This is the best moment I've had in football, the highlight of my career," he said.

The second half opened with Liverpool far more effective. Rijkaard's reaction was characteristic, if reckless, and defensive resilience vanished from their midfield as Iniesta took over from Motta. When substitute Giuly passed back into his own area Valdés impetuously picked the ball up to give away a free-kick. It was touched to Gerrard and, although the goalkeeper blocked his drive, Liverpool were so full of verve that Arbeloa swept in a dashing cross which Kuyt headed on to the bar.

Barcelona did get an invitation to regain the lead immediately before they fell behind. In the 73rd minute Saviola wormed his way through and, when the ball ran free after being blocked by Reina, Messi was set to finish until Arbeloa heroically got in the way. Moments later Gerrard fed Kuyt and, although the Dutchman miscontrolled, Valdés hesitated and Márquez

inadvertently knocked the ball down to Bellamy, who squared for Riise to lash into the net with a right-foot drive.

A late free-kick by Deco bounced off the far post, but Liverpool clung on to secure a famous victory.

"It was destiny for both of us to score, I think," conceded Riise in the aftermath, his fierce right-footed finish seared on the memory. "Both Bellamy and myself have had a difficult run-up [to the game], but we've put it behind us when it mattered. The team is happy. I'm happy for Craig that he scored. As for my goal, I don't think I've ever scored with my right foot. I just played on instinct – I could have taken a touch with my left, but when I got the ball from Bellamy I just thought 'Smash it'."

Barcelona's preparations had also been thrown into chaos by striker Samuel Eto'o, who had recently returned after four months out with a knee injury and played for nine minutes in a league game against Osasuna, but his apparent refusal to play against Racing Santander made headline news.

> **"We have the team to beat Liverpool and at moments like this I prefer to stay optimistic."**
> **Joan Laporta, Barcelona President**

Amid confusion, Craig Bellamy's header has been allowed to roll over the line by goalkeeper Valdes

John Arne Riise lashes home the winner from Bellamy's pass

Asked if he would apologise, Eto'o, alluding to divisions within the camp, said: "I don't have to give any explanations to anyone. I will only give an explanation to the club if they ask me. If I come out and speak then people will see what is going on. I can forgive, but not forget."

The striker's outburst lifted the lid on divisions at the reigning champions, with the media speculating that the rivalry between Eto'o and Ronaldinho could prompt one of the players to leave at the end of the season.

Liverpool's victorious players made a point of suppressing their public celebrations after the match, perhaps mindful that Barcelona's last visit to Anfield had ended in a 3-1 victory. Captain Steven Gerrard said: "We've got to be realistic. We're facing the best side in Europe, a team full of world-class players, even if they're not playing at top form of late."

"The job is not done," Benítez stressed. "We have a good chance now, but we need to be careful. But it's a wonderful result and I'm very happy for the players, and for Craig and John in particular. It is a coincidence that they should both score [after what happened in Portugal], but I'm pleased for them."

Barcelona president Joan Laporta urged his players to put the defeat behind them. "(We need) to forget this game, where we have let in some strange goals," he said on Barca TV. "We have the team to beat Liverpool and at moments like this I prefer to stay optimistic."

Bellamy explained what had happened on the Algarve: "It started when we were all doing a bit of karaoke. I only sang one song and that was Red, Red Wine by UB40. That was because Jerzy Dudek was drinking it. That's how silly it all was. A lot of the lads wanted Riise to get up there next because he hadn't turned up at the dinner earlier and I tried to get him up, too. I wasn't that bothered whether he wanted to sing or not so I sat back down but he wasn't too happy about me trying to get him to sing so he let me know about it. The situation was calmed down then, but when I was walking back to the hotel with Steve Finnan, who I was rooming with, I lost control for a few seconds. I went and confronted 'Ginger' and I said to him 'don't be doing that in front of the players again'. And that was really about it. Straight away the next morning we were training together. There's no problem now."

Norwegian international Riise believed it was fitting that the two men who brought Liverpool into disrepute should repair the Merseyside club's reputation at the home of the European champions. Riise said: "We both had a tough week after Portugal, but we had the courage to put all the problems behind us. We are both men. We are both mature. We are both team players. Of course we spoke about what happened, but the important thing was we agreed to put it behind us. You could see from our celebrations we're good team-mates."

Porto 1 v Chelsea 1
Estadio do Dragão
Attendance: 49,000

Raul Meireles (L) celebrates with Bruno Alves after scoring Porto's goal

PORTO 1 v **CHELSEA 1**

Referee
Massimo Busacca (SUI)

Assistant Referee
Matthias Arnet (SUI) Stéphane Cuhat (SUI)

Fourth Official
Carlo Bertolini (SUI)

UEFA Referee Observer
Volker Roth (GER)

Scorers			
12'	Meireles	Shevchenko	16'

Teams

Porto		Chelsea	
01	Helton	Cech	01
14	Alves	Bridge	18
13	Fucile	Ricardo Carvalho	06
03	Pepe	Terry	26
18	Assuncao	Ballack	13
12	Bosingwa	Diarra	19
08	González	Essien	05
16	Meireles	Lampard	08
07	Quaresma	Makelele	04
09	López	Drogba	11
23	Postiga	Shevchenko	07

Substitutes

	Porto	Chelsea	
56'	> 05 Cech < 16 Meireles	16 Robben > 26 Terry <	13'
65'	> 29 Moraes < 13 Fucile	12 Mikel > 16 Robben <	45'
77'	> 23 Adriano < 23 Postiga	21 Kalou > 07 Shevchenko <	88'

Discipline

	Porto	Chelsea	
90'	Pepe	Makelele	36'
		Essien	42'
		Cech	70'
		Ballack	82'

Porto		Chelsea
1	Yellow cards	4
0	Red cards	0
5	Shots on target	3
3	Shots off target	10
9	Fouls committed	17
3	Corners	4
6	Offsides	1
27' 36"	Ball. Poss. (time)	29' 22"
48%	Ball. Poss. (%)	52%

Despite securing a draw at his former club, Porto, with whom he won the Champions League in 2004, Jose Mourinho's Chelsea future was in doubt.

Mourinho may have won consecutive Premiership titles, but he had been knocked out of the Champions League at semi-final and last-16 stages in the last two seasons and relations between himself and Roman Abramovich had not been warm since the January failure to purchase players in the transfer window and what he perceived as interference in his duties.

Meanwhile Chelsea's season had been hugely disrupted by repeated injuries to their captain, John Terry, and the prolonged absence of the goalkeeper Petr Cech. Ashley Cole and Joe Cole had also suffered long-term injuries, while summer signings Andriy Shevchenko and Michael Ballack had failed to live up to expectations. Both would begin their return to some kind of form in this tie.

Mourinho was defiant under questioning about his future: "I have a happy family, my kids are healthy, I have a lot of friends and I live a good life. I have won a lot of things in my career. I cannot win

> ## "We have the quality to win the Champions League."
> ### Andriy Shevchenko, Chelsea

Arjen Robben's introduction changed the shape of the game and brought Chelsea's equaliser

DID YOU KNOW?
Chelsea midfielder Michael Ballack was a European Cup finalist with Bayer Leverkusen in 2002 and is a three-times German Footballer of the Year

> **"Even if I don't score until the end of the season it won't matter if we win the Champions League and the FA Cup."**
> **Didier Drogba**

every time, every year, every week. But no-one could have done a better job in this club this season."

Mourinho praised his players for sticking together and been prepared to play out of position in crucial games in both domestic and European competition and that spirit stood them in good stead at the Estadio do Dragão. Michael Essien looked a world-class performer as an emergency centre-half, pressed into service after John Terry departed early with yet another niggling injury.

With Terry lying on the sidelines having turned his ankle making an innocuous clearance, Raul Meireles made the breakthrough, reacting quickest to Makelele's weak headed clearance and volleying past Petr Cech, via the boot of Frank Lampard.

John Obi Mikel had his tracksuit off when Porto's goal went in, yet it was Arjen Robben who replaced the injured Terry for the restart and this time Mourinho's decision proved inspired. Within minutes the winger had put Andriy Shevchenko through on goal and the Ukrainian rifled past the despairing Helton with his left foot. It

silenced the vociferous home crowd but Porto responded well, with Chelsea right-back Lassana Diarra, making his first start in the competition, struggled to cope with the lively Ricardo Quaresma and Hélder Postiga.

Only the quick reactions of Petr Cech denied Lisandro López after he was put through by Hélder Postiga midway through the half, before it was, inevitably, crowd favourite Ricardo Quaresma who rattled the crossbar with a stunning long-range strike using the outside of his boot.

Porto began the second period in a similar vein, as they sought to replicate the 2-1 reverse dealt to Mourinho on his first return to the Dragão two seasons ago. The teaser posed by a large Porto banner on the halfway line: "Esta noite seremos..." (Tonight we will be) appeared to have a positive ending just around the corner.

But the Premiership title-holders slowly found their shape with Mikel, who had come on for Robben at the break, providing more fortitude in midfield, cutting off the supply to Porto's dangerous left flank and freeing up space for Chelsea's quiet strikers. With 13 minutes remaining, Drogba might have stolen an unlikely win when he thumped his attempt against the post from an acute angle, but Porto held on.

"It was an intense and very tight match, but a positive one," said Jesualdo Ferreira, Porto's coach. "We were the better team in the first half – we started well, scored and controlled the play. Robben's entrance was decisive."

Shevchenko, the scorer of Chelsea's vital equaliser, said: "We have the quality to win the Champions League. The Ukrainian striker was still a big fan of Milan and remained close friends with club President Silvio Berlusconi, who is the godfather of his son. There had been reports linking the former Dynamo Kiev star with a return to Milan, but he declared he had no intention of going back. "I speak with President Berlusconi often," said Shevchenko. "For me, it was extremely difficult to tell the President that I wanted to leave. I'll never forget Milan. For me, it was a very important experience and one which has allowed me to become the player I am. But I made my choice, I arrived in England and now I want to continue on this path."

Strike partner Didier Drogba, by contrast, had been full of goals all season, but insisted it would mean nothing to finish as top scorer in the Champions League if the Blues failed to win it. The Ivory Coast international smashed 29 goals in all competitions so far and was on course to become the first Chelsea player since Kerry Dixon to score 30 in a season. Drogba's sensational season saw him crowned African Player of the Year and silence the boo-boys who once slammed the £24m acquisition as a diver and a cheat. But he declared that all he cared about was the team, not personal records. Drogba said: 'It would be nothing special if we don't win the Champions League. I know how big Kerry Dixon was for Chelsea and it will be something great for me to reach his record. But there is no interest for me to score if we don't win. I want my team to win and everybody to be happy. Even if I don't score until the end of the season it won't matter if we win the Champions League and the FA Cup."

> "It was an intense and very tight match, but a positive one."
> Jesualdo Ferreira, Porto coach

DID YOU KNOW?
The most disruptive part of Chelsea's season came when Petr Cech and John Terry were simultaneously injured – 10 goals were conceded in nine games

Andriy Shevchenko scores the vital away goal to ease the pressure on Mourinho

INTER MILAN 2 v **VALENCIA 2**

Referee
Martin Hansson (SWE)

Assistant Referee
Fredrik Nilsson (SWE) Henrik Andren (SWE)

Fourth Official
Martin Ingvarsson (SWE)

UEFA Referee Observer
Zoran Petrovic (SRB)

Scorers

29'	Cambiasso	Villa	64'
76'	Maicon	Silva	86'

Teams

12	César	Canizares 01
16	Burdisso	Ayala 04
02	Cordoba	Marchena 05
13	Maicon	Miguel 02
23	Materazzi	Moretti 24
04	Zanetti	Albelda 06
19	Cambiasso	Albiol 20
07	Figo	Silva 21
05	Stankovic	Angulo 10
18	Crespo	Morientes 09
08	Ibrahimovic	Villa 07

Substitutes

31'	> 15 Dacourt < 19 Cambiasso	16 Hugo Viana > 09 Morientes <	76'
68'	> 09 Cruz < 18 Crespo	15 Joaquin > 10 Angulo <	83'
89'	> 21 Solari < 07 Figo	18 Jorge Lopez > 21 Silva <	90'

Discipline

85'	Burdisso	Albelda	28'
90'	Zanetti	Marchena	41'

2	Yellow cards	2
0	Red cards	0
10	Shots on target	8
8	Shots off target	2
16	Fouls committed	10
2	Corners	3
5	Offsides	1
28' 41"	Ball. Poss. (time)	30' 03"
48%	Ball. Poss. (%)	52%

Inter Milan 2 v Valencia 2
San Siro
Attendance: 65,000

Inter's Julio Cesar is beaten by David Villa's long range strike to level the scores at 1-1

Inter led in both halves of an engaging encounter, but goals from midfielders Esteban Cambiasso and Maicon were nullified by long-range efforts from David Villa and David Silva as Valencia refused to concede defeat.

Inter's fans may have been reduced in number by UEFA's restriction on supporters in the San Siro, but that only served to ramp up the volume in the Curva Nord and the home side responded by carving out some fine early opportunities. Their first chance came as a result of a mistake by Santiago Cañizares, whose attempted clearance rebounded off Zlatan Ibrahimovic and looped back over his head towards goal. Roberto Ayala was on hand to spare his blushes with a crucial clearance.

From the ensuing throw-in, Maicon's curling cross was met by a glancing header from Ibrahimovic but this time it was the post and then Raúl Albiol that came to the Spanish goalkeeper's rescue.

Along with Zanetti and Cambiasso, Luís Figo was justifying his selection with an excellent performance and, after luring David Albelda into a foul on the right flank on 29 minutes, the 34-year-old delivered a curling free-kick which was touched goalwards by Ibrahimovic. Cañizares made a fine reaction save, but the reflexes of Cambiasso were even quicker as he stooped to head in the rebound.

"We should have prevented their second goal and would have if we'd paid more attention."
Roberto Mancini, Inter Milan coach

Valencia, seemingly affected by an injury-depleted squad, were largely reduced to chasing shadows and the hosts should have doubled their lead a minute earlier when Crespo dived headlong to send Dejan Stankovic's centre narrowly wide.

The second half continued in the same vein as Figo squandered two openings, first finding his shot blocked by Albiol following another sweeping Nerazzurri move, then failing to make clean contact with an angled attempt from ten metres. Valencia barely threatened, but, against the run of play, pulled themselves level on 64 minutes when Villa unleashed a venomous strike from a free-kick 30 yards from goal.

Valencia's tails were up and they began to pass the ball around with confidence, but with a quarter of an hour remaining, they conceded again. Maicon, excellent all night, set off on another foraging right-wing run, exchanged passes with substitute Julio Cruz and side-footed the ball in from six metres for a goal his selfless industry merited.

The Primera División team were not done yet, though. They grabbed a lifeline

Esteban Cambiasso opens the scoring for Inter past a stricken Santiago Canizares

Silva celebrates with his team-mates

> ## "It was a very good result for us. I'm satisfied with the way we managed to keep possession of the ball."
> ### Quique Sánchez Flores, Valencia coach

four minutes from time when Silva volleyed in from the edge of the area following a half-cleared corner to secure a second away goal and leave the tie weighted in Valencia's favour.

Roberto Mancini, Inter Milan coach said: "We should have prevented their second goal and would have if we'd paid more attention. However, we know we have enough quality to go there and get a result."

"It was a very good result for us," said Valencia coach Quique Sánchez Flores. "I'm satisfied with the way we managed to keep possession of the ball, especially in the second half. I think the game went pretty much as we were hoping."

Inter's Luis Figo fights for the ball with Valencia's David Albelda

AS Roma 0 v Lyon 0
Stadio Olimpico
Attendance: 55,000

AS Roma's Simone Perrotta fires in a shot past Lyon's Sébastien Squillaci in a tight goalless draw

AS ROMA 0 v **LYON 0**

Referee
Mike Riley (ENG)

Assistant Referee
Roger East (ENG) Peter Kirkup (ENG)

Fourth Official
Mark Clattenburg (ENG))

UEFA Referee Observer
Mario van der Ende (NED)

Teams

32	Doni	Coupet	01
21	Ferrari	Abidal	20
05	Mexes	Clerc	02
02	Panucci	Cris	03
16	De Rossi	Squillaci	29
30	Mancini	Malouda	10
20	Perrotta	Juninho	08
07	Pizarro	Tiago	21
11	Taddei	Toulalan	28
22	Tonetto	Fred	11
10	Totti	Govou	14

Substitutes

76'	> 04 Wilhelmsson < 30 Mancini	07 Baros > 11 Fred <	74'
86'	> 23 Vucinic < 11 Taddei		

Discipline

02'	Mexes	Juninho	12'
07'	Panucci	Govou	45'
18'	Pizarro	Toulalan	49'
43'	Mancini		
57'	Taddei		
82'	Totti		
89'	Tonetto		
90'	De Rossi		

8	Yellow cards	3
0	Red cards	0
2	Shots on target	5
4	Shots off target	7
24	Fouls committed	33
5	Corners	5
7	Offsides	0
23' 20"	Ball. Poss. (time)	24' 38"
48%	Ball. Poss. (%)	52%

Both teams struggled to find their rhythm in a tense affair which was interrupted by a series of free-kicks and a record 11 yellow cards from English referee Mike Riley.

What few chances there were came from set pieces, with Roma's Francesco Totti the first to catch a glimpse of goal in the 10th minute with a 20-yard free-kick which went high of the mark.

Minutes later, another foul allowed Juninho a free-kick for Lyon, and the visitors came close to opening the scoring when home midfielder Rodrigo Taddei headed the ball onto the right post from the centre of a crowded penalty area.

Neither goalkeeper had had much to do so far in the match, but that changed for Alexander Doni towards the end of the half with the Roma custodian first holding onto a Florent Malouda bullet before fumbling a second strike from the French international moments later.

The visitors carried that momentum into the second half and Fred should have done better with a right-footed drive which flashed past the post.

Perrotta responded for Roma with a lob of his own which dropped over the crossbar, before Lyon goalkeeper Gregory Coupet was called upon to make his first real save of the match with an agile dive to tip another Totti free-kick around the post.

But, six minutes later, Coupet almost gifted Roma an opening goal when he failed to get a proper grip on

> **"The draw is not a bad result for us, even if we are going to play the second leg away from home."**
> **Luciano Spalletti, Roma coach**

Roma's Philippe Mexes (L) challenges Lyon's Fred

Totti's testing free-kick before atoning for his error by retrieving the ball as it trickled toward the goalline.

Set pieces continued to provide the best opportunities for both sides as the clock ticked down, and seven minutes from time an inswinging corner from Juninho was swept off the line by defender Christian Panucci.

And Lyon almost snatched the win in the final minute with another free-kick from Juninho which dipped just too late and landed on the roof of the net.

Roma coach Luciano Spalletti was satisfied with his team's performance. "The game was open, there were a lot of scoring chances for both sides, and I'm largely happy with how my team played. We didn't keep the ball very

Roma coach Luciano Spalletti gets his point across to his team

Mike Riley adds Francesco Totti to his record list of cautions, finishing with a record 11 in the game

well, but we played well enough. The draw is not a bad result for us, even if we are going to play the second leg away from home."

"The result is a fair one," agreed Lyon coach Gérard Houllier. "It was a typical Champions League game between two teams who tested each other out and were evenly matched. We hit the post and I think overall the Roma goalkeeper was more involved than Grégory Coupet. I'm satisfied with the score and for me, it's a step forward towards the quarter-finals."

DID YOU KNOW?
Roma had now gone nine games unbeaten at home in European competition

DID YOU KNOW?
English referee Mike Riley broke the record for the most yellow cards in a single UEFA Champions League match in the match between Lyon and Roma. A total of 11 yellow cards (8 to Roma and 3 to Lyon) were issued

"For me, it's a step forward towards the quarter-finals."
Gérard Houllier, Lyon coach

First Knockout Round
Tuesday 6 March 2007 – Second Legs

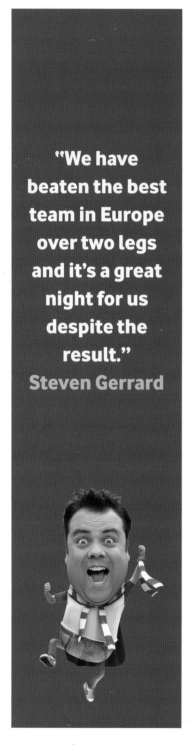

> "We have beaten the best team in Europe over two legs and it's a great night for us despite the result."
>
> **Steven Gerrard**

Liverpool 0 v Barcelona 1
(aggregate 2-2; Liverpool won on away goals)
Anfield
Attendance: 41,000

Liverpool's players celebrate knocking out the holders

Such was Liverpool's achievement in dispatching the reigning champions Barcelona that it drew "hear hears" when it was brought up by one member of parliament during Prime Minister's questions the next day.

Liverpool's inspired and unexpected victory over two legs sent a message of intent to Europe's leading clubs. The elimination of the reigning European Cup holders, on an electric night of high emotion at Anfield, made Liverpool a force to be feared in the last eight. "We feel we have laid down a marker here," said Gerrard. "We have beaten the best team in Europe over two legs and it's a great night for us despite the result."

Liverpool deserved to go through after dominating the first half, hitting the crossbar twice through John Arne Riise and Mohamed Sissoko and drawing several fine saves from Víctor Valdés. It was not until Gudjohnsen was introduced as a substitute that Barcelona attacked with zest. The former Chelsea striker gave the visitors hope when he beat José Reina with 15 minutes remaining, but Liverpool held on.

Eidur Gudohnsen slides the ball past Pepe Reina but the goal was not enough to rescue Barcelona

LIVERPOOL 0 v BARCELONA 1

Referee
Herbert Fandel (GER)
Assistant Referee
Carsten Kadach (GER) Volker Wezel (GER)
Fourth Official
Peter Sippel (GER)
UEFA Referee Observer
Jørn West Larsen (DEN)

Scorers

	Gudjohnsen	75'

Teams

25	Reina	Valdés	01
05	Agger	Márquez	04
02	Arbeloa	Oleguer	23
23	Carragher	Puyol	00
03	Finnan	Thuram	21
06	Arne Riise	Deco	20
14	Alonso	Xavi	06
08	Gerrard	Iniesta	24
22	Sissoko	Ronaldinho	10
17	Bellamy	Eto'o	09
18	Kuyt	Messi	19

Substitutes

67'	16 Pennant / 17 Bellamy	08 Ludovic / 09 Eto'o	61'
77'	12 Aurelio / 06 Riise	07 Gudjohnsen / 21 Thuram	71'
90'	15 Crouch / 18 Kuyt		

Discipline

17'	Arbeloa	Thuram	29'
20'	Sissoko		
80'	Pennant		
81'	Reina		

4	Yellow cards	1
0	Red cards	0
9	Shots on target	4
6	Shots off target	0
12	Fouls committed	11
2	Corners	4
3	Offsides	1
25' 32"	Ball. Poss. (time)	32' 47"
43%	Ball. Poss. (%)	57%

Frank Rijkaard was magnanimous in defeat, the Barcelona manager admitting that his side had struggled to counter Liverpool's "lively" style in the opening half. "They have got a lot of depth, they get forward quickly, they are very direct and they create danger and they did that tonight. They put in a great performance. It's full of concentration, full of mentality and teamwork and they do it quite well. I think they have possibilities."

In the directors' box, George Gillett and Tom Hicks sat entranced by the football phenomenon and the ear busting din at the end. "I've seen a lot of sporting events all around the world," said Hicks, "but nothing comes close to that."

Even in defeat, their first taste of a game as co-owners of the "Liverpool Reds" could not have been more enthralling as power was symbolically changing hands in the boardroom. Gillett and Hicks had already purchased some 62.2% of the club's shares and anticipated securing a 75% stake by 12 March, a financial commitment effectively amounting to £435m. But this was also David Moores' last match as chairman and the end of an era. Moores had seen it as a chance "to go out with a bang".

Gillett stood dumbstruck during the bellowed pre-match rendition of You'll Never Walk Alone, and again when it rang out in stoppage-time. "That was like nothing I've ever seen or heard," he said. They had watched the first leg from a Canadian ski resort.

Liverpool had 10 shots by the time Barcelona mustered their first, a horribly awkward volley spooned over the bar by Ronaldinho met with howls of derision from the stands. The millionaires erupted in laughter at the crowd's reaction. "Will I always have this much fun when I come to Anfield?" asked Hicks. "I'd heard so much about the fans, but that was spectacular. The Kop was just special." Twice in the first half the party in the directors' box joined the fans by rising as one as Riise and then Sissoko rattled the Barcelona bar.

DID YOU KNOW?
This was Liverpool's third consecutive 1-0 home defeat in all competitions

The Kop rejoices at the final whistle

New co-owner Tom Hicks enjoys the show

You just wondered how the Americans took in the away-goal rule! Victory in defeat. It could only be a British trait.

Liverpool should have hit the net in stoppage time, when Peter Crouch put a volley over the bar after being found by his fellow substitute Jermaine Pennant.

Riise revelled in the space on the left and went past a static Oleguer to hit the bar with a drive in the 11th minute. The same piece of woodwork was shuddering again after 32 minutes when the goalkeeper Victor Valdés shanked a clearance to Sissoko. The Malian, seeking the first goal of his Liverpool career, dispatched it back first-time, but it scraped the top of the bar with the keeper unable to recover to get anywhere near it.

It was in defence Liverpool excelled. Carragher made classic tackles on Deco, Messi and Eto'o, and Pepe Reina had not been called upon for a save by half-time. "Over the two legs, Carra has been phenomenal," said Gerrard. "I look at the defenders across Europe and the rest of the world and I really don't see anyone who's better than him. I definitely wouldn't swap him for anyone."

"He has a never-say-die attitude, but it isn't just that with Carra," added Crouch. "He's a determined, whole-hearted player and a top-class defender and we're so pleased to have him. Carra always has a lot to say before and during games, always shouting and barking orders. He is a leader. I don't think anybody would relish playing against him."

Liverpool's regret was the caution for Sissoko, following a foul on Deco, meaning he would be banned for the first leg of the quarter-final.

Both sides had their chances. With 26 minutes gone, Bellamy's hook shot was fended away by Valdés and the goalkeeper parried a follow-up from Kuyt before the subsequent flying long range header from Riise was cleared off the line by Puyol. After 53 minutes, Ronaldinho wheeled across the Liverpool defence, got round Arbeloa and fired against a post. The breakthrough came when Gudjohnsen rounded Reina after a Xavi pass. Arbeloa hung back to keep the Icelander onside. It was a small revenge for the Icelander as he had missed narrowly two years previously when a goal at Anfield would have sent Chelsea to the 2005 UEFA Champions League final.

> ## "I've seen a lot of sporting events all around the world, but nothing comes close to that."
> ### Tom Hicks, co-owner Liverpool

Chelsea 2 v Porto 1
(Chelsea won 3-2 on aggregate)
Stamford Bridge
Attendance: 39,041

Lampard, Ballack and Essien celebrate qualification for the quarter-finals

CHELSEA 2 v **PORTO 1**

Referee
Roberto Rosetti (ITA)

Assistant Referee
Alessandro Stagnoli (ITA)
Cristiano Copelli (ITA)

Fourth Official
Andrea De Marco (ITA)

UEFA Referee Observer
Rune Pedersen (NOR)

Scorers

48'	Robben	Quaresma	15'
79'	Ballack		

Teams

Chelsea		Porto	
01	Cech	Helton	01
06	Ricardo Carvalho	Alves	14
03	A Cole	Cech	05
13	Ballack	Costa	02
19	Diarra	Fucile	13
05	Essien	Pepe	03
08	Lampard	Assuncao	18
04	Makelele	González	08
16	Robben	Meireles	16
11	Drogba	Quaresma	07
07	Shevchenko	López	09

Substitutes

45'	> 12 Mikel < 04 Makelele	06 Ibson > 16 Meireles <	56'
66'	> 20 Ferreira < 19 Diarra	28 Adriano > 05 Cech <	56'
85'	> 21 Kalou < 07 Shevchenko	20 Moraes > 09 López <	82'

Discipline

35'	Robben	Quaresma	58'
61'	Diarra	Fucile	83'
		Adriano	87'

2	Yellow cards	3
0	Red cards	0
3	Shots on target	2
9	Shots off target	0
17	Fouls committed	18
5	Corners	0
0	Offsides	3
34' 28"	Ball. Poss. (time)	25' 27"
57%	Ball. Poss. (%)	43%

Didier Drogba celebrated a fabulous Chelsea fight-back after a first half which had given fans plenty of cause for concern.

Drogba said: "We dug deep and found the strength to win and to get through to the next round. Maybe we didn't play well, but to win a cup game you don't really need to play well."

Chelsea were trailing 1-0 at the interval when Mourinho asked his side to relish the pressure of having to fight back. They did so with goals from Arjen Robben and Michael Ballack. "Psychologically I told my team to think a bit that at that moment we are out of the competition and that we could enjoy it or be scared of it. I said that if we were scared, we would go out. I said, 'Let's enjoy being under pressure.' This is possible sometimes, to show quality and personality. Our reaction was very

positive and when we came out to score in minute three of the second half it gave extra confidence. We were very, very strong mentally."

Having taken an away goal from the first-leg trip, Mourinho's confidence was well placed. Without their captain John Terry, Chelsea had become vulnerable to the long pass and Porto were alive to its potential.

Essien advanced as high as the halfway line and was sucked in to challenge Gonzalez. Essien scrambled back, but Lucho played his perfectly measured pass through the gap between him and Carvalho. Quaresma advanced and slipped the ball under Cech. Chelsea were stunned.

Ashley Cole produced little on the left wing, Lampard was uncharacteristically hurried in midfield and Arjen Robben, who had made several runs at the defence, similarly lacked composure

Ricardo Quaresma hails his goal as Porto take a shock lead at Stamford Bridge

Michael Ballack finds the net to win the tie for Chelsea

when, shortly before half-time, he set himself up on the edge of the area only to shoot well wide.

Mourinho addressed the possession problem by withdrawing Makelele for Mikel John Obi at the interval and advancing Lassana Diarra into midfield. The dividends were instant. Diarra pushed into the outside-right channel, dragging it back for Robben. The speculative effort was covered by Da Silva Helton at his near post, but the goalkeeper somehow allowed the ball to bobble over him for the equaliser. "I was cool because naturally if we don't score in the 48th minute we score in the 49th," said Mourinho. "It was our natural tendency to win the game because our experience would make sure."

From that moment, each time the ball approached Helton, who had twice dropped or ducked crosses, he was subjected to a crescendo of mocking that utterly unnerved him.

Mourinho had Michael Ballack to thank for Chelsea's continuing interest in the competition, the German repaying the depth of faith his manager has placed in him.

Finally, Cole's high diagonal ball found Drogba on the edge of the area. His header across goal for Shevchenko was returned to Ballack, who clinched the tie with just 11 minutes remaining with a hooked shot from close in. "It's good for him because his goal has put Chelsea in the quarter-finals," said Mourinho.

Even though he has had his own trauma to cope with over the last few months, Petr Cech, still had sympathy for his Porto counterpart whose mistake gave Chelsea the vital equaliser on a plate. He said: "It's always difficult for a keeper when you make a mistake and the goal changed the game. It's difficult for your colleague because you know what he feels like. I said to myself 'Don't make the same mistake' and it was important for me to finish the game having let in just one goal."

Cech believed that the whole team has had to stand up and be counted this season. "Of course you miss

Jose Mourinho feels the pressure building on his shoulders as the stand off with Abramovich continued despite victory over Porto

> **"It was a fair result, but I'm very proud of my team."**
> **Jesualdo Ferreiria, Porto coach**

players like JT. But this season we've had difficult moments without injured players and I think we've done well in that situation."

After seeing his side come so close to knocking out the English champions Porto coach Jesualdo Ferreiria sang their praises: "It was a fair result, but I'm very proud of my team. Our club is strong and we'll aim to do well in the Champions League next year and remain positive despite this loss. I have a way of playing which gets results, and this was a match either team could have won."

Mourinho paid tribute to both sides' qualities: "The game was intense and Chelsea had a higher intensity – we can thank playing in the English Premiership for that. We deserved the result for our very strong second-half performance, but Porto should be proud of the work they did."

> **"We deserved the result for our very strong second-half performance, but Porto should be proud of the work they did."**
> **Jose Mourinho**

LYON 0 v AS ROMA 2

Referee
Manuel Mejuto González (ESP)

Assistant Referee
Juan Carlos Yuste Jimenez (ESP)
Antonio Artero Gallardo (ESP)

Fourth Official
Bernardino Gonzalez Vazquez (ESP)

UEFA Referee Observer
Karl-Erik Nilsson (SWE)

Scorers
	Totti	22'
	Mancini	44'

Teams
Lyon	Roma	
01 Coupet	Doni	32
20 Abidal	Cassetti	77
03 Cris	Chivu	13
12 Reveillere	Mexes	05
29 Squillaci	De Rossi	16
15 Diarra	Mancini	30
10 Malouda	Perrotta	20
08 Juninho	Pizarro	07
21 Tiago	Taddei	11
11 Fred	Tonetto	22
14 Govou	Totti	10

Substitutes
45' > 06 Kallstrom < 15 Diarra	14 Faty > 30 Mancini <	89'
45' > 22 Wiltord < 14 Govou		
69' > 19 Benzema < 12 Reveillere		

Discipline
57'	Tiago	Perrotta	79'
63'	Cris	Pizarro	90'
76'	Kallstrom		

Lyon		Roma
3	Yellow cards	2
0	Red cards	0
6	Shots on target	3
9	Shots off target	5
26	Fouls committed	15
9	Corners	4
0	Offsides	8
30' 50"	Ball. Poss. (time)	20' 19"
60%	Ball. Poss. (%)	40%

Lyon 0 v AS Roma 2
(AS Roma won 2-0 on aggregate)
Stade de Gerland
Attendance: 40,000

Roma's players acclaim their stunning 2-0 victory over Lyon to knockout one of the tournament favourites

Roma coach Luciano Spalletti hailed his players as "extraordinary" following their 2-0 victory in Lyon. Goals from Francesco Totti and Brazilian midfielder Mancini saw the Giallorossi advance to the last eight.

Spalletti said: "I am delighted, my players have been extraordinary. They played the perfect game. It was a performance of great maturity from my players."

Mancini's goal was the highlight of the evening, the South American bamboozling Anthony Reveillere before lashing the ball high into the net for the vital second goal. "When I saw Reveillere,

I danced the samba," said Mancini. "Few believed we could do it, but the criticism has been an added motivation for us. Now we are among the top eight in the Champions League and we will do everything we can to go as far as possible. The Champions League is a marvellous thing."

Lyon coach Gérard Houllier admitted the result was a "failure and a disappointment", but was the first to accept Roma deserved to progress. "It was the team that was more realistic and more efficient that won the game," the former Liverpool boss said. "We were beaten by a stronger side. "Both teams had their chances, but it was Roma who knew how to take theirs. I wish them good luck in the next round. It is a failure and a disappointment, especially for our supporters and the people who follow us. But when you enter the elimination stage, you know there are no easy matches. The turning point, for me, was the second goal. If we had gone into the dressing room just one goal behind, I think we could have won. But we were a bit broken after that."

The visitors played the perfect game of counter-attacking football and had the ball in the net from their first corner on six minutes, but Daniele De Rossi's close-range header was ruled out for a push by Totti. At the other end, Sébastien Squillaci nodded Juninho's free-kick tamely at Doni, before Sidney Govou directed a corner from the Brazilian over the bar.

Lyon were producing little from open play, as David Pizarro and De Rossi stamped their authority on midfield. Indeed, it came as little surprise when Roma scored the opening goal of the tie on 22 minutes. Max Tonetto raced beyond Anthony Réveillère on the left and delivered a perfect cross for Totti who, after ghosting between Squillaci and Cris, headed powerfully past Grégory Coupet.

Then came Mancini's wonder goal and the tie was effectively dead and buried.

> **"It was a performance of great maturity from my players."**
> Luciano Spalletti, coach Roma

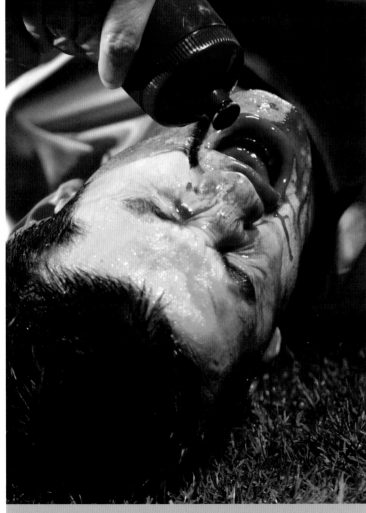

Roma's Christian Chivu receives treatment for a painful blow on the nose

DID YOU KNOW?
Roma reached the quarter-finals of the UEFA Champions League for the first time

VALENCIA 0 v **INTER MILAN 0**

Referee
Wolfgang Stark (GER)

Assistant Referee
Jan-Hendrik Salver (GER)
Sönke Glindemann (GER)

Fourth Official
Manuel Gräfe (GER)

UEFA Referee Observer
Leslie Irvine (NIR)

Teams

01	Canizares	César	12
04	Ayala	Burdisso	16
05	Marchena	Maxwell	06
02	Miguel	Cordoba	02
24	Moretti	Maicon	13
20	Albiol	Materazzi	23
08	Baraja	Zanetti	04
21	Silva	Dacourt	15
10	Angulo	Stankovic	05
09	Morientes	Crespo	18
07	Villa	Ibrahimovic	08

Substitutes

37'	> 16 Hugo Viana < 08 Baraja	09 Cruz > 18 Crespo <	58'
67'	> 14 Vicente < 09 Morientes	07 Figo > 15 Dacourt <	64'
77'	> 15 Joaquin < 10 Angulo	11 Grosso > 06 Maxwell <	75'

Discipline

30'	Canizares	Ibrahimovic	30'
69'	Angulo	Materazzi	73'
		Cordoba	79'
	•	Maicon	88'

2	Yellow cards	4
0	Red cards	0
4	Shots on target	2
11	Shots off target	4
15	Fouls committed	18
5	Corners	2
1	Offsides	5
27' 42"	Ball. Poss. (time)	26' 41"
50%	Ball. Poss. (%)	50%

Valencia 0 v Inter Milan 0
(aggregate 2-2; Valencia won on away goals)
Mestella
Attendance: 50,000

Things get a bit heated at the final whistle as Inter's Marco Materazzi (L) and Zlatan Ibrahimovic (C) argue with Valencia's Roberto Ayala

UEFA charged Valencia and Inter's players with improper conduct after the post-match brawl which marred their game. The second leg tie finished goalless, with Valencia progressing on away goals following the 2-2 draw at the San Siro, but Valencia substitute David Navarro sparked a melée in the aftermath by breaking Inter's Nicolas Burdisso nose. Inter's incensed players chased Navarro all the way down the tunnel.

Navarro apologised, telling Spanish radio station Cadena Ser: "I saw that they were trying to attack a team-mate, and I lost my nerve. I have never behaved in this fashion before, and I will never do it again. I am very sorry and ashamed. I have not yet been able to

DID YOU KNOW?
UEFA banned David Navarro for SEVEN months after Valencia's brawl with Inter Milan. The Spanish side's reserve keeper would not play again until October after breaking Nicolas Burdisso's nose. The punch sparked a mass brawl at the end of the tie. UEFA also fined Valencia and Inter around £105,000 each but opted against imposing a stadium ban on the Spaniards. Inter defenders Burdisso and Maicon were also banned for six matches, while Valencia defender Carlos Marchena received a four-match suspension. Inter defender Ivan Cordoba and striker Julio Cruz were hit with three and two-match bans respectively. UEFA asked FIFA to extend Navarro's suspension to international level, so that it applied to all football competitions

see the images, nor the reaction of the Inter players in our changing room," continued Navarro. "It was a lamentable incident. I want to apologise to those affected by my actions."

Navarro, who was a non-playing substitute in the goalless draw at the Mestalla, was involved in a post-match fracas that spilled over from the pitch and into the tunnel. He came onto the field following an altercation between Valencia midfielder Carlos Marchena and Inter's Nicolas Burdisso, and punched Burdisso.

Burdisso then fell to the ground, nose splayed. That sparked a free-for-all, with some of the visiting team attempting to trip Navarro up as he ran off the pitch, while a handful of Inter players also tried to get into the Valencia changing room following the incident.

Valencia coach Quique Sanchez Flores tried to play down the incident, saying: "I hope that the punishment is minimal and affects us as little as possible. The tension of football generates these situations and affects our good sense."

Inter coach Roberto Mancini was less than impressed with Navarro's actions. "Now I have seen the footage, I can say that the Valencia player is a coward," reflected Mancini. "There's nothing else you can say about someone who throws a punch like that then runs away."

Valencia's Italian defender Emiliano Moretti expressed his surprise at his team-mate's actions. "Navarro is a perfectly normal person and I don't know what would cause him to do such a thing," he told Sky Italia.

Navarro added: "I feel very bad, all my family are having a bad time as well, I wish the day could be erased, so it did not have to exist. My dad is very bad, I spoke with him all night at home. I could not sleep at all and I feel very bad. It is logical that UEFA will punish me. I am trying to locate Burdisso, to ask him for forgiveness, and if necessary I will go to Italy to do it in person. I don't know what the club will do. What I have done is not good."

The incident overshadowed what should have been a memorable night for Valencia, as they booked their place in the quarter-finals in a tense atmosphere on and off the pitch. Inter controlled midfield, but could not find the creative spark to make the most of chances for Zlatan Ibrahimovic. Hernán Crespo snapped at a loose ball in the area and the goalbound shot bounced off Albiol on the goalline. The Inter forward called for a penalty, but referee Wolfgang Stark was well-placed to decide it had hit the defender's thigh not his hand.

Just before the break both Santiago Cañizares and Ibrahimovic were booked for a bout of push and shove which involved several players, as referee Stark defused the tension. The second half was furious for footballing reasons and brought chances. Maicon delivered a centre to the back post which Stankovic could only volley into the sidenetting. Moments later, Villa spotted his left-back in the penalty box, but Emiliano Moretti guided the free header into César's hands.

Inter's best opportunity came when Materazzi outjumped everyone at a corner, beating Cañizares only to see Carlos Marchena control the ball on his stomach and the goalkeeper clutch possession gratefully. A massive roar greeted that save and was matched for every tackle as the Mestalla urged their favourites, successfully, into the last eight.

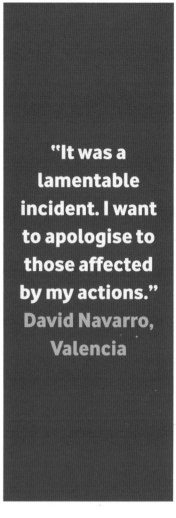

"It was a lamentable incident. I want to apologise to those affected by my actions."
David Navarro, Valencia

Inter's Hernan Crespo grimaces after missing a chance

First Knockout Round
Wednesday 7 March 2007 – Second Legs

> "Of course I'm going to say we can go all the way. I'm not going to say the quarter-finals are as far as we can go. We've a good team with good players and we can make it a great season."
>
> **Edwin van Der Sar, Manchester United**

Manchester United 1 v Lille 0
(Manchester United won 2-0 on aggregate)
Old Trafford
Attendance: 75,182

Henrik Larsson takes off after netting in his last appearance at Old Trafford, a goal which turned out to be the winner

Henrik Larsson, the 35 year-old Swede, rose to nod in the 72nd minute goal that took United into their first Champions League quarter-final for four years.

But the hero was not going to stick around to help United into the final. Larsson's loan spell at Old Trafford was over after United's FA Cup tie at Middlesbrough and he returned to his club Helsingborg.

Larsson said, "It has been a wonderful experience at a great club. It's something I'll always be grateful for."

Alex Feruguson bemoaned losing the Swede saying, "He's got his family, so there's no point in going on about it. I've spoken to the man and he's going back. That, unfortunately, is that."

This was the Swede's ninth start in his loan spell and his decisive header, from a sublime run and cross by Cristiano Ronaldo, was his third goal

MAN UTD 3 v **LILLE 0**

and his last competitive touch in the red shirt at Old Trafford.

In the space of a week, as United entered the final stages of what remains a possible treble, Sir Alex lost three strikers. Louis Saha's scan on his hamstring on the morning of this game discovered damage that would keep him out for a month – up to six matches. That followed the loss the previous week of Ole Gunnar Solskjaer to knee surgery. With regulations forbidding the calling back of Giuseppe Rossi from loan at Parma, it was symbolic that when Larsson departed to a rousing ovation, Alan Smith was his replacement. Smith was lively and sharp in his 15 minutes, but during his rehabilitation from a horrendous leg break he has begun just two games this season, both in the Carling Cup.

There was also a new injury to Darren Fletcher in training that will mean two months out and Mikaël Silvestre dislocated a shoulder in a heavy fall. He was carried off on a stretcher. United's European progress has its problems mounting.

United dominated an otherwise largely uneventful game. From a corner O'Shea Larsson rose unchallenged to nod a header on to the crossbar. Odemwingie bloodied the nose of Vidic after 27 minutes. Shortly before that Makoun wasted a promising headed chance for Lille and there was then a comedy moment when Scholes attempted to take a quick free-kick in the style of Giggs. The stadium laughed as Lille flapped. But the ground fell quiet at the start of the second half. Lille, it appeared, had to score when Odemwingie, just two minutes in, miscued a header that fooled van der Sar and struck a post. An away goal then and the whole occasion would have been changed.

Larsson provided the missing inspiration when, spinning on to a short pass, he found Scholes, who switched the ball out to Ronaldo. Booked earlier for an apparent dive, Ronaldo burst

Referee
Luis Medina Cantalejo (ESP)

Assistant Referee
Victoriano Giraldez Carrasco (ESP)
Jesus Calvo Guadamuro (ESP

Fourth Official
Alfonso Perez Burrull (ESP)

UEFA Referee Observer
Nikolay Levnikov (RUS)

Scorers

72'	Larsson

Teams

01	van der Sar	Sylva	01
05	Ferdinand	Chalmé	21
02	Neville	Plestan	25
22	O'Shea	Tafforeau	20
27	Silvestre	Tavlaridis	04
15	Vidic	Bastos	08
16	Carrick	Dumont	29
07	Ronaldo	Makoun	17
18	Scholes	Obraniak	35
17	Larsson	Kader Keita	23
08	Rooney	Odemwingie	14

Substitutes

75'	> 14 Smith < 17 Larsson		02 Debuchy > 08 Bastos <	45'
80'	> 13 Park < 08 Rooney		13 Fauvergue > 14 Odemwingie <	74'
82'	> 23 Richardson < 07 Ronaldo		27 Mirallas > 29 Dumont <	74'

Discipline

42'	Ronaldo	Makoun	31'
86'	Richardson	Kader Keita	36'
		Chalmé	36'
		Tafforeau	50'
		Plestan	62'

2	Yellow cards	5
0	Red cards	0
4	Shots on target	6
3	Shots off target	7
17	Fouls committed	17
4	Corners	2
1	Offsides	2
30' 11"	Ball. Poss. (time)	24' 24"
55%	Ball. Poss. (%)	45%

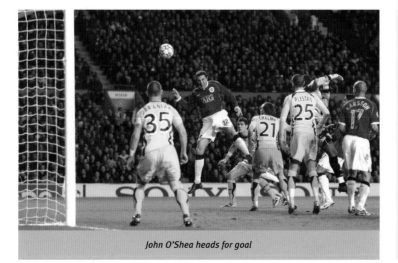

John O'Shea heads for goal

Larsson scores with a header

past his marker, reached the byline and sent in a perfect cross; right on the button for Larsson's forehead and a wonderful finish.

Sir Alex was pained at lifting the European Cup only once. Fergie confessed, "There is disappointment in my mind about United's record in Europe. I still think the Champions League is the thing we should be measured by. Although for many years we have painted lovely pictures about European nights with the likes of Barcelona and Juventus and some success, we have only ever won it twice. Clubs like Ajax and Bayern Munich have won it four times, Liverpool five and AC Milan six. And then, of course, there is Real Madrid. I am disappointed with our record, it should be better. The material is certainly here for it to be done in the future even if not in my time."

"It has been a wonderful experience at a great club. It's something I'll always be grateful for."
Henrik Larsson, Manchester United

Arsenal 1 v PSV Eindhoven 1

(PSV Eindhoven won 2-1 on aggregate)
Emirates Stadium
Attendance: 60,073

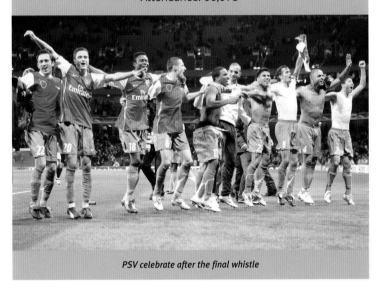

PSV celebrate after the final whistle

ARSENAL 1   v   PSV EINDHO'N 1

Referee
Alain Hamer (LUX)

Assistant Referee
Eric Castellani (FRA) Francis Crelo (LUX)

Fourth Official
Fredy Fautrel (FRA)

UEFA Referee Observer
Vitor Manuel Melo Pereira (POR)

Scorers			
58'	Alex (og)	Alex	83'

Teams		
01	Lehmann	Gomes 01
22	Clichy	Alex 04
10	Gallas	Feher 22
05	Toure	Salcido 23
19	Gilberto Silva	Xiang 28
09	Baptista	Cocu 08
15	Denilson	Culina 15
04	Fabregas	Mendez 11
13	Hleb	Simons 06
08	Ljungberg	Farfan 17
25	Adebayor	Arouna Koné 10

Substitutes				
66'	14 Henry / 09 Baptista	20 Afelley / 10 Koné	41'
76'	02 Diaby / 08 Ljungberg	18 Addo / 17 Farfan	89'
85'	32 Walcott / 10 Clichy	07 Väyrynen / 11 Mendez	90'

Discipline			
81'	Fabregas	Feher	55'

Arsenal		PSV
1	Yellow cards	1
0	Red cards	0
6	Shots on target	1
8	Shots off target	5
18	Fouls committed	15
7	Corners	4
1	Offsides	9
35' 11"	Ball. Poss. (time)	25' 05"
58%	Ball. Poss. (%)	42%

Arsène Wenger confessed that the past two weeks had been "horrendous", after his side were eliminated from the FA Cup and Champions League as well as losing the Carling Cup final.

It was another night of missed chances for Arsenal, who once again failed to match their excellent approach play with clinical finishing.

Worse still for Arsenal's season, Thierry Henry would be missing for the foreseeable future after the striker succumbed to yet another injury. Henry, who has been dogged by sciatica this season and began on the bench, tore his groin and his stomach muscles during his cameo appearance at the end. "It's a different injury to the previous one," said Wenger. "I think he did it when he tried to cross the ball. It was a cruel night, but you could see that the games have caught up with us," Wnger admitted. "We were less sharp than two weeks ago, physically, and we lacked quality in the final third.

It was a PSV Eindhoven defender, owned by Chelsea, who scored twice – one at each end. Brazilian centre-half Rodrigo Alex put PSV 1-0 down with an own goal to balance the aggregate score at 1-1, but in the 83rd minute he produced a gigantic leap above substitute Abou Diaby to head home Edison Méndez's free-kick. The Brazilian, who is nicknamed The Tank, was outstanding. Coach Ronald Koeman, aware of cross-capital rivalries, appreciated the irony of the situation. "I think Chelsea will be happy tonight," he said. "Normally, they'd like the English team to go through, but I know about the occasional, not disagreements but let's say miscommunications sometimes between Jose Mourinho and Arsène

DID YOU KNOW?
Wenger's team had not been eliminated from the Champions League so early since the 1999/00 season

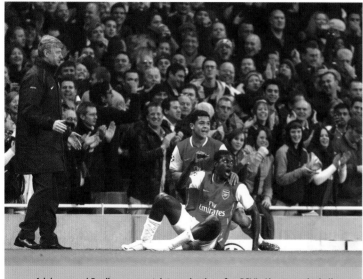

Adebayor and Denilson congratulate each other after PSV's Alex turns the ball into his own net to put the Gunners level on aggregate

Cristiano Ronaldo is beaten to the ball by Lille keeper Tony Sylva

Wenger. We're proud Alex plays for our team, but he's only PSV's player until the end of this season. After that, we will be talking to Chelsea about the player's situation. But that's the truth at this moment."

Extraordinarily, the Brazilian could legitimately line up against Mourinho's side in this competition should Chelsea be drawn against PSV. Quite how the Chelsea manager would react is intriguing. "He can play against them because he is registered to us for the whole season," said Koeman. "People said they may try and bring him to England in January, but the deal was for 12 months, so we would have tried to keep him. He is a fantastic defender and played so well tonight. In the really big games, the best players show themselves. He enjoyed the level this game was played at."

Alex shot to prominence as a 20 year-old during his first season with Santos in 2002, his uncompromising style and capacity for scoring goals. He found the net three times in his first season and upped that to nine the following campaign. His leadership has taken PSV to the Champions League semi-finals in 2005 and the last eight this season.

Freddie Ljungberg reckoned poor finishing and slack defending had cost Arsenal dear this season. "We made a mistake and they scored. It is not the first time something like this has happened. We knew that they would defend and would not create a lot. So it was important not to give away any free-kicks where they could put up Alex

> **"All credit to PSV because they are a good side – but we should still have won the game."**
> **Freddie Ljungberg, Arsenal**

or people who can go up for the headers. We had opportunities to kill off the game and had them on the brink of defeat. We eased off a bit. When they equalised with five minutes to go it killed the rest of the game. All credit to PSV because they are a good side – but we should still have won the game."

DID YOU KNOW?
Arsenal were now unbeaten in 15 Champions League home games since losing to Chelsea in a quarter-final second leg three years ago. They had not lost any of their 21 competitive games at their new Emirates Stadium this season, but had been forced to fight back after falling behind 11 times

DID YOU KNOW?
Thierry Henry scored a total of 42 goals in 84 UEFA Champions League games for Arsenal

Manager Wenger can barely believe what he has seen

AC MILAN 1 v **CELTIC 0**

Referee
Konrad Plautz (AUT)

Assistant Referee
Egon Bereuter (AUT) Markus Mayr (AUT)

Fourth Official
Fritz Stuchlik (AUT)

UEFA Referee Observer
Michel Piraux (BEL)

Scorers

93"	Kaka

Teams

	AC Milan	Celtic	
01	Dida	Boruc	01
25	Bonera	McGeady	46
03	Maldini	Naylor	03
44	Oddo	O'Dea	48
23	Ambrosini	Telfer	02
08	Gattuso	Jarosik	20
22	Kaká	Lennon	18
18	Jankulovski	McManus	44
21	Pirlo	Nakamura	25
10	Seedorf	Sno	15
09	Inzaghi	Vennegoor of Hesselink	10

Substitutes

73' > 11 Gilardino < 09 Inzaghi		16 Gravesen > 20 Jarosik <		62'
79' > 32 Brocchi < 08 Gattuso		37 Beattie > 15 Sno <		97'
117' > 17 Simic < 44 Oddo		09 Miller > 25 Nakamura <		105'

Discipline

42'	Ambrosini	McManus	41'
		Naylor	56'
		McGeady	86'
		Lennon	104'

1	Yellow cards	4
0	Red cards	0
9	Shots on target	3
20	Shots off target	4
22	Fouls committed	29
11	Corners	3
3	Offsides	4
42' 32"	Ball. Poss. (time)	35' 15"
54%	Ball. Poss. (%)	46%

AC Milan 1 v Celtic 0
After extra time
(AC Milan won 1-0 on aggregate)
San Siro
Attendance: 65,000

Celtic's traveling army salute their heroes who came so close to defeating mighty AC Milan

Celtic came within extra-time of making it into the uncharted territory of the Champions League quarter-finals, when an individual goal from the outstanding Kaka, three minutes into the extended period, finally separated the teams.

Celtic were rarely an attacking threat, but their powers of containment and Gordon Strachan's tactical approach worked well.

"If there was a trophy for sheer guts and determination then we'd have a chance of winning it," said Gordon Strachan. "It was a fantastic evening in a great stadium with a great atmosphere, between two teams — one with a bit more technique, but the other with incredible heart, will and determination."

Strachan opted for the brawn of Jiri Jarosik instead of the pace of Kenny Miller to support Jan Vennegoor of Hesselink in attack, and the decision

> **"If there was a trophy for sheer guts and determination then we'd have a chance of winning it."**
> **Gordon Strachan**

almost paid dividends inside six minutes. Jarosik should have won a penalty as Paolo Maldini used his hands to block a shot from the Czech player. Two minutes earlier the Celtic goalkeeper, Artur Boruc, had made a spectacular diving save to halt Kaka.

The Scots made a surprising choice not to train at San Siro on Tuesday evening, on a playing surface only three weeks old. An afternoon deluge rendered conditions far from perfect, but Milan came within a saving Lee Naylor tackle of opening the scoring midway through the opening half after a delightful move involving Kaká and Clarence Seedorf; Filippo Inzaghi was poised to score before Naylor's intervention.

Milan's ambitions to be crowned European Champions for a seventh time were highlighted when Naylor's 55th-minute foul on the Milan striker, given as a free-kick, should have resulted in a penalty as the defender tugged Inzaghi just inside Celtic's penalty area. Boruc saved smartly from Maldini.

Kaká rattled a shot off the crossbar as Milan pushed on. Yet, Strachan's men somehow doggedly held on for extra-time. But within 180 seconds Evander Sno cheaply conceded possession in midfield and Kaká raced forward, brushing past Neil Lennon to slide the winning goal underneath Boruc.

Milan's relieved manager, Carlo Ancelotti, said: "It was hard. We are delighted, but it was worthwhile; our happiness will recharge us."

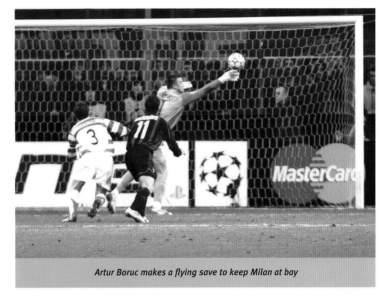

Artur Boruc makes a flying save to keep Milan at bay

Kaká celebrates his winning goal

"It was hard; our happiness will recharge us."
Carlo Ancelotti, Milan coach

BAYERN MUN. 2 v REAL MADRID 1

Referee
Lubos Michel (SVK)

Assistant Referee
Roman Slysko (SVK) Roman Csabay (SVK)

Fourth Official
Richard Havrilla (SVK)

UEFA Referee Observer
Hugh Dallas (SCO)

Scorers

01'	Makaay	van Nistelrooy (pen)	83'
66'	Lucio		

Teams

01	Kahn	Casillas	01
03	da Silva	Roberto Carlos	03
21	Lahm	Helguera	21
02	Sagnol	Sergio Ramos	04
05	van Buyten	Gómez	38
23	Hargreaves	Diarra	06
20	Salihamidzic	Emerson	08
31	Schweinsteiger	Gago	16
17	van Bommel	Raúl	07
10	Makaay	Higuaín	20
11	Podolski	van Nistelrooy	17

Substitutes

69'	> 14 Pizarro < 10 Makaay		14 Guti > 08 Emerson <		32'
85'	> 18 Görlitz < 02 Sagnol		18 Cassano > 20 Higuaín <		45'
87'	> 06 Demichelis < 11 Podolski		10 Robinho > 16 Gago <		75'

Discipline

24'	van Bommel	Sergio Ramos	08'
45'	Podolski	Guti	55'
82'	van Bommel	Diarra	61'
		Diarra	82'

3	Yellow cards	4
1	Red cards	0
8	Shots on target	4
6	Shots off target	6
25	Fouls committed	19
7	Corners	4
3	Offsides	5
32' 04"	Ball. Poss. (time)	32' 46"
49%	Ball. Poss. (%)	51%

Bayern Munich 2 v Real Madrid 1
(4-4 on aggregate Bayern Munich won on away goals)
Allianz Arena
Attendance: 69,500

Roy Makaay celebrates after scoring the crucial goal for Bayern just 10 seconds after kick-off

Fabio Capello's time as coach of Real Madrid yet again appeared to be drawing to a close following his side's departure from the Champions League. After defeat on away goals at the Allianz Arena, Real's sporting director, Predrag Mijatovic, refused to confirm that Capello would be in charge for the next match against Barcelona.

Asked if Capello would take charge on Saturday, Mijatovic replied: "For the moment he is our coach."

DID YOU KNOW?
Madrid's record in Munich is poor having lost eight of their previous nine encounters there and drawn just one

Out of the Champions League at the first knockout stage and lying fourth in La Liga, six points behind the leaders Sevilla, Capello's Madrid had scored only 32 goals in 25 league matches and drawn their past three games in La Liga, including at home to Real Betis and Getafe. Patience with Capello was exhausted. There had been calls from fans for the coach and the club's president, Ramón Calderón, to resign.

Real's attempts to defend the first leg lead got off to the worst start as they fell behind after 10 seconds to the fastest goal in Champions League history, scored by Roy Makaay. To add to the humiliation Real kicked off. Fernando Gago played the ball back to Roberto Carlos, whose control let him down. Hasan Salihamidzic seized possession and crossed for Makaay to slide a shot past the goalkeeper, Iker Casillas.

"The early goal changed the match completely," said Capello. "All our plans and preparation went out of the window. For them to score a goal like this was incredible. We gave them an incredible present."

Lucio scored Bayern's second with a header from a corner in the 66th minute before Real's goal, a van Nistelrooy penalty, set up a frantic finale. Bayern's Mark van Bommel and Real's Mahamadou Diarra were sent off after receiving second yellow cards for jostling on the edge of the penalty area like two silly schoolboys refusing to give up an inch of space outside of the area before the spot-kick.

Sergio Ramos thought he had snatched victory for Real when he smashed the ball past Oliver Kahn from the edge of the box, but he was adjudged to have handled in controlling the ball.

Capello, however, clung on by his fingernails and, using this early departure from the UEFA Champions League found a way to stoke his 'Galacticos' including a resurgent David Beckham, into action. By the end of the Spanish League season Real had come back from the dead, defeated Barcelona and somehow managed to steal the title for a record 30th time from under their noses by virtue of having a better head-to-head record, following a dramatic late comeback in the final league match against Real Mallorca.

> "For them to score a goal like this was incredible. We gave them an incredible present."
> **Fabio Capello, Real Madrid coach**

Makaay nets the vital opener

Quarter-Finals
Tuesday 3 April 2007 – First Legs

Magnificent Seven

Manchester United thrash Roma on an astonishing night at Old Trafford to overturn a 2-1 first leg deficit and make a rare recent appearance in the quarter-finals

Blue Heaven

Chelsea recover from a disappointing first leg to record a rare defeat for Valencia in the cauldron of the Mestella

Dutch Masters

Liverpool canter to an easy 4-0 aggregate victory over PSV Eindhoven, winning 3-0 in the first leg in Holland

> "We want to see Stevie scoring goals, Carra playing a lot of games and the team winning."
> **Rafa Benitez**

PSV Eindhoven 0 v Liverpool 3
Philips Stadion
Attendance: 36,500

John Arne Riise crashes home the second goal of the game for Liverpool

PSV EINDHO'N 0 v LIVERPOOL 3

Referee
Referee: Bertrand Layec (France)

Assistant Referee
Christian Thoison (France)
Eric Dansault (France)

Fourth Official
Stéphane Lannoy (France)

UEFA Referee Observer
Aron Schmidhuber

Scorers

	Gerrard	27'
	Riise	49'
	Crouch	63'

Teams

01	Gomes	Reina 25
14	Da Costa	Agger 05
02	Kromkamp	Aurelio 12
23	Salcido	Carragher 23
08	Cocu	Finnan 03
15	Culina	Riise 06
11	Mendez	Alonso 14
06	Simons	Gerrard 08
07	Väyrynen	Mascherano 20
17	Farfan	Crouch 15
26	Tardelli	Kuyt 18

Substitutes

45'	> 28 Xiang < 17 Farfan		32 Zenden > 06 Riise <	66'
51'	> 09 Kluivert < 11 Mendez		11 Gonzalez > 12 Aurelio <	75'
68'	> 22 Feher < 02 Kromkamp		16 Pennant > 15 Crouch <	85'

Discipline

64'	Kluivert	Mascherano	39'
72'	Feher	Kuyt	90'

2	Yellow cards	2
0	Red cards	0
2	Shots on target	6
8	Shots off target	5
15	Fouls committed	14
2	Corners	2
5	Offsides	2
35' 11"	Ball. Poss. (time)	27' 28"
56%	Ball. Poss. (%)	44%

Rafael Benitez described Liverpool's performance as "almost perfect" and went so far as to declare that his 2007 crop were better than the champions of two years earlier. He enthused, "We knew what to do and that was the key. We knew PSV had problems. We had to do the right things and profit from their mistakes. To score three goals and to get a clean sheet is almost perfect."

The result virtually guaranteed the club's place in the semi-finals, although Benítez warned against complacency in the second leg. But for all the manager's caution – "we must be careful and approach the second game seriously" – a semi-final against Chelsea or Valencia

beckoned, evoking memories of their journey to Istanbul and that memorable final against Milan two years ago. "This team is better than the team that won the Champions League," claimed Benítez. "We have got to play one more game and after I hope the semi-final."

PSV coach Ronald Koeman had declared beforehand that 0-0 "would be a good result" and that lack of ambition was evident throughout. Gerrard, outstanding again, put Liverpool ahead in the 28th minute with a bullet header set up by Steve Finnan. John Arne Riise propelled a 35-yard shot into the top corner before Crouch headed in a third, his fourth goal in as many days, after a hat-trick in the 4-1 league demolition of Arsenal.

Victory was never in doubt from the moment Gerrard scored and Liverpool

---

DID YOU KNOW?
Steven Gerrard's goal was his 15th in the Champions League, one more than legendary Anfield goalscorer Ian Rush managed in the European Cup

Peter Crouch bags the third goal, which virtually ended the tie

PSV coach Ronald Koeman faces up to facts; his team have been steamrollered by Liverpool

> **"We want to see Stevie scoring goals, Carra playing a lot of games and the team winning."**
> **Rafa Benitez**

could not have imagined a smoother passage into the last four. "We came here not to concede and to get a goal," said Crouch. "To get three is even better. I don't know if it's about rotation, but perhaps we are peaking at the right time."

So impressive in jettisoning Arsenal in the previous round, PSV were crushed, the illusion that English sides unravel when confronted by Koeman exposed as a sham.

The goal that eased Liverpool ahead began when Javier Mascherano sliding a pass in behind the gasping left-back Carlos Salcido for the overlapping Steve Finnan to gather. The full-back had time to glance up and spin his cross to beyond the penalty spot where Gerrard, unattended, thumped a header into the net.

On 48 minutes Riise scored a sensational goal. A poor clearance fell to the Norwegian 30 yards out, and he took one stride before unleashing a thunderous drive that crashed past a startled Gomes.

And the third soon followed. Another Finnan overlap on 62 minutes produced a cross that saw Crouch jump high above his marker to head powerfully into the top corner.

Koeman flung Patrick Kluivert on in desperation, but there was no papering over such gaping deficiencies at the back.

The victory was so comfortable that Dirk Kuyt, already having a yellow card from a previous game, needlessly encroached on a free-kick late on to ensure he picked up a booking that meant he would be suspended for the

DID YOU KNOW?
Jamie Carragher reached a new landmark in this match, his 58th appearance in the UEFA Champions League, surpassing Phil Neal's club appearance record in the competition

return leg at Anfield, but available for the semi-finals.

When the club's flight returned to John Lennon airport around 4am, the weary VIPs on the plane applauded their heroes as they landed. George Gillett had flown in from a family holiday in Austria to witness Liverpool's advance in Holland, having seen the 4-1 mauling of Arsenal four days earlier – his and Tom Hicks' first match as official joint-owners. Ex-chairman David Moores, now just a plain director, but still the figurehead of the trip, stood wistfully by the baggage carousel considering the difficult feelings of no longer being at the helm. He said: "Yes, it's a strange feeling after all these years being chairman. But the club had to move on and I believe it is in good hands."

The family essence of Liverpool was shown as Moores warmly embraced Gerrard, the club skipper giving Moores' wife Marjorie a peck on the cheek as the team were whisked away. Liverpool would never be the same again after a momentous week.

As the Liverpool squad touched down at John Lennon International in the small hours of the morning, the talk was about reaching the final in Athens. "We are getting that same feeling we had in 2005 when we won this trophy, but I am also telling myself to slow down and realise that we have a lot more work before we can think about getting to Athens," said Gerrard.

"There's no denying we're in a great position," said Finnan, who set up two of the goals. "We were in a great position when we beat Barcelona in Spain in the last round but we can't let our standards slip. I'd be very disappointed if we didn't go through but we have to be focused and do the right thing next week."

The only sour note was an injury to Fabio Aurelio. There was nobody near the Liverpool left-back when he collapsed to the ground clutching his leg. He was taken from the field on a stretcher and, after leaving the ground on crutches, a scan revealed that Aurelio, who was beginning to make his mark after a slow start following his move from Valencia, would not play again this season and would need surgery on the achilles tendon he had ruptured in his right leg.

John Arne Riise had been used on the left wing, ahead of Aurelio, in recent weeks, but would return to full-back for the remainder of the campaign after the Brazilian's injury. After being declared bankrupt over an unpaid debt of £100,000, Riise had the order lifted at Liverpool County Court. His financial problems stemmed from a dispute with his former agent, Einar Baardsen, over the way the player's earnings of £40,000 a week had been invested.

> ### "We are getting that same feeling we had in 2005 when we won this trophy."
> **Steven Gerrard**

DID YOU KNOW?
This 3-0 win was Liverpool's biggest ever success in the Champions League proper

The one black spot for Liverpool; Fabio Aurelio is stretchered off

AC MILAN 2 v BAYERN MUN. 2

Referee
Yuri Baskakov (Russia)

Assistant Referee
Tikhon Kalugin (Russia)
Anton Averianov (Russia)

Fourth Official
Stanislav Sukhina (Russia)

UEFA Referee Observer
David Elleray

Scorers

40'	Pirlo	van Buyten	78', 90'
84'	Kaká (pen)		

Teams

01	Dida	Rensing	22
03	Maldini	Lahm	21
13	Nesta	Lucio	03
44	Oddo	Sagnol	02
23	Ambrosini	van Buyten	05
08	Gattuso	Hargreaves	23
22	Kaká	Ottl	39
18	Jankulovski	Salihamidzic	20
21	Pirlo	Schweinsteiger	31
10	Seedorf	Makaay	10
11	Gilardino	Podolski	11

Substitutes

72'	> 09 Inzaghi < 11 Gilardino		30 Lell > 02 Sagnol <	68'
85'	> 20 Gourcuff < 10 Seedorf		14 Pizarro > 11 Podolski <	68'
87'	> 04 Kaladze < 18 Jankulovski		24 Santa Cruz > 10 Makaay <	86'

Discipline

53'	Gilardino	Salihamidzic	33'
		Lucio	84'

1	Yellow cards	2
0	Red cards	0
4	Shots on target	5
4	Shots off target	4
10	Fouls committed	11
3	Corners	5
1	Offsides	1
30' 26"	Ball. Poss. (time)	34' 12"
47%	Ball. Poss. (%)	53%

AC Milan 2 v Bayern Munich 2
San Siro
Attendance: 77,700

On a dramatic and controversial night, Bayern Munich's players remonstrate with Russian referee Yuri Baskakov after he awarded a late penalty against them, but to no avail

Daniel van Buyten had failed to cause much of a stir in Manchester during his five appearances for City three years ago when on loan from Marseille; now he had become a big-money purchase for Bayern. The Belgian got himself noticed at the San Siro with two late equalisers.

Van Buyten's second, over three minutes into injury-time, gave Bayern a striking away-goals advantage and took some of the glare off the Russian referee, Yuri Baskakov, whose 84th-minute penalty award to Milan infuriated the Germans. Lucio perfected a ball-winning challenge on Kaká six minutes from the end. Kaká went to ground as if felled. Baskakov was close by, yet pointed to the spot.

Bayern's manager Ottmar Hitzfeld had said pre-match that he was worried about Baskakov; he was right to be. Kaká converted the penalty as Carlo Ancelotti's side looked sure to take a crucial one-goal lead to Bavaria. "You can see clearly on television that Lucio got the ball," Hitzfeld said. "It was no penalty," conceded Ancelotti.

But Bayern had scored two late goals at the San Siro in the group stage, against Inter, and they had shown the fight to claw their way back once already. That was when van Buyten got his first equaliser, in the 78th minute, capping a 20-minute period of Munich pressure.

Owen Hargreaves and Lucio were central to Bayern's recovery, but as Ancelotti put it: "We lacked the necessary clarity in front of goal."

DID YOU KNOW?
Milan were the only club of last season's quarter-finalists to appear in the last eight this time around

The main culprit, centre-forward Alberto Gilardino, endured jeers from 67,000 fans, and when he did manage to get an effort on target he found Michael Rensing in impressive form in the Bayern goal. Rensing was playing only because Oliver Kahn was suspended for not providing the required urine sample after their victory over Real Madrid in the previous round. When Gilardino beat Rensing in the 53rd minute, the goal was ruled out for offside and the Italian was booked, missing the return leg, though with Filippo Inzaghi back from injury and able to come on as Gilardino's replacement, Milan were not devastated.

Hitzfeld conceded Milan looked sharper in the first half and deserved the 40th-minute lead supplied by Andrea Pirlo's looping header. But their threat petered out after Kaká squandered a great chance nine minutes into the second half when the Brazilian failed to make contact to an Ambrosini centre from four yards out.

That enabled Bayern to begin sustained probing for the first time. Hargreaves was the source, with solid help from Andreas Ottl. Gradually they began to find the hitherto isolated Roy Makaay and, when the wooden Lukas Podolski gave way to Claudio Pizarro with 25 minutes left, Bayern had the impetus and Milan were fraying – "We tired ourselves out," admitted Ancelotti – and when Hasan Salihamidzic fired in a deep cross in the 78th minute, Pizarro jumped highest and won it. The ball ran to van Buyten, who showed coolness to guide the ball beyond Dida.

Sadly for Bayern they had just lost their stand-in captain Willy Sagnol to injury and the French international may need an operation on his knee.

> **"We lacked the necessary clarity in front of goal."**
> **Carlo Ancelotti, AC Milan coach**

Kaká is chased by Bayern's Lucio

Kaká nets the penalty which he, and all Milan fans, thought had brought them victory

Baskakov's 84th-minute penalty award for Lucio's non-foul on Kaká was one of those decisions that inevitably recalls events when Milan were docked eight points at the start of the season for pressurising match officials. But then, three minutes and 39 seconds into injury-time and with Bayern forward in numbers, the ball again fell to van Buyten. From a narrow angle, close to the touchline, he again beat Dida with a smacked volley.

"Their goals were lucky goals," said right-back Massimo Oddo of van Buyten's equalisers, "and we had a lot of bad luck. I think we'll make good in Munich and progress to the semi-finals."

> **I think we'll make good in Munich and progress to the semi-finals."**
> **Massimo Oddo, AC Milan**

Hasan Salihamidzic celebrates Bayern's last minute goal

Alessandro Nesta comes to terms with van Buyten's late equalizer

Oddo's colleague at left-back, Marek Jankulovski, concurred: "Above all we were lacking a bit of luck, as we could have been two or three up at half-time. Unfortunately Bayern scored on two hopeful crosses to the back post and we have to make up for that now."

The pair had been drawn together for the second successive season with the German giants having last year been knocked out of the tournament 5-2 on aggregate at the first knockout round stage. Post-match Bayern chairman Karl-Heinz Rummenigge admitted his players had been looking for revenge: "Last year we lost convincingly 4-1 here and so we had something to make up for," he said. 'We know them well and have had the advantage of playing the first leg away. We will have to see if our dreams are still alive after the return game."

Bayern coach Ottmar Hitzfeld "It was a very exciting night with lots of opportunities to score on both sides. Milan played well, but I knew from early in the game that they could not keep up such a high tempo for the whole 90 minutes. Tonight's result was fully deserved because we defended well and we only showed 70 per cent of our potential. We will not defend in Munich, we want to score."

However, on this evidence Sir Alex Ferguson's representatives will have departed quietly confident that Manchester United would be able to overcome either side... if they get past Roma.

> **"We will not defend in Munich, we want to score."**
> **Ottmar Hitzfeld, Bayern Munich coach**

Quarter-Finals
Wednesday 4 April 2007 – First Legs

> "It was a tough job, but we're happy with the result. We knew once we got the away goal that it will be very tough for Roma to come to Old Trafford."
>
> **Wayne Rooney**

AS Roma 2 v Manchester United 1
Stadio Olimpico
Attendance: 78,000

Paul Scholes sees red on a devastatingly disappointing night for Manchester United and British football

Prior to the game, with around 4,500 supporters expected to make the trip, and after incidents of crowd violence in Italy earlier this season – as well as problems for their own supporters in Lens, United issued travel advice. "We have sent out our usual letter to supporters, but with more information contained than perhaps in the past," said Phil Townsend, United's Director of Communications. United told supporters to use transport to the Olympic Stadium recommended by the Italian authorities. They also warned them to keep away from areas which attract a build-up of home fans. United found themselves facing demands for an apology from, among others, the mayor of Rome, Walter Veltroni. He was among those to have been upset by the club's decision to warn their fans of the "real danger" of being attacked by Roma's "Ultras".

Roma coach, Luciano Spalletti, described himself as "extremely annoyed by this slur" and Mayor Veltroni revealed that he had made an official complaint to the city's British ambassador, Edward Chaplin.

The hostility spilled over in the Stadio Olimpico as Paul Scholes found himself dismissed for two yellow cards in the first half and then fans clashed. UEFA announced an immediate investigation after violence erupted and ten English fans found themselves in hospital with stab wounds. Further confrontations broke out inside the stands between

AS ROMA 2   v   MAN UNITED 1

Referee
Herbert Fandel (Germany)

Assistant Referee
Carsten Kadach (Germany)
Volker Wezel (Germany)

Fourth Official
Peter Sippel (Germany)

UEFA Referee Observer
Peter Sippel

Scorers

44'	Taddei	Rooney	60'
66'	Vucinic		

Teams

32	Doni	van der Sar	01
77	Cassetti	Brown	06
13	Chivu	Ferdinand	05
05	Mexes	Heinze	04
02	Panucci	O'Shea	22
16	De Rossi	Carrick	16
30	Mancini	Giggs	11
20	Perrotta	Ronaldo	07
11	Taddei	Scholes	18
04	Wilhelmsson	Rooney	08
10	Totti	Solskjaer	20

Substitutes

62'	> 23 Vucinic < 04 Wilhelmsson		24 Fletcher > 20 Solskjaer <	72'
82'	> 28 Rosi < 11 Taddei		09 Saha > 11 Giggs <	77'

Discipline

42'	Perrotta	Scholes	26'
		Scholes	34'
		Solskjaer	70'
		Heinze	87'

1	Yellow cards	2
0	Red cards	0
9	Shots on target	4
13	Shots off target	3
20	Fouls committed	19
9	Corners	3
3	Offsides	2
27' 18"	Ball. Poss. (time)	21' 06"
56%	Ball. Poss. (%)	44%

United fans and Italian police, after missiles were thrown, with local police firing teargas to deal with the problems.

Sir Alex Ferguson refused to comment on the trouble, but United claimed local police 'handed out indiscriminate beatings to United supporters'. It was an ugly incident which claimed headlines for days afterwards.

Sir Alex Ferguson claimed Manchester United were playing "against 12 men" in an outburst against the German referee Herbert Fandel. Ferguson was incensed by Fandel's performance at the Stadio Olimpico claiming that "a good referee" would not have sent off Paul Scholes. "Considering we played with ten men – mostly against 12 men – for over an hour, this is a good result for us. I don't think we got a decision all night but that is European football, I'm afraid."

Fandel has been one of Ferguson's least favourite referees since he officiated their Champions League tie against Porto in 2003 and, in the eyes of the United manager, allowed Jose Mourinho's players to get away with some of the worst gamesmanship he has ever seen in a European tie. Ferguson remonstrated with the fourth official, Peter Sippel, on several occasions and later complained that Fandel was not equipped to take control of such a big match. "I can't have any complaints about [Scholes's] first booking, but I do have complaints about the second one. In a big game like that, a good referee would not have sent him off, " said Ferguson, before turning his attention to the Roma defender Cristian Chivu, who appeared to give Fandel the thumbs up when Scholes was shown a second yellow card. "In my opinion Chivu got Scholes sent off because of his reaction to the referee. The referee told us before the game that if anyone

Rodrigo Taddei opens the scoring for Roma

Roman police clash with Manchester United fans in a controversial incident on an unhappy night

attempted to get another player booked they would be sent off themselves. But that wasn't the case at all and it left us in a very difficult position."

Even though Ferguson complained about Fandel's refereeing, the midfielder had already been lectured for two late tackles before his first yellow card. That came in the 26th minute when he scythed down Christian Wilhelmsson on the touchline and, when he clipped Francesco Totti eight minutes later, Fandel brandished red. Scholes felt

DID YOU KNOW?
Rooney's classy 60th-minute goal was his first in the Champions League since a debut hat-trick against Fenerbahce in September 2004

aggrieved because there was only minimal contact.

Within eight minutes of Scholes' dismissal, Roma broke menacingly, Mancini crossed from the left and Taddei scored with a deflection off Wes Brown.

In the second half United counterattacked, willing to press forward despite their numerical disadvantage with Ronaldo able to occupy the Roma defenders and he was instrumental in Rooney's goal, skipping past a couple of challenges and moving the ball to Ole Gunnar Solskjaer. His cross picked out Rooney at the far post and the striker controlled the ball on his chest, showing brilliant composure, before side-footing the ball past Doni. The United fans could be heard celebrating, but Roma's response was swift. Van der Sar had been in imperious form, but his first mistake of the night was to parry out Mancini's shot, when he could have flicked it over, and the ball fell invitingly for Vucinic to lash in the rebound.

The Italians missed chances to add to the goals from Taddei, their Brazilian midfielder, and Mirko Vucinic, a second-half substitute, but Serie A's second-placed club celebrated at the final whistle.

Despite defeat Ferguson refused to consider Roma as favourites to

progress to the semi-finals. "I think 2-1 is a good result for us. We're experienced enough to know that playing at home is a big advantage when you are in Europe. Over the years there have been some great games back at Old Trafford and we are in for another one now. We have come out with a good result here and if we score at Old Trafford we will go through. The away goal is invaluable in these two-legged fixtures. We have been impressed by Roma from what we have seen of them this season. We knew it would be tough, and it was tough. They made it difficult for us because they had an extra player, but in the end it's a good result for us."

Ferguson identified Wayne Rooney for special acclaim after the striker had scored his first Champions League goal in 18 matches. "The great thing is that Wayne is only 21 yet he showed fantastic composure in front of goal. It would have been easy for him to rush his shot, but he took it down and took his team before picking out his spot." Rooney later described it as "one of the hardest games" he had ever been involved in, but he, like Ferguson, believes 2-1 is a result that can stand in United's favour. "It was a tough job, but we're happy with the result. We knew once we got the away goal that it will be very tough for Roma to come to Old Trafford. We have the home advantage next week and it's not a bad position to be in."

As he left the Stadio Olimpico, Ole Gunnar Solskjaer remarked: "Losing is never a good result, but we have to win 1-0 at Old Trafford to get into the Champions League semi-finals. We'd have taken that six months ago."

Solskjaer felt particularly encouraged by Rooney scoring his first European Cup goal since 2004: "He showed great composure in that instant. He's not been affected by all the talk and his confidence has never dropped." Eight months earlier most people doubted Solskjaer would ever play again because of his persistent knee injury, but now the Norwegian is back. "Europe's special," he said. "I've been waiting a long time to play in these big games."

Chelsea 1 v Valencia 1
Stamford Bridge
Attendance: 38,065

Chelsea fans get into the mood for a cracking quarter-final, but they went home frustrated at their team's inability to shine

CHELSEA 1 v **VALENCIA 1**

Referee
Frank De Bleeckere (Belgium)

Assistant Referee
Peter Hermans (Belgium)
Mark Simons (Belgium)

Fourth Official
Serge Gumienny (Belgium)

UEFA Referee Observer
Jaap Ullenberg

Scorers

53'	Drogba	Silva	30'

Teams

01 Cech	Canizares 01
06 Ricardo Carvalho	Ayala 04
03 A Cole	Del Horno 03
26 Terry	Miguel 02
13 Ballack	Moretti 24
19 Diarra	Albelda 06
08 Lampard	Albiol 20
12 Mikel	Joaquin 15
11 Drogba	Silva 21
21 Kalou	Vicente 14
07 Shevchenko	Villa 07

Substitutes

74'	> 10 J Cole < 12 Mikel	10 Angulo > 14 Vicente <	58'
75'	> 24 Wright-Phillips < 21 Kalou	16 H Viana > 15 Joaquin <	87'
		18 Jorge Lopez > 07 Villa <	90'

Discipline

45'	Drogba	Silva	36'
86'	Diarra	Albelda	44'
		Ayala	72'

2	Yellow cards	3
0	Red cards	0
3	Shots on target	2
6	Shots off target	4
12	Fouls committed	19
7	Corners	5
6	Offsides	0
31'54"	Ball. Poss. (time)	24'36"
56%	Ball. Poss. (%)	44%

Before Chelsea's tie with the only remaining Spanish representatives, Valencia, talks of a rift at Stamford Bridge were rife in the media, and Andriy Shevchenko was at the root of it all.

German website sport.ARD.de. claimed that Shevchenko, so disappointing since his arrival in England, had spoken of the tensions within the club. "It's true I have complained about Mourinho, but there are a lot of things which drove me to that," Shevchenko was quoted as saying. "A few months ago I suddenly became his dartboard because he was having a spat with the President [Abramovich] at the time."

Failing to find his form since his high-profile move from AC Milan, Shevchenko showed his hand by allegedly saying: "I'm an employee of the club, so I do what the President says. The manager never spoke to me or played me in the position where my strengths lie. It's also no secret that I was more on Mr Abramovich's wish list than the manager's."

Shevchenko denied that he had said anything of the sort, but the damage was done and the tension which had encompassed Stamford Bridge since the Christmas slump, injury crisis and fall out amongst senior members of staff was hardly eased when Jose Mourinho confirmed he had not met Roman Abramovich for more than two months. Abramovich had stopped visiting the dressing room after matches and had not been to the training ground, where he used to be a regular visitor. The Russian billionaire was last seen by the players or manager in person after the Boxing Day home draw against Reading.

DID YOU KNOW?
After this draw Valencia were unbeaten in eight successive matches against English competition, having dispatched Arsenal and Leeds United en route to the final in 2001

> **"If we win, we go to the semi-final. If we lose, there is wrestling at Earls Court on the day of the semi-final, so if we're not playing I'll go to Earls Court with my kids."**
> **Jose Mourinho**

Interestingly Valencia's season had been overshadowed by an injury crisis, boardroom turmoil and ambiguity over the future of their coach and their best players, all issues familiar to Chelsea fans. David Albelda, captain and midfield enforcer, a veteran of the Valencia side who reached the 2001 Champions League final, missed three months of the season after tearing knee ligaments back in October. The injury list regularly reached double-figures and included former Chelsea defender Asier del Horno and ex-Arsenal midfielder Edu. The captain acted as peace-maker in the simmering row between sporting director Amedeo Carboni and coach Quique Sanchez Flores. Carboni had been a surprise appointment after his retirement as a player last summer and admitted that he only got the job because of his friendship with president Juan Soler. But he had not forgiven Sanchez Flores for leaving him on the substitutes' bench for most of last season and the pair bickered all year, with Carboni refusing Sanchez Flores's request for transfer funds to be made available in the January window and openly looking for a new coach for next season. The pair even disagreed over Valencia's involvement in the post-match fight with Inter Milan in the last round. When Sanchez Flores, sickened by the violent scenes had said his players "were not worthy of a big club like Valencia", Carboni countered that, saying "it's a logical reaction to defend your team-mates".

Meanwhile Valencia striker David Villa denied he was joining Chelsea in the summer. The 25 year-old said that he would "only think about my future once the Chelsea games are over". With bidding likely to start around £20m and Real Madrid and Barcelona not expected to be among the interested parties, Villa's options seem to be to leave Spain or stay at Valencia.

Mourinho planned to be ringside at Earls Court, watching the WWE wrestlers with his children if Chelsea failed to reach the semis. "If you ask me 'Will we make the semi-final?' then I would say 'yes'," he said. "If we win, we go to the semi-final. If we lose, there is wrestling at Earls Court on the day of the semi-final, so if we're not playing I'll go to Earls Court with my kids."

Valencia, though, had the first fall in this contest thank to their away goal. The 2000 and 2001 finalists took the lead on the half-hour in west London, Silva producing an unstoppable strike out of nowhere from what looked an unpromising

DID YOU KNOW?
After this draw Valencia were unbeaten in eight successive matches against English competition, having dispatched Arsenal and Leeds United en route to the final in 2001

DID YOU KNOW?
This was top scorer Didier Drogba's first goal for a month and it made him the first Chelsea player since Kerry Dixon in 1985 to reach 30 goals in a season

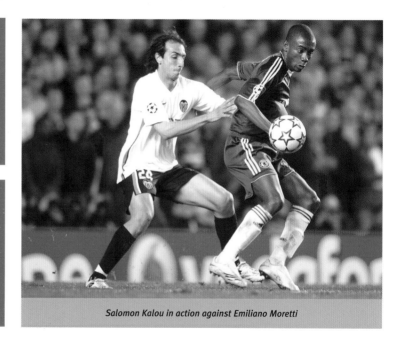

Salomon Kalou in action against Emiliano Moretti

Drogba heads home Chelsea's equalizer

Chelsea can draw 2-2, even 1-1 and go to extra-time. We can come through this."

John Terry was equally defiant, "With Didier scoring goals, I'm sure we can get a few. We just need to keep a clean sheet. We've shown in the Champions League before we can go away, pick up a result and go through."

Under pressure Mourinho insisted: "I think if someone has to win this game it should be Chelsea because we attacked more. They were lucky to get that amazing goal because they didn't create a lot. The result was correct, but this was a game in which Chelsea did everything to try to win, but Valencia only tried to draw. We had bad luck when Kalou hit the post in the first half and then Shevchenko clashed with Ayala and got nothing. But we cannot worry too much because the game is still there to win. We are in the same position as we were in the last round when we drew 1-1 with Porto in the first match. And then we saw what happened in the second. We must now go to the Mestalla and perform 1-1, 2-2 or get the win. The fact is the game can still go each way."

Valencia coach Quique Flores Sanchez warned: "It's natural that we will attack more when we are at home and you will see more of David Villa in the second match. Our approach will be very different to the one you saw in London."

Dutch legend Johan Cruyff seriously questioned if Chelsea had the credentials to win the competition. "I doubt if the winner of the Champions League will emerge from the three English clubs – especially given the way Chelsea play," he said.. "They only start playing when they're losing! They have enough quality in the squad, which is why they often get things right under Jose Mourinho. But what frustrates me is that Chelsea feel such little need to please the public."

position on the Valencia left. Silva got a lucky break off John Obi Mikel following a Valencia throw-in, giving the 21 year-old room to advance. He was still outside the penalty area and at an unfavourable angle when he unexpectedly let fly and was rewarded as the ball arrowed into the far corner of Chelsea's net.

Chelsea levelled through Drogba's sixth goal in the competition this season – his 30th of the campaign. After Ashley Cole punted a long ball forward, Ayala was less than his usual immaculate self, failing to cut out the bouncing ball and inviting Drogba to nod over the goalkeeper and bring Chelsea level.

Drogba had been devastated to lose to Valencia while wearing Marseille colours in the 2004 UEFA Cup final. "It remains a really painful memory for me. That defeat in Gothenburg left its mark

on me like nothing else." His goal went part of the way to dimming the pain.

And it might easily have been a Chelsea victory. With six minutes remaining Ricardo Carvalho's drive was blocked and Andriy Shevchenko, following up with an overhead kick, was foiled as Miguel cleared over his own bar. Earlier Shevchenko had driven in from the left after 10 minutes and been blatantly bodychecked by Roberto Ayala just inside the area, Kalou turned on the loose ball and clipped the top of the bar.

Despite his side's failure to find a winning goal, Mourinho still believed. "Maybe Valencia are enjoying this result, but, if I was in their place, I would be very cautious. If we have a good referee and he is not influenced by the enthusiastic atmosphere of the Mestalla, why can't we get a result? It's 1-1, we're not 3-0 down.

Quarter-Finals
Tuesday 10 April 2007 – Second Legs

> "Hopefully it's not a one-off, but the quality of goals was so high it is difficult to think we could ever get that again."
> **Sir Alex Ferguson**

Manchester United 7 v AS Roma 1
(Manchester United won 8-2 on aggregate)
Old Trafford
Attendance: 74,476

Michael Carrick notches the first of three United goals in a devastating five minute spell during the rampage to a seven goal humiliation of Roma

> "It was a night I won't forget for a long while. It was awesome to be part of it."
> **Michael Carrick, Manchester United**

Sir Alex Ferguson savoured his greatest night of European football as Manchester United destroyed Italy's reputation of possessing the world's most accomplished defences. "The quality of our game was so high that once we scored the second and third goals I was in the dugout thinking 'this could be something really big here'. But even so, I wasn't expecting that," glowed the ecstatic manager.

Ferguson used the word "uncanny" and he shook his head with disbelief, "Hopefully it's not a one-off, but the quality of goals was so high it is difficult to think we could ever get that again. It was a fantastic performance; the speed of our play, the penetration, the confidence we showed, the clinical nature of our finishing. It was a special night and we can't wait for the semi-finals now because it will give the club a real lift."

Ronaldo and Rooney came of age, according to Sir Alex while Michael Carrick produced his best ever display. And the manager identified Alan Smith, making only his fourth start of the season after recovering from the broken leg and dislocated ankle he suffered

> **DID YOU KNOW?**
> This was only the second time United had made it into the quarter-finals since winning the trophy in 1999

Wayne Rooney celebrates scoring the third goal

MAN UTD 7   v   **AS ROMA 1**

Referee
Lubos Michel (SVK)

Assistant Referee
Roman Slysko (SVK) Martin Balko (SVK)
Vladimir Vnuk (SVK)

Fourth Official
Zoran Petrovic (SRB)

UEFA Referee Observer
Manuel Diaz Vega

Scorers

11', 60'	Carrick	De Rossi 69'
17'	Smith	
19'	Rooney	
44', 49'	Ronaldo	
81'	Evra	

Teams

01	van der Sar	Doni	32
06	Brown	Cassetti	77
05	Ferdinand	Chivu	13
04	Heinze	Mexes	05
22	O'Shea	Panucci	02
16	Carrick	De Rossi	16
24	Fletcher	Mancini	30
11	Giggs	Pizarro	07
07	Ronaldo	Wilhelmsson	04
08	Rooney	Totti	10
14	Smith	Vucinic	23

Substitutes

52'	03 Evra / 22 O'Shea	14 Faty / 16 De Rossi	86'
61'	20 Solskjaer / 11 Giggs	28 Rosi / 04 Wilhelmsson	88'
73'	23 Richardson / 16 Carrick	35 Chuka / 30 Mancini	90'

Discipline

40'	Smith	Cassetti	76'
42'	Ferdinand	Mexes	82'

2	Yellow cards	2
0	Red cards	0
15	Shots on target	8
7	Shots off target	8
20	Fouls committed	17
3	Corners	2
5	Offsides	2
26' 34"	Ball. Poss. (time)	31' 45"
45%	Ball. Poss. (%)	55%

against Liverpool 14 months earlier, for special acclaim. "He deserves it more than anyone. His attitude is absolutely wonderful, but the greatest qualities he has shown are his patience and his perseverance," said Ferguson.

But the night had begun rather less gloriously as the residual ill-feeling from the first leg spilled over again. Hundreds of supporters were caught up in ugly scenes outside Old Trafford before the game as a standoff ensued between rival fans who were separated by riot police and dog handlers. Police arrested 21 supporters – 14 English and seven Italian. "The police said they dealt with a few small, isolated incidents and there was nothing on the scale of what happened to Manchester United fans in Rome last week," commented Sean Bones, of the Manchester United Supporters' Trust. The police's

match commander, Superintendent Charlie Coxon, said officers were forced to use batons, horses and dogs to contain a "very small minority" of United fans intent on causing trouble in revenge for the previous week's troubles. "It's important to realise that the vast majority of the 75,000 crowd did exactly what United and GMP asked for, which was to come to Old Trafford and enjoy another exciting night of European football," he said.

And that's exactly what they got as United stormed into a 3-0 lead inside 20 minutes in a display of staggeringly swift passing, dynamic movement and clinical finishing.

Even before the start Roma were in trouble. Rodrigo Taddei took ill so close to kick-off that the team sheet had to be redrafted. His place went to Mirko

UEFA Champions League Thrashings In The Competition's Latter Stages

Milan 4 Barcelona 0 final, 1994
Ajax 5 Bayern Munich 2 (agg. 5-2) semi-final, 1995
Manchester United 4 Porto 0 (agg. 4-0) quarter-final, 1997
Kaiserslautern 0 Bayern Munich 4 (agg 0-6) quarter-final, 1999
Barcelona 5 Chelsea 1, (agg. 6-4) quarter-final, 2000
Valencia 5 Lazio 2 (agg. 5-4) quarter-final, 2004
Deportivo La Coruña 4 Milan 0 (agg. 5-4) quarter-final, 2004
Lyon 7 Werder Bremen 2 (agg. 10-2) first knockout round, 2005
Lyon 4 PSV Eindhoven 0 (agg. 5-0) first knockout round, 2006

Vucinic, who had delivered the winner in the 2-1 success a week earlier.

Ferguson, unexpectedly, adopted the same 4-2-3-1 formation as Roma with Rooney on the left, Smith the lone striker, even though he had not started a Premiership fixture in the current campaign.

With 12 minutes gone Ronaldo jinked inside and set up Carrick, whose bending finish from outside the area confused the static goalkeeper Doni and beat him at his near post. Five minutes later Heinze advanced on the left and picked out Giggs in the middle, Chivu failed to cut out the Welshman's through-ball and Smith was clear to accept the chance.

In the 19th minute a mesmeric move by Ronaldo, followed by Smith's ball to Giggs, allowed the veteran winger to centre and Rooney knocked in the third. To set the seal on a devastating first half Ronaldo cut inside from the right and beat Doni at the near post just before the break.

United did not relent after half-time. Four minutes in Roma lost the ball in defence, Giggs picked it up on the left and, while Smith could not quite connect with a low delivery, Ronaldo at the far post forced it home. "Are you City in disguise?" bayed the crowd.

With an hour gone, United switched a move to the left, Heinze laid the ball back and Carrick placed it high past Doni from 20 yards for his second. In a rare Roma attack Daniel de Rossi

'Stunned, Destroyed, Humiliated' – The Verdict In Rome

Italy's front-page headline writers delivered the scale of Manchester United's 7-1 Champions League slaughter of Roma. "A historic rout for Italian football," screamed the football daily La Gazzetta dello Sport, while La Repubblica led a front page editorial with "Goodbye dreams, Roma humiliated in Manchester." La Stampa ran "Roma Hell", compared to Il Messaggero's "Oh No".

The editorials referred back to Juventus's 7-0 humbling at the hands of Austria's Wiener SK in 1958. "I do not recall such an apocalyptic quarter-final or such a devastating first half," wrote La Stampa's Roberto Beccantini, adding that Roma were "stunned, then swept away, then destroyed, then humiliated."

Looking ahead, La Repubblica worried what Cristiano Ronaldo, scorer of two goals, might unleash on the "dinosaurs" in the Milan defence were he to confront them in the semi-final. Contending with Ronaldo's dribbling, the Roma players "looked like car-sick kids who vomit their elevenses at the first sharp curve," the paper wrote. Francesco Totti, christened "Captain Disaster" by La Gazzetta Dello Sport and accused by La Repubblica of going missing on big nights, described it as the saddest night of his life. "Describing each goal would just be sadistic," wrote Corriere della Sera, going on to quote the Roma coach, Luciano Spalletti, who was rather less reticent. "Every shot finished in the back of the net," he said incredulously, adding: "What would I change if I could do it again? Stay at home."

netted a volley from a Totti cross in the 69th minute.

Then with ten minutes to go, Patrice Evra, on as a substitute, collected a pass from Solskjaer, advanced to the edge of the area and squeezed his shot between two defenders and past Doni, once again at the near post.

It was, to put not too fine a point on it, carnage.

Shell-shocked Roma captain Francesco Totti struggled to come to terms with his team's humiliating defeat. "It is the saddest night of my sporting career," admitted Totti. "I had never conceded seven goals in a Champions League match before. Each shot they took, they found the target."

The result was also a hammer blow for the 5000 Giallorossi fans that travelled with the team to Manchester. "I have to thank our travelling fans," said Totti. "They showed a lot of heart

by coming here to support us. Unfortunately, we have come across a better team."

Totti was overshadowed by Cristiano Ronaldo, who stole the limelight. Ronaldo scored two goals and was a menace all night and 36 year-old Dutch goalkeeper Edwin van der Saar watched in awe. The Dutch custodian purred: "The way we played in that first 19 minutes is unlike anything I have seen in my whole career. Every chance we created we scored. The second goal which Alan Smith scored was just brilliant one-touch football all the way. It wasn't that Roma played badly, we were just very good. It gives us great confidence to go all the way."

England midfielder Michael Carrick said: "I'll get the DVD of the game and it will be coming out once or twice, you can be sure of that. It was an incredible night. We asked the fans to get behind

DID YOU KNOW?
Alan Smith's goal was his first since 15 November 2005

DID YOU KNOW?
United's 7-1 victory was the biggest win in the quarter-finals of the European Champion Clubs' Cup since Real Madrid's wins in 1958 (8-0 against Sevilla FC) and in 1959 (7-1 against Wiener Sportclub)

Roma keeper Doni contemplates the seventh goal

us and there was a big build-up to the game. But for it to go like that was unbelievable and it was a night I won't forget for a long while. It was awesome to be part of it."

Ferguson went on to declare the presence of three English teams in the semi-finals signified that the Premiership could now be considered as the strongest league in Europe. "A few years ago I would have said that Spanish football was the best but the evidence this season is that Barcelona and Real Madrid are nowhere near as strong as they have been in previous years. The quality of the English game has improved and everyone can see that now because it is very probable there will be three of us in the semis and, hopefully, an all-English final. I think English football has to be recognised as the best in Europe now."

Even that Anglo-sceptic Johan Cruyff, member of the Ajax and Holland 'Total Football' sides of the Seventies that perfected the style of attacking from all areas of the field enjoyed United's performance, "I was on the edge of my seat.

It was one touch, total football. It was absolutely breathtaking. Ronaldo can dribble and show blistering pace at the same time. That's a rare combination. The most fantastic thing about the way United played against Roma was that the Italians were even beaten at their own game. The Italians were second best in every area of the pitch. Everything the United players touched turned into gold. It was a joy to watch."

Cristiano Ronaldo bamboozles Roma's Christian Wilhelmsson

> "What would I change if I could do it again? Stay at home."
> Luciano Spalletti, Roma coach

VALENCIA 1 v **CHELSEA 2**

Referee
Kyros Vassaras (Greece)

Assistant Referee
Dimitrios Bozatzidis (Greece)
Dimitris Saraidaris (Greece)

Fourth Official
Vladimir Vnuk (SVK)

UEFA Referee Observer
Francesco Bianchi

Scorers

11'	Morientes	Shevchenko	52'
		Essien	90'

Teams

01	Canizares	Cech 01
04	Ayala	Ricardo Carvalho 06
03	Del Horno	A Cole 03
02	Miguel	Terry 26
24	Moretti	Ballack 13
06	Albelda	Diarra 19
20	Albiol	Essien 05
15	Joaquin	Lampard 08
21	Silva	Mikel 12
09	Morientes	Drogba 11
07	Villa	Shevchenko 07

Substitutes

65'	> 10 Angulo < 09 Morientes	10 J Cole > 19 Diarra < 45'
72'	> 16 Hugo Viana < 20 Albiol	04 Makelele > 08 Lampard < 90'
		21 Kalou > 07 Shevchenko < 90'

Discipline

45'	Del Horno	Essien	03'
51'	Albelda	Ballack	21'
60'	Ayala		
62'	Moretti		

4	Yellow cards	2
0	Red cards	0
4	Shots on target	6
3	Shots off target	9
22	Fouls committed	10
4	Corners	8
1	Offsides	5
19' 21"	Ball. Poss. (time)	28' 27"
40%	Ball. Poss. (%)	60%

Valencia 1 v Chelsea 2
(Chelsea won 3-2 on aggregate)
Mestalla
Attendance: 53,000

Chelsea's players gleefully celebrate Michael Essien's last minute winner

A last-minute winner from Michael Essien, following Andriy Shevchenko's equaliser, contrived an excellent fight-back after Valencia had taken a first-half lead through Fernando Morientes.

John Terry let on that the Portuguese had reprimanded his players at half-time. That, coupled with the introduction of Joe Cole's clever talents and Michael Essien's withdrawal to the right-back slot, changed the game in Chelsea's favour.

Terry observed, "The belief in ourselves has been there all season long, we'll go right to the final whistle – that's what we're all about. Things are going well for us at the moment. We're not getting carried away but we're looking fit, we're looking sharp and strong and so the Quadruple is a possibility. We certainly hope this is our season." There were extraordinary scenes captured on TV of Mourinho leaping on his skipper to congratulate him, while Terry was conducting an interview!

Frank Lampard expressed his admiration at the way Mourinho turned the game with his half-time team talk and tactical double substitution. Lampard said: "He is one of the best in the world and I don't see many better than him out there. I am fortunate enough to work with him every day and have a very good relationship with him. I love working with the man. He is the focal point and leader of our group so the things he does make a big, big difference. Of course the players have to go out and perform but the manager is fantastic. Huge credit to him for what

DID YOU KNOW?
Chelsea won with the 22nd goal they scored in the last 10 minutes of a match this season

Fernando Morientes fires home Valencia's opener

he did in Valencia. You can't talk highly enough about the moves he makes because many times they work for us."

"I think the second half was amazing," Mourinho said. "We were very dominant. I am proud of our group because this season is special. Nobody has had so many problems as us; we have had surgery problems with more than 50% of the team and we have resisted it mentally."

Roman Abramovich was conspicuous by his absence and his governorship of Chukotka was given as one of the reasons for his no show. But the Russian has long since given up his post-match visits to the Chelsea dressing room, a fact Lampard insists the players cannot hold against him. The midfielder said: "He has every right to do whatever he wants, whether he is here or not. If he is

not around, his people are there and it is not an issue for us."

Although Chelsea started with assurity, suddenly Valencia came close on the counter, a burst of pace from David Villa down the left had Carvalho twisting and turning before the Valencia winger sent a precise square ball to Morientes. His control was immaculate, his left-foot shot cracked against left the upright, bringing a loud 'oooohhh!' from Valencia's raucous home support.

Valencia went in front on 32 minutes through Morientes on a ground where they had not lost to English opposition for 40 years and where only Francesco Totti had scored a visiting goal in Europe this season. Joaquin was

Fortress Mestella

Prior to Chelsea's remarkable comeback win, since January 2000, Valencia's European record at their formidable Mestalla Stradium read: P43, W32, D7, L4. Their record in UEFA Champions League and La Liga matches this season showed only two defeats in 19 home matches. On the way to their second successive Champions League final in 2001, they had won seven of their nine home matches, drawing the other two. Since 2000, British sides have visited seven times. Arsenal (twice), Liverpool, Leeds and Celtic all suffered defeats.

Valencia won six of their last 10 home encounters against Premiership teams and their last defeat at the Mestalla against English opposition dated back to 1967.

DID YOU KNOW?
It was the first time an English club had beaten Valencia on their own patch in 12 attempts

"Chelsea have a good chance because Barcelona, who in my opinion are the best team in Europe right now, are out, alongside Inter Milan."
Gianfranco Zola

Michael Essien lashes in his late, late winning goal

granted room to find a cross that dropped over the Chelsea defenders and fell on the six-yard line. A sense of anticipation had returned to the stadium and Morientes matched it with a sliding diversion that took the ball beyond Petr Cech. But despite further Valencia pressure, Chelsea went in only one down and, when they re-emerged, Shevchenko quickly made it 1-1 seven minutes into the second half after Drogba had caused more physical confusion inside the box and the ball fell invitingly to the Ukranian just a couple of yards form the line. From a few feet Shevchenko could not miss. It was his 14th goal of the season for his club.

When Ballack rose to meet a Lampard 84th-minute free-kick with a deft flick that was flying towards the far corner, Cañizares produced a Gordon Banks of a save to thwart them and extra-time felt certain. But then came Essien, striding down the right to smash an angled drive past Cañizares at his near post.

Valencia full-back Asier del Horno believed his former club were worthy Champions League semi-finalists. "The whole team is gutted," said Del Horno afterwards. "To concede a goal in the 90th minute is hard to take because you have no time to reply to that. We gave everything we had but it was not enough, we had bad luck."

Stamford Bridge legend Franco Zola, now assistant coach of Italy's Under-21s, was willing Chelsea on to win the trophy. He said: "Chelsea have a good chance because Barcelona, who in my opinion are the best team in Europe right now, are out, alongside Inter Milan. So they have a great chance – and it's all down to them now. John Terry and Frank Lampard are really the soul of the team, always pushing them."

Mourinho lets loose as Essien's shot hits the back of the net

Quarter-Finals
Wednesday 11 April 2007 – Second Legs

Liverpool 1 v PSV Eindhoven 0
(Liverpool won 3-2 on aggregate)
Anfield
Attendance: 41,447

Peter Crouch celebrates his winning goal

> **"I've got a few goals in the Champions League this season and I'm happy with my form."**
> **Peter Crouch**

> **"Getting to the quarter-finals is a success for a small club like PSV."**
> **Ronald Koeman, coach PSV Eindhoven**

Liverpool completed the formalities with their task being made even easier after a red card for PSV's young debutant Dirk Marcellis. Peter Crouch then scored his 18th goal of the season to set the 2005 Champions on a collision course with Chelsea and a repeat of that season's all English semi-final against the Blues.

LIVERPOOL 1 v **PSV EINDHO'N 0**

Referee
Roberto Rosetti (Italy)

Assistant Referee
Cristiano Copelli (Italy)
Alessandro Stagnoli (Italy)

Fourth Official
Paolo Tagliavento (Italy)

UEFA Referee Observer
Bo Karlsson

Scorers

67'	Crouch

Teams

25	Reina	Gomes	01
05	Agger	Addo	18
02	Arbeloa	Feher	22
04	Hyypia	Marcellis	39
06	Riise	Salcido	23
14	Alonso	Cocu	08
16	Pennant	Culina	15
22	Sissoko	Simons	06
32	Zenden	Väyrynen	07
17	Bellamy	Farfan	17
15	Crouch	A Koné	10

Substitutes

17'	> 09 Fowler		28 Xiang >		63'
	< 17 Bellamy		22 Feher <		
72'	> 11 Gonzalez		09 Kluivert >		63'
	< 14 Alonso		17 Farfan <		
78'	> 29 Paletta		38 van Eijden >		71'
	< 05 Agger		10 A Koné <		

Discipline

	Salcido	42'
	Marcellis	64'

0	Yellow cards	1
0	Red cards	1
6	Shots on target	3
5	Shots off target	1
6	Fouls committed	18
2	Corners	4
1	Offsides	3
31' 40"	Ball. Poss. (time)	31' 03"
50%	Ball. Poss. (%)	50%

The Kop in full cry

Dominant Sami Hyypia heads clear

Roberto Rossi dismisses Dirk Marcellis, albeit somewhat harshly

Crouch said, "I've got a few goals in the Champions League this season and I'm happy with my form. Hopefully we can keep our form going in the semi-final and make it really special."

Marcellis slid in with studs showing on Boudewijn Zenden in front of the dug-outs midway through the second period, the challenge truly warranting yellow, but receiving red. PSV's resistance was broken. By the end the Kop were chanting their appreciation of the Dutch fans, with the game reduced to little more than an exhibition match.

History was against PSV even before the youngster's dismissal. Liverpool had conceded three goals on only two occasions in 126 previous European home games. Patrick Kluivert, a late substitute here, had featured for

Barcelona in inflicting one of those defeats, back in 2001.

With PSV still re-organising following the dismissal of their right-back, Zenden's cross was flicked goalwards by Crouch, with Heurelho Gomes pushing the attempt away. Robbie Fowler, a first-half substitute, collected the loose ball and returned it into the six-yard box where his partner slammed Liverpool ahead, ending the game as a contest.

Liverpool were now gunning for a semi-final hat-trick against Chelsea, having also dumped them out of the FA Cup a year ago, while Mourinho still awaited his first Champions League win over the Reds in four games, after three draws on top of that Anfield showdown. Midfielder Xabi Alonso "They'll be talking about revenge, but, at the

> ## "We are a better team now than we were two years ago."
> ### Xabi Alonso

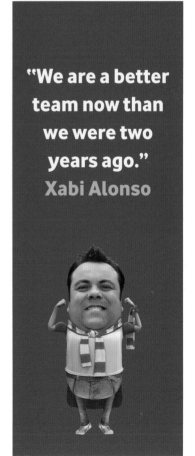

DID YOU KNOW?
PSV Eindhoven have only once scored three away goals in a UEFA Champions League tie courtesy of a Ruud van Nistelrooy hat-trick against HJK Helsinki in November 1998

moment, we're a confident team. They've done a good job to beat Valencia, but we both know it's going to be very close again. We know Chelsea very well because we'll now have faced them three years in a row in semi-finals – and we'll be looking to repeat those results. We are a better team now than we were two years ago, but that doesn't mean we'll play better or get the same result. To do that we must prepare in exactly the same way and show the same commitment we did in those games when we were successful."

Coaches Benítez and Mourinho have become regular foes since arriving in this country three years ago and the semi-finals would be the 14th and 15th times they have confronted each other. Post-match Benetiz spoke mischievously of "Chelsea's millions" and of their "five years of spending big money". Then he added, "We were good friends until we started beating them."

Conversely Mourinho regularly makes digs about Liverpool's purported "long ball" style or "direct" approach.

The phoney war leading up to the titanic clash had begun.

PSV boss Ronald Koeman felt that English clubs were rather richer than ever before. "Getting to the quarter-finals is a success for a small club like PSV," he observed. "English clubs have the money, so they also have some very good players and some very good coaches. England is very strong at the moment. I think it's a great success of English football to have three semi-finalists. It means you have at least one English team in the final, it's a success for England. Liverpool deserved the result more than us, but they are very difficult to play against and keep a lot of men behind the ball."

As a Spaniard who worked in La Liga when it was the envy of Europe, Rafa Benítez feels the European power balance has shifted England's way. "To see three English teams in the semi-finals means that the Premiership is really, really strong. I think it's the best league in Europe now – and it's really, really important we show that the Premiership is really strong in the semi-finals."

Steve McClaren, the beleaguered England manager who watched from the directors' box, must ponder the paradox that has seen his country produce three UEFA Champions League semi-finalists and a national side that struggles.

DID YOU KNOW?
A seventh European Cup goal of the season moved Crouch alongside Roger Hunt and Steven Gerrard as the club's most prolific scorer in a single campaign

Crouch scores to clinch the 4-0 aggregate victory

Bayern Munich 0 v AC Milan 2

(AC Milan won 4-2 on aggregate)
Allianz Arena
Attendance: 66,000

Filippo Inzaghi expresses his joy at scoring Milan's clinching second goal

 BAYERN MUN. 0 v AC MILAN 2

Referee
Manuel Mejuto González (Spain)

Assistant Referee
Juan Carlos Yuste Jiménez (Spain)
Antonio Artero Gallardo (Spain)

Fourth Official
Bernardino Gonzalez Vazquez (Spain)

UEFA Referee Observer
Karl-Erik Nilsson

Scorers

Seedorf	27'
Inzaghi	31'

Teams

01	Kahn	Dida	01
21	Lahm	Maldini	03
30	Lell	Nesta	13
03	Lucio	Oddo	44
05	van Buyten	Ambrosini	23
23	Hargreaves	Gattuso	08
39	Ottl	Kaká	22
20	Salihamidzic	Jankulovski	18
17	van Bommel	Pirlo	21
10	Makaay	Seedorf	10
11	Podolski	Inzaghi	09

Substitutes

45'	> 24 Santa Cruz < 39 Ottl	27 Serginho > 09 Inzaghi <	70'
61'	> 14 Pizarro < 10 Makaay	20 Gourcuff > 10 Seedorf <	80'
86'	> 18 Görlitz < 30 Lell	02 Cafu > 08 Gattuso <	87'

Discipline

47'	van Bommel
63'	Salihamidzic

1	Yellow cards	2
0	Red cards	0
8	Shots on target	5
8	Shots off target	2
14	Fouls committed	12
7	Corners	1
2	Offsides	5
38' 52"	Ball. Poss. (time)	28' 13"
57%	Ball. Poss. (%)	43%

Milan eased past a disappointing Bayern thanks to first-half goals from Clarence Seedorf and Filippo Inzaghi, which set up a semi-final against Manchester United.

Sir Alex departed Bayern's vast arena having witnessed a Milan clinical in both attack and defence. Yet, no Italian side relished meeting United after the walloping inflicted on Roma. Conversely maybe they would, seeking revenge and the restoration of national pride

Bayern's President, Franz Beckenbauer, pronounced on the big transfer story of the week, saying on television before kick-off that he would contemplate selling England midfielder Owen Hargreaves to Manchester United "for £25m". Hargreaves had been excellent in Milan, but he laboured along with his colleagues as Milan controlled the game, looking to hit Bayern on the break, even though Mark van Bommel and Oliver Kahn both returned from suspension.

Kahn was fortunate to be playing as he had almost blotted his copybook once again three days ahead of the Milan game. Kahn swung an elbow at an opposing centre-forward in a Bundesliga match and appeared lucky to have earned only a yellow card. Had it been red, stand-in Michael Rensing would have been looking forward to an extended run in the team. His form deserved it. Rensing is 22, 15 years Kahn's junior, and lately he knew that the former Germany No. 1 and national captain will retire at the end of next season. "The position at the club is plain and it's not going to alter because of a single game," said Rensing after the 2-2

DID YOU KNOW?
Bayern have never knocked AC Milan out of the competition – the closest they came was in 1990 when they lost on away goals

Milan's wonderkid Yoann Gourcuff (left) takes on Bayern's Philipp Lahm

> **"This game is important because it allows us to get one step closer to the Champions League final, which has always been our aim."**
> **Carlo Ancelotti**

draw in Milan. "But I will wait. I've always wanted to be Bayern's No. 1 keeper."

Van Bommel made his returning presence felt with a smart eighth-minute cross that bypassed Maldini and Nesta and picked out Lukas Podolski, coming in at pace. He could only stab the ball goalwards, but it was beating Dida until Oddo cleared it a yard from the line. Soon afterwards a lovely reverse pass from Makaay found Podolski unmarked on the 18-yard line,

but his fierce shot was too close to Dida.

On 27 minutes the game was chaged by Milan brilliance. Kaká cut inside from the right and ran smoothly until supplying Seedorf. The experienced Dutchman jinked away from Lucio before shooting through the legs of van Buyten and into the bottom corner. Kahn was nowhere.

Just four minutes later, neat passing from Jankulowski and Kaká was followed by a creator's backheel from

The brilliant Kaká was Milan's inspiration. Here his progress is halted unceremoniously by Bayern's Lucio

Seedorf that freed Inzaghi to bear down on the ageing Kahn before finishing high into the net.

The home side piled on the pressure, but that gave the visitors, now focused almost entirely on defence, the occasional opportunity on the break, Kahn stretching out a leg to deny Kaká after a typical piece of wizardry from the Brazilian maestro. Van Bommel, Salihamidzic and Pizarro all battered away at the disciplined Milanese ranks, but too many Bayern crosses fell short of their intended targets a s Milan killed off Bayern with solid defence.

DID YOU KNOW?
AC Milan had failed to reach the last four only once in the past four seasons

DID YOU KNOW?
This was both Oliver Kahn and Paolo Maldini's 103rd UEFA Champions League appearance

DID YOU KNOW?
Bayern had not lost at home in Europe for 11 matches, stretching back three years

Two-goal hero from the first leg Daniel van Buyten struggles to come to terms with defeat

It's all too much for Bayern's Mark van Bommel

Semi-Final
Tuesday 24 April 2007

Manchester United 3 v AC Milan 2
Old Trafford
Attendance: 73,820

MANCHESTER UNITED

Scorers

05'	Ronaldo
59', 90'	Rooney

Team

01	van der Sar
06	Brown
03	Evra
04	Heinze
22	O'Shea
16	Carrick
24	Fletcher
11	Giggs
07	Ronaldo
18	Scholes
08	Rooney

Substitutes

Discipline

42'	Evra
62'	Giggs

Super Ron

Ronaldo gives United an early lead thanks to Dida's slip

Referee
Kyros Vassaras (GRE)
Assistant Referee
Dimitrios Bozatzidis (GRE)
Dimitrios Saraidaris (GRE)
Fourth Official
Christoforos Zografos (GRE)
UEFA Referee Observer
Manuel López Fernández (ESP)

AC MILAN

Scorers

Kaká	22', 37'

Team

Dida	01
Maldini	03
Nesta	13
Oddo	44
Ambrosini	23
Gattuso	08
Kaká	22
Jankulovski	18
Pirlo	21
Seedorf	10
Gilardino	11

Substitutes

25 Bonera > 03 Maldini <		45'
32 Brocchi > 08 Gattuso <		53'
20 Gourcuff > 11 Gilardino <		84'

Discipline

Kaká	62'
Bonera	74'

11	Shots on goal	4
11	Shots wide	10
17	Fouls committed	14
10	Corners	2
2	Offsides	2
37' 24"	Ball. Poss. (time)	30' 36"
55%	Ball. Poss. (%)	45%

First Leg

Rooney is enveloped by provider Paul Scholes and Darren Fletcher after levelling the scores

> **"I was particularly impressed with the singing of the Manchester fans at half-time, especially as their team was 2-1 down."**
> **Kaká, AC Milan**

A pulsating, dramatic game ended with the kind of twist that makes European football the most exciting, dynamic competition around.

After dragging United back on level terms with an instinctive second-half strike from Paul Scholes' inspired chipped pass, Wayne Rooney then latched on to a Ryan Giggs through ball before lashing a phenomenal first-time effort past a startled Dida in the Milan goal to send Old Trafford ballistic.

Sir Alex hailed Rooney after the striker conjured a spectacular last-gasp winner; the seoncd of his two goals. "Wayne was a threat to Milan all night," said the United boss. "We played him up front on his own because we wanted to stretch their defence. It meant he wasn't going to get the greatest involvement in the match but he still made some fantastic runs between the two central defenders and of course, the winning goal was an incredible hit. He didn't take a touch on it, just hit it first-time. It was a brilliant goal. On an occasion like tonight, we needed our big players to hit the heights."

The victory was all the more remarkable because United were without six key players, including three-quarters of Ferguson's first-choice defence. Ronaldo had given United the perfect start when he met Giggs' corner

Rooney slots his first goal following a superb flick by Paul Scholes

Kaká celebrates his second goal to put Milan 2-1 ahead

with such power Dida was unable to keep it out despite two attempts. At that stage, another handsome win appeared to be on the cards, only for Milan's own boy-wonder, brilliant Brazilian Kaká, to turn the game on its head with a well-taken double which exposed United's defensive frailties.

Somehow United clung on and, thanks to Rooney, grabbed a precious lead and Ferguson was in thrall to his team's titanic efforts. "I don't think anyone expected us to fold when we fell behind,' said Ferguson. 'We have an outstanding chance now because, with the speed of our game, I believe we will score in Italy. Whether it will be enough I don't know. It will not be easy – but it will not be easy for them either.'

The one regret for United was the booking Patrice Evra picked up which ruled him out of the second leg. Ferguson acknowledged it was a serious blow to lose Evra for the San Siro. "We don't know at this moment if we can get any of our injured defenders back, but we will do our best. It's too early for Nemanja Vidic, but hopefully Rio Ferdinand will be OK. He is crucial to us now."

Milan coach Carlo Ancelotti had problems too, with Maldini almost certainly out as well with a knee injury and influential midfielder Gattuso facing a race against time to recover from a toe problem, which forced him off midway through the second-half at Old Trafford. "Manchester United probably do have a slight advantage," conceded Ancelotti, bewildered at the turnaround in fortunes during the second half. "We are disappointed about their winning goal because I felt we had the match pretty much in hand. It seemed we were going to get a good result, but that goal has complicated matters."

DID YOU KNOW?
AC Milan announced, just 24 hours after the first leg, that the return leg at the San Siro had sold out with all 67,500 tickets snapped up

Wayne Rooney kneels in ecstasy after smashing home the last gasp winner against Milan

Sir Alex backed his side to win the trophy as they had an outstanding chance of reaching their first European final in eight years. Ferguson was disappointed by the concession of what he described as "two terrible goals", but the United manager, his ambition firmly set on a treble of Champions League, the Premiership and the FA Cup, paid tribute to the rich quality of his team's performance. "We were the better team," he said. "To come back from 2-1 down against a team of that standard is difficult, but I told the players at half-time to persevere with their football and keep playing at that speed because that would be the difference. There

were some mistakes and some bad decision-making, but we also played some great football and we showed that we can go on and win this competition. There was some bad defending from us in the first half, but we got a great second goal and that gave us the incentive to go on and win the match. After that, there was only going to be one winner, albeit it needed the last kick of the game."

Rooney's vital goal surprised Dida at his near post as the pugnacious striker took a first-time shot on the run, and half turn. He had the opportunity not only because of Giggs's through ball but also because

DID YOU KNOW?
United's recent away record in the Champions League was actually quite disturbing, with only two wins in their past 13 games. Ferguson's team had lost at FC Copenhagen, Celtic and Roma this season and Milan had not dropped a point in a home game in Serie A since a scoreless draw against Torino on December 10

"It was a brilliant goal. On an occasion like tonight, we needed our big players to hit the heights."
Sir Alex Ferguson

With three English clubs through to the semi-finals, there were understandable claims that the Premiership is now the best in Europe. Dutch legend Johan Cruyff suggested we wait before becoming arrogant. "The dominance of English clubs in the Champions League is clearer than ever before, but it does not mean it will stay like that. Too often I have seen great sides change and fall. Only if the top English clubs can maintain this level of success for the next couple of seasons can we say that English football rules Europe. Don't forget most of the players are foreign at Chelsea and Liverpool, if less so at United and that all reflects in the national team, which is struggling."

> **"It seemed we were going to get a good result, but that goal has complicated matters."**
> **Carlo Ancellotti, AC Milan coach**

the winger had won a tackle to start the attack.

Perhaps Milan rued the decision that Dida was fully fit following a shoulder problem and Ancelotti can curse his luck that Gattuso departed after 53 minutes, while captain Paolo Maldini was another injury victim.

At one point or another in this game both sides seemed in complete disarray. United's start was reminiscent of the 7-1 mauling of Roma, with the early goal exposing serious flaws in Milan's experienced, but arguably ageing defence. But the resemblance stopped there. Milan took over midway through the half, with Gattuso biting into challenges and Kaká increasingly influential in general play. And is was Kaká who scored both Milan goals. With 22 minutes gone, the mercurial Brazilian broke away from Carrick to take Seedorf's pass before gliding wide of Heinze to striker a perfect low shot into the far corner of the net. Fifteen minutes later Kaká was outnumbered as he chased down the left, but he slipped inside Fletcher and lobbed the ball over Heinze, who was then flattened by a frantic Evra leavng Kaká free to tuck a shot behind van der Sar. Now it was United in disarray.

With the lone striker Gilardino unimpressive, the source of menace was obvious yet it could not be stopped. With Milan in the lead with critical two away goals, midway through the second half Scholes came to the rescue with an inspirational moment as he flipped a delightful pass with the outside of his right foot from the edge of the area and Rooney, just onside, racing back into the box as Milan cleared their lines, controlled it with his chest before beating Dida. The goalkeeper had, to his credit, pulled off a few impressive saves, with a particularly convincing response to a Fletcher drive. The late winner merely rubbed Milan's noses in the Old Trafford mud as they left empty handed save for two potentially vital away goals.

Milan defender Massimo Oddo rued his side's failure to convert a couple of chances early in the second half. "We were stupid. We played a great first half and their second goal was fine but then we missed several opportunities to make it 3-1," he said.

"It's a very bitter result that gives us little margin for error, but I'm convinced Milan can go through," Kaká told La Gazzetta dello Sport. "After the 2-2 draw with Bayern Munich we had to get a great result away from home. Now we have to win but we've got the advantage of playing at home. We will have to play like United did against us. We will have to show we've got great personality and enormous energy because we face a real battle."

> **"I believe we are favourites.**
> **We are going to go for the kill in the San Siro."**
> **Kaká, AC Milan**

Dida rejoices after Kaka's second goal

Kaká hailed United's fans for their vocal performance, "I was particularly impressed with the singing of the Manchester fans at half-time, especially as their team was 2-1 down. This is one of the great things about Premiership fans. They have such passion for their team. I love that kind of atmosphere." "Fantastique Manchester United" was one headline in France that greeted this contest as United emerged as the most exhilerating attacking side in Europe.

Yet, with two away goals, nothing could be taken for granted in the second leg. "I believe we are favourites," Kaká said ominously in the bowels of the stadium. "We are going to go for the kill in the San Siro, to win outright."

DID YOU KNOW?

In the aftermath of the first leg defeat, an angry AC Milan fan put Dida up for sale on the internet. The 33 year-old, who joined Milan in 2000, was a hero after the shootout win over Juventus in the 2003 Champions League final, but his popularity had slumped after a series of errors. He was criticised in the defeat at Old Trafford, when he flapped a Ronaldo header into his own net and then left his near post exposed for Rooney to blast home a stoppage-time winner.

Dida failed to attract great interest on ebay. The price, before the Brazilian international was removed from the auction site, had reached 71 euros after 25 bids.

Ancelotti commented, "People have criticised our goalkeeper for making mistakes for two of United's goals, but only when I believe Dida has become a problem will I make a change. At this time he still has all my confidence."

> "It's time to step up to the plate."
> John O'Shea,
> Manchester United

Semi-Final
Wednesday 25 April 2007

Chelsea 1 v Liverpool 0
Stamford Bridge
Attendance: 39,483

CHELSEA

	Scorers
29'	J Cole

Team

01	Cech
06	Ricardo Carvalho
03	A Cole
20	Ferreira
26	Terry
10	J Cole
08	Lampard
04	Makelele
12	Mikel
11	Drogba
07	Shevchenko

Substitutes

76'	> 21 Kalou < 07 Shevchenko	
85'	> 24 Wright-Phillips < 10 Cole	

Discipline

Blue Is The Colour

Chelsea supporters revel in a 1-0 lead

Referee
Markus Merk (GER)

Assistant Referee
Jan-Hendrik Salver (GER)
Carsten Kadach (GER)

Fourth Official
Felix Brych (GER)

UEFA Referee Observer
Nikolay Levnikov (RUS)

LIVERPOOL

Scorers

Team

Reina	25
Agger	05
Arbeloa	02
Carragher	23
Riise	06
Alonso	14
Gerrard	08
Mascherano	20
Zenden	32
Bellamy	17
Kuyt	18

Substitutes

15 Crouch > 17 Bellamy <		52'
16 Pennant > 14 Alonso <		83'

Discipline

Mascherano	77'

4	Shots on goal	4
10	Shots wide	9
9	Fouls committed	19
1	Corners	5
5	Offsides	2
26' 40"	Ball. Poss. (time)	31' 21"
46%	Ball. Poss. (%)	54%

First Leg

Frank Lampard shoots

For the sixth time a Rafa Benítez side left Stamford Bridge after failing to score.

After Petr Cech, now fully recovered from his horrific injury in the Autumn and sporting natty protective headgear, pawed away a stinging Steven Gerrard attempt early in the second half Benitez cursed to the heavens, then moved back into the dugout with hands buried deep in his pockets; fuming.

Benítez, actually, was grateful to his goalkeeper Reina for keeping the score down to one, as Chelsea dominated the vast majority of the game, permitting them hope in the Anfield cauldron. The goalkeeper denied Lampard in each half.

After the disappointing defeat, the usually softly-spoken Rafa Benitez laid into his team. Benitez said: "I was very angry after the game. I was angry with myself, my staff and my players because we had not performed. From the outside people think I am calm and often that is the best way to get your message across even if you are angry inside. But this was the semi-final of the Champions League and I had to shout to get through to the players that they were wasting an opportunity. I cannot analyse the future of a player in one or two games, but some

> **"If Craig Bellamy had scored, maybe we would have been talking about other things ..."**
> **Rafa Benitez**

> **"Joe Cole is Joe Cole. He is a good player and he gave a good contribution."**
> Jose Mourinho

DID YOU KNOW?
Since Bruno Cheyrou's goal in January 2004, Liverpool have spent more than 500 minutes trying in vain to score at Stamford Bridge

players must realise that they are playing for a European Cup Final and for their futures. Things can change quickly and decisions over whether you stay with a top side or leave do depend on these next weeks."

A number of Liverpool players were left shocked by Benitez's uncharacteristic rant and worried for their futures. Was it merely a motivational ploy for the vital second leg at Anfield?

His opposite number Jose Mourinho was so determined not to upset Chelsea's remarkable team spirit that he preferred to dwell on his side's amazing

resilience rather than applaud Joe Cole's winner against Liverpool.

Although as a spectacle this fare did not compare with the first semi-final, at least the 29th minute goal was breathtaking.

On this occasion Didier Drogba turned provider. After Ricardo Carvalho, commanding in defence, broke forward at pace to supply Drogba in a wide position, the centre-forward twisted and turned before slotting across a pass for Cole to convert on the stretch from close range with the Liverpool defence

Joe Cole nets the only goal of the game much to the joy of the supporters behind the goal

stretched to breaking point. It was a superb, sweeping three-man move.

It was only Cole's second start since he fully recovered from the stress fracture of the foot which ruined his season but Mourinho was more concerned with praising a side that continues to defy the critics and the spectre of fatigue. Mourinho said: "Joe Cole is Joe Cole. He is a good player and he gave a good contribution. But I have to praise every player – everybody gave a top contribution."

Chelsea's resilience was proving to be unbreakable with another example of a bond that transgressed the normal team camaraderie.

Liverpool fans are absorbed in the contest

DID YOU KNOW?
The last time Liverpool overturned a first-leg deficit in European competition was in November 1991, in a UEFA Cup tie against Auxerre. However, this was only the sixth first-leg match Liverpool had lost since then

DID YOU KNOW?
This was Andriy Shevchenko's fourth European Cup semi-final in five years; the other three with Milan

Rafa Benitez makes his point as Liverpool struggle to make an impact on the game

Andriy Shevchenkoi finds no way past Jamie Carragher

The Liverpool manager was not alone in being unhappy at some aspects of this ultimately disappointing match. Mourinho was in yet another of his dark moods, and launched a bitter complaint about a penalty — no doubt unaware that the replays showed a handball to be outsde the area! Mourinho moaned about the failure of German referee, Markus Merk, to award a penalty when Arbeloa used his arm to control a mis-hit clearance — a certain handball. However, Mourinho failed to take into account that the Liverpool right-back had been two feet outside the penalty area. "I don't understand how we don't have penalties," he told Sky television, reprising a theme he had opened on Sunday after a ball struck Stephen Carr's arm in the goalless draw at Newcastle United. "When the penalties are so clear, I don't understand. I go for the facts and it's a fact. In the Champions League this season we have good referees and to be fair to Mr Merk he was comfortable. But the penalty is a big chance for us to be 2-0. Then it would be a completely different game and a different story. I feel it is not fair."

Mourinho emphasised that controversy had cost his side in the teams' last Champions League semi-final meeting in 2005 when a goal was awarded even though William Gallas cleared García's shot from the line. "They had their mistake, but it was not a penalty. I hope after the second leg we are not crying and thinking again about a big decision. Two years ago we were. I hope we are not looking back on the penalty."

Benítez was dismissive. "If he says it was a penalty, I am sure it was a penalty!"

But the Liverpool manager also commented more seriously, "We gave the ball away far too easily, and not because Chelsea were playing particularly well, but because we were not playing well enough. We couldn't control the game. We were better after the interval when we had a target man to hit, and that offered more possibilities." Asked whether the omission of Peter Crouch had been a mistake, his response betrayed regret. "If Craig Bellamy had scored, maybe we would have been talking about other things ..."

The withdrawal of Steve Finnan with a stiff neck had effectively disrupted the entire side, though Liverpool also lacked the leggy energy of Momo Sissoko to offer them an outlet. Only when Gerrard drove them forward in the frenzied early stages of the second half did they threaten, and then sporadically.

Benítez, though, insisted on being upbeat, "Playing at Anfield will be really good for us, even if we know Chelsea's strengths on the counter, so we'll have to be careful. We need to beat a good team in the second leg, but we can achieve that."

In fact Liverpool were the last side to defeat Mourinho, albeit 22 matches ago, and a repeat of the 2-0 Premiership success in January would be enough to get them to Athens.

> **"I was angry with myself, my staff and my players because we had not performed."**
> **Rafa Benitez**

Semi-Final
Tuesday 1 May 2007

Liverpool 1 v Chelsea 0
Aggregate: 1-1 (Liverpool win 4-1 on penalties)
Anfield
Attendance: 42,554

LIVERPOOL

Final Countdown

CHELSEA

Liverpool		Chelsea	
Scorers		**Scorers**	
22'	Agger		
Team		**Team**	
25	Reina	Cech	01
05	Agger	A Cole	03
23	Carragher	Ferreira	20
03	Finnan	Terry	26
06	Riise	J Cole	10
08	Gerrard	Essien	05
20	Mascherano	Lampard	08
16	Pennant	Makelele	04
32	Zenden	Mikel	12
15	Crouch	Drogba	11
18	Kuyt	Kalou	21

Liverpool Substitutes

78'	> <	14 Alonso 16 Pennant
105'	> <	17 Bellamy 15 Crouch
118'	> <	09 Fowler 20 Mascherano

Chelsea Substitutes

16 Robben 10 J Cole	> <	98'
24 Wright-Phillips 21 Kalou	> <	107'
14 Geremi 04 Makelele	> <	118'

Liverpool Discipline

| 62' | Agger |
| 110' | Zenden |

Chelsea Discipline

| A Cole | 28' |

John Arne Riise
congratulates goalscorer
Daniel Agger after the
Dane's shot found the
back of Cech's net

Referee
Manuel Mejuto González (ESP)

Assistant Referee
Juan Carlos Yuste Jiménez (ESP)
Jesus Calvo Guadamuro (ESP)

Fourth Official
Alberto Undiano Mallenco (ESP)

UEFA Referee Observer
Pierluigi Collina (ITA)

Liverpool		Chelsea
2	Yellow cards	1
0	Red cards	0
6	Shots on target	4
7	Shots off target	6
32	Fouls committed	21
5	Corners	6
3	Offsides	5
38' 6"	Ball. Poss. (time)	32' 16"
54%	Ball. Poss. (%)	46%

Second Leg

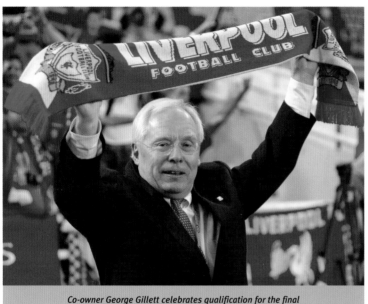

Co-owner George Gillett celebrates qualification for the final

Liverpool had won the 2005 UEFA Champions League on penalties and headed to Athens by the same method – with Pepe Reina the hero.

Steven Gerrard praised Reina for his role in taking the Anfield team to a second Champions League final in three years in a penalty shoot out. The Spanish goalkeeper saved penalties from Arjen Robben and Geremi. Dirk Kuyt converting the decisive kick as shoot out specialists Liverpool took their tally to 11 victories in 12 competitive penalty shoot outs. "We have the best goalkeeper in the world," said Gerrard. "We saw his penalty saves before he came, so we knew all about him." Reina

follows his father to European final – he kept goal for Atlético Madrid in the 1974 final. "Because of my father, football is naturally in my blood," he said. "Just because my father was a goalkeeper didn't automatically mean I was going to become one too. I've got five brothers and I'm the only one who is a goalkeeper. Knowing he played in a European Cup final has been special to me and, if we can win the trophy, it would mean a lot. He would be the proudest father in the world."

Chelsea capitulated to their second Champions League semi-final defeat to Liverpool in three years. "The first time was special, but to do it again from being a goal down against a magnificent squad like Chelsea is fantastic,"

> **"The first time was special, but to do it again from being a goal down against a magnificent squad like Chelsea is fantastic."**
> **Steven Gerrard**

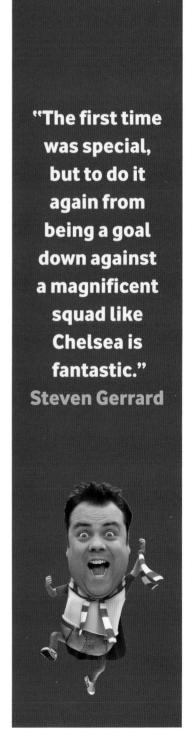

Penalty Shootout		
Liverpool	Score	Chelsea
Zenden (score)	1 – 0	
	1 – 0	Robben (miss)
Alonso (score)	2 – 0	
	2 – 1	Lampard (score)
Gerrard (score)	3 – 1	
	3 – 1	Geremi (miss)
Kuyt (score)	4 – 1	

Reina saves Arjen Robben's penalty, and the Dutchman reacts to his failure

> "Everywhere Tom and I go it is the same: people are pleased and so welcoming. I wanted to shake their hands, to embrace them at the end because they had been magnificent for their team."
>
> George Gillett, Liverpool owner

said Gerrard. "The manager's tactics were spot on. We crossed that line and stuck together out there. The players fought for every ball together. If we are through to the final it has made all of that hard work worthwhile."

Liverpool levelled the tie on aggregate through Daniel Agger's goal in the 22nd minute. Joe Cole, a booking short of suspension, was relieved when referee Manuel Mejuto González did not raise a yellow card for his foul on Gerrard. With Chelsea, in the absence of the injured Carvalho, anticipating the routine high ball aimed at Crouch, a well worked free-kick caught them out. Gerrard pulled the free-kick back low and the onrushing

Agger side-footed a first time shot low into the net at the near post. The centre-half had suffered at Stamford Bridge and this was an ideal reposte.

Liverpool were outstanding as the back, but there was a shortfall in creativity from Chelsea. Drogba, inevitably, had the best chance. After 32 minutes, a pass from Mikel John Obi slipped the Ivorian striker in behind Agger, but his first touch took the ball half a yard too far, the angle narrowed and he blasted straight at the keeper who was well placed to push out the fierce drive.

Liverpool had the better chances to win the tie inside the 90 minutes. Dirk Kuyt hit the bar and had a goal disallowed

DID YOU KNOW?
As Liverpool reached a seventh European Cup final, Chelsea have yet to qualify for one, and still no London club has won the biggest prize of all

for a marginal offside. Jermaine Pennant, up against his old friend Ashley Cole, produced a deep cross after 56 minutes and Crouch leapt above Ferreira for a header which was blocked by the legs of Cech. In the 71st minute, Terry misjudged a long ball which skidded off his head and Pennant's goalbound drive ricocheted from the makeshift centre-back Essien for a corner.

Andriy Shevchenko, still out of favour or sidelined with a groin injury depending upon which spin you believed, sat watching from the stands, but given his form it is doubtful whether he would have made an impact. Chelsea's only real second half chance came when Jamie Carragher diverted an Ashley Cole cut-back over his own crossbar after 76 minutes.

In extra-time, Mourinho finally made late changes, first Robben, then Wright-Phillips for pace down the flanks, and Wright-Phillips' low cross was almost met by Drogba in a rare opening for Chelsea. But the stalemate could not be broken.

The drama of the penalty shoot out was somewhat dimmed by Chelsea's failure from 12 yards. Of their three takers only Frank Lampard found the back of Reina's net. The Spaniard's two saves gave Dirk Kuyt the opportunity to send Liverpool to Athens by netting Liverpool's fourth and he duly obliged.

American George Gillett, the new Liverpool co-owner, was seen shaking hands with fans in front of the directors' box as the Kop celebrated raucously. Later Liverpool's players tried to dunk Gillett into the team bath during their post-match celebrations – but they settled for showering the American in champagne instead. "It was quite messy in the dressing room afterwards," admitted Peter Crouch. "One of the owners [Gillett] came into the dressing room, but I don't think he saw much because his glasses kept steaming up. We tried to throw him in the bath at one point, so he's had a real welcome to English football. It seems to me we have the spirit of 2005 in this team. I remember watching it on television and seeing them come back from 3-0 down feeling so amazed. Now I want to be part of another great triumph."

Gillett was full of praise for his Special One, Benitez, as he said: "We knew of Rafa, but I don't think we realised how good he was. Not only is he a brilliant coach, but he is a very sharp, savvy businessman. He knows what he wants and how to get it. The more we have seen of him the more impressed we have become." Gillett and Hicks were "hugely impressed" at how Liverpool's fans had welcomed them into the Anfield family following the buyout. "They are amazing," said Gillett. "Everywhere Tom and I go it is the same: people are pleased and so welcoming. I wanted to shake their hands, to embrace them at the end

"This is the lowest point of my career."
Petr Cech, Chelsea

PEPE REINA

In his last season at Villarreal before joining Liverpool penalty specialist Pepe Reina saved seven from nine spot-kicks, before making the decisive stop from Anton Ferdinand in the 2006 FA Cup final shoot-out.

"My penalty record is down to luck, but you have to like football too," said Reina. "The more you watch games, the more information you learn. I didn't do too much different than I would normally do ahead of the Chelsea game, but it is important to know what their players do at other moments. It depends always on the situation of the game – many things. I won't say too much more because that is my secret.

I don't watch videos of the rival team or anything. I just wait as long as possible, concentrate on the penalty-taker and try to intuit where the ball is going by the run-up."

Since arriving at Liverpool his team-mates have kept him on his toes. "We had the players practising in every session on penalties," said Rafa Benítez. "Two or three of the players practise penalties every day. We had the confidence in the penalty shoot-out against Chelsea because we have the best goalkeeper in the world. You need your keeper in penalty situations as a bonus and he was superb. Pepe is always good with penalties and in the final of the FA Cup he was fantastic."

Reina had also conjured a post-war club record 55 clean sheets in his first 100 games for Liverpool to go alongside his phenomenal shoot out record.

"I don't watch videos of the rival team or anything. I just wait as long as possible, concentrate on the penalty-taker and try to intuit where the ball is going by the run-up."

Liverpool's players give it large after Kuyt's winning penalty, while skipper John Terry leads his team off the Anfield pitch, head held high

"I guess when you've invested £500m it's a fantastic season to win the League Cup."
Rick Parry, Liverpool Chief Executive

DID YOU KNOW?
Rafa Benitez at one point struggled to find the English words to describe opposite number Jose Mourinho. So the Spaniard reverted to his mother tongue: "No ofende quien quiere sino quien puede." He even spelled the words out in a reporter's notebook. "It means, 'You can talk, but it is not offensive for me, because it is not an offence'. I don't know whether you have a saying similar to this one?"

because they had been magnificent for their team."

Benitez allowed his players to go out into Liverpool city centre. Three of them – Alonso, Carragher and Gerrard – partied until the early hours with supporters at the fashionable Sir Thomas Hotel. "We've not only underlined our great history, we've shown our present and future can be even better," Gerrard said. The Liverpool captain claimed the achievement was greater than defeating Chelsea at the same stage of the competition two years ago. "I remember on that night it was all about digging in and defending for our lives. We did that this time when we had to, but this time you could see there was more quality to our play throughout the team, from the goalkeeper, through to the defence, midfield and strikers.

Semi-Final
Wednesday 2 May 2007

AC Milan 3 v Manchester United 0
AC Milan won 5-3 on aggregate
San Siro
Attendance: 78,500

AC MILAN

Scorers

11'	Kaká
30'	Clarence Seedorf
78'	Alberto Gilardino

Team

01	Dida
04	Kaladze
13	Nesta
44	Oddo
23	Ambrosini
08	Gattuso
22	Kaká
18	Jankulovski
21	Pirlo
10	Seedorf
09	Inzaghi

Substitutes

67'	> <	11 Gilardino / 09 Inzaghi
85'	> <	02 Cafu / 08 Gattuso
86'	> <	19 Favalli / 22 Kaká

Discipline

75'	Ambrosini
83'	Gattuso

Masters Of Milan

Kaká acclaims his opening goal

Referee
Frank De Bleeckere (BEL)
Assistant Referee
Peter Hermans (BEL) Mark Simons (BEL)
Fourth Official
Paul Allaerts (BEL)
UEFA Referee Observer
Marc Batta (FRA)

MANCHESTER UNITED

Scorers

Team

van der Sar	01
Brown	06
Heinze	04
O'Shea	22
Vidic	15
Carrick	16
Fletcher	24
Giggs	11
Ronaldo	07
Scholes	18
Rooney	08

Substitutes

09 Saha	>	77'
22 O'Shea	<	

Discipline

Ronaldo	84'

7	Shots on goal	2
6	Shots wide	11
14	Fouls committed	22
4	Corners	5
2	Offsides	2
32' 42"	Ball. Poss. (time)	35' 21"
48%	Ball. Poss. (%)	52%

Second Leg

Ryan Giggs gets no change out of Massimo Oddo

Carlo Ancelotti was immensely proud after his side outplayed Manchester United and won a place in their second final in three years. "Watching your team playing as we did in the first half is the dream of every coach. In the first 45 minutes we played the perfect football. We built our victory from a great start."

There would be no Champions League final between Premiership clubs...much to the relief of the Athens police. Instead, The final was be a repeat of the 2005 defeat by Liverpool, and on the quality and intensity of this performance Ancelotti was naturally confident his side could avenge that match in Istanbul two years ago, when they threw away a

three-goal lead and lost on penalties to Rafael Benítez's side. "It will be a very fascinating match against Liverpool," said Ancelotti. "They are a more physical side compared to Manchester United. Champions League football is peculiar but I think Milan are the best side in Europe in playing this kind of games." Ancelotti added, "What happened two years ago has no weight on the upcoming final. We want to win it."

Milan president and former Italian Prime Minister Silvio Berlusconi, however, set his sights on revenge. "Tonight Milan reminded everybody of our mission: being the best team in world. We are going to Athens to take back from Liverpool the cup they took from our hands two years ago. Two years ago we lost an incredible game

> **"In the first 45 minutes we played the perfect football."**
> **Carlo Ancelotti**

*Gennaro Gattuso and Ryan Giggs battle it out,
but the Italian midfielder ruled the roost in the San Siro*

AC Milan's Kakha Kaladze and Wayne Rooney fly into a challenge

and we have been hypnotised by a dancing clown goalkeeper but this time we will be ready also for that. We will not give anything for granted'

Paolo Maldini, the club captain who was ruled out of facing United by injury, joined in the pitch-side celebrations embracing his team-mates with little concern about his designer suede jacket being soaked with the sweat his colleagues had generated while out-chasing and out-playing England's prospective champions. He was also preoccupied with the thought of facing Liverpool again. "My team-mates made me a great gift because I wanted so much to play that final against Liverpool. The memory of Istanbul still hurts. We are in great physical condition in the right moment of the season. It will be a very tough game, but we fear nobody at this stage."

Sir Alex regretted his team were unable to get through the first 25 minutes without "cutting our own throats" by conceding goals to Kaká and Clarence Seedorf. "The atmosphere was fantastic and they caught us on the back foot. But I still think we can do better at coping with that. The name of the game in Europe is that you don't give the ball away. Milan kept the ball far better than us. They've been together for many years and that great experience is not to be dismissed. Compared to that, my team lacks experience. You only get that by keeping a team together over a long period. But the nature of our football is that we recover from disappointment. We've had to do it before after big European nights and we'll do it again."

United rarely threatened. Rooney might have demanded a penalty as he was jostled while attempting a bicycle kick, but United did not force Dida to a testing save. In defence, Sir Alex, lacking a fully fit Ferdinand, risked a comeback for Vidic, while Ferdinand was on the bench in reserve. Maybe United would have given Milan a far more stringent examination had their squad been as near to full strength as Ancelotti's.

The rain and thunder should have made United feel at home, but Milan were full of the attacking flair normally associated with Sir Alex's side. Milan were in front after 11 minutes when Seedorf headed down a long ball, cleverly back into the path of Kaka, who from 22 yards, drilled a low left-foot shot across van der Sar into the corner.

After 30 minutes Heinze played a brainless pass to Vidic, who slipped on the greasy turf havng been put under pressure by his team-mate. He cleared only as far as Pirlo, who squeezed over a cross just before the ball crossed the by-line which the Argentine defnder should have prevented. Vidic met it with a tame header towards Seedorf, who forced himself away from Fletcher. The Dutchman then skipped wide of Vidic's sliding tackle before picking the same spot as Kaká with a volley.

Kaka, in search of his fourth goal of the tie, turned inside Vidic in the 53rd minute and drew a good parry from van der Sar as Rooney and Ronaldo made little impression.

Milan established the 3-0 lead in the 78th minute after Sir Alex made attacking changes, bringing on Saha for O'Shea, leaving huge gaps at the back. Ambrosini's pass from the left on the counter attack was exquisite and the substitute Gilardino was unmarked and clear through to finish past van der Sar.

Kaká was estatic at Milan's performance and relished the opportunity for revenge, "We have played a perfect game. I am extremely happy with the way the team has played, we were the best side on the pitch and we deserved to go through. The final against

Alberto Gilardino slots the ball past Edwin van der Sar to end the game as a contest with the third goal

> **"There is an element of revenge with Liverpool. We were waiting for this. I think it will be a beautiful final."**
> **Silvio Berlusconi, AC Milan President**

Liverpool will be a unique game. I sincerely hope it will be different from that of 2005."

Gennaro Gattuso, in his beany hat and trainers, was sure the well-organsied Liverpool would be harder to beat then the flamboyant United, "It is very different to Manchester, who are a real footballing team. Liverpool are like an Italian team of 10 years ago. All they try to do is defend together, with everybody behind the ball. United have far more technical players, who are quick. Liverpool do not have those individuals. What they have is a way of playing as a team."

An hour after Milan's victory their president Silvio Berlusconi was savouring the opportunity to put matters right.

"I am a happy man," Berlusconi said. "I was thinking to myself, 'I want a Liverpool win, to meet them again after two years'. And we will have, with all the appropriate respect due to a great club like Liverpool, an enormous desire to win back a cup that we lost in those unbelievable circumstances." Berlusconi then demonstrated his Dudek shuffle. "That's why we lost, you know. The goalkeeper was trying to disturb our players' concentration. This time we'll be practising penalties against moving goalkeepers!"

Berlusconi described this win as the latest step in a genuine comeback, an unlikely finale to a campaign that had started in July with a Rome tribunal that found a Milan employee to have

Milan's players thank the crowd for their support as they celebrate reaching the final

had a fringe role in the scandal over manipulating Serie A match officials that would see Juventus relegated as a punishment. Milan were docked eight points — "a heavy injustice," says Berlusconi. Since January, though, Berlusconi has "begun to see again our great capacity to recover". He added, "There is an element of revenge with Liverpool. We were waiting for this. I think it will be a beautiful final. But I hope to win without penalties."

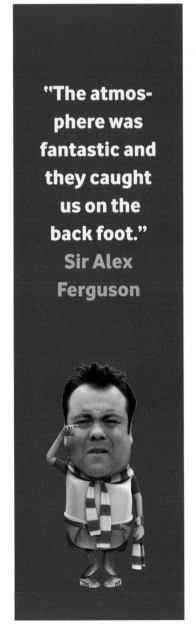

> **"The atmosphere was fantastic and they caught us on the back foot."**
> **Sir Alex Ferguson**

The realization hits Alex Ferguson that he will have to try once again to emulate his achievement of 1999

Champions League Classic Match

LIVERPOOL 3 V AC MILAN 3
(Liverpool win 3-2 on penalties)

Champions League Final

Wednesday 25 May 2005 ◆ Atatürk Stadium, Istanbul ◆ Attendance 65,000

Teams

Jerzy Dudek	Dida
Steve Finnan (Sub. Dietmar Hamann)	Cafu
Djimi Traore	Paolo Maldini
Sami Hyypia	Jaap Stam
Jamie Carragher	Alessandro Nesta
John Arne Riise	Gennaro Gattuso (Sub. Rui Costa)
Steven Gerrard	Clarence Seedorf (Sub. Serginho)
Xabi Alonso	Andrea Pirlo
Luis Garcia	Kaka
Milan Baros (Sub. Djibril Cissé)	Andriy Shevchenko
Harry Kewell (Sub. Vladimir Smicer)	Hernan Crespo (Sub. Jon Dahl Tomasson)

Scorers

Gerrard 54, Smicer 56, Alonso 59 ◆ Maldini 1, Crespo 39, 44

Referee

Mr M Gonzalez

"We all dream of a team of Carraghers." That song echoed about Liverpool and, memorably, Turkey after Jamie's heroics in Istanbul in May 2005 wrote him indelibly onto the hearts of the club's fans. Rafa Benitez would probably concur that a team of Carraghers would guarantee a side with an impeccable will to win. Jamie has become recognised as one of Europe's finest defenders and his part in Liverpool's 2005 UEFA Champions League success left a number of quality strikers to vouch for his thirst for snuffing out their threat. Not bad for a boy from Bootle. Here Jamie recalls the incredible night in 2005 when Liverpool clinched their fifth title.

"The room was quiet. Nothing was being said. Nothing could be said. We were 3-0 down in the biggest game of our lives. We were getting beat; make that getting slaughtered and. for now. what could any of us say? The only noise was the manager working away on the board trying to rectify the team and its tactics.

Suddenly, through the silence you could hear You'll Never Walk Alone as our fans incredibly found their voice once more. I'd like to say that it inspired me and made want to go out and claw the three goals back, made us turn in the performance of our lives to pull off that incredible comeback; but if I'm honest it just made me feel that much worse. "They're doing their bit, but we haven't done ours," I thought. I was gutted. I felt like crying for them at that point.

They were singing away despite thinking that they were going to lose. I spoke to some after and the odd one was like, "I knew we were going to win", but I don't believe that for a minute. I certainly didn't think we could do it. But we did and what a night. What a crazy, unforgettable, amazing night.

There was no sign of a Liverpool revival at half-time when many fans left the stadium and others struggled to come to terms with what had happened in a whirlwind first half assault by Milan

It's got to go down in history as one of the best ever finals. People rightly go on about the 1960 game between Real Madrid and Eintracht Frankfurt and I think that the night in Istanbul will be the same. In twenty, no thirty-years time people will still be talking about what was an incredible match. I have got about seven or eight years left of my career and I think if I am going to ever top that I'll have to play in a World Cup Final and score a hat-trick!

The start was incredible. We kicked off and then boom, we're losing. It was our kick off! How did they score a goal from our bloody kick off? Djimi Traore was a bit nervous and he lost the ball and then gave away a foul. From that free-kick they scored. We had built up for this for ten days, and then within a minute we were 1-0 down. You might as well as be in a second-leg of a tie, and a goal down. None of us had had a kick and it's killed everything. The game plan, the atmosphere, it's all gone.

> ## "You don't go 3-0 down before half-time in a European Cup final. It's not done."

Soon though, the manager had even more to think about. Not only were we a goal down, but now Harry Kewell was clearly struggling and would have to come off. It was all going wrong out there. As Harry limped off there were some boos from the fans and that was tough. Replacing Harry was Vladi Smicer. It was a surprise to us that Vlad came on. I thought that Didi Hamann would be the replacement, but at only 1-0 Rafa wanted to keep his original shape. Vlad went onto the right and Luis played off Baros. It was to be an incredible night for Vlad, in what was his last game for the club.

We had our moments and Luis looked to have been fouled for what we thought was a penalty to us, but there was no time to dwell on it because the game hadn't stopped and suddenly you've got Kaka, Shevchenko and Hernan Crespo running at you. It was an amazing break. Kaká put Shevchenko in and he crossed it past me for Crespo to score. I was lying on the turf thinking "2-0, that's it." At 1-0 I thought "We're doing OK here, we might even get back in this", but 2-0 in a European Cup final, "This is going to be difficult."

Difficult was about to turn into nigh on impossible. Kaká played through a brilliant pass which I stretched for, but couldn't intercept. At the time I thought, "Oh, I've made a mistake there", but I've watched it back and realise it was just a class ball. I wasn't sure whether I could have stayed on my feet and got it, but it's such a great pass there was nothing I could do. Crespo's finish was incredible and at 3-0 it's a rout.

Now I was just embarrassed. When you watch finals, no matter how big the gulf between the teams, they are always tight. You don't go 3-0 down before half-time in a European Cup final. It's not done. When the whistle went for the end of the half, I couldn't get in the dressing room quick enough.

If someone had said to me then "This'll finish 3-0", I would have taken it.

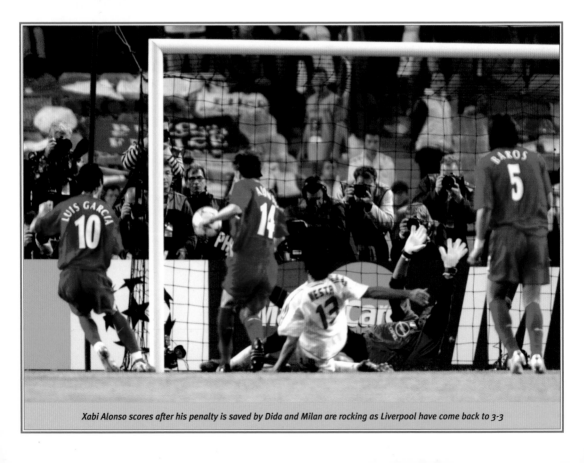

Xabi Alonso scores after his penalty is saved by Dida and Milan are rocking as Liverpool have come back to 3-3

Captain Steven Gerrard leads the celebrations after one of the most incredible comebacks of all time

That sounds mad now that we won, but at the time I just wanted to stop the rot. I really was thinking that this could finish six.

The manager was calm. There was no big talk or anything. He just got on with sorting out the tactics and said "Let's try and get the first goal". He was all set to bring Djimi off. He hadn't had the best of games, although he'd been better towards the end of the half. Djimi was all undressed and ready to get in the shower when Steve Finnan said his knee was sore and so Djimi's had to get dressed again, get his boots on and get ready to play another half.

We got out there, but again looked shaky and I remember Jerzy let an easy ball ricochet off his knees for a needless corner. I gave him a talking to for that one. He made amends with a fantastic save from a Shevchenko free-kick and then Xabi Alonso had a good shot go just wide. The fans were lifted slightly, but it wasn't as if we'd piled on the pressure. After half-time if anyone was going to score it was going to be them again. It wasn't like we came out flying.

But then we did score.

Stevie's goal didn't have me celebrating. I calmly made my way back into position hoping that it had stopped the rot. But maybe in hindsight it just brought the Milan players down a bit.

They'd blown it the year before in the quarter-final against La Coruna after being 4-1 up from the home leg and PSV had come so close to beating them in the semi-final, so in their minds there must have been a niggling worry. If you look at their performance in the second half it would suggest that they lost it. We were good, but they were bad. For six or seven minutes they seemed so dazed. Their manager, Carlo Ancelotti, later called it "Six minutes of madness." In fact after that first goal went in I could sense their fear.

Then Vlad went through. They were screaming for offside, but the ref was just played an advantage because they had the ball, that was all. They gave it away and Vlad cracked a shot just inside the post. 3-2.

We were right back in it. I still didn't celebrate; I was urging us all on and

> **"It was adrenaline keeping us going."**

Jamie Carragher celebrates as Jerzy Dudek saves from Andriy Shevchenko to clinch an astonishing 3-2 victory on penalties.

from that moment each and every one of us wanted the ball, we were all so up for it and you couldn't help but feel that that we were going to get that third goal. I surged forward again and played the ball into Milan Baros, who touched it in to Stevie. Milan didn't get the credit for that touch; it was great. He just nudged it round the corner and Steve's clear; flying towards goal. You knew it was going to be a penalty because Steve's run was taking him across the defender and he's obviously going to be fouled. I still think Gattuso should

have been sent off, mind. He was the last man.

It had been agreed before the game that Xabi would be on them. He had never taken one in anger, but to be honest we didn't have a regular penalty taker. I gave the ball to him and then stood half-way in the Milan half and watched. It all happened so quickly. Dida saved it low to his right, but you didn't have time to be gutted, Xabi's knocked in the rebound and we're back level. Unbelievable.

I didn't sprint over to Xabi; again I just got back into position. I was ecstatic but I needed a breather because I realised this was about to get tougher. At 3-2 it was all adrenaline and you're hungry. At 3-3 I'm thinking "We'd better watch ourselves here." That's when the fear arrived on our side of the fence. Now we've got back in it you dread throwing away all that hard work. Riise had a shot a couple of minutes later, but then Milan emerged from their daze, got themselves sorted out and started to get their game together.

It was adrenaline keeping us going. In injury time I played a poor cross-field pass that handed them possession. From that they broke into our box and had a man over. I had sprinted back thinking "Please don't score from my cock-up". I knew the fella couldn't score from the angle he had, so there was no point me closing him down because he would have just pulled it back to Shevchenko. I read what he had to do and managed to block Shevchenko's shot and we won a goal-kick. That's my job. Block things, tackle.

It was to be extra-time and I was having treatment for cramp and focusing on the most important thirty minutes of my career, but as I lay there I was taken by the fans who were still giving it their all. They had played such a massive part in not only the final but over our entire run to get there. Olympiakos, Juventus, the Chelsea games. They had been incredible.

The first-half of extra-time was very tight. Tomasson had one chance but Djimi did enough to put him off. The second period was all about us holding on. I stretched to stop a Serginho cross and my groin and my calves tightened with cramp. I was splayed out on the turf in pain. According to one TV pundit, who shall remain nameless, I had cramp in both groins.

In the last moments, Shevchenko had a header that we could do nothing about. He knocked it goalwards and from there it's slow motion again, you're just waiting for the net to bulge and to this day I can't believe he's missed it. Credit to Jerzy, he pulled off one amazing save and then followed up with another block, but it's a bad miss. I couldn't believe that once again we were still in the game and I just grabbed Jerzy and told him I loved him. I meant it too.

That was the end. It was penalties. Before we got going I ran over to Jerzy and gave him the pep-talk. I don't care what you call it, cheating, gamesmanship, I just wanted to win the European Cup and I told him to do his best to put them off. It worked. Jerzy's giving it the Grobbelaar and they've missed their first two penalties and we've scored ours. When Cissé made it 2-0 you're starting to allow yourself to think "We might win this". That was the first time I really did that.

Then it all changed again.

Tomasson made it 2-1 and John Arne Riise was up next for us. Riise's was a great pen, beautifully placed, but it was another great save. Dida blocked it. Because it's John, we all expected him to blast it, he's got a bit of a shot on him you know, but he's placed it and it hasn't gone in.

That let them back in and Kaká made it 2-2, so Vlad's penalty was vital. If he scored his, we really had a great chance. He knocked it in and went mad. He was celebrating like we'd won and I was telling him to come back and calm down. I didn't want him to get carried away because it can come back to haunt you. All their players are watching him and I just thought this could get embarrassing. I remembered the Munich players getting a bit cocky in 1999 and then United came back to win, so you have to be careful.

They had to score their next penalty. I was standing next to Stevie and we see it's Shevchenko coming up to take it. There's no way he's missing, surely. Steve was up next for us, so I was saying to him, "Come on lad, you can win this for us." You don't expect the likes of Shevchenko to miss, but to be honest it was one of the worst penalties I've ever seen. It looks like he's trying to dink it, but it was nothing really. Jerzy got a good hand to it.

Pandemonium.

Suddenly my cramp's gone and I was off. I ran towards Jerzy, but then changed my mind and just wanted to be with the fans. Somehow I found my friends and family. I didn't have a clue where they were in the ground; I just ran and ran and then stopped and was grabbed by the supporters in the stand. My mates had come to the front. We did our celebrating and then, when I'd calmed down a but, I went over and shook the Milan guys hands. Stam came over and said "Well done." They have to take some credit because they took it very well. I would have been suicidal.

To see that trophy with our red ribbons around it was unbelievable. I have always watched foreign football and I never thought I'd be playing in a Champions League Final. Half-way through the season we were losing at Southampton, Crystal Palace, Birmingham, and Burnley even. You don't even entertain ideas that you could be involved in a night like this.

UEFA's president Lennart Johansson actually made to give me the trophy. He thought I was the skipper! Some of those old UEFA guys haven't got a clue, I don't think. Steve had probably been rehearsing that moment since he was a kid and can you imagine if I had lifted it. There would have been hell to pay.

We took the cup around to our fans and it was just singing and dancing. Johnny Cash's Ring of Fire had become our theme tune and all of us were banging it out. That song had started on one of the coaches that my dad had been on. They would bring music for the away games and that was on this tape. They started singing it and it's taken off. They play it at Anfield now. It's become our theme tune. All the players had a CD with it on and it's still funny to see the Spanish guys all humming away to Johnny Cash.

We had a room at the top of our hotel where we had a big party. I couldn't really enjoy it because my phone was going off every two minutes with people wanting to get in. I kept having to go down to the fella on the door and lie, saying that this was my brother and could he come in. "You have very big family," he remarked. I do, but it's not that big!

Coming home was amazing. The way we had won the game touched everyone and brought them out in their hundreds of thousands. On rooftops, hanging out of windows, standing on cars. Superb.

My medal sits proudly in the house. My dad has been taking it around the local schools for the kids to have photos taken with it. I still have to double take though when I see the words LIVERPOOL, EUROPEAN CHAMPIONS, but that's what that night made us and no-one can take that away.

I got married just weeks after the final and had the trophy at my wedding. They allowed me to bring it along and we had it on the top table. What a guest of honour."

"To see that trophy with our red ribbons around it was unbelievable."

section
six

the final

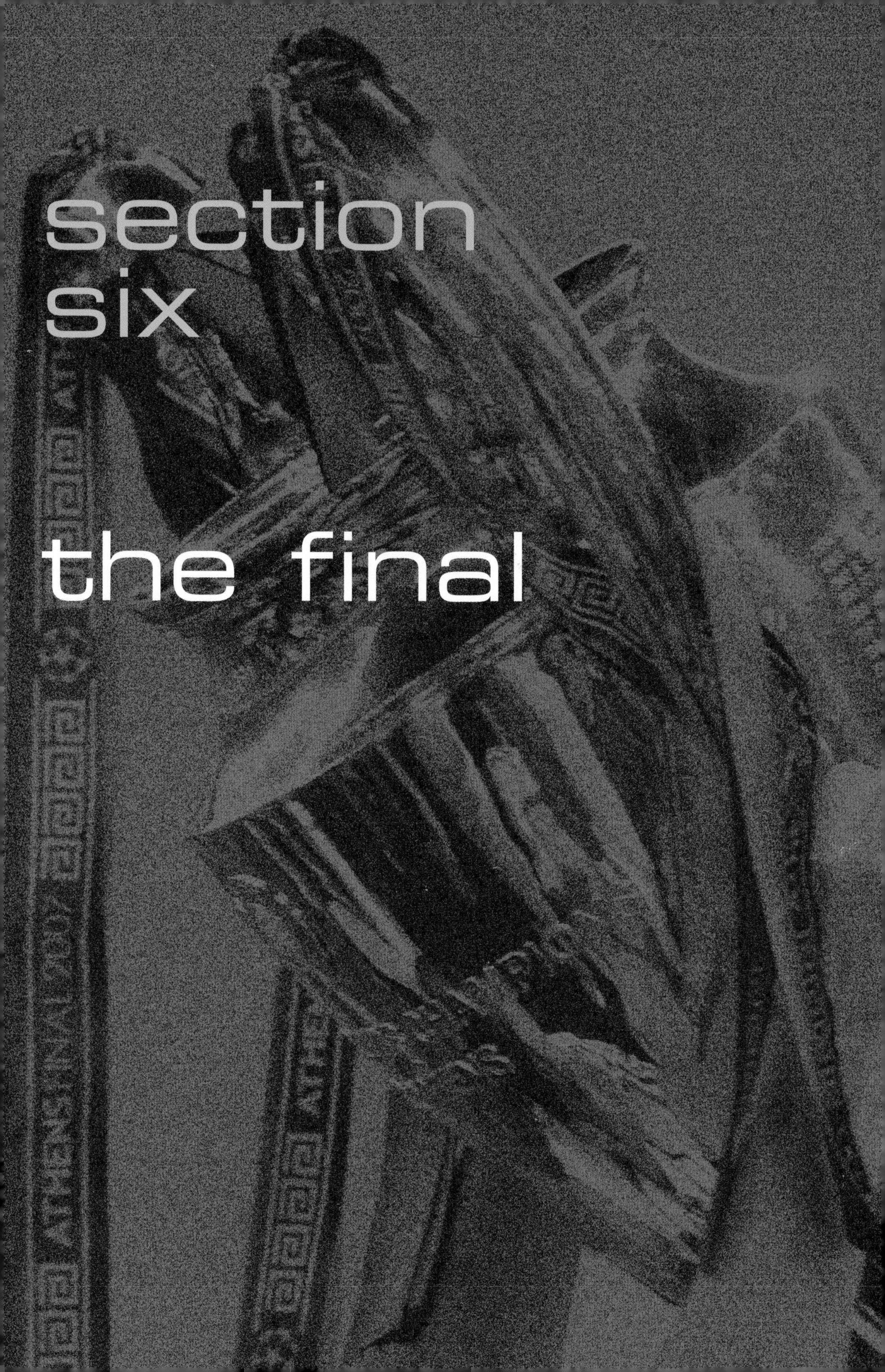

The Preamble

The scramble for tickets and flights to the final in Athens got under way immediately the finalists were known with black market seats on sale for nearly £2,000, more than seven times their face value. Airlines began to finalise arrangements to lay on scores of special charter flights and British police readied contingency plans to cope with thousands of fans descending on the Greek capital.

The two finalists were each allocated 17,000 tickets in the Olympic Stadium, but Liverpool's chief executive, Rick Parry, voiced concerns over security issues as many supporters were expected to travel without tickets. When Liverpool played in the 2005 final in Istanbul, more than 35,000 fans travelled from Merseyside. Officials at Liverpool John Lennon Airport held a special meeting to discuss the number of charter flights with more than 20,000 fans expected to use the airport.

Fans had to dig deep to pay for the trip; charter flights for Liverpool fans were being advertised at £599 for a flight and two-night accommodation package. A scheduled flight from Manchester, including a stopover at Brussels, the day before the final and returning the day after, was advertised at £1,347. Hotel accommodation was scarce. Websites indicated no availability at some 170 hotels in Athens.

The Association of Chief Police Officers liaised with their counterparts in Athens to finalise arrangements. Greece's entire 20,000-strong police force were deployed for the final, building on security plans that were prepared for the 2004 Olympics.

From the board room to the dressing room, revenge was the key note in the build up to the Final. Gennaro Gattuso commented, "I know I am supposed to say that Istanbul is long forgotten and

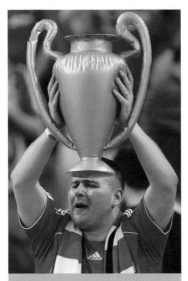

Liverpool fans clamoured for tickets to the Champions League final as it was predicted that even more than the 35,000 who traveled to Istanbul for the 2005 final would make their way to Athens

this game has nothing to do with what happened two years ago, but it's not true. It was not easy to come to terms with what happened and this is a chance to put things right."

One of the most mouth-watering prospects of the Final was the midfield head to head between Gattusso and Gerrard. As Gerrard stormed into the Liverpool dressing-room at half-time in Istanbul two years earlier, he let rip a string of expletives at the cocky Milan players. Gerrard accused Gattusso of smirking as Liverpool fell three goals behind. The reasons for Liverpool's remarkable recovery, pulling back to 3-3, forcing extra time and then winning on penalties, ranged from the fans' rendition of You'll Never Walk Alone to Rafa Benitez's speech about showing pride in the shirt.

Milan's premature celebrations, embodied by Gattuso's expression, stoked Liverpool's fire. Gerrard used his autobiography to detail his anger with the Italian international. "He had a smirk on his face leaving the pitch at half-time," Gerrard wrote. "I saw it. F*** you. A couple of other Milan players waved at their fans and family. That disgusted me. OK, Milan were battering us, but you never behave like that to opponents. I was steaming as I arrived in the dressing room."

Asked about Gerrard's accusations Gattuso shrugged his shoulders and

Gattuso and Gerrard were prepared for a battle royal in the centre of midfield

pleaded innocence. "No, we didn't do that at all," he insisted in decent English acquired from his days with Rangers. "It was wrong to say that."

Gerrard, however, added in his book, "I wasn't worried about Gattuso before the game, during the game, or after. People rate the Italian for some reason. For me, he is all mouth. He looks aggressive, but he is as scary as a kitten. I swear I wouldn't mind playing against Gattuso every week. He doesn't hurt you. I have never seen Gattuso play a killer ball. He won't nick a goal either. Gattuso just plays for the fans – theatrical and emotional."

Pepe Reina was out to exorcise his own family demons, in the final after his father's mistake had cost Atlético Madrid a vital goal in the 1974 final

DID YOU KNOW?
Milan chose to wear their change all white strip despite winning the right to don their traditional red and black stipes. Keen to 'exorcise the demons' of Istanbul, Milan selected the white strip, not only because they had worn it during the defeat in Aistanbul, but also because 5 of their 6 victories in the competition had come whilst wearing white

'Pepe' Reina joined a select band of just three fathers and sons to appear in European Cup finals. Miguel Sanchez and his son, also called Miguel, achieved that feat for Real Madrid, as did Cesare and Paolo Maldini for Milan, and now Miguel and Jose Reina, for Atlético Madrid and Liverpool respectively.

It was 33 years since Georg Schwarzenbeck's optimistic shot from distance beat Miguel Reina's despairing dive in the final minute of extra-time to haul Bayern Munich level against Atlético Madrid. He then let in four in the replay. "Luck was against our family that time," said Reina the younger. "After what happened then, this competition owes us."

No other goalkeeper can match Reina's 19 clean sheets in his 35 Premiership appearances this season; 56 of his 103 games for the club have culminated in shut-outs.

Coach Carlo Ancelotti called on Milan to set the seal on a season that had seen his team overcome unprecedented setbacks. The Italian courts' decision to deduct 44 points from last season's total in punishment for their involvement in the Calciopoli scandal might have precluded Milan's participation in this season's tournament. It meant Milan's pre-season preparations were conducted in a state of turmoil, despite the punishment's reduction on appeal to 30 points. That softening of the sentence granted Milan a place in the qualifying stages of the tournament, from where they had now reached their eighth final in 20 years. "Milan reached this final deservedly," said Ancelotti. "Perhaps more than the other teams because in Serie A we had points docked and we have come back [mentally] from that. So if we win I think we truly deserve it. This has been the most difficult year since I have been at Milan. We have had to face problems we have never had in the past; there have been injuries and, well, I won't go into

the detail. What's emerged is the great harmony I've had with the team and the club. We never looked for an alibi or to blame anyone. We have tried to face our problems and solve them. These problems have given us a lot of strength for this season and for this final."

Patrick Vieira put a different point of view. The former Arsenal midfielder was adamant the disgraced Italian giants should never have been allowed into the competition. Milan had been caught up in the match-fixing scandal which had seen Vieira's former club Juventus relegated, but were allowed to retain their Serie A status and compete in the Champions League. That prompted Vieira to insist the punishment did not fit the crime. He said: "I don't understand why Milan were even allowed to compete in the Champions League. They were given the green light and now they are in the final. It is a great achievement for them and I must say their performances have been magnificent. But if it's decided that what happened last year was wrong they should have been punished properly. How can a team be found guilty and then still be allowed into the Champions League? They were part of a scandal that hurt Italian football."

Javier Mascherano could hardly believe his luck at being part of the UEFA Champions League final after his disastrous spell at Upton Park

Final referee Herbert Fandel of Germany

transfer window after a nightmare spell alongside his countryman Carlos Tevez at West Ham United.

"I was at West Ham, going nowhere, doing nothing. I was depressed, at my lowest ebb, and wondering what had happened to me. And now here I am about to play in the biggest club game in the world. It is surreal," said Mascherano. "That is the only way I can describe it — weird. After what I have been through this season, I find it unbelievable to be involved."

The outstanding player of the tournament, Kaka, is a contender for European Player of the Year with 10 goals in the Champions League. Kaká was confident Liverpool will not pay him special attention. "I believe they won't man-mark me," he said. "I have never been man-marked in the competition. I think it will be the same against Liverpool. This is a great opportunity for me. I am hoping to do something important tomorrow, so I can leave my trace on history."

Javier Mascherano's route to the final was unusual to say the least. He joined the Merseyside club in the January

German referee Herbert Fandel was handed the privilege of taking charge of the final. The 43 year-old German

Milan's Kaká had designs on greatness in the build up to the final

Fans congregate on the day of the final in Athens city centre

pipped Slovakia's Lubos Michel to the honour. The Italian media made much of the fact that Liverpool had not won with Fandel as their referee in three matches, while Milan had won five matches out of five with the German in charge. It would be the first time that he had handled a game in Athens.

This season, he had been the referee of Milan's 4-1 win over Anderlecht at the San Siro – which meant that he finally saw AC Milan concede a goal at the fifth attempt. Conversely he had never seen Liverpool score a goal. He handled their 2-0 defeat in Valencia in September 2002; the goalless draw away to Chelsea in December 2005; and the 1-0 home defeat by Barcelona at Anfield in March's quarter-final second leg. He had officiated at 69 internationals after becoming an international referee in 1998.

Black and Asian Liverpool fans descended on Athens. Liverpool has become a popular team amongst ethnic minorities across the UK. Many younger black and Asian fans from London, Birmingham and other major cities, developed their footballing loyalties in the seventies and eighties, when Liverpool had been last

at the summit of European football. Worries about racism in the stands meant that many did not attend games and became 'armchair supporters', choosing the most exciting teams to cheer on rather than the ones closest to their homes. As football has become safer, minorities have become more confident about attending matches and following local sides.

Other sides with 'national' follow-ings amongst black fans include Arsenal and Manchester United.

An estimated 70,000 Liverpool fans travelled to Athens to get behind the Reds, with 40,000 due to attend the game. Many gathered in the historical Syntagma Square in the centre of Athens, with large numbers of Asian fans in particular visible amongst them. Last year, Liverpool captain Steven Gerrard commented on the number of Asian fans attending Anfield when he spoke to Kick It Out, "The other players and I are aware that we have loads of Asian fans that come to games every week. I guess they love the club for the same reason every Liverpool fan does. We have always played good football and entertain people. I think that's always going to attract people who love the game."

Idris Mohammed, a life-long Liverpool fan from the North West, was one of the lucky few to get a final ticket. "The atmosphere is absolutely electric – thousands of Liverpool fans are taking over the city. I've seen lots of groups of Asian fans and quite a few black fans checking out the city and proudly wearing their Liverpool tops. Black and Asian fans are definitely part of the make up of Liverpool these days. Not everyone will get to go to the game, but I think for a lot of us we are just happy to be out here and a part of what could be yet another memorable night. All we need now is for the boys to deliver on the pitch."

DID YOU KNOW?
Cafu's real name is Marcos Evangelista de Moraes

The Final
Wednesday 23 May 2007

AC Milan 2 v Liverpool 1
Spiros Louis Stadium
Athens
Attendance: 63,800

AC MILAN

Scorers	
45', 82'	Inzaghi

Team

01	Dida
03	Maldini
13	Nesta
44	Oddo
23	Ambrosini
08	Gattuso
22	Kaká
18	Jankulovski
21	Pirlo
10	Seedorf
09	Inzaghi

Substitutes

80'	> 04 Kaladze	< 18 Jankulovski
89'	> 11 Gilardino	< 09 Inzaghi
90'	> 19 Favalli	< 10 Seedorf

Discipline

41'	Gattuso
54'	Jankulovski

Milan Become Champions Of Europe For The Seventh Time!

Filippo Inzaghi celebrates his opening goal

Referee
Herbert Fandel (GER)

Assistant Referee
Carsten Kadach (GER) Volker Wezel (GER)

Fourth Official
Florian Meyer (GER)

UEFA Referee Observer
Bo Karlsson (SWE)

LIVERPOOL

Scorers	
Kuyt	89'

Team

Reina	25
Agger	05
Carragher	23
Finnan	03
Riise	06
Alonso	14
Gerrard	08
Mascherano	20
Pennant	16
Zenden	32
Kuyt	18

Substitutes

07 Kewell	>	59'
32 Zenden	<	
15 Crouch	>	78'
20 Mascherano	<	
02 Arbeloa	>	88'
03 Finnan	<	

Discipline

Mascherano	59'
Carragher	60'

3	Shots on goal	4
1	Shots wide	6
15	Fouls committed	27
4	Corners	6
3	Offsides	3
27' 24"	Ball. Poss. (time)	24' 5"
53%	Ball. Poss. (%)	47%

*Paolo Maldini prepares to lift the UEFA Champions League Trophy
for the second time and collect his fifth winner's medal*

> "We've been the best team in Italy, Europe and the world over the last 20 years and the cycle hasn't ended yet."
>
> Paolo Maldini, AC Milan captain

In an absorbing final Milan gained sweet revenge for the travails of Istanbul with two goals from veteran striker Filippo Inzaghi.

While Milan lifted the European Cup for a seventh time, Paolo Maldini won the hallowed trophy for the fifth time and the second as captain in his remarkable career. The defender considered the

achievement further evidence that his team are the best in the business. "This club has provided me with a lot of amazing emotions and this is another example. We've been the best team in

Carlo Ancelotti applauds Milan's ecstatic fans

have rather different highlights to reflect upon this summer. "I said I would go blond, but only after Italy's internationals in June." The World Cup winner now has a second Champions League medal to add to his 2003 success and was relieved to have avenged the 2005 final defeat by Liverpool. "Two years ago in Istanbul it was us who were in tears," he said. "Now it's their turn to cry."

The Italian press were universal in their praise of Milan's seventh European crown with La Gazzetta Dello Sport printing their traditionally pink front page in the red and black of the Rossoneri. "Hooray!!!!!!!" ran the headline, the exclamation marks making the point in no uncertain terms.

The Milan president, Silvio Berlusconi, who has witnessed five UEFA Champions League wins during his 21-year ownership of the club, claimed a chunk of the credit. Despite having tried to persuade Ancelotti to start with Alberto Gilardino instead of Filippo Inzaghi, Berlusconi said: "I told Inzaghi he would score two goals and I was right. It is particularly wonderful to win this, as we have gone some way to wiping away the pain of Istanbul, which was still weighing heavily upon us."

Kaká expressed his delight at claiming the cup after his experiences of Istanbul, "It is very nice to win the Champions League, I'm very happy because in 2005 we lost. What happened then was strange. For just six minutes we played not so good and paid for that. We knew that if we had played that Istanbul match a thousand times it would not have happened again. So, after Kuyt's goal, we knew it would not be the same and today we could do what we want. This is a beautiful side."

Liverpool, however, dominated the first half, keeping Milan at arm's length, with Javier Mascherano, who had won Olympic gold with Argentina on this ground in 2004, a key factor in the Merseysiders successful smothering operation.

In attack Liverpool threatened. Jermaine Pennant in particular rose to the challenge. The speedy former Arsenal man was by far the Reds most effective performer and visibly rose in

Italy, Europe and the world over the last 20 years and the cycle hasn't ended yet. We've got something different to other clubs. We've had this special mentality for some time."

The Rossoneri's all-time European record is second only to the nine-times winners Real Madrid. But while Madrid's dominance lay mainly in the 1950s, in the past two decades Milan have won the trophy five times, been runners-up three times and reached the semi-finals nine times.

Carlo Ancelotti, himself a four-time winner, twice each as Milan player and coach, claimed this to be his sweetest success, given a trying start to the season in which at one point his side were thrown out of the Champions League as

part of their punishment for the Calciopoli match-fixing scandal. "It is our greatest victory," he said. "We've done something extraordinary. I tried to get the best out of every player, but motivating them wasn't difficult. This win was born last November, which was the toughest moment of the season. We could have lost everything, but we didn't, and from then on we started something special."

Ancelotti must now keep a promise he made in the build-up to the final. A prodigious smoker all of his adult life, the 47 year-old declared he will kick his 30-year habit. "I made a vow before the final that if we won I'd quit smoking. It won't be easy, but I'll have to do it now."

Another with a pledge to honour is midfielder Gennaro Gattuso, who will

> "We've done something extraordinary.
> I tried to get the best out of every player,
> but motivating them wasn't difficult."
> **Carlo Ancelotti, AC Milan coach**

confidence after having one early shot parried away by Dida. He gave the Rossoneri defence a torrid time, providing the cross which Gerrard, asked to provide the main attacking support to lone striker Dirk Kuyt, volleyed over.

Gerrard was his usual energetic self, but, without direct involvement in the midfield skirmishes, struggled to exert the kind of influence he would have wished. Instead, Pennant continued to torment Jankulovski, indirectly creating the opportunity Xabi Alonso fizzed wide just before the half hour, then cutting inside to set up John Arne Riise, who drilled over.

The winger linked with Gerrard to set up Kuyt, only for Alessandro Nesta to block. At that point, with the snarling Gennaro Gattuso booked for one borderline tackle too many on Alonso, Liverpool were by far the more likely scorers.

But the Reds were hit by a 45th-minute sucker-punch from Inzaghi. Alonso fouled Kaká in the most opportune position for Milan, some 20 yards from the target. Andrea Pirlo's 20-yard free-kick hit the Milan striker and wrongfooted Reina before hitting the back of the net.

Ripping intended interval team talks up against Milan is nothing new

for Benitez and in the knowledge Liverpool's position was nowhere near as acute as the one he faced before, he opted not to change things until close to the hour mark.

By that stage two years ago, Benitez's side had thrillingly drawn level. This time, not only were they still behind, Milan were starting to get on top. The arrival of Harry Kewell at least gave the Italians something else to think about, although the momentum was now with Milan and had Pirlo curled home a 20-yard free-kick instead of dipping it over the bar, Liverpool would surely have been doomed.

The ball is on its way into the back of Pepe Reina's net for the opening goal right before half-time

Inzaghi rounds Reina to put Milan 2-0 ahead

Pirlo's near-miss ignited Gerrard's fire and Liverpool's talisman should have levelled when he sped onto Kuyt's pass, then flashed past Nesta, only for Dida to save a precise shot aimed at the far post. It was the Reds' clearest opportunity before Inzaghi raced onto Kaka's inspired through ball, rounded Reina and tapped home Milan's second.

The tension grew by the second as the game entered its last ten minutes.

Then, immediately after Benitez had gone for broke by replacing the effective Javier Mascherano with Peter Crouch, Kaká found space to release Inzaghi, who skipped around Reina to put Milan 2-0, coolly rolling the ball into the net.

Kuyt's close-range header on 89 minutes gave the travelling Reds fans hope, but it was too late.

Ancelotti substituted Inzaghi in the 88th minute so the forward could wallow in a personal ovation. Within

seconds Pennant's corner from the left was flicked on by Agger and headed in by Kuyt. A few Italian hearts must have stopped, but there was to be no recreation of Istanbul here, even though Crouch, with the sort of effort not usually associated with him, had Dida tipping an attempt from distance over soon after Inzaghi's clincher.

Benitez was annoyed that the full three minutes of added time was not played at the end of the game, and made his feelings known to Fandel and the new UEFA president Michel Platini as he went up to collect his loser's medal, but admitted: "It's not a reason, we lost against a good team with top-class players. The first half we played really well, but conceded a goal, a deflection, through bad luck. It was luck, but that is football. Then we were pushing and pushing and you leave a space and they have quality and it was the difference. We were trying to keep the ball and press high but you need to take your chances."

Inzaghi had an alternative viewpoint about the fortune of his first goal. "It was something that we rehearsed in training," said Inzaghi with a grin. "I scored with it against Empoli. Sometimes it just comes off."

Whether it was deliberate or not, there was little doubt it was the turning point of the match, and it was fitting that Inzaghi was involved. The 33 year-old suffered from a number of injuries over the last couple of years and missed Milan's defeat on penalties by Liverpool in Istanbul. This season, his scoring form was mixed, with four goals from 11 games in the UEFA Champions League before the Final, including two in the qualifiers, and just two goals in 20 Serie A outings.

Before the final, there had been much debate about whether Ancelotti would play Inzaghi or Gilardino up front. Inzaghi's double strike repaid his coach's confidence. "I have a very special relationship with, Milan," he said. "A couple of years ago I missed a lot of games through injury, but the club kept faith in me and when I was fit again they welcomed me back with open arms. They showed real trust in

Liverpool fans watching in the city centre look on aghast as the final drifts away

Dirk Kuyt's header came too late for Liverpool to mount an Istanbul-style comeback

"Two years ago in Istanbul it was us who were in tears. Now it's their turn to cry."
Gennaro Gattuso, AC Milan

"It's a feeling of great joy. There aren't words to describe it... I feel like it's all a dream."
Filippo Inzaghi, AC Milan

me." If Inzaghi's first goal had a touch of good fortune, there was no doubting the quality of his second. "The first goal opened up the game, but the second was certainly better," he said. Summing up his emotions, Inzaghi added: "It's a feeling of great joy. There aren't words to describe it...I feel like it's all a dream."

Jamie Carragher's cold assessment of Liverpool's failure in Athens was brutally clear: "There's no point making excuses, Milan just about deserved it. But nobody remembers the runners-up, we know we did not do enough. I am not going to moan about things that went against us. We did not do enough and we must pick ourselves up and have another go next season."

In the immediate aftermath of the final UEFA launched an investigation into security problems at the Stadium after Greek police arrested over 200 people for possessing or selling forged tickets. Many others – mostly English – forced their way past the security perimeters around the Olympic Stadium hours before kick-off.

The British government demanded an explanation from the Greek authorities over the treatment of Liverpool fans who were baton-charged after being denied entry to the final. Chaotic disturbances outside the ground soured the evening, as fans with legitimate tickets were turned away and sprayed with tear gas by riot police. Police also used batons against fans who had genuine tickets for the game.

Supporters were angered after being told the ground was full to its 63,800 capacity, and trouble erupted as they attempted to find a way around police cordons. Officers at the scene told the fans it was not their fault, and it appeared that supporters with forged tickets had got into the stadium earlier. Around 2,000 people were still outside the ground when the final kicked off.

More than 25,000 Liverpool fans and around 17,000 Milan fans were estimated to be in the city for the match, with 8,500 police officers on duty.

UEFA's communications chief, William Gaillard, put the blame squarely on Liverpool supporters. "Unfortunately in Britain it is the behaviour. Liverpool fans are responsible for the problems before, during and after the game."

A total of 230 people who had been detained with forged tickets were released the next day, with a promise that no further action would be taken against them. Police said 216 of them were from the UK, and nine from Italy.

The row would rumble on over the summer, with UEFA also releasing a report which named Liverpool fans as 'the worst in Europe'.

Milan supporters, however, partied long into the night both in Athens and northern Italy to celebrate their team's incredible achievement of going from Champions League outcasts to winners.

Milan are champions once again...
...while Steven Gerrard and Jermaine Pennant trudge off to contemplate defeat

The Finalists

AC Milan

DIDA

Doubters will tell you that Dida was to blame for Liverpool's win in the 2005 final. He should have done better with Steven Gerrard's header that looped over him to drag the Reds back into the game. He should have got down for Vladimir Smicer's second. Those doubters would have been at full volume just a few minutes into this year's semi-final first leg at Old Trafford when Dida let a Ryan Giggs corner evade him for United's first goal. But it was the Brazilian goalkeeper who had the last laugh, making himself big on several occasions in the final and getting those imposing hands on a second Champions League winners medal.

PAOLO MALDINI

There are certain things you expect from a Champions League final these days; a balmy spring evening, two colourful sets of fans with massed banners and the odd flare thrown in, the omnipotent UEFA Champions League anthem filling the night air, and Paolo Maldini on the pitch. The Italian defender has now played in an incredible seven finals, more than any other man in the history of the tournament. Maldini was as imperious as ever and, despite missing his side's impressive 3-0 win over Manchester United in the semi-final second leg, there was no way Carlo Ancelotti was going to leave his captain out of the final.

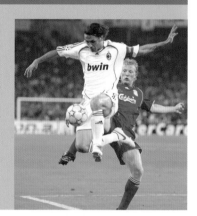

KAKHA KALADZE

Milan's Georgian defender had a stamp bearing his image issued in his home country in 2003 when the club won the Champions League and he became the first man from the tiny former Russian state to pick up a winners medal. Whilst he didn't get to start the final in Athens, Kaladze's overall contribution and his last ten minutes as a substitute will have furthered his heroic status back home. Kalazde was in and out of Ancelotti's starting line-up, but he filled in at centre-half for the injured Paolo Maldini in the semi-final second leg against Manchester United and helped keep Messrs Rooney and Ronaldo more than quiet.

ALESSANDRO NESTA

Nesta, along with Maldini, may have breathed a sigh of relief when he realised that Liverpool would be playing only one centre-forward in the Final, but there was still a job to do and Nesta was in majestic form in Athens. Milan's World Cup winning centre-half was injured before Christmas and missed most of the group stages, but his return to the defence for the quarter-final against Bayern Munich helped galvanise the team, his very presence settling what had been hitherto a tentative campaign. In the final he more than matched Dirk Kuyt's strength and fully deserved his new contract with the Rossoneri that will keep him at the San Siro until 2011.

MAREK JANKULOVSKI

Marek took part in all 13 of Milan's 2006/07 Champions League matches, starting in each of the knock-out matches, the final and proving that once Maldini does retire, that the left-back slot will be passed on to his more than capable hands. The Czech defender may not have the tactical awareness of his master, but he more than makes up for that with his lung-busting bursts upfield and throughout the campaign he gave the Milan attack an extra dimension. In the final itself he seemed to be struggling with Jermaine Pennant in the first-half, but after the break, with his team 1-0 up, he nullified the Englishman's threat as Milan took control.

CAFU

Officially Cafu is 37 years-old, but many think he is much older. Whilst he may not be the dominating influence he once was, the Brazilian legend (he has 141 caps) was still a prominent part of the winning squad. Throughout the campaign, Cafu came off the bench to calm his side's nerves. How re-assuring must it be to have a man of his stature and experience to bring on when a lead is there to be protected, and how demoralising it must be to see him getting warm when you are the team chasing that deficit.

CHRISTIAN BROCCHI

Brocchi spent the season before last on loan at Fiorentina, who in summer 2006 were keen to make the move permanent. Milan, though, knew the 31 year-old's worth and, while he is far from a regular in the midfield, he offers great support and was a valuable member of the winning squad. Brocchi started most of the group games before the trio of Pirlo, Gattusso and Ambrosini all gained full fitness. He made a valuable contribution from the bench against Celtic at the San Siro and it was his energy that in extra-time kept Gordon Strachan's men at bay. He didn't get off the bench in Athens, but was well worth his medal.

DANIELE BONERA

The Italian defender didn't have the most memorable of Champions League campaigns. Sent off in October during the group stage match at Anderlecht, Bonera struggled to oust Kakha Kaladze as the third choice centre-half and his cause was far from helped at Old Trafford in the semi-final first-leg. Just after half-time Paulo Maldini limped off to be replaced by Bonera. The defender had to put up with a torrid United display that saw them equalise and grab a winner after he arrived. Come the second leg, Bonera, despite Maldini's injury, was left out and couldn't even get on the bench in Athens.

MASSIMO ODDO

Oddo is a trained hairdresser and actually styled a lot of his World Cup winning team-mates last summer, earning him the nickname 'The Barber of Berlin' and should he ever open a salon after he retires, the walls will be decorated with much more than just that World Cup winner's medal. Oddo has become a fixture at right-back for the Rossoneri, playing in every knock-out match and offering Milan much needed width down the right. Oddo in the final had the ineffectual Zenden to deal with, but the more dangerous John Arne Riise was also kept quiet to great effect.

GENNARO GATTUSO

There are silkier players at Milan, there are players who can light up football stadia with their deft touch and eye for the spectacular, but if you ask a Milanese supporter who is the heartbeat of their team, who makes the parts tick, they will raucously tell you that it is Gennaro Gattuso. Called 'a kitten' by Steven Gerrard in his autobiography, it was Gattuso who had the last meow as his efforts allowed both Pirlo and Kaká to dominate the midfield in Athens. Gattuso's greatest game in the campaign was against Manchester United at the San Siro, where his tireless running and tackling paved the way for a famous win.

CLARENCE SEEDORF

On the way to Athens, Seedorf, Milan's much travelled Dutch midfielder, scored two vital goals. The first came in Munich to put his team in front and ensure the pendulum of control had swung Milan's way. The second was in the second leg of the semi-final against Manchester United. Milan had made a stirring start to the match and taken the lead through Kaká after a great nod back by the Dutchman, but it was Seedorf's goal that killed off United and ensured a trip to Athens. In the final he was full of energy in a tightly fought midfield and was a worthy winner of a fourth winner's medal.

YOHANN GOURCUFF

Nicknamed 'Petit Zizou' (Little Zidane) Gourcuff is one for the future, but the 20 year-old Frenchman showed enough flashes of brilliance in the Champions League to suggest that Milan have a real star on their hands. A goal in the group stages against AEK Athens at the San Siro underlined his potential, whilst a more than competent performance in the cauldron of Celtic's Parkhead that earned a valuable 0-0 draw showed a more steely side to his game. This season was too soon for Gourcuff to make the 16 for the final, but with the Milan midfield ageing, his time will soon come.

KAKA

What can you say? 2006/07 was without a doubt the year of the Kaka. His skills lit up the UEFA Champions League and the European game, his goals took Milan all the way to the final. The ten scored by the Brazilian made him the competition's top scorer, but they are just an added bonus to his all-round game. The two he notched at Old Trafford and the opener against Manchester United at the San Siro were all different, but all excellent. In the final he was well shackled by Javier Mascherano, but as soon as the Argentinean had been substituted he broke free, slipped the ball through Liverpool's back four for Inzaghi to score and the game was won. In a word, brilliant.

ANDREA PIRLO

Another one of Milan's 2006 World Cup winners, Pirlo enjoyed yet another fantastic season for the Rossoneri, pulling the strings in Carlo Ancelotti's midfield. Whilst the likes of Seedorf, Gattuso and Ambrosini are all strong athletic players, Pirlo is the brains of the outfit, using his wide range of passing to open teams up and most importantly get Kaká going. He managed one goal in the 2-2 draw with Bayern Munich, but it was his free-kick right on half-time in Athens that deflected off Inzaghi to give Milan a precious lead.

MASSIMO AMBROSINI

Whilst injury forced Ambrosini out of much of last season and Italy's victorious World Cup campaign, the midfielder eventually recovered to settle firmly into a new look midfield that Carlo Ancelotti decided very much needed his vice-captain. With another ball winner in there, Kaká was allowed an even freer role and from the second round onwards Ambrosini was a regular. It was his pass that set free Gilardino to score the third past Manchester United at the San Siro and it was his energy that meant the likes of Gerrard and Alonso were kept quiet in Athens.

RICARDO OLIVEIRA

Having finally got his move to AC Milan from Real Betis in Spain, 2006/07 was far from a memorable season for the Brazilian forward Oliveira. The £15m that Milan paid for him looks like bad business given that he scored just twice all season, neither of them coming in the Champions League, but there were reasons for his slump. Oliveira will point to the fact that his sister had been kidnapped and wasn't released until March this year, but he will have to drastically improve if the likes of Inzaghi are to be threatened by his presence.

ALBERTO GILARDINO

In the end, Gilardino had done enough to make Carlo Ancelotti seriously consider who to play up front in the final, but not enough to get the preference over eventual Man of the Match Filippo Inzaghi. Yet Gilardino can take heart from a fine season in the Champions League, and his two goals in the competition underlined a potentially brilliant prospect. He pushed Inzaghi hard, his goal against Manchester United looked like even getting him the nod in Athens, but it wasn't to be. At just 24, though, his time will come.

FILIPPO INZAGHI

You would have to have a heart of steel to begrudge Inzaghi his success this year. Often belittled for his tendency to stray offside, and missing through injury in 2005 when Milan lost the Champions League final, the 33 year-old (quite aged for a centre-forward) grabbed his chance this time out and left the Olympic Stadium in Athens a hero. It was Inzaghi's goal back in August that beat Crvena Zvevda in the third qualifying round and four more sealed his famous season.

CARLO ANCELOTTI

Ancelotti's Champions League legend is now written in stone. As a player he won the old trophy twice and now he has matched that as a coach, joining an elite club of managers to have won it more than once. Ancelotti quite rightly is now up there with the likes of Ernst Happel, Bob Paisley and Ottmar Hitzfeld as a coach of multiple European Cup winners. His team may be getting old, but his system of playing four tireless midfielders behind the mesmeric Kaká worked a treat, especially against Manchester United in the semi-final second leg where the Champions of England were simply outclassed.

Liverpool

JOSE REINA

It had been hard for Jose 'Pepe' Reina. A good goalkeeper, he had been bought by Rafa Benitez as a replacement for Jerzey Dudek. The only problem was that Dudek had only just pulled off his heroics in Istanbul; heroics that had helped Liverpool win the UEFA Champions League. No matter how well Reina did, his number two always had that one crazy night in Turkey over him. Until this season that is. Against Chelsea in another famous semi-final win Reina saved two penalties and suddenly the shadow of Dudek was lifted. The Spaniard enjoyed a fine campaign and is now regarded as one of the best in Europe.

ALVARO ARBELOA

Bought on the last day of the January 2007 transfer window, Arbeloa had played one Premiership match when Benitez threw him into the side for the small matter of an away game at Barcelona's Nou Camp. The Spanish right-back was asked to fit into the left-back berth to keep an eye on Lionel Messi, who has a tendency to cut in from the right onto his stronger left foot. It was tactically brilliant, Arbeloa (in both legs) was tidiness personified and Messi didn't get a sniff. Arbeloa went on to appear in later rounds at his more favoured right-back spot, but ironically never looked as potent. One for next season?

STEVE FINNAN

Ask many Liverpool fans to name their Player of the Year and they will opt for the ever dependable Steve Finnan. He is certainly the most unsung. Bought in 2003, Finnan was a decent Premiership defender, but in 2005, and this season especially, he has blossomed into a great right-back, capable of dealing with the world's best players. Ronaldinho, shackled, Joe Cole, frustrated; not only that, but he can also attack and it was his run and cross that led to Steven Gerrard's opening goal at PSV Eindhoven in the first leg of the quarter-final.

SAMI HYYPIA

2006/07 was the season that the seemingly unmovable wall that is Sami Hyypia was finally breeched. The arrival of Daniel Agger at centre-back saw Liverpool's giant Finnish international make way from a defence he has marshalled so fervently for seven years. Not that he didn't play his part. Hyypia was still dominating things in the first half of the season and it was with him in the team that Benitez's men qualified with such authority from their group. Agger's form, though, meant that soon Hyypia would be warming the bench. But he remains a strong part of the squad and there are some who believe his experience was greatly missed in the final.

JAVIER MASCHERANO

The 24 year-old's first game in the Champions League was in the quarter-final first leg in Eindhoven and immediately you could tell that this type of football was tailor made to his game. The Argentine is a tenacious tackler, who possesses brilliant distribution and can disrupt the most imagnitive of midfields. He was fantastic against Chelsea at Anfield, working tirelesslesly for the cause and frustrating Frank Lampard amongst others with that ability to break up attacks. The final saw him shackle Kaká and it was only when he was taken off that the Brazilian was able to express himself and set up Inzaghi's second goal.

JERMAINE PENNANT

It says a lot about Jermaine Pennant's ability that his manager Rafa Benitez gave him the responsibility of attacking Milan's left-back in arguably the biggest game on the world club calendar. Pennant could have gone into his shell, just happy to be there, but he was one of Liverpool's brighter and more inventive players in the final, especially in the first half when he got in behind the Italians on a few occasions and could well have scored. The lack of an end product, though, dogged his season at Liverpool and his goal scoring must improve.

JOHN ARNE RIISE

In the cauldron that is the Nou Camp in Barcelona, with the ball sitting up on the edge of the home team's penalty area and a hush descending , a fan or a manager could wish for no player other than John Arne Riise to be rushing into take the vital shot. In the 74th minute of Liverpool's second round match against Barcelona, that is what happened and, of course, the Norwegians shot was clean, vicious and ended up slamming into the net. Riise had another fine campaign in Europe, but suffered from Aurelio's injury as he was then asked to concentrate on his defensive duties in the final rather than marauding forward at Milan's back four.

JAMIE CARRAGHER

You could accuse Jamie Carragher of being greedy. Not in the sense that most deem footballers to be these days, but because he just receives more and more adulation from Liverpool's smitten fans. He had already given them 2005 - when he had them dreaming of a "team of Carraghers" — but then this season he once more played with dominance and doggedness. At Anfield in the 2nd leg of the semi-final against Chelsea he scrapped, blocked and frustrated until Didier Drogba seemed to visibly submit. It was one of the great European displays and a fitting night to break Ian Callaghan's long held record of 88 European appearances for the club.

STEVEN GERRARD

It was so close. Not since Emlyn Hughes in 1978, had a Liverpool captain lifted the European Cup for a second time. Gerrard once more dragged his team to the final with a series of fine performances that confirmed his position as one of Europe's most influential players. In Barcelona he struggled initially, but as he got a grip so did his team. In Eindoven he was brilliant and his opening goal settled nerves and broke their hosts's spirit. But it was against Chelsea at Anfield in the semi-final that he was at his commanding best. He was everywhere, cajoling team-mates to ignore fatigue and setting up the vitsal goal. Unfortunately, that effort wasn't enough in Athens, but look at his face as he trudged off that night. He wants that trophy again.

XAVIER ALONSO

It says a lot about the standards set by the 25 year-old Spaniard that despite another tidy season, he would be the first to admit that he can do much better. Alonso at his best dictates a game, pulls the strings with his exquisite passing and lets his more marauding team-mates do their thing. There were times this season when that passing range deserted him, so much so that for the semi-final against Chelsea at Anfield, Benitez saw fit to drop him. Still, he rose to that challenge, and won his place back for the final where he had a tidy game, almost scoring in the first half with a long range effort.

MARK GONZALEZ

The Chilean winger had had to wait a long time for his dream move to Anfield, and in the first game of the season, a Champions League qualifier against Israeli champions Maccabi Haifa, that wait continued as he sat on the bench and watched his new team struggle to break down an organised Israeli side. With just five minutes left and the score at a frustrating 1-1, Rafa Benitez sent on the speedy Gonzalez and with his first touch he raced clear and won the tie for Liverpool, effectively easing the club into the important and lucrative group stages. That was as good as it got for Gonzalez, who despite some cameo performances along the way, never quite set the continent alight.

DANIEL AGGER

When Daniel Agger upset the Carragher-Hyypia apple-cart he finally achieved what so many top European strikers have tried and failed to do for years. It was always going to take something special to dislodge Sami Hyypia, but in Agger, Liverpool have stumbled across a centre-back strong in defence but smooth on the ball and he looks likely to figure at their heart of the back four for a long time to come. Agger came in for the 3-2 win over Galatasary at Anfield and from then on the position was his. He was fantastic at the Nou Camp, but it was the 2nd leg of the semi-final against Chelsea that he came into his own. The Dane had struggled in the 1st leg, but at Anfield it was his early goal that got Liverpool level and on their way to Athens.

FABIO AURELIO

In the second half of Liverpool's quarter-final first leg in Eindhoven, Rafa Benitez must have sat, watched and, as much as a perfectionist like him can, thought "life is sweet". His team were three goals up, playing brilliantly and another semi-final beckoned. In the 75th minute, however, his Brazilian left-back Fabio Aurelio went down and clung, clearly in pain, to his achilles tendon. It was clear he was badly hurt, so hurt it turned out he wouldn't play again that season and that was a massive blow. After a slow start, Aurelio was showing some excellent form and his ability to defend and over-lap with John Arne Riise was causing the best of teams all sorts of problems. Liverpool fans, along with Benitez will be wishing their Brazilian a speedy recovery.

CRAIG BELLAMY

Unfortunately for Craig Bellamy he will be remembered more for what he did with a golf club in Europe during the 2006/07 season than what he did with a football. It's a shame because the Welshman was instrumental in the win over Barcelona at the Nou Camp, scoring the vital equaliser and brilliantly setting up John Arne Riise (the man he was alleged to have attacked prior to the game) for the winner. Bellamy's pace upset many defenders, but he couldn't add any more goals to his repertoire and that proved costly as he had to watch the final in Athens from the bench in what turned out to be his last game for the club before moving to West Ham.

MOHAMED SISSOKO

2006/07 season was another frustrating season for Sissoko, who once more had to endure injury disappointment and struggled to gain any real momentum in the Liverpool line-up. He was at his dynamic best in the group stages and played out of his skin at the Nou Camp in the Second Round (it was possibly his best performance in a red shirt and he deservedly won the Man of the Match award). But with the arrival of Mascherano Momo often had to sit games out, never fully recovering from niggling blows. He sat out the final due to a knock, but he has signed a four-year contract, underlining his fighting spirit.

PETER CROUCH

The goalscoring table doesn't lie, and for a long time this season Peter Crouch was the best goalscorer in Europe. Kaká beat him to that crown eventually, but this was the season that Crouch went from Premiership plodder to UEFA Champions League master. The overhead kick against Galatasary, the two goals against PSV in the knockout stages; in all the seven goals he scored made him more than just a handful and it says much about him that many think Benitez got it wrong not starting, or at least not utilising him earlier, in the final.

BOUDEWIJN ZENDEN

The much-travelled Dutchman had a strange European campaign with Liverpool. His place in the team for vital games (including the semi-final and final) puzzled fans who showed concern for his lack of invention, but by Benitez, the master tactician, he was lorded for his work ethic and the balance he gave the side. Whatever your view you can't question that work rate and whilst not setting the world alight he was especially effective against Chelsea at Anfield where he shackled the Blues and put his penalty in the shoot-out away with aplomb. Zenden moved on to join Olympique Marseille in the summer of 2007.

DIRK KUYT

The Dutch striker's only goal in the campaign was the late consolation against Milan in Athens, but that fact belies what a great impact he had on his new team over the season in Europe. Kuyt's ability to hold the ball up, bring others into play and generally wreak havoc amongst European defences meant it was he who was charged with single-handedly leading the line in the final. He could have done with more support against two wily centre-backs like Maldini and Nesta but anyone who saw his dejected face at the final whistle will tell you that his competitive will stand the club in good stead for seasons to come.

RAFA BENITEZ

Whatever the club's shortcomings in their domestic league, Rafa Benitez has the European game firmly in hand and was clearly disappointed not to add another Champions league trophy to his impressive European collection. The Spaniard once more took on the continent's best and came away with unexpected wins. No-one gave his team a chance in Barcelona, but they outplayed the Champions League holders. Chelsea and his nemesis Jose Mourinho were supposed to gain revenge for 2005, but once more it was Benitez holding the tag of 'Special One'. Some might say he was over-cautious in the final against an ageing Milan defence and, whilst that may be true, it is he that clubs all over Europe covet as the brains behind their European campaigns.

Fan Behaviour
By Tom Green

While the financial might of the UEFA Champions League comes thanks to television, and it is the players, managers and club owners who reap the rewards, arguably the greatest asset to the competition is the fans.

The truly memorable European nights are about atmosphere. Be it at Anfield, the San Siro or in Istanbul, there is nothing quite like the noise, colour and passion of a UEFA Champions League match. That's what makes the spine tingle. That's what makes hundreds of millions of people around the world tune in to watch.

Last season, however, that asset threatened to become a fatal flaw. The highest profile problems came with Manchester United's trip to Roma, but that outburst of violence on the terraces merely served to highlight how much potential for trouble among supporters remains, right across the continent.

The headlines caused by the clashes in Rome demonstrated the sensitivity in England to any apparent outbreak of hooliganism. Violence in

French riot police react to the crushing among the Manchester United fans during the second round game at the Felix-Bollaert Stadium, Lens against Lille

domestic games has been more-or-less eradicated, but at first glance this looked like a flashback to the 1980s when English teams were banned from European competitions for five years following Liverpool fans part in the Heysel stadium tragedy of 1985.

In fact, it turned out that Manchester United fans were, on the whole, victims rather than protagonists. Eyewitness accounts told of over-crowding, aggressive policing and near panic that could have had disastrous consequences. Although both United and Roma were fined by UEFA for their fans' behaviour, most commentators agreed that the incident primarily reflected deep-rooted problems in the Italian game.

The issue of terrace violence has been a sensitive one in Italy since the death of a policeman in riots after a match in Sicily in February. The authorities suspended all matches for a week and talked of taking far-reaching action to challenge the so-called Ultras – core groups of supporters who are usually responsible for any violence and sometimes have links to the club hierarchy.

The trouble at Roma, however, like the very similar clashes between police and Tottenham fans in Seville for a UEFA Cup match the following night, seemed more down to approach than any formal regulations. The Italians are introducing a stewarding system, modelled on that

Roma's Ultras provoked trouble before and during both legs of the quarter-final tie against Manchester United

used at British grounds, aiming to control crowds before any trouble can start, but initial reports suggest some scepticism as to how effectively this is being implemented by the clubs.

While Italy clearly has some serious problems with fan behaviour and policing, they are by no means alone. English supporters might not have been culpable in Rome or Seville, but there have been enough incidents over the years to caution against any complacency. Meanwhile, elsewhere in Europe, several countries have experienced difficulties in the past twelve months.

The Dutch club Feyenoord, for example, were thrown out of last season's UEFA Cup after their fans rioted before a match against Nancy. It was the latest of several incidents involving Feyenoord supporters, although the club's financial director, Onno Jacobs, insisted that they were "being punished for the misbehaviour of people we have nothing to do with."

Even more seriously, in March all team games in Greece were suspended for two weeks by the domestic authorities following the death of a supporter in fights between rival Panathinaikos and Olympiakos supporters. Action has been promised to crack down on troublemakers but, as in Italy, there are serious questions about whether the will exists to really tackle the fan culture that gives rise to such clashes.

There are also the persistent problems of racism in European football. According to the English organisation Kick It Out, a number of clubs have been targeted by neo-Nazi groups with the worst affected being Lazio and Verona in Italy, Paris Saint-Germain in France, and Real Madrid and Real Zaragoza in Spain. Targets can vary, but black players in many European countries have been subject to racist taunting.

Every country must find its own solutions to the issues racism and violence on the terraces, but the first step is to admit that there actually is a problem. That's what English clubs did following the Hillsborough and

Despite their brand new Allianz Arena, Bayern Munich fans still have to watch games from behind bars

Heysel tragedies and it led to them address everything from the layout of grounds to ticketing, stewarding and policing.

For European matches the key seems to be cooperation between clubs and police forces. In Seville, Spurs fans reported that it was the presence of their own stewards that finally helped calm the situation.

English police have worked with foreign forces for many years to advise about potential troublemakers and perhaps now, with cheap flights making mass support at away games more feasible, that help needs to be stepped up.

Indeed, UEFA President Michel Platini has already announced the creation of a Europe-wide initiative to increase cooperation on stewarding and policing. The success of the Fan Fest viewing areas in Germany during the 2006 World Cup shows that large numbers of fans – even drunk English ones – can be accommodated safely if the approach is right.

The fans make the UEFA Champions League, but they also have the potential to undermine it. Football administrators must act swiftly to make sure that last season's problems remain isolated incidents rather than marking the start of a destructive trend.

It's not all bad. Chelsea and Celtic fans gloried in their teams' achievements during 2006/07

section
seven

2007/08
uefa
champions
league

Olympic Arena

All who enter September's group stage will be aiming to make it to the final at the Luzhniki Stadium in Moscow on 21 May 2008. The Russian capital has never before staged a European Champion Clubs' Cup final, making this the most easterly showcase in the tournament's history. The 84,745-seat arena was the setting for the 1980 Olympics under its former name, the Grand Arena of the Central Lenin Stadium.

Spartak Moscow's Luzhniki Stadium will be free of snow for the first UEFA Champions League final to be hosted in Russia

Past Performance Key

Andorra, San Marino and Montenegro feature in the tournament's access list for the first time following a decision by the UEFA Executive Committee. The access list is based on performances over the previous five seasons and determines the number of spots each national association have in the following campaign's UEFA Champions League, and also UEFA Cup.

2007/2008 UEFA CHAMPIONS LEAGUE COMPETITOR CLUBS

IOC	Entry Stage	Club	Coefficient
TH	Grp	AC Milan	133.808
ESP2	Grp	FC Barcelona	119.374
ENG3	Q3	Liverpool	112.618
ITA1	Grp	Inter Milan	107.808
ENG4	Q3	Arsenal	104.618
ESP1	Grp	Real Madrid	104.374
ENG1	Grp	Manchester United	99.618
ENG2	Grp	Chelsea	99.618
ESP4	Q3	Valencia	99.374
FRA1	Grp	Olympique Lyonnais	95.706
POR1	Grp	FC Porto	89.107
ESP3	Q3	Sevilla	87.374
NED1	Grp	PSV Eindhoven	81.995
ITA2	Grp	AS Roma	78.808
POR3	Q3	Benfica	67.107
NED2	Q3	Ajax	65.995
GER3	Q3	Werder Bremen	63.64
SCO1	Q3	Celtic	62.064
GER2	Grp	Schalke 04	60.64
GER1	Grp	VfB Stuttgart	58.64
ROU2	Q2	Steaua Bucharest	55.255
RUS1	Grp	CSKA Moscow	53.92
POR2	Grp	Sporting Lisbon	52.107
ITA3	Q3	Lazio	51.808
FRA2	Grp	Olympique de Marseille	51.706
SCO2	Q2	Rangers	47.064
UKR2	Q2	Shakhtar Donetsk	44.726
TUR2	Q2	Besiktas	43.791
GRE1	Grp	Olympiakos	42.415
BEL1	Q3	RSC Anderlecht	41.638
UKR1	Q3	Dynamo Kiev	38.726
BUL1	Q2	Levski Sofia	38.112
CZE1	Q3	Sparta Praha	37.851
TUR1	Q3	Fenerbahçe	36.791
GRE2	Q3	AEK Athens	36.415
ROU1	Q3	Dinamo Bucharest	34.255
CZE2	Q2	Slavia Praha	32.851
NOR1	Q2	Rosenborg BK	31.509
RUS2	Q3	Spartak Moscow	27.92

2007/2008 UEFA CHAMPIONS LEAGUE COMPETITOR CLUBS – CONTINUED

IOC	Entry Stage	Club	Coefficient
SRB1	Q2	Crvena Zvezda	19.256
DEN1	Q2	FC København	19.129
FRA3	Q3	Toulouse	17.706
CRO1	Q1	Dinamo Zagreb	17.533
BEL2	Q2	KRC Genk	15.638
HUN1	Q2	Debreceni VSC	11.675
SUI1	Q3	FC Zürich	9.869
AUT1	Q2	Salzburg	9.104
CYP1	Q1	APOEL FC	6.492
ISR1	Q2	Beitar Jerusalem FC	6.338
POL1	Q2	Zaglebie Lubin	5.609
SVN1	Q1	NK Domzale	5.272
SWE1	Q1	IF Elfsborg	4.478
BIH1	Q1	FK Sarajevo	4.19
LVA1	Q1	FK Ventspils	3.86
SVK1	Q1	MSK Zilina	3.575
IRL1	Q1	Derry City FC*	3.145
ISL1	Q1	FH Hafnarfjördur	2.65
FIN1	Q1	Tampere United	2.42
LTU1	Q1	FBK Kaunas	2.42
MDA1	Q1	FC Sheriff	2.365
GEO1	Q1	FC Olimpi Rustavi	1.98
MKD1	Q1	FK Pobeda	1.925
BLR1	Q1	FC BATE Borisov	1.54
ALB1	Q1	KF Tirana	1.265
EST1	Q1	FC Levadia Tallinn	1.21
ARM1	Q1	FC Pyunik	1.155
AZE1	Q1	FK Khazar Lenkoran	1.045
KAZ1	Q1	FK Astana	0.77
NIR1	Q1	Linfield FC	0.715
WAL1	Q1	The New Saints FC	0.66
MLT1	Q1	Marsaxlokk FC	0.55
LUX1	Q1	F91 Dudelange	0.55
FRO1	Q1	HB Tórshavn	0.55
MNE1	Q1	FK Zeta	0
AND1	Q1	Rànger's	0
SMR1	Q1	S.S. Murata	0

* Shelbourne FC won the title but did not apply to enter the UEFA Champions League after being relegated for financial reasons. Derry inherited their place in the competition as Irish runners-up.

Red = seeded in the Group stage of the competition

2007/2008 DRAW

1st Qualifying Round

1	Lenkoran	v	Dinamo Zagreb
2	APOEL	v	BATE
3	Sheriff	v	Rànger's
4	Hafnarfjördur	v	HB
5	The New Saints	v	Ventspils
6	Pobeda	v	Levadia
7	Olimpi	v	Astana
8	Zeta	v	Kaunas
9	Tampere	v	Murata
10	Dudelange	v	MSK Zilina
11	Linfield	v	Elfsborg
12	Derry City	v	Pyunik
13	Marsaxlokk	v	Sarajevo
14	NK Domzale	v	Tirana

2nd Qualifying Round

1	Winners Match 12	v	Shakhtar Donetsk
2	Crvena Zvezda	v	Winners Match 6
3	Rangers	v	Winners Match 8
4	Debrecen	v	Winners Match 11
5	Zaglebie Lubin	v	Steaua Bucharest
6	Racig Genk	v	Winners Match 13
7	Winners Match 5	v	Salzburg
8	Winners Match 7	v	Rosenborg
9	Winners Match 4	v	Winners Match 2
10	Copenhagen	v	Beitar Jerusalem
11	Winners Match 10	v	Slavia Prague
12	Winners Match 9	v	Levski Sofia
13	Winners Match 14	v	Winners Match 1
14	Besiktas	v	Winners Match 3

3rd Qualifying Round

14/15 Aug, 28/29 Aug 2007

Group Phase

18/19 Sep, 02/03 Oct, 23/24 Oct, 06/07 Nov, 27/28 Nov, 11/12 Dec 2007

First Knockout Round

19/20 Feb, 04/05 Mar 2008

Quarter-finals

01/02 Apr, 08/09 Apr 2008

Semi-finals

22/23 Apr, 29/30 Apr 2008

Final

21 May 2008

Champions League Diversity
by Steve Menary

Many's the time in recent years that fans from the biggest nations in Europe have bemoaned the sterility at the top of their domestic leagues which sees the qualification places for the UEFA Champions League persistently fall into the same hands. In the English Premier League, for example, since the turn of the century, only Leeds United, Newcastle United and Everton have broken the domination of the big four of Manchester United, Chelsea, Liverpool and Arsenal over the top four qualifying spots.

In Italy the two Milan clubs, Roma, Juventus and Lazio vie for the four available places almost exclusively with only Chievo Verona having achieved a top four finish in the last five years outside these clubs. And in Spain only six different clubs have qualified in the past five seasons.

Hearts brought some new blood to the 2006/07 Champions League from a Scottish perspective, breaking the duolpoly of Celtic and Rangers. But their sojourn didn't last much longer than Saulius Mikoliunas's opening goal against AEK Athens

However, for countries joining the Champions League recently the story is vastly different. They are providing the greatest diversity in terms of teams playing in Europe's premier club competition as it expands to become as broad a church as it has ever been, something new UEFA President Michel Platini has set as one of his major goals for his term of office.

A survey shows that five different teams have represented Kazakhstan in the six seasons since the country joined UEFA from the Asian confederation and started entering teams in the one place on offer in the Champions League. Also, the first champions of the Bosnia-Herzegovina league entered the competition in 2000/01 and six different teams have taken the eight slots on offer since then.

The research (see table) covers the 11 seasons since 1997/98, when clubs from smaller countries were reinstated to the UEFA Champions League after a brief period in exile in the UEFA Cup making a true league of all Europe's Champion clubs, plus those of major leagues who finish in qualification positions.

This season, 2007/08, sees three new UEFA members entering the Champions League with the champions of Montenegro, newly accepted into UEFA earlier this year, playing along with the champions of Andorra and San Marino respectively.

UEFA have helped Andorra and San Marino develop club leagues since the two countries joined in the 1990s. As a result, Massimo Agostini, a Serie A veteran with Roma, Napoli, Parma and AC Milan, will return to the Champions League this season at the age of 43 with San Marrinese SS Murata's debut in Europe's top club competition.

Agostini's former club AC Milan won the Champions League last season and netted a thumping €39.6 million (£26.2 million). That, of course,

is a massive fillip for clubs like AC Milan; and getting knocked out of before the group stages is a disaster for teams from bigger countries such as Italy, but just getting that far is a major prize for sides from places such as Luxembourg.

All clubs that qualify for the competition, but fail to reach the league stages receive €160,000 (£108,000), but teams that simply qualify for the first qualifying round then get knocked out – regardless of the score – also get another €100,000 (£67,300). That was the fate of Luxembourg's champions for 42 years until the 2006/07 Champions League, when F91 Dudelange recovered from a 0-1 home defeat to NZ Zrinjksi to score a shock 4-0 win away from home in the return leg in Bosnia-Herzegovina. The Luxembourg side, which was only founded in 1991, went out to Austrians SK Rapid Wien in the next qualifying round, but pocketed at least €360,000 (£242,300) from that experience.

Marc Diederich of the Luxembourg Football Federation says: "Dudelange is the club with the highest budget, but the solidarity payment from the CL helps our clubs a lot. This is one of the most important money income sources for our clubs. May be for Dudelange this money increases the budget about 25 per cent to 30 per cent." Perhaps this shows that the increased diversity, so heralded by Platini during his election campaign, is truly underway.

Dudelange has won the Luxembourg championship for the past three seasons.

In some countries, such as Switzerland, there is a huge diversity of teams qualifying for the UEFA Champions League despite the rewards on offer to entrants.

In the last 11 seasons, nine different Swiss clubs have taken up the 14 Champions League slots on offer –

making Switzerland, in fifth place, the most diverse place in the survey of countries that have been awarded more than one Champions League place in one season.

The rewards on offer from the competition can, however, help teams in other UEFA members turn their leagues into a formality. In Moldova, local newspaper Sport Plus even offered 100 litres of beer to the team that could break Sheriff Tiraspol's iron grip on the domestic championship, which has seen the team take every Champions League place on offer to that country since the 2001/02 season.

Skonto Riga took Latvia's sole Champions League place for nine seasons in a row from 1997/98, but this iron grip was broken two seasons ago by Liepajas Metalurgs, and Ventspils will represent the Latvians this season.

Rosenberg's domination of the Norwegian league has also been broken in recent seasons and in 2006/07 Norway's perennial champions did not even make either of the country's UEFA Champions League qualification slots, although they are back again this season.

The least diverse UEFA member is the Ukraine, where only Dynamo Kiev and Shaktar Donetsk have taken up the total 19 Champions League places on offer since the 1997/98 season.

Platini's desire to see a more widespread participation will be tested to the limit as he tries to push through the much heralded reforms which will see the big countries deprived of some places in the competition. Ultimately, with only two of the last eight winners of the competition doing so as national champions, the UEFA Champions League needs to be as inclusive as possible, allowing the competition to be won on the pitch, rather than merely via a hefty bank balance. That won't change the attraction of the biggest clubs in Europe to top players, but when clubs who face adversity such as AC Milan win the competition, it shows that there is far more to being the Champion Club of Europe than merely money, although it does help.

UEFA CHAMPIONS LEAGUE DIVERSITY INDEX

	Ranking	Total apps	No. of Clubs	INDEX
Kazakhstan	1	6	5	1.20
Bosnia-Herzegovina	2	8	6	1.33
Sweden	3=	11	8	1.38
Belarus	3=	11	8	1.38
Switzerland	5	14	9	1.56
Hungary	6	11	7	1.57
Azerbaijan	7	9	5	1.80
Poland	8=	11	6	1.83
Malta	8=	11	6	1.83
Slovakia	8=	11	6	1.83
Albania	11=	11	5	2.20
Finland	11=	11	5	2.20
Georgia	11=	11	5	2.20
Republic of Ireland	11=	11	5	2.20
Macedonia	11=	11	5	2.20
Northern Ireland	11=	11	5	2.20
Norway	11=	11	5	2.20
Austria	18=	16	6	2.67
Armenia	18=	11	4	2.75
Bulgaria	18=	11	4	2.75
Cyprus	18=	11	4	2.75
Estonia	18=	11	4	2.75
Faroe	18=	11	4	2.75
Faroe Islands	18=	11	4	2.75
Lithunia	18=	11	4	2.75
France	26	31	11	2.82
Israel	27=	12	4	3.00
Serbia & Montenegro	27=	12	4	3.00
Denmark	29	13	4	3.25
Czech Republic	30	20	6	3.33
Belgium	31	17	5	3.40
Spain	32	41	12	3.42
Germany	33	35	10	3.50
Latvia	34=	11	3	3.67
Luxembourg	34=	11	3	3.67
Moldova	34=	11	3	3.67
Slovenia	34=	11	3	3.67
Wales	34=	11	3	3.67
Romania	39	12	3	4.00
Croatia	40	13	3	4.33
Italy	41	40	9	4.44
Turkey	42	20	4	5.00
Holland	43	26	5	5.20
Russia	44	16	3	5.33
England	45	38	7	5.43
Scotland	46	17	3	5.67
Portugal	47	25	4	6.25
Greece	48	23	3	7.67
Ukraine	49	19	2	9.50

*Liechtenstein do not enter teams in the Champions League. Andorra, Montenegro & San Marino excluded as first entry was 2007/08.

Young Guns

The UEFA Champions League thrives on the introduction of new talent. In recent years the likes of Wayne Rooney, Lionel Messi and Michael Essien rising to prominence with dazzling performances on the European stage to add to their already growing domestic stock. Champions League Yearbook takes a look at four young players aged 23 or under to watch out for in 2007/08.

YOANN GOURCUFF

Team: AC Milan
Date of Birth: 11 July 1986
UEFA Champions League Appearances: 4
UEFA Champions League Goals: 1

Yoann Gourcuff was born in Ploemeur, Morbihan, Brittany. Having started out with local club FC Lorient (whose manager was his father, Christian Gourcuff, who won Ligue 2 in 2005/06 to promote his team to the top flight of French football for the first time where they finished 14th), at a young age, Gourcuff signed a youth contract with Stade Rennais in 2001, followed by a professional contract two years later after turning 17.

Making only 9 appearances in the 2003/04 season, the following seasons were more successful, as he scored 6 goals in the 2005/06 season, helping Rennes to finish 7th in Ligue 1 and winning them a place in the 2006 Intertoto Cup.

Having been linked with a host of big name European clubs such as Ajax Amsterdam, Valencia CF and Arsenal F.C., at the end of the 2006 season, Gourcuff moved to A.C. Milan where his contract runs until 2011.

He has been capped for France at schoolboy level and was part of the winning French team at the 2005 European Under-19 Football Championship.

He started his Milan career by scoring a goal and being one of the best players on view in Milan's first UEFA Champions League match against AEK Athens in September 2006.

Gourcuff is being talked of by many as Zinédine Zidane's heir apparent due to his similar height, build, movement, and skill. Others have named him rather as the next Youri Djorkaeff. He is certainly a major talent, and being at Europe's current Champion club he has the quality players around him to bring him on.

Yoann Gourcuff could be the new Zidane, or the new Djorkaeff. Take your pick. But he's certainly a phenomenal talent

THEO WALCOTT

Team: Arsenal
Date of Birth: 16 March 1989
UEFA Champions League Appearances: 6
UEFA Champions League Goals: 0

Theo Walcott shot to prominence when then England coach Sven-Goran Eriksson selected him as one of only four England strikers for the 2006 World Cup at the tender age of 17, without him having made a single first team appearance for Arsenal. His Gunners manager, Arsène Wenger, has adopted a much slower method of bringing the young buck on. Using his pace and skill in the latter stages of Champions League games, Wenger has allowed Wallcott to develop his innate ability to beat his man on the right wing and deliver quality crosses into the box.

As a kid, the young Walcott scored more than 100 goals in his one and only season for Newbury, before rising to prominence Southampton. He was so highly thought of that Nike agreed to a sponsorship deal with Walcott when he was 14 years-old. Walcott became a Southampton first team player aged 16, scoring three goals in the week following his full debut. His rapid rise to fame soon attracted attention from the British media, and a host of top clubs including Arsenal, Chelsea, Liverpool, Manchester United and Spurs, as well as foreign clubs such as Real Madrid, Juventus, AC Milan and Barcelona.

Walcott ultimately signed for Arsenal on 20 January 2006 for an initial fee of £5 million, rising to a possible £12 million based on appearances for club and country, making him the most expensive 16 year-old in the history of British football. On 16 March 2006 (his 17th birthday), Walcott signed a professional contract worth a reported £1 million a year. He scored after three minutes of his debut for England Under-21s, becoming the youngest player ever to score for that team, in a 2-2 draw with Moldova, and then netted two scorching goals against Germany to seal qualification for England to the Under-21 European Championships in the summer of 2007.

Walcott's Champions League debut came in the second leg of Arsenal's third qualifying round match against Dinamo Zagreb in August 2006, when he became the youngest ever Arsenal player to appear in European competition, a record previously held by Cesc Fabregas. During stoppage time his cross beat the Dinamo defence and Mathieu Flamini scored. He has continued to have an impact as a substitute in both Champions League and Premiership and is now looking to cement his place in the starting line-up in the Gunners' post-Henry era.

Walcott scored his first goal for Arsenal in the Carling Cup Final against Chelsea, becoming the second-youngest goalscorer in a League Cup final. After a full recovery from surgery on his shoulder in the summer of 2007, his pace, balance and body swerve mark him as a player who is sure to unlock even the tightest of European defences in years to come.

Theo Walcott celebrates his first Arsenal goal, in the Carling Cup final in February 2007

CARLOS TÉVEZ

Team: Manchester United
Date of Birth: 5 February 1984
UEFA Champions League Appearances: 0
UEFA Champions League Goals: 0

Forget all the problems, forget all the controversy, Carlos Tévez is ready to take the UEFA Champions League by storm – now 'The Bull' has finally joined Manchester United.

Tévez has had an incredible 2007, on and off the pitch, and now his future is resolved in the famous red shirt, if he manages to put all the silliness which has accompanied his stay in England so far behind him, Europe had better watch out.

Tévez has always stood out. His prominent scar from right ear to chest was as a result of being scalded by boiling water when a young boy. He declined plastic surgery as a football-mad lad since he would have to be out of the playground for four months and later refused an offer from Boca Juniors to have the scars cosmetically improved, saying that they were a part of who he was.

A child star, Tévez joined Boca at the age of thirteen and in 2003 won the Argentine Championship, Copa Libertadores and Intercontinental Cup, then followed it up in 2004 with the Copa Sudamericana. Following Argentina and Tévez's personal success at the 2004 Olympic Games, he was named Futbolista latinoamericano más destacado ("Most notable Latin American footballer") in 2003 and the Argentine Football Writers chose him as Footballer of the Year and Sportsman of the Year 2004 at the age of just 20.

In December 2004, Tévez transferred to Brazilian giants Corinthians for $20 million; the biggest transfer ever in South American football. He became captain and star of the team that won the 2005 league title, winning the award of best player of the tournament from the Brazilian football federation, the first non-Brazilian player to win that award since 1976.

On 31 August 2006, European transfer deadline day, Tévez sensationally signed for West Ham United along with countryman Javier Mascherano. The deal shocked the football world and controversy surrounded the move's exact nature.

It turned into something of a nightmare as West Ham seemed destined for relegation and the two Argentinians struggled. Mascherano soon moved on to Liverpool, but Tévez remained and almost single-handedly kept the Hammers in the Premiership, scoring the decisive goal at Old Trafford on the final day of the season which assured safety.

Over the summer of 2007 Tévez was pursued by United, but the problems which had surrounded his initial signing, and the Premier League's decision not to deduct points from West Ham and thus relegate the club, resurfaced. Tévez had his heart set on Old Trafford and, while the transfer drama raged on, helped Argentina reach the final of the Copa America, where they succumbed 3-0 to Brazil.

You can imagine the relief which securing his desired move will bring the young buck. And given the freedom to express his undoubted talents by Sir Alex Ferguson, Tévez will assuredly destroy many of Europe's best defences this season. The Bull is about to take Europe by the horns.

Tévez enjoys a giggle, but European defences won't be laughing when he, Rooney and Ronaldo are bearing down in them

JOÃO MOUTINHO

Team: Sporting Lisbon
Date of Birth: 8 September 1986
UEFA Champions League Appearances: 6
UEFA Champions League Goals: 0

It would be easy to believe that, after Manchester United's recent shopping spree, all of the best young talent in Portugal has been bought. Wrong. Case in point: João Filipe Iria Santos Moutinho.

The 20 year-old Sporting playmaker is one of the best young midfield talents in Europe and will be the next young Portuguese star to thrill the world.

Moutinho is a product of the renowned Sporting youth system. After showing great promise as a boy playing for his hometown club, Portimonense, encouraged by his sports-mad parents who knew of the youth system's reputation, he signed with Sporting at the age of 13.

From the moment the Algarve-born midfielder broke into Sporting's first team aged 17, few onlookers doubted they were in the presence of a very special player. The instant hit quickly grew into a polished performer. Despite his lack of height – Moutinho is only 1m 70cms – his box-to-box dynamism, pinpoint passing and tremendous determination quickly made him a firm fans' favourite. Indeed the fans have a special song for him: "Ele é o 28, ele é baixinho, João Moutinho, João Moutinho!" (He's number 28, he is short... João Moutinho, João Moutinho!).

His performances in 2004/05, especially in the UEFA Cup where Man of the Match displays against Feyenoord and Newcastle United helped the Lions reach the final of the competition, made him a star.

Since then, he has also featured for Portugal's senior national team and is currently a stud on the U21 side, scoring the last minute goal which ousted Italy from the 2006 Under-21 Championships.

In his second season Moutinho's incredible consistency (the midfielder was the only player in Portugal in 2005/06 to play every minute of every league match in the) was one of the few bright spots in an otherwise disappointing season for Sporting. It was fitting that Moutinho should net his team's final goal of the campaign in a 1-0 win over Braga to ensure a return to UEFA Champions League football for the Lisbon club.

In 2006/2007, following the departure of veteran Sá Pinto, Moutinho was made vice-captain at just 19.

Sporting recently tied João Moutinho to a contract until 2013, but that probably won't prevent bigger clubs from trying to sign him. The reported asking price is £15 million and potential suitors include the usual suspects like Inter Milan, Barcelona and Manchester United. It was reported in the British press that Moutinho has been the subject of a £15 million bid from English giants Arsenal.

After his club finished as runners-up in the 2006/07 domestic league, just one point behind Champions Porto, and lifted the Portuguese Cup, Moutinho will again have the chance to pit his wits against Europe's best midfielders as he continues to mature.

Sporting's Joao Moutinho (C) holds up the Portuguese Cup with team-mates Ricardo Pereira (R) and Custodio Castro (L) after winning the final against Belenenses at the Jamor stadium in Lisbon in May 2007

We hope you have enjoyed the inaugral Champions League Yearbook and that the UEFA Champions League 2007/08 is already capturing your imagination. If so, then you can pre-order your copy of the 2008/09 Champions League Yearbook by photocopying the form below and sending it to us at Know The Score Books Ltd, 118 Alcester Road, Studley, Warwickshire, B80 7NT, along with payment. Or go online to www.knowthescorebooks.com.

Order now and receive your copy of next season's book before it is available in shops and have it delivered to your door post free for just £19.99.

Name

Address

Postcode

Telephone

Email address

Please send me ___ copy(s) of the 2008/09 Champions League Yearbook post free and in advance of the book being available in shops.

Please enclose your cheque made out to Know The Score Books Ltd for £19.99 per copy.

Or call 01527 454482 to pay by card, or visit www.knowthescorebooks.com